THE CAPITOL

ALSO BY BRIAN JAY JONES

THE

CAP

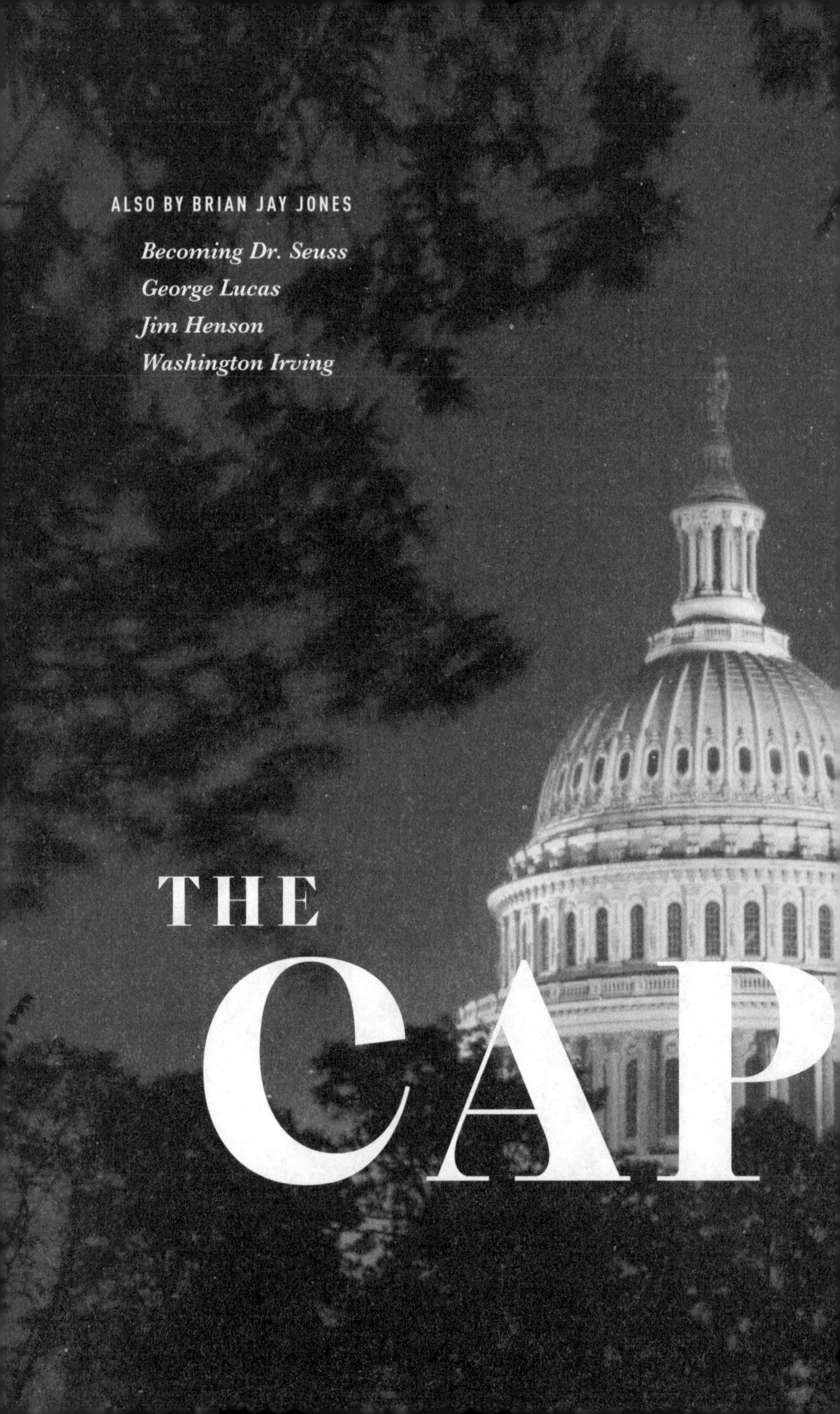

THE SURPRISING
BIOGRAPHY OF AN
AMERICAN BUILDING

BRIAN JAY JONES

ITOL

DUTTON

DUTTON
An imprint of Penguin Random House LLC
1745 Broadway, New York, NY 10019
penguinrandomhouse.com

Book design by Lorie Pagnozzi

Library of Congress Cataloging-in-Publication Data has been applied for.

ISBN 9780593185001 (hardcover)
ISBN 9780593185025 (ebook)

Printed in the United States of America
1st Printing

The authorized representative in the EU for product safety and compliance is Penguin Random House Ireland, Morrison Chambers, 32 Nassau Street, Dublin D02 YH68, Ireland, https://eu-contact.penguin.ie.

Contents

For the Old PVD Gang

★

THE CAPITOL

Computer-assisted reproduction of Pierre Charles L'Enfant's 1791 manuscript plan for the City of Washington, produced by the U.S. Geological Survey for the Library of Congress. Details are revealed here that are obscured by the varnish that was misguidedly applied to the original in the mid-19th century.

Published by the Library of Congress in 1991 with support from the National Geographic Society, the U.S. Geological Survey, and the National Park Service.

Perpendicular height of the source of Tiber Creek, above the level of the tide in said Creek
F. I. Pts
236. 7. 5/8
Perpendicular height of the West branch, above the tide in Tiber Creek
F. I. Pts
115. 7. 3/8
The perpendicular height of the Ground where the Congress house stands, is above the tide of Tiber Creek, 78 feet.
New Road to Bladensburg
Lat. Congress House, 38. 53. N.
Long. 0. 0.
Bridge
EASTERN BRANCH.
PART OF MARYLAND, WITHIN THE FEDERAL DISTRICT.
References.
F. Grand Cascade, formed of the Water from the sources of the Tiber.
G. Public walk, being a square of 1200 feet through which Carriages may ascend to the upper Square of the Federal house.
H. Grand Avenue, 400 feet in breadth, and about a mile in length, bordered with Gardens, ending in a slope from the houses on each side. This Avenue leads to the Monument A, and connects the Congress Garden with the
I. President's park, and the
K. Well improved field, being a part of the walk from the President's house, of about 1800 feet in breadth, and 3/4 of a mile in length. Every lot, deep coloured red, with Green plots, designates some of the situations which command the most agreeable prospects, and which are the best calculated for spacious houses and gardens, such as may accommodate foreign Ministers, &c.
L. Around this Square, and all along the
M. Avenue from the two bridges to the Federal house, the pavement on each side will pass under an arched way, under whose cover, Shops will be most conveniently and agreeably situated. This Street is 160 feet in breadth, and a mile long.
N.I.

Pages x–xi: Architect Pierre "Peter" Charles L'Enfant's 1791 plan for the newly created Federal city—not yet called Washington, D.C.—included carefully chosen sites for the President's House and a "Congress House" located atop Jenkins Hill. Thomas Jefferson would scratch out the term "Congress House" and replace it with "Capitol."

CHAPTER 1

Grandeur, Simplicity, and Beauty

1790–1794

In Thomas Jefferson's opinion, there was something about the map of the new Federal city that wasn't quite right.

There was no denying it was capably, even elegantly drawn by its draftsman, Pierre L'Enfant, a talented thirty-six-year-old French-born military engineer who had served with distinction on the staff of General George Washington during the American Revolution. Now, eight years after independence, with the nascent nation still learning to appreciate and navigate the nuances of its newly installed Constitutional government, President Washington had personally assigned L'Enfant the task of mapping out a home for that same government along the banks of the Potomac River.

In truth, L'Enfant had practically begged for the job. When the opening session of the first Congress had met in New York City in March 1789, it had been L'Enfant who had converted the city's old courthouse into a tasteful meeting place worthy of the new legislative body, earning the admiration of the Congress, New Yorkers, and George Washington himself. Emboldened by his rave reviews, L'Enfant, in his usual shaky English, wrote to Washington in September 1789 asking that he be assigned the task of designing the new, still unnamed Federal city, along with any buildings that might be needed to house the president and the Congress. It was an opportunity, he explained with faux modesty, to enhance his own reputation with a high-profile project. "Your Excellency will not be surprised that my ambition and the desire I have of becoming a useful citizen should lead me to wish to share in the undertaking," he wrote.[1]

Perhaps against his better judgment—there were other, more accomplished and qualified architects who had also presented to the president their own enthusiastic letters of introduction—Washington handed L'Enfant the job. While L'Enfant had come highly recommended by well-placed friends like Treasury Secretary Alexander Hamilton and Secretary of War Henry Knox, Washington had selected L'Enfant largely on the merits of two points in his favor: one, he was a relatively quick draftsman, and two—and perhaps even better—he was available immediately.

And Washington was in a hurry. Since he had settled on the location of the new Federal district in the summer of 1790—a decision that, for now, had resulted in an uneasy détente between Northern and Southern interests—skeptics were already convinced that the project was nothing more than an expensive boondoggle never to be completed. Some strongly suggested that the new seat of government remain in Philadelphia, where it had moved after vacating New York City in August 1790.

Washington, then, was determined not only to get the new district mapped out, but also to get to work as quickly as possible designing and constructing government buildings—especially the President's House and the workplace for the Congress. When it came to "projecting public works; and carrying them into effect," wrote Washington, L'Enfant was "better qualified than anyone who had come within my knowledge."[2] Not the most ringing endorsement exactly, but Washington was sending a clear message: L'Enfant was his man, and his man had better get to work *now*.

As L'Enfant arrived in the Federal district in March 1791, the formal boundaries were still being surveyed and staked out by Andrew Ellicott, a skilled and amiable Pennsylvanian who was a clockmaker by training but a surveyor and astronomer by profession. Ellicott, like L'Enfant, had been recommended to Washington by well-heeled friends—in his case, it was Benjamin Franklin—and as he had done with L'Enfant, Washington put Ellicott quickly to work, sending him out into the Maryland countryside to mark the boundaries of the new Federal district.

It was a project that came with a pedigree like perhaps no other in American history; the specifications, after all, had been explicitly laid out in 1787 in the text of the United States Constitution. Under Article I, Section 8, Clause 17, the Congress of the United States was given explicit authority over a federal "District (not exceeding ten Miles square) as may . . . become the Seat of Government of the United States." Ellicott's marching orders had come directly from the Founders themselves.

George Washington, too, had taken a personal interest in the landing spot for the Federal city, preferring the location on the Potomac not only for its convenience for Congressmen from Southern states—no one south of Maryland liked that long trip to New York City—but also for its proximity to his home at Mount Vernon, about twenty miles away in northern Virginia. After personally selecting the site along the Potomac for the new Federal district, then, Washington directed that the region be surveyed and marked starting on the Virginia side of the river, at the tip of a cape called Jones Point.[3] And so Ellicott—with the help of a free Black surveyor and astronomer named Benjamin Banneker—proceeded from there, marking out the boundaries of the Federal district in a tilted square straddling the Potomac, placing boundary stones every mile—thus "milestones"—along each ten-mile side.

While Ellicott and Banneker were off surveying in the distant woods, L'Enfant's job was to focus on the layout of the Federal city itself, keeping it huddled close to the banks of the Potomac, well inside the borders of the new district. After consulting with Washington, L'Enfant began riding the hills within view of the river, closely examining the grounds just east of the busy port of Georgetown, cradled between Rock Creek to the west and the Anacostia River[4] to the east.

He liked what he saw. While Washington, D.C., would later suffer the indignity of being derided as a city built on a swamp, that descripton wouldn't be apt for at least another century, when portions of the District's waterfront were filled and graded to extend the city beyond its natural boundaries. In 1791, the Federal city was mostly a series of low wooded hills rolling north in increasingly steep steps from the Potomac, with low cliffs along the river's edge. On March 11, L'Enfant wrote to Secretary of State Thomas Jefferson informing him that he had seen "many spots which appeared to me really beautiful"[5]—so beautiful, in fact, that he was having a hard time deciding where to put the capital's two showcase buildings.

After further consideration, L'Enfant found the ideal location for the Congressional building along the western end of a thickly wooded hill with sweeping views to the south and west; L'Enfant called the area Jenkins Heights[6]—he would also casually refer to it as Jenkins Hill, a name that stuck. Why L'Enfant attached the name "Jenkins" to the site is still unclear;[7] more accurately, it should probably have been called "Carroll Hill," as the land L'Enfant was eyeing for the Capitol was within a five-hundred-acre parcel of land belonging to Daniel Carroll of Duddington, a well-heeled Marylander with relatives whose signatures could have been found on the Declaration of Independence, the Articles of Confederation, and the Constitution. After surveying the area, L'Enfant enthusiastically reported to Washington that Jenkins Hill—and most of Carroll's land—was perfect; he "could not discover one [location] in all respects so advantageous." In fact, he told the president, Jenkins Hill was practically "a pedestal waiting for a superstructure."[8]

For the President's House—and the French-born draftsman couldn't help but refer to it as a "presidential palace" in his correspondence[9]—L'Enfant would select a flat spot a little more than a mile west of Jenkins Hill, which put it about halfway between the Congressional building and Georgetown. With the key sites now selected, he began sketching a map of the Federal city around them. L'Enfant's design was strongly influenced by the layout of the French town of Versailles, with streets laid out on a grid and intersected diagonally by avenues radiating away from the presidential palace and the Congressional building, each of which L'Enfant now clearly labeled on his map as "President's House" and "Congress House." While L'Enfant promised he'd share drawings of the two key buildings with everyone in due time, he actually had no plans, not even rough sketches. It's unlikely that they existed anywhere but in L'Enfant's head—he would, in fact, never produce a single drawing, no matter how much George Washington badgered him.

In front of Congress House, L'Enfant envisioned rerouting the shallow Tiber Creek to the foot of the building and having it flow prettily down Jenkins Hill—an ambitious plan and another design piece he had lifted from Versailles. Then, at the base of the hill itself, he had drawn what he identified as a "Grand Avenue, 400 feet in breadth, and about a mile in length" extending due west toward the Potomac.[10] This public avenue—the primitive precursor to today's museum-and memorial-lined Mall in Washington, D.C.—would be edged mostly by gardens and end directly in front of the President's House with a public square featuring at its center a gigantic equestrian statue of George Washington—to be designed by L'Enfant, of course.

The president was impressed with L'Enfant's plan—so much so that after receiving the map at his home at Mount Vernon in June 1791, he made very few corrections. There was a bit of fussing with some of the boundary lines as well as a slight scooting of the President's House to give it a better view of the river—and L'Enfant would later note with amusement that the president had deliberately and perhaps symbolically faced the house to look almost directly south toward Mount Vernon. After completing his own review, Washington next handed the map over to Jefferson for further evaluation.

Thomas Jefferson—a lifelong student of architecture and planning who had already spent more than two decades designing and constructing his perpetually unfinished neoclassical home near Charlottesville, Virginia—also approved of L'Enfant's work, at least for the most part. "I am happy that the President has left the planning of the town in such good hands," he wrote to L'Enfant, "and have no doubt it will be done to general satisfaction."[11] But Jefferson *wasn't* satisfied. Something, he thought, still wasn't quite right.

Jefferson began lightly marking up L'Enfant's plan, striking through several wordy descriptions of roads and rivers. Where L'Enfant had identified the river with the more archaic name "Potowmack"—an already corrupted spelling of the name of the nearby Patawomeck tribe—Jefferson slashed out the "w" and changed the spelling to "Potomac." He then turned his attention to his real source of annoyance: the central portion of the map, where L'Enfant had carefully located and labeled the "Congress House."

Jefferson considered the words closely; something about calling it a "Congress House" wasn't right. Most states operated their legislative bodies out of a "statehouse." But the United States was something new. As a nation rooted in the ideals of a democratic republic, it deserved more than just another public office building; it demanded a seat of government that reflected its hard-won place at the center of a republic governed by the people.

In a deliberate nod to the Roman temple of Jupiter Optimus Maximus, which stood as the focal point of that ancient republic's cultural and civic life from its perch on Capitoline Hill, Jefferson scratched out every mention of "Congress House" and wrote in its place a more majestic and, he thought, a much more appropriate term.

Capitol.

Conflict and controversy are built into the very foundation of the United States Capitol building. Like the nation it embodies, the Capitol was founded and built on debate and compromise, heated arguments and bruised egos, hurt feelings and loud disagreement—and often violence and chaos. Our own imperfections as a nation and as human beings have shaped its structure since it was little more than a proposal or a pencil sketch. In the beginning, perhaps because of the way eighteenth-century Americans preferred to be governed—mostly regionally, nearly always frugally, and overly deferentially to the authority of individual states—the construction of the Capitol and the governance of the new capital city were left mostly to determination, imagination, and improvisation.

Even the location of the city itself was a matter of furious, and fiercely regional, debate and passionate political compromise. While the U.S. Constitution had explicitly authorized the creation of a new Federal district, independent—or so it was hoped—of the whims and politics of state legislatures, it had provided no guidance on where exactly to put it.

In 1784, during the waning days of the Articles of Confederation—under which the cobbled-together alliance of newly independent states were shakily governed after the American Revolution—the Congress had selected New York City as its capital city, mostly because of its existing infrastructure and easy access to a large port. However, with the formal ratification of the Constitution in June 1788—and the very specific marching orders in that document to create a new Federal district—several Congressional delegations immediately began lobbying to relocate the national capital to their home states. Members feverishly pled their cases for locations like Baltimore, Philadelphia, Trenton, or Dover—but with no site able to muster a clear majority, Congressman James Madison, stalling for time, convinced his fellow Congressmen—and they were all men—to keep the capital in New York and pick up the conversation again later.

George Washington, who still very much wanted the capital in a more southern location, initially blanched at that strategy—but Madison assured the president that New York remained an unpopular and impractical site and that it would be easier to convince members to move the capital away from New York City than it would be to rip it from a sentimental favorite like Philadelphia. Madison was certain the Congress would take up the issue again when the first session of the new Congress met in March 1789, but he warned Washington, "The business of the seat of government is become a labyrinth."[12]

That was putting it mildly. The bickering began soon after Congress convened in its New York quarters, with every faction suspecting the others, fairly or not, of subterfuge and backroom conspiracies that would steal the capital away to their state. Eventually, two lead contenders emerged: Pennsylvania, with a site on the banks of the Susquehanna, and Virginia, which was hoping to locate the new Federal district somewhere on the river Jefferson would later rename the Potomac. With President Washington aligned with the interests of Virginia, Pennsylvania Senator William Maclay was certain the fix was in. "It is in fact the interest of the President of the United States that pushes the Potomac," Maclay fumed in his diary. "He by means of Jefferson, Madison . . . and others urges this business."[13]

But when the Congress adjourned in autumn, most members went home believing Pennsylvania had the inside line, although there had been some dithering over the details. Before adjourning in the fall, the House of Representatives had approved the Residence Act, formally recommending the district be moved to the tiny town of Columbia, Pennsylvania, about eighty miles west of Philadelphia but easily accessible from the Susquehanna River; the Senate, meanwhile, had gone off script and suggested Germantown, a small town located just north of Philadelphia but nowhere *near* the Susquehanna River. Thanks to Madison, the final bill would again be postponed—but as Congress reconvened in early 1790, it seemed clear that the Federal district was going to go *somewhere* in Pennsylvania.

Debate would come to a standstill in January 1790, however, when Treasury Secretary Alexander Hamilton presented to the Congress his

First Report on Public Credit, in which he outlined his proposed system for paying off the debts incurred during the American Revolution. Hamilton's plan—and thus the official strategy of the Washington administration—was for the new federal government to assume the debts of all thirteen states, a total of about $20 million, in a move Hamilton hoped would help establish the credit rating of the United States and shore up the new nation's fiscal standing. But Southern states balked; assumption was a *Northern* problem, they insisted, pointing out that their debts were largely paid while also fuming that Hamilton's proposal was nothing but a ploy to seize power for a centralized government—an accusation similarly leveled at Hamilton by Secretary of State Thomas Jefferson. Consequently, Hamilton's debt plan quickly bogged down the Congress along regional lines, even as it similarly fractured President Washington's cabinet.

Deadlocked on the issue of the debt, Congress turned to the consideration of a new version of the Residence Act, this one introduced at the end of May by Senator Pierce Butler of South Carolina. Butler had simply left blank the location for the Federal district in the text of his bill and opened the floor for debate. But the Senate stalemated, again along mostly regional lines, with members unable to agree on Baltimore, Wilmington, or somewhere on "the easterly bank of the Patowmack." Between the assumption bill and the Residence Act, the United States Congress, barely a year old, had officially ground to a halt.

For the moment, the Founders were flustered—and it was more than just state debts or the location of the new Federal district that was on the line; a deadlocked Congress this early in the new American experiment was not only a potential cause of national discord, dividing the country along geopolitical lines, but also a probable source of international embarrassment. How did this new nation expect to be taken seriously by the rest of the world when its attempt at self-governance was already stalled by something as petty as regional politics? Privately, even Vice President John Adams confessed it wasn't a good look. "We are about founding a City which will be one of the first in the World," he wrote in his diary, "and We are governed by local and partial Motives."[14]

On Saturday, June 19, 1790, outside George Washington's New York City residence on Broadway, Jefferson, as he reported later, found Hamilton looking "somber, haggard, and dejected."[15] The two struck up a conversation directly in front of the president's front door and paced back and forth in the street for nearly half an hour as Hamilton pled his case for compromise, urging his stubborn colleague to at least present a unified front within the president's cabinet. "He observed that the members of the administration ought to act in concert," wrote Jefferson, ". . . that the President was the center on which all administrative questions ultimately rested, and that all of us should rally around him."[16] Jefferson agreed to further discussion and suggested that Hamilton and "another friend or two" dine with him at his quarters at 57 Maiden Lane the following evening. "I thought it impossible that reasonable men, consulting together coolly, could fail, by some mutual sacrifices of opinion, to form a compromise which was to save the union," Jefferson wrote later.[17]

At dinner the next evening, Jefferson's "friend or two" turned out to be James Madison, who favored a Southern-based capital and opposed assumption but who could also be counted on to do the necessary head counting and floor management to shepherd any compromise through Congress. Jefferson later claimed that Hamilton and Madison had done most of the talking, but however the deal was cut—and none of those in attendance would ever reveal the details—by the end of the evening, Hamilton and Madison had arrived at a compromise. Hamilton agreed to a Residence Act that would relocate the new Federal district to the banks of the Potomac by way of a temporary ten-year stay in Pennsylvania—a bit of political appeasement to the Pennsylvanians, who would suddenly find the rug yanked out from under them—while the new Potomac-based capital city was prepared and the Capitol building was constructed. In return, Madison would help steer Hamilton's assumption bill through Congress, which would involve some serious buttonholing of his exceedingly skeptical fellow Southerners. While George Washington hadn't been in attendance at the decisive dinner, as the three negotiators parted that evening, they felt certain there would be no objections from the chief executive; the so-called Compromise of 1790, which had been forged in Jefferson's dining room, gave him everything he wanted.

When debate on the previously deadlocked Residence Act resumed in late June, the still suspicious Senator Maclay sensed movement in the legislative logjam—and he wasn't certain he liked it. Thanks to some backroom negotiating by Hamilton and Madison—who had already predetermined the outcome—"the Pennsylvania delegation had . . . agreed to place the permanent residence [of the Congress] on the Potomac, and the temporary residence to remain ten years in Philadelphia," fumed Maclay, who huffed in his diary, "I know nothing of any such agreement."[18] And yet, with or without him, the deal was falling into place—and Maclay thought he knew whom to blame. "The President of the United States has (in my opinion) had a great influence in this business," he wrote.[19]

Maclay was right—Washington's weight was enough to sway even the most stubborn of skeptics and holdouts. On July 16, 1790, the president of the United States signed the Residence Act into law; the assumption bill would follow two weeks later, making the terms of the Compromise of 1790 the official policy of the new federal government. Under the terms of the residency bill—officially titled An Act for Establishing the Temporary and Permanent Seat of the Government of the United States—the capital was to relocate immediately to Philadelphia, where it would remain until the first Monday in December 1800, at which point the seat of government would be transferred to the new Federal district on the Potomac.

With his signature on the Residence Act, President Washington had just started the clock. The capital city—and the Capitol—had to be ready for the Congress to occupy by Monday, December 1, 1800, a little more than ten years away.

While the Residence Act authoritatively placed the new capital on the Potomac,[20] it punted on nearly every other detail regarding the management of the new Federal district, leaving most decisions to the president of the United States. James Monroe, seated as Virginia's newest Senator in the fall of 1790, considered that a wise strategy. "If they have plac'd . . . the business under the direction of the Executive," Monroe wrote to Jefferson, "it will most probably succeed."[21]

Among the explicit tasks assigned the president was the appointment of a three-member commission to oversee the entire capital—and Capitol—project. In January 1791, Washington appointed his trio of commissioners, placing in the first seat Virginia doctor David Stuart, who had married the widow of Washington's stepson. Into the second seat went Thomas Johnson, a former governor of Maryland as well as a longtime friend and colleague from the Revolutionary era. For his third pick, Washington selected Daniel Carroll of Rock Creek—another member of the prominent Carroll family of Maryland and a relative of Jenkins Hill resident and landowner Daniel Carroll of Duddington—who had just lost his seat in the Congress for voting in favor of assumption. The three men were decent, well-connected, and capable—if often disinterested—appointees whose major qualification was their devotion to the first president of the United States.

And so, it would be President Washington who would lead the commission through its paces, as the commissioners mainly nodded their approval at his selection of the precise location for the Federal district on the Potomac, quietly assented as he handed Andrew Ellicott the job of surveying the site, and willingly consented as he tasked Pierre L'Enfant with laying out the capital city. But while Congress had given Washington considerable leeway in his administration of the capital city, the one thing they hadn't given him was money. There would be no federal funding involved; Congress expected the Federal city and its buildings to be entirely financed through the sale of land within the district that had been divided into hundreds of developable lots, along with any loans interested developers might be lucky enough to secure. As costs of the capital city began to swell over the next decade—and as tepid land sales and rampant speculation depleted the commission's coffers—Washington would become less involved, and increasingly frustrated, with the city's financing. It would be left to others to persuade the Congress to abandon this unreliable funding mechanism in favor of federal appropriations.

Washington would also deliberately avoid the discussions of what to name the new Federal district and its capital city, perhaps suspecting—and rightly so—that his name would be involved. One early visitor to the region had suggested calling the district "Washingtonople," a terrible idea that, thankfully, went nowhere.[22] Madison and Jefferson felt certain they could do better than that, and on September 8, 1791, they convened the three commissioners at a tavern in Georgetown, where they all agreed that the name of the capital city would be "Washington," and that the Federal district itself should be designated as "Columbia"—formally written as "Washington, District of Columbia."

As for the design and construction of the Capitol building itself, Washington was content for the moment to leave that in L'Enfant's hands. But while plans for the city were going well, L'Enfant was stubbornly refusing to hand over any designs for either the President's House or the Capitol, assuring the commissioners that while he was too busy to draw anything, he had everything worked out in his head.[23] The commissioners shrugged to Washington that they were certain L'Enfant would send his drawings "as soon as he finds himself disengaged" from putting the final details on the city map.[24] But when Washington pressed

L'Enfant for a final version of the map of the Federal city—incorporating Jefferson's label changing "Congress House" to "Capitol" and, perhaps just as important, showing the city divided into lots that might interest potential buyers—L'Enfant simply ignored the president's request.

Operating with his typical brashness, L'Enfant began clearing portions of Jenkins Hill to make room for the foundation of a Capitol building no one had seen and laying out roads drawn on a map that hadn't been published. He ran into trouble almost immediately when he declared that an existing structure was encroaching on the right of way of one of the major avenues he was surveying near the site of the Capitol. The offending structure was a wall belonging to Daniel Carroll of Duddington, who, on a parcel of family property, was constructing a home that intruded seven feet into a roadway that L'Enfant had designated as New Jersey Avenue.

It was not a smart fight for L'Enfant to pick. As one of the largest landowners in the region, Daniel Carroll of Duddington had graciously deeded to the government property that L'Enfant had selected for the site of the Capitol; in return, Carroll received about $67 per acre—a bargain for the federal government. Carroll's motives weren't entirely patriotic—he felt certain that other land he owned within the vicinity of the Capitol, including the parcel on which he was now building his family home, would significantly appreciate in value (it would, but not in his lifetime). Nonetheless, his generosity had earned the gratitude and respect of Washington and Jefferson, giving him two powerful allies and advocates. None of that seemed to matter to L'Enfant, who intended to plow through the wall that Carroll—who, thanks to L'Enfant, had no maps of the city to consult—had extended out into the still unmarked roadway.

Rather than negotiate with Carroll—or keep the commission in the loop—L'Enfant simply warned him that "his house must come down"[25] and sent his men to tear down Carroll's property. Stunned, Carroll appealed directly to Washington, who tried to keep the peace, promising to compensate Carroll for his loss and warning L'Enfant about the dangers of overstepping his authority. "Having the beauty and regularity of your plan only in view," wrote Washington, "you pursue it as if every person and thing were *obliged* to yield to it."[26] The president was a patient man, but the ice beneath L'Enfant was thinning quickly. "*He must know* there is a line beyond which he will not be suffered to go," the exasperated president told Thomas Jefferson.[27]

Washington reminded L'Enfant that he served at the pleasure of the commissioners and had to keep them informed of his activities—especially as "the commissioners have many circumstances to attend to, some of which, perhaps, may be unknown to you." Yet L'Enfant brashly chose to ignore the president's advice and privately groused to friends that he would never take orders "from men so ignorant and unfit as the commissioners."[28] Instead, L'Enfant suggested to Washington that the commissioners had no authority over him whatsoever and recommended that he be put entirely in charge of the design and construction of the Capitol—and even over the administration of the capital city itself. All he needed, L'Enfant told the president, was a thousand men and a million dollars.

Washington could hardly believe the colossal nerve. "The conduct of Maj[o]r L'Enfant and those employed under him astonishes me beyond measure!" he wrote incredulously to Jefferson.[29]

And still L'Enfant refused to hand over any designs for the Capitol—if any actually existed—or to finalize his map of the District. It would fall to surveyor Andrew Ellicott to finish up the map and prepare it for publication; he finally placed the document in Washington's hands on February 20, 1792. The layout would be all L'Enfant's: streets overlaid on a grid—with north-south streets named with numbers and east-west ones with letters—and bisected at regular intervals by wide diagonal streets that he had named for the then current fifteen states, including the newly approved Kentucky, which would be formally admitted in June. Ellicott would neaten up L'Enfant's pencils and place the now correctly labeled "Capitol" prominently in a large clearing on Jenkins Hill, bisected diagonally by Maryland, Pennsylvania, New Jersey, and Delaware Avenues, all converging on the building, which served as the center of the asterisk of streets. As directed, he had broken the city down into more than eleven hundred numbered and irregularly sized parcels, all of which would be put up for sale. Ellicott had also drawn true east-west and north-south lines, cleverly intersecting them with the Capitol at the center and creating what would later be known as the "Washington meridians," which marked ground zero for the nation's capital.

At the moment, however, there were no actual streets crossing the site from any direction; Jenkins Hill was a mostly empty plateau. About four acres of heavy woods had been cleared by axmen enslaved by Daniel Carroll of Duddington, though most of the downed trees had yet to be hauled away—long a sore spot with L'Enfant. The area remained open to future, unrelated development as well. Several homes—most belonging to Carroll—were visible in the surrounding woods; in a short time, wealthy investor William Mayne Duncanson would build six blocks to the south a stately Federal-style house he called the Maples, complete with stables and housing for enslaved workers. George Washington would hail it as "a fine house in the woods."[30]

Around the same time Ellicott handed his map to Washington, Jefferson hinted to L'Enfant that the commissioners were still waiting for drawings of the Capitol. "The advance of the season begins to require that the plans for the buildings and other public works at the Federal city should be in readiness,"[31] Jefferson reminded L'Enfant as gently as he could. But Jefferson, too, would be stonewalled as L'Enfant insisted the task of "chang[ing] a wilderness into a city . . . is an undertaking vast as it is novel."[32]

Washington's patience was at an end. On the evening of February 26, the president directed his personal secretary, Tobias Lear, to visit L'Enfant and present him with an ultimatum of sorts, asking whether he intended to acknowledge the authority of the commissioners. L'Enfant tartly informed Lear that "he had already heard enough of this matter"[33] and that he had no intention of submitting to commissioners he didn't respect.

The next morning, Pierre L'Enfant was officially fired by the very commissioners he didn't respect. To the suddenly contrite L'Enfant, Washington made it clear that if he wanted his old job back, he had to ask the commissioners for it—a not-so-subtle reminder to the defiant draftsman that it was the commissioners who had always been his boss and not the president.

Despite his sacking, L'Enfant's fingerprints remain on the District of Columbia to this day, with the city's modern layout—including the National Mall and, to the continued annoyance of D.C. drivers, the intersecting diagonals—still mostly adhering to L'Enfant's original design. But as L'Enfant skulked out of the District of Columbia in the late winter of 1792, he also took with him—at least in his head—whatever plans or ideas he might have had for the designs for the President's House and the Capitol.

And the clock was ticking; it had been nearly fifteen months since the passage of the Residence Act of 1790—but due in no small part to L'Enfant's stubbornness and ego, there wasn't a single scrap of paper to be found containing even a hint of what the new Capitol building might look like.

Thomas Jefferson, however, had an idea.

"It is necessary to advertise immediately for plans for the Capitol and the President's House," Jefferson wrote to the commissioners on March 6, 1792.[34] It was the word "immediately" that carried the most weight; Jefferson worried L'Enfant's dismissal might give the appearance of a Federal city in disarray—which was close to the truth—and thus give anti-Potomac Congressmen an excuse to reopen debate on the location of the Capitol. It was vital, then, for the commissioners to make it look as if everything was proceeding according to plan. Otherwise, argued Jefferson, detractors might "take advantage of the retirement of L'Enfant, to trumpet an abortion of the whole."[35]

Jefferson's solution was a national contest, announced in the nation's major newspapers, calling for submissions of designs for the Capitol building, including detailed plans for its exterior and interior. The ad, as drafted by Jefferson, specified that the Capitol should be made of brick and contain a chamber for the House of Representatives—large enough to accommodate at least three hundred people—as well as a Senate chamber of twelve hundred square feet and at least twelve rooms, six hundred square feet each, for committees and offices.[36] The winning design would see its creator receive a parcel of property within the District as well as "500 dollars, or a Medal of that value." There was no mention of a preferred architectural style, though privately Jefferson was looking to "the models of antiquity which have had the approbation of thousands of years," preferably something similar to the Roman Pantheon.[37] Washington, however, just wanted something big. "The building . . . ought to be on a scale far superior to anything in this country," he told Jefferson.[38]

The advertisement, officially approved and submitted by the three city commissioners, went into newspapers in Boston, Baltimore, Charleston, Richmond, Philadelphia, and New York on March 24, 1792, and set Sunday, July 14, as the deadline for entries. As the deadline closed in, more than thirty entries had been submitted[39]—$500 in 1792 was a substantial prize, equivalent to nearly $20,000 today,[40] and certainly more than enough to pique the interest of even the most aspiring of amateurs. But Washington and Jefferson were quickly discouraged by what they were seeing. "If none more elegant than these [designs] should appear," groaned Washington, "the exhibition of architecture will be a very dull one indeed."[41]

The idea of a national competition asking for architectural plans for a major public building or project was a concept that dated back at least as far as ancient Greece. In 448 B.C., Athenians had sponsored a public contest, looking for designs for the Acropolis—and Jefferson likely felt if such an architectural competition was good enough for democracy-loving ancient Greeks, it was more than fitting for their eighteenth-century American heirs. The new nation's grandest public building deserved public input, and Jefferson was confident that the commissioners would be dazzled by the architectural imagination of modern Americans.

Unfortunately, in 1792, there were very few professional architects in the United States, which meant most entries were submitted by dabblers and dilettantes—"common builders," snickered L'Enfant.[42] While Americans did indeed have imagination, few had any real ability to draw a building that could exist in three dimensions or that had an interior that matched the exterior. Thus, submitted designs for the Capitol ran the gamut from the hilarious to the merely competent; some followed Jefferson's directions to the very letter, while others disregarded the ad's instructions entirely—the size of the Senate chambers seemed to be the biggest wild card, with one aspiring architect submitting an interior floor plan that was mostly a cavernous warehouse. Many were hampered by an inability to draw with any sense of perspective or proper scale; one drawing, submitted by a Mr. James Diamond, featured a large sculpture—or perhaps it was a weather vane—with a gigantic bird that dwarfed the rest of the building.

Still, among the stack of submitted drawings were several designs with elements that caught the president's eye, including one from George Turner, a judge in the Northwest Territory, whose drawing, while amateurish, was topped by a dome that immediately grabbed Washington's attention. Washington admitted he was "more agreeably struck with the appearance of" Turner's plan, though he wasn't willing to declare it the winner. But that dome! "The Dome . . . would, in my opinion, give beauty & grandeur to the pile," wrote Washington.[43]

Only one submission had come from a professional, a French-born, classically educated thirtysomething[44] architect named Étienne Sulpice Hallet, who had recently settled in Philadelphia, where he went by the Americanized name of Stephen. Washington and Jefferson generally liked the layout envisioned by Hallet—with a domed center section flanked by wings on each side serving as formal meeting places for each body of Congress—though both also found Hallet's design more ostentatious than inspiring. Washington *did* like the look of Hallet's dome, however—that element, similar to the one in Turner's drawing, had quickly distinguished it from the rest of the pack. For the moment, Hallet seemed to be the front-runner, even as the president quietly extended the deadline for entries for another year, hoping for a larger pool.

But while the winner of the Capitol competition was still officially undecided, the President's House was in good hands; a similar contest had the commissioners enthusiastically endorsing the plans submitted by James Hoban. The highly skilled Hoban was an Irish-born architect living in South Carolina, where he had designed the tasteful Charleston County Courthouse—a building that influenced the look of his drawings for the President's House. To Washington's likely disappointment, however, Hoban had not submitted an entry for the Capitol.

With the encouragement of Jefferson and the commissioners, Hallet would spend much of the rest of 1792 redrawing and revising his nearly there Capitol concept. He continued to believe that, in due time, he would be declared the winner of the competition, even as the commissioners continued to pick apart his drawings—though always reassuring Hallet that his "design may perhaps be improved into approbation."[45] Despite the revisions, Hallet's design was still a bit too expensive, too European, and too stuffy for Washington's taste—it was with good reason his plan would come to be casually referred to as the "fancy piece." But if Hallet thought the job was his—he was, after all, the only trained architect in the running—he would soon have reason to watch his back;

with the competition still open, another promising design, drawn by a physician and amateur architect named William Thornton, was submitted to the commissioners in January 1793—and immediately charmed both Washington and Jefferson.

A native of the island of Tortola, thirty-three-year-old William Thornton was a liberal, rational, civic-minded man of many interests, from botany to phonetics. He had trained as a surgeon, completing his education at the University of Aberdeen in 1781, though medicine would always be more of a pastime than a profession for him. Naturally curious, Thornton had traveled widely, including extended trips to London, Paris, and Scotland—and his excursions through European cities had strongly influenced his tastes in architecture. As a Quaker, Thornton struggled with the horrors of slavery; he opposed the inhumane practice even as his family's sugar plantation in Tortola relied on the labor of enslaved people, and he would remain for his entire life an outspoken crusader for their freedom and resettlement in West Africa.

It was partly his distaste for slavery, in fact, that had prompted him to leave the plantation in Tortola to settle first in Delaware and then in Pennsylvania, where he was inspired by Benjamin Franklin to become an inventor and dilettante, drawing up plans for a steam-powered gun, among other far-out contraptions. In 1787, he had brazenly entered a contest seeking architectural designs for the building to house the Library Company of Philadelphia. Despite lacking any architectural training and never having designed a building before, the self-taught Thornton, a skilled artist, wowed the judges with his elegant drawings of a brick building with a peaked roof, executed in the Georgian style. It would be left to a local builder to carry out the actual construction of the building; Thornton was a draftsman, not a foreman.[46]

The drawing of the Capitol that had caught both the president's and Jefferson's eyes was actually Thornton's second effort; an earlier design, which Thornton had completed in Tortola in July 1792, was mostly a series of large but opulent warehouses, uninspiring and impractical.

Four months later, Thornton had been back in Philadelphia, where he ran into an old acquaintance, Judge George Turner, who informed Thornton that, based on the feedback he'd received on his own entry, he knew President Washington was looking for a dome. With this bit of valuable inside information, Thornton asked the commission if he could try again. He was told he definitely could.

His latest design for the Capitol, then, submitted in early January 1793, was both inspired and inspirational; it included elements like a center dome and a portico executed in the neoclassical manner that Jefferson admired, and fused them with two wings, one for each legislative body, reflecting the Georgian style that Washington preferred. Without quite meaning to, Thornton had landed in the sweet spot between competing architectural styles and tastes that appealed to the two most important critics, Washington and Jefferson. Thornton had included as the dominant feature of his plan a central domed rotunda—the one feature that he knew would really catch the president's eye—and carefully merged it with a simple but tasteful central portico, topped by a triangular pediment that extended the building's center face outward.

Thornton's jutting portico stood in stark contrast to the east face of Hallet's fancy piece, with its recessed front, which made the entire structure look as if it were holding its breath. When the drawings were put side by side, Hallet's prim fussiness just couldn't compete with Thornton's airy elegance. Thornton's concept would also provide the basic template that would remain at the heart of the Capitol's design and structure through countless modifications and expansions: a domed central structure flanked by identical wings for each legislative body. And while Thornton's dome wasn't much—a simple push button, compared to the soaring, columned dome that would be added six decades later—it gave the building a grounded elegance and a sense of order. Thornton's Capitol was a building suited to a new nation built on ideals of soaring optimism. In short, it was American.

Washington loved it; Thornton's design, he declared, had "Grandeur, Simplicity, and Beauty."[47] Jefferson, too, was impressed, calling the design "simple, noble, beautiful, excellently distributed, and moderate in size."[48] While the final decision for the winning design was officially in the hands of the commissioners, Jefferson knew the real final word lay with one man "whose decision is the most important."[49] Few were surprised, then, when Washington himself directed the commissioners to promptly inform Hallet that "Doctor [Thornton]'s plan may be preferred to his."[50]

On April 6, 1793, the decision was made public as Thornton was officially announced as the winner of the contest. Anxious to finally get started on construction, the commissioners immediately asked Thornton to turn in more detailed plans, including specific measurements of rooms and corridors and a list of materials to be used in the building's interior as well as meticulous drawings of the exterior. That level of detail, however, far exceeded the skills of the untrained Thornton. What was needed, then, was an experienced draftsman who could review Thornton's plans, determine their practicality, then convert the two-dimensional drawings into the detailed architectural plans required to construct a three-dimensional structure. The commissioners thought they knew just the man for the job: Stephen Hallet.

Curiously, George Washington, normally the most astute of men, agreed with the commission's recommendation. While Washington had a soft spot for Hallet, even making certain he received a generous cash prize for placing second in the contest, Washington should have known that putting the runner-up in charge of executing someone else's winning design was a big mistake—one that was bound to result in bruised egos, backstabbing, and endless delays, which, in the end, is exactly what happened.

As directed by the commission, Hallet reviewed Thornton's drawings for the Capitol to assess their feasibility in three dimensions and determine costs for construction. Surprising no one, Hallet decided that

Thornton's design was too impractical and too expensive to build—and even if it *could* be built, he was certain there was no way it would ever be completed by 1800. To be fair, some of Hallet's concerns were legitimate. Thornton's drawings *were* impractical in the sense that his interiors as designed didn't always fit into his exterior, especially once ventilation and lighting needs were taken into consideration. But with his ego smarting, Thornton refused to budge, insisting that Hallet's criticisms were "trifling" and snarking that he would have been happy to address each of Hallet's complaints individually, if only "Mr. Hallet's report had been written in a more legible hand."[51]

Washington didn't want to hear any of it—and yet Hallet had successfully planted seeds of doubt in the president's mind. Sighing that it was "unlucky that this investigation of Dr. Thornton's plan and estimate of the cost had not preceded the adoption of it,"[52] Washington nevertheless wanted work on the Capitol to begin as quickly as possible. On June 30, the president looked to the mediator who had helped broker the compromise on the matter of the Capitol's location, instructing Thomas Jefferson to convene a similar meeting between Hallet and Thornton to try to resolve their differences. "The case is important," Washington wrote. "A Plan must be adopted; and good, or bad, it must be entered upon."[53]

Several weeks later, Jefferson brought together in Philadelphia a small commission to listen to Hallet's objections, inviting not only Hallet and Thornton to the conversation but also James Hoban, who was supervising the construction of the President's House, and two experienced local builders who were counted on as neutral parties. So important was the need for the commission to come to an agreement that even Washington dropped in on their meetings from time to time, lending his gravitas and calm to the often heated discussions.

The commission would eventually reach a wobbly compromise, agreeing to take an interior design by Hallet and jam it somehow into Thornton's award-winning exterior—a solution that annoyed Hallet, who still insisted that his exterior, with its recessed eastern front, was the superior design. That particular feature, however, remained a nonstarter with Washington, who grumbled to Jefferson that "the recess which Mr. Hallet proposes . . . strikes everyone . . . unpleasantly."[54]

If the true measure of a good compromise is that it makes no one happy, then one other element of the agreement was a rousing success—and would cause continued strife and foot-dragging over the next year. While Thornton would forever have the distinction of being the first Architect of the Capitol—a title that would take on increasing responsibilities over the next two centuries—it would be Hoban who would be formally appointed as the superintendent overseeing the work at both the President's House and the Capitol building. But with Hoban's attention mostly on the President's House, the commissioners also agreed that Hallet would serve as the project's on-the-ground foreman, managing the actual day-to-day construction. To Washington's annoyance, that particular chain of command would give Hallet the opportunity to tinker with certain design elements of the building—such as the repeatedly rejected recessed eastern front—before a single brick had been laid.

The agreement struck by the commission would come to be known as the "conference plan"—and like with the United States itself, which had seen its Founders establish the structure of Congressional representation on the back of the messy Connecticut Compromise in 1787, and with the uneasy Compromise of 1790, which had fixed the location of the capital city, the very design of the Capitol building was also the product of negotiation, politicking, and compromise. Due mostly to the continued meddling of Hallet, it would remain a shaky arrangement for some time to come.

On Wednesday, September 18, 1793, the largest public works project in the United States to date got underway officially.[55] It began at ten a.m. with the arrival of President Washington on the shores of the Virginia side of the Potomac River, across from the site on the District side where carpenters and bricklayers were already at work on the President's House under the watchful eye of James Hoban. The mood in the capital city that morning was one of general pride, though tempered with concern; a surge of yellow fever was burning through the Northern states, with Washington receiving word from Secretary of War Henry Knox that a hundred Americans were dying daily in Philadelphia. The District of Columbia so far had been mostly spared.

Washington was rowed across the Potomac to be met by members of Masonic lodges in Virginia and Maryland as well as by Masons from a new federal lodge that had just been established in the Federal district. Together they began to march east two at a time "with music playing," reported the local newspaper, "drums beating, colors flying, and spectators rejoicing." Their destination: Jenkins Hill, about a mile and a half away, where a large crowd had gathered to watch Washington preside over a Masonic ceremony to lay the cornerstone of the Capitol.

The president was accustomed to such pomp and circumstance; he had been a Mason for more than forty years since joining the Freemasonry Lodge at Fredericksburg, Virginia, in 1752 when he was twenty years old. Now, at age sixty-one and in his second term as president, Washington participating in the laying of the cornerstone would be about more than just Masonic ritual; by presiding over the ceremony, the man who was the very embodiment of the new nation was literally helping to lay the foundation of the monument to its representative government. Senator Daniel Webster, perhaps the most prominent statesman and orator of the next century, would reflect on the moment with his typical elegance when commemorating the ceremony more than sixty years later: "Who does not feel that, when President Washington laid his hand on the foundation of the first Capitol, he performed a great work of perpetuation of the Union and the Constitution?"[56]

Arriving at Jenkins Hill, the group assembled at the southeast corner of the foundation, near a deep, freshly dug trench. The president stood with the Grand Masters of the Virginia and Maryland lodges next to the gigantic cornerstone, which was to be lowered into the trench, while the rest of the group fanned out in a circle. Washington, wearing his Masonic leather apron, was solemnly presented with a silver plate prepared by Caleb Bentley, a Georgetown silversmith who had etched into its surface a note of recognition that the Capitol's cornerstone

> was laid on the 18th day of September, in the thirteenth year of American Independence, in the first year of the second term of the Presidency of George Washington, whose virtues in the civil administration of his country have been as conspicuous and beneficial, as his Military valor and prudence have been useful in establishing her liberties. . . .[57]

Washington stepped down into the trench, placed the silver plate on the soil at his feet, then carefully guided into place the enormous cornerstone as it was slowly lowered and set atop the silver plate. Using the tools of their order—the trowel, the square, the level, and the plumb rule—the Masons deemed the cornerstone to be "well-formed, true, and trusty" and duly consecrated it with corn, wine, and oil.[58] As Washington emerged from the trench, the ceremony crescendoed into celebration, with artillery gunfire and speeches, and culminated in an enormous barbecue at which a five-hundred-pound ox was roasted and messily devoured well into the evening. As newspapers reported later, all in attendance "generally partook, with every abundance of other recreation."[59]

While the cornerstone ceremony has been well-documented, one key detail is missing from all accounts: the precise location of the cornerstone itself. Visitors to the Capitol will still find in the building's north wing a large wall plaque mounted during the Capitol's centennial celebration in 1893; it informs tourists with confidence that the cornerstone lies just below. Unfortunately, later investigation failed to turn up any evidence of the stone or its silver plate beneath the centennial anniversary plaque.

A hundred years later, while preparing for the building's 1993 bicentennial, historians and engineers went spelunking in the foundations again, searching for exactly *which* of the building's many southeast corners might be the correct one. While the effort unearthed an enormous chunk of granite resembling a cornerstone, metal detectors and soil samples still showed no signs of the silver plaque. "We will leave it to future generations to use their technology to look for it," Capitol historian William C. Allen sighed at the time, "because it will always hold a fascination."[60]

As expected, putting Hallet in charge of executing Thornton's design was a bad idea. Despite the repeated objections of the president of the United States himself, Hallet remained committed to his idea of a recessed east front. But if Washington was going to continue to insist on an eastern portico jutting out beyond the face of the building, Hallet would try to skirt the issue on a technicality, nudging the eastern front forward, as Washington asked him to, but leaving a large central courtyard open behind it. That meant the dome would no longer be centered on the Capitol's middle section; instead, Hallet wanted it scooted toward the west front, putting it over a rear conference room instead of a central rotunda and upsetting the visual balance of the building. Without consulting Washington, Hoban, or the commissioners, Hallet instructed his laborers to begin laying the building's foundations accordingly. "Mr. Hallet was desirous of altering not merely what might be improved," wrote Thornton later, "but even what was most approved."[61]

Washington was not amused. While the commissioners diplomatically warned Hallet that he reported to Hoban and thus did not have the authority "to introduce into the building any departures from Dr. Thornton's plan,"[62] the president was less inclined to be polite: as Thornton reported, "[Washington] expressed his disapproval in a style of such warmth as his dignity seldom permitted."[63] The president wanted Thornton's design constructed exactly as it had been drawn, including the extended eastern portico and the central dome, and he accused Hallet—rightly—of trying to leave his own fingerprints on the building for posterity.

Hallet refused to budge. In fact, he insisted that he had never agreed to accept Thornton's design in the first place. Rather, he informed Washington, "I misunderstood your mind as to the Plan." He then advised the commission that he intended to continue constructing the Capitol according to his own designs—which, he was certain, they would thank him for later. "I claim the original invention of the plan now executing," he informed the commissioners in June 1794, "and beg leave to lay it hereafter before you and the President the proofs of my right to it."[64]

This complete disregard for Thornton as the primary Architect of the Capitol might have been Hallet's intention all along. Not only did Hallet not want Thornton getting any credit for the building's design, but he had also already taken steps to tamper with the historical record. The silver plaque that had been placed under the cornerstone nine months earlier—inscribed after the terms of the conference plan had been agreed to by all parties—contained no mention at all of Thornton as the Architect of the Capitol, crediting instead only Hoban and Hallet. It's possible that, with the intention of moving forward with his own design, Hallet might have used his influence with Caleb Bentley to deliberately omit the engraving of the name of his competitor from the silver plaque—a petty maneuver indeed.

Whatever Hallet's motivation, Washington had seen enough; on November 15, 1794, Hallet was fired. Like L'Enfant before him, his ego had been his undoing—and like L'Enfant, Hallet would leave in a huff without handing over any of his detailed drawings or architectural plans. Laborers would continue work on the Capitol's north wing, which was intended for the Senate, but all construction on Hallet's revised, and unsanctioned, central section would cease.

While it was certainly good riddance, Washington had to be nervous—the clock had now been ticking for four years with not much to show for it up on Jenkins Hill. Eyeing the calendar and tiring of seeing most of the big decisions about the Capitol punted to him by the deferential commissioners, Washington made two major pronouncements. First, he made it clear the Capitol *had* to be completed by December of 1800, even if it meant concentrating mostly on the building's exterior, with the bulk of the interior to be completed after the arrival of Congress. "The internal work—and many of the ornamental parts without, may be finished gradually, as the means will permit," wrote Washington.[65] The president wasn't concerned about whether the building was pretty, but he was determined that there would at least be four walls and a roof to house anxious legislators.

Next, to his three commissioners—who, he thought, lacked focus on the matters at hand—Washington issued an ultimatum: each of them had to live in the Federal city or lose their seats. The president knew it was a lot to ask; in 1794, the Federal district was mostly one of temporary wooden structures with no real roads to speak of. Even Pennsylvania Avenue, intended to be the grand thoroughfare linking the President's House with the Capitol, was still just a dusty trail hacked into the wooded countryside. A few churches had sprung up in the region, and Georgetown College, the brainchild of Father John Carroll, had been accepting and teaching students for three years—but so far, there were no theaters, no newspapers, and no real neighborhoods. Washington, D.C., was, for all intents and purposes, a ghost town. As compensation for the inconvenience, Washington promised each commissioner an annual salary of $1,600, about $48,500 today.

It wasn't enough for commissioners Thomas Johnson and David Stuart, both of whom submitted their resignations immediately; the third commissioner, Daniel Carroll of Rock Creek, agreed to remain on board only for as long as it took for a replacement to be found. Washington quickly appointed Maryland attorney Gustavus Scott to fill Johnson's seat and eventually replaced Carroll with former Virginia Congressman Alexander White. But finding replacements was difficult; the requirement that commissioners reside in the District was a lot to ask—even Washington's personal secretary, Tobias Lear, refused an entreaty from his own employer to take a seat on the commission.

Both Lear and Thomas Jefferson, however, thought it might be worthwhile to have a conversation with William Thornton, who not only had a personal interest in the Capitol, but also—thanks mostly to bad investments and a weakness for raising expensive horses—desperately needed a job. Lear found Thornton to be "a very sensible, genteel and well-informed man, ardent in his pursuits," though he cautioned the president that Thornton and Hoban were likely to clash on some matters involving architecture.[66]

A kind word from Jefferson was all it took for Thornton to move his wife and mother-in-law from Philadelphia to a house in Georgetown. As a member of the commission, Thornton would officially have "very extensive" oversight not only of the Capitol but also of the President's House and the entire District of Columbia. He was determined to make the most of it and to use his new position to make his mark on posterity. "I must do more than I have ever done," he explained, "or my name too will die."[67]

The president was also glad to have Thornton on the commission, convinced that with the dismissal of the constantly improvising Hallet, the Capitol would at last be built according to Thornton's designs without further question or conflict.

He would be wrong.

Physician and amateur architect William Thornton submitted the winning drawing in a national contest that asked Americans to design their own Capitol building. His elegant illustration featured a central structure that had a portico under a low dome—a feature that immediately caught George Washington's attention—that was flanked by wings for the House of Representatives and the Senate. Thornton's design still defines the basic layout of the building more than 230 years later.

CHAPTER 2

A Durable and Honorable Monument of Our Infant Republic

1795–1812

Appointing the man who had designed the Capitol to the commission tasked with overseeing its construction wouldn't be the panacea George Washington had been hoping for. For one thing, William Thornton's fellow commissioners didn't like him very much. Thornton would always be the self-proclaimed smartest guy in the room, and commissioners Gustavus Scott and Alexander White wasted no time in mocking Thornton as "a little genius at everything" while complaining to Thomas Jefferson that he was also a bad project manager.[1]

In fairness, it wasn't all Thornton's fault; the Capitol in early 1795 was mostly just a series of trenches still being filled with foundation stone. At that moment, workers were slowly putting in place the solid base needed for the construction of the building, following the plan agreed to in the summer of 1793, which would put Thornton's eye-catching exterior over Hallet's more practical interiors. But even under Hallet's supervision, much of the foundation stone had been laid carelessly and would eventually have to be either squared again or pulled out and relaid entirely.

And it wasn't just the foundation that would require the use of heavy stone; George Washington himself had decreed that both the Capitol and the President's House would be made of stone instead of brick, which had been used for most public buildings at that time. The decision was as much about symbolism as it was materials: these structures were meant to be grand ones built to last for the long life of a republic.

Fortunately, the sandstone Hallet had chosen to build with was in constant supply, due mostly to the work of day laborers and enslaved workers who were cutting stone as fast as they could at several quarries in the region—including one near Georgetown at Foggy Bottom and a larger one farther downriver near Fredericksburg where Aquia Creek emptied into the Potomac. Even with construction at the Capitol slowing as old foundations were torn out and relaid, the commissioners were determined to keep the stone coming quickly, warning one quarry owner to "keep the yearly hirelings at work from sunrise to sunset—particularly the Negroes."[2]

Stonecutting was grueling and miserable work, especially at the Aquia site in Virginia, which was often overrun with snakes and swarmed by mosquitoes. Quarrying involved hacking a series of cavities directly into a stone outcropping about ten or twenty feet apart, with each cavity about two feet wide and five feet high—just large enough for a man to stand in. Next, a perpendicular trench was slowly chopped—by hand—into the rock to connect the cavities, forming large chunks of stone about ten or twenty feet long and five feet high. Using chisels and iron wedges, stonecutters then split the stones into enormous rectangular blocks, which could be further trimmed to the desired size. Cut stones were then loaded by cranes onto sailing ships and ferried forty miles upriver to the docks just south of the Capitol. There, they would be slowly scooted on wooden sleds up Jenkins Hill to the construction site, where they would be further hacked and cut and shaped before being eased into place. The weights of individual blocks could vary widely, depending on size—a cubic foot of sandstone weighs about a hundred twenty pounds;[3] in January 1796 alone, more than 142 tons of rough-cut stone was shipped from Aquia to the Federal city.[4]

Even with the help of ropes, cranes, and sturdy horses, moving the stones was tough. It could take two days for six enslaved workers to unload a small ship and another three days for eight to load the stone onto the wooden sleds.[5] Over the course of the project, countless heavy stones would crash over the sides of the boats or slip off their sleds to be lost in the waters of the Potomac at the foot of Jenkins Hill. At another point, a ship groaning under the weight of nearly forty tons of stone sank near the Aquia quarry in twelve feet of water.

The labor for such a grand project was expensive—and with no money coming in from the Congress, the commissioners chose to rely on the cheapest labor they could find. As early as 1792, the commissioners had resolved "to hire good labouring negroes by the year, the masters clothing them well and finding each a blanket, the commissioners finding them provisions and paying twenty-one pounds a year."[6] Eager for the windfall, some area enslavers hired out their enslaved laborers for the project, putting them to work at both the President's House and the Capitol as carpenters, masons, painters, brickmakers, mortar mixers, and glazers.

Some of the most backbreaking labor was done in the saw pits on Jenkins Hill, where the enslaved were expected to put in brutal hours—working through the day and well past dark and without a break on the weekends—to cut trees into boards five to seven feet in length and several inches in thickness. Carpenters would then plane each board to ensure a smooth and level fit for floors or doors and window frames. Brickmaking, as a semiskilled trade, was a task often assigned to enslaved women or teenagers who molded bricks out of clay, sand, and water, then baked and cured them, sometimes for days, in gigantic fires that burned as hot as 2,000 degrees Fahrenheit. The making of mortar and plaster, which depended largely on enslaved labor, too, relied on a recipe of crushed oyster shells sifted with sand and mixed with water to create a sticky, spreadable paste.

According to records, between 1795 and 1801, payments were made for 385 enslaved laborers, providing their enslavers with about $60 per worker annually. Meanwhile, unskilled white laborers, who worked alongside the enslaved, were paid $70.[7] Starting in 1808, nonresident enslavers—which was most of them—were taxed on the income derived from the contracted use of enslaved labor, which caused considerable grumbling among enslavers, resulting in a marked decrease in the use of enslaved labor. The use of enslaved labor would be discontinued at the Capitol only because it was seen as unprofitable, not unprincipled.[8]

It was not lost on the relatively enlightened Thornton that the monument to freedom and democracy that he had designed would be built partly on the backs of those who would neither experience freedom nor participate in democracy. When the commissioners struggled with the need for more skilled stonecutters, Thornton saw it as an opportunity to reconcile a bitter reality with his ideals of emancipation or relocation; while he acknowledged the need for enslaved workers, he suggested they be permitted to work for their freedom and be granted "their liberty at the expiration of 5 or 6 years."[9] His suggestion was dismissed by his fellow commissioners.

Still, there were some enslaved laborers who were permitted to share in at least part of the payment allocated to their enslavers for their work, which they could use to purchase supplies—or, if they were lucky, their freedom. One such individual was a Maryland-born enslaved laborer named George Pointer, who had been rented out by his enslaver to the Patowmack Canal Company to assist with the construction of the canals running alongside the Potomac River. Pointer so impressed the directors of the company with his talents and reliability that they urged his enslaver to permit him to buy his freedom—which Pointer eventually secured for $300. As a freeman, Pointer would serve as one of the many boat captains who would ferry sandstone, marble, and other materials for the Capitol up and down the Potomac River to the docks near Jenkins Hill.[10]

Despite the reliance on cheap labor, there would never be enough money for the project—and by the beginning of 1795, the commissioners were fretting about a lack of progress, noting that despite the expenditure of £20,000 on the project, there wasn't much to show on Jenkins Hill, apart from a few outbuildings and some piles of raw materials. Growing concerned about the deadline, the commissioners determined that it was best to concentrate on getting at least one wing completed by 1800. They recommended concentrating on the north one, which was sturdier than the south wing—the foundation of which was still mostly a disaster—and had been designed with more rooms, making it more functional. But doing so would mean slowing work on the central rotunda and its dome, much to Washington's disappointment.

The commission also decided that the project needed a full-time supervisor and recruited English-born architect George Hadfield, who not only came highly recommended by artist John Trumbull but also had the advantage of being the brother of Thomas Jefferson's former lover, Maria Cosway. Hadfield had recently fallen into both a personal and a professional funk—there was some speculation he'd had his heart badly broken by a countess—and he took the position without hesitation, eventually arriving in the Federal district in October 1795.

Hadfield was immediately alarmed by what he saw. For one thing, when his predecessor, Stephen Hallet, had departed the city in an angry snit, he had taken with him any architectural plans or rough sketches that would have provided even the slightest bit of guidance for his replacement on how to proceed. "I find the building begun," reported Hadfield, his head spinning, "but do not find the necessary plans to carry on a work of this importance."[11] Hadfield's challenge, like Hallet's before him, was to figure out how to squeeze Hallet's interior into Thornton's exterior—a problem the baffled Hadfield thought could be remedied by simply removing the basement.

Perhaps predictably, Thornton objected and griped to Washington that the Englishman was trying to undermine his authority and reputation as the designer of the Capitol. He further informed the president that all great buildings had basements in them, a practice "adopted by many of the first architects."[12] Washington wisely refused to take a stance on the issue of basements and left it to Thornton and James Hoban, still overseeing work at the President's House—where things were proceeding in a much more orderly fashion—to determine the most appropriate course of action to take with Hadfield and his proposal.

With Thornton and Hoban piling on, Hadfield attempted a preemptive resignation in protest, then thought better of it, agreeing to remain on under the conditions imposed by the commissioners, the main one being that he "was engaged to superintend the execution of the plan without alteration."[13] In other words, he had to give Thornton his basement, just as Thornton had drawn it. By the end of the year, the basement of the north wing would be complete.

Thornton had done much to ensure he would prevail in such disputes; while Washington had balked at weighing in on the basement debate, he genuinely liked Thornton and was, for the most part, nearly always willing to give him the benefit of the doubt—and his way. It was a relationship Thornton worked hard to cultivate, partly by making sure he took the time to accompany the president on his regular rides from the capital to Mount Vernon as well as by keeping Washington well stocked with rum made from the sugar grown on Thornton's Tortola plantation. More important, Thornton had recently put his crew up on Jenkins Hill to work ripping out the foundation Hallet had laid for his square courtyard. Instead, he now had them slowly installing a foundation to support a central dome—the one architectural touch Thornton knew the president had his mind set on.

In early 1796, a message arrived in the Congress updating them on the progress being made in the Federal city. The report had been transmitted and signed by George Washington himself rather than by the commissioners, another sign of the president's increasing involvement as well as of his growing concern that the city might not be ready in time for the arrival of the Congress in 1800. Washington perhaps had some reason to be worried; while he had not yet announced it publicly, he had no intention of standing for a third term as president, and he was concerned his successor, whoever it might be, wouldn't share a similar zeal for the Capitol and the capital city. Before his term ended in March 1797, then, Washington wanted to ensure everything was in motion for the Capitol's timely completion.

As always, there was a problem with money. The initial plan to fund the construction of the Capitol using private funds raised from the sale of city lots had failed to generate much revenue. After several unsuccessful attempts to secure loans from banks at home or abroad, Washington was now appealing directly to a skeptical Congress for a guaranteed loan, though he left it to the Congress—and a special committee—to determine what the actual costs for completion might be.

It was just the excuse the Congress needed to delay and question every decision that had been made by the commission for the last two years, from the very design and size of the building to the speed of the work. Through it all, much of the complaining was done by Congressmen who had neither set foot in the District nor seen the Capitol building itself. To Washington's likely annoyance, the special committee also fussed over the dome, eventually concluding, noncommittally, that "the grand vestibule may or may not be covered with a dome; architects differ in opinion with regard to covering it."[14] The committee finally recommended providing the commissioners with a loan of $300,000—down from an initial suggestion of $500,000—and then put its faith in George Washington to see the project through.

It was mostly enough. With the money flowing again, work proceeded up on Jenkins Hill. But it was slow going; there was a shortage of workers in the summer of 1796, due mostly to a lack of sufficient or affordable housing, and Hadfield and the commissioners, frequently at odds, were engaged in a game of cat and mouse in which the persnickety architect repeatedly threatened to submit his resignation and the commissioners just as repeatedly threatened to accept it. Through it all, Washington calmly urged his commissioners to stay the course, and as the president's political career came to a voluntary end in early 1797, Washington reminded Thornton and the commissioners that it would now be largely up to them to ensure the Capitol was ready for the Congress in three years—especially as his successor, John Adams, had zero interest in maintaining the same kind of nearly daily oversight of the Capitol that Washington had. "[T]here are many who intermix doubts with anxiety, lest the principal building should not be in a situation to accommodate Congress," Washington warned the commissioners.[15]

The commissioners and Hadfield took Washington's admonition to heart, putting most of their bickering aside long enough to see to it that much of the north wing, which was to serve as the meeting place for the Senate, was in good shape by late summer. By now the basic structure was mostly complete, with the shingled roof—carefully and cleverly planned by Thornton so it was sloped enough for drainage but not high enough to be seen above the balustrades around the edge of the building—being loudly hammered into place. In the heat of the building below, carpenters toiled to lay wooden floors that had been carefully cut to fit together tightly, then sanded smooth by increasingly skilled enslaved laborers.

Curiously, at this moment, Commissioner Alexander White noted that the commissioners had intended for the central section of the building to be capped with not one dome but *two.* On the western half of the central section would be a columned dome, similar to those seen on temples, soaring over a large conference room, with a shorter, more traditional dome directly to its east and over "a grand circular vestibule."[16] It was an odd idea, one that had been suggested in a floor plan by Hallet and embraced by Thornton, who enthusiastically drew plans reflecting this new recommendation. It was a bad idea that gave the entire structure an odd, unbalanced, and thrown-together look. Congress seemed to agree; when Commissioner White traveled to Philadelphia in early 1798 to show Thornton's latest drawings and ask for yet more funding, the Congress reluctantly agreed to a loan of $100,000—it still refused to fund the project outright—but made clear that the money came on the condition that the clumsy, and ugly, double dome be scrapped. Thornton's elegant single dome was the look everyone preferred.

The progress, while slow, wasn't enough to save the cantankerous Hadfield. In May 1798, after months of his threatening to resign, weary commissioners pulled the plug on the architect and fired him for being too difficult to work with—though the commission's official dismissal merely noted that they considered him "deficient in practical knowledge of architecture."[17] In his place the commissioners installed the reliable James Hoban to oversee day-to-day operations at the Capitol, assigning him the same job up on Jenkins Hill that he was successfully doing over at the President's House. But with funds again drying up and only a little more than a year until the arrival of the Congress, Hoban was reminded that his priority, as directed by President Washington, was the completion of the Capitol's north wing. Both the Senate and the House would be expected to work out of the finished structure—a tight fit, to be sure, but Hoban was certain it could be done.

Hoban worked quickly, often relying on Thornton to provide architectural drawings—or at least rough sketches—to guide him as he oversaw completion of the roof, finished the brickwork, and set sandstone in place on the exterior walls. As the months wore on, Thornton became increasingly uninterested in providing detailed drawings; he huffily declared that Hoban—who had been given the official title of surveyor of public buildings, a designation that made Thornton positively jade with envy—should be responsible for creating such drawings. Soon, Thornton would provide Hoban with only vague descriptions of the work, informing him rather unhelpfully, for instance, that a particular wall was to be "very pale blue in fresco."[18] Hoban would eventually stop asking for Thornton's input.

Hoban would also put his management skills to work supervising the construction of two boardinghouses going up just to the north of the Capitol that were meant to provide incoming members of Congress with a place to stay as well as a bit of rental income for their owner and landlord: George Washington. The houses had been designed by Thornton, but it would be Washington who caught the criticism for their lack of curb appeal, with one District resident complaining that the structures had been "badly planned and conducted" and that Washington "knew how to give liberty to his country, but was wholly ignorant of art."[19]

By spring 1799, Hoban had plasterers at work inside the Capitol, putting the finishing touches on the interiors as they slathered nearly twenty tons of plaster onto the walls in corridors and committee rooms. While interior columns and window trim were in place—and in some rooms, false doors had been installed to ensure a proper sense of symmetry—a lack of reliable funding meant there would be little in the way of elaborate decoration; there would be no statues, no sculptures, no ornate finishes. The same was true of the exterior, where the only visible adornments were several lightning rods. That was fine by Washington, who had been asking his architects to concentrate on the north wing's infrastructure rather than its art—and once again, the design compromises had worked in the building's favor, with the lack of ostentation giving the structure a dignified and uniquely American simplicity rather than a European extravagance.

Still, setbacks would continue. The glass that had been ordered for the windows arrived broken—and what wasn't cracked or shattered was deemed to be of such poor quality that the commissioners returned it to the English supplier without payment. A miscalculation in the amount of raw materials needed to complete the north wing left the surrounding grounds strewn with nearly thirty thousand unused bricks and five hundred tons of unlaid stone.

But perhaps the biggest setback occurred on Saturday, December 14,

1799. That evening, between ten and eleven p.m., George Washington died in his upstairs bedroom at Mount Vernon. The Capitol's most enthusiastic supporter—as well as its most powerful advocate—was dead at the age of sixty-seven. He would see neither the building he had championed completed nor the Federal city that bore his name occupied by the United States government.

When Washington fell ill with a throat infection, Thornton was summoned to Mount Vernon in hopes that he might be able to provide the gasping president with some relief by performing a tracheotomy—a relatively new procedure in which the European-trained Thornton had some expertise. To his lifelong sorrow, Thornton—who lamented that Washington was "the best friend I ever had"—arrived too late to see the president alive, but he made the bizarre suggestion that he be permitted to reanimate the recently deceased Washington by slowly warming his body, inflating his lungs with air, and pumping him full of lamb's blood. "I was not seconded in this proposal," Thornton later wrote with some disappointment even as he continued to insist that "there was no doubt in my mind that his restoration was possible."[20]

If he couldn't restore his best friend to life, Thornton was determined to honor his memory in the next best way he knew how: by prominently entombing Washington in the very building whose cornerstone the president had laid just six years earlier. At Thornton's urging, on December 23, 1799, the Congress passed a resolution asking Martha Washington to approve interring the late president's body under "a marble monument . . . at the capitol of the city of Washington."[21]

As envisioned by Thornton, the remains of the president—and eventually those of Mrs. Washington—would be interred in a burial chamber two stories below the still unbuilt rotunda, placing the president both literally and figuratively at the center of the nation's capital. Just above the burial chamber, in the central room designated in his floor plans as a "Grand Vestibule," Thornton suggested erecting an enormous marble statue of Washington—the "marble monument" of the

Congressional resolution—and then cutting a ten-foot circular opening in the floor of the rotunda one story above it to permit visitors to view the statue from the chamber above.

It was a grandiose plan—and it didn't matter to Thornton, or the Congress, that Washington himself had explicitly requested in his will that he be buried on his beloved Mount Vernon estate. Nevertheless, after receiving the resolution in late December, Mrs. Washington penned a magnanimous response to President John Adams agreeing to allow her late husband's body, already entombed at Mount Vernon, to be relocated to the Capitol. "Taught, by that great example which I have so long had before me, never to oppose my private wishes to the public will," she wrote to Adams, "I must consent to the request made by Congress." Then, in a heartbreaking coda, she added that "in doing this, I need not, I cannot, say what a sacrifice of individual feeling I make to a sense of public duty."[22]

President Adams referred Mrs. Washington's response back to the Congress on January 8, 1800—but while Thornton would immediately begin drawing up plans for the presidential crypt and its accompanying marble monument, the Congress, at least for the moment, would take no further action. The president's final resting place would remain a matter of uncertainty, and debate, for the next three decades.

On Thursday, April 24, 1800, President John Adams formally approved legislation relocating the federal government from Philadelphia to its new home on the banks of the Potomac River. For the first time, Congress provided federal funding rather than a loan, laying out $9,000 to buy furniture and to cover the costs of moving as well as another $5,000 to secure "such books as may be necessary for the use of Congress"—an afterthought of a clause from which would later spring the gigantic Library of Congress. When Congress adjourned on May 15, Adams further instructed the members of his cabinet to ensure that all federal departments were packed, relocated, and operating out of their new D.C. offices thirty days later. While some government offices would remain in Philadelphia, the city's term as the nation's capital officially came to an end on June 11, 1800.

For many, making the transition from the relatively refined Philadelphia to the still undeveloped, muddy backwoods of Washington, D.C., was culture shock. As she made the trip to the Federal city, First Lady Abigail Adams lamented that "[w]oods are all you can see from Baltimore until you reach the City, which is only so in name."[23] With the arrival of the government, the population swelled up toward three thousand—but with fewer than four hundred houses, one new resident moaned that the District was merely "the scattered buildings of the desert."[24] Even members of Congress would have a hard time finding anywhere to stay, and many rented rooms in boardinghouses—like the two George Washington had built—where they often slept two to a bed. "I do not perceive how the members of Congress can possibly secure lodgings," remarked Treasury Secretary Oliver Wolcott Jr., "unless they will consent to live like Scholars in a college or Monks in a monastery, crowded ten or twenty in one house."[25] And so they would.

It would be just as crowded in the Capitol building, where the lone north wing was expected to serve as the meeting place and workspaces for both the Senate and the House of Representatives—and eventually the Supreme Court and the Library of Congress. But making room for the Congress alone was going to be difficult enough; the entire building, just slightly over two stories high, measured only 126 feet by 121.5 feet—barely forty yards long on a single side. The thirty-two-member Senate was provided with a meeting chamber that took up most of the northeastern corner of the ground floor and was under a high ceiling that vaulted up into a second-floor observation gallery. The 106-member House of Representatives, meanwhile, was assigned to a second-floor room intended for the Library of Congress: a cavernous chamber—eighty-six feet long, twenty-five feet wide, and thirty-six feet high—that occupied nearly the entire western half of the top floor and was directly across from the Senate's observation gallery. The remaining space on both floors was crammed with offices for clerks and meeting rooms for committees.

Outside, Thornton already had crews at work laying the circular foundations for the central rotunda and constructing the basement of the south wing. As suggested, the exterior of the north wing remained unadorned—and, in fact, its south-facing wall was still just unfinished red brick, which could more easily be attached to the center building as the structure was constructed. And on the lawn a short distance away was another vital structure: a gigantic privy, seventy feet long, eight feet wide, and fourteen feet high, recently completed at a cost of $234. (Given the status of its users, it's likely that seating was individual, with private chambers rather than communal facilities.) With the Congress preparing to move in for the opening of its next session on November 17, the north wing of the Capitol—at the moment the *only* wing of the Capitol—was ready for occupancy. Thornton—and L'Enfant and Hallet and Hadfield and Hoban—had met their deadline.

On November 22, 1800, President Adams addressed the Congress from the floor of the Senate, an elegant chamber framed by thin wooden walls that had been gracefully curved to shape the room into a semicircle. At the front of the chamber, the seat of the vice president—officially the Senate's presiding officer, as designated by the Constitution—looked out toward twelve Ionic columns forming another graceful arc defining the Senate floor. Vice President Jefferson had made a point of asking Thornton to design the chamber with enough room for Senators to walk *behind* his chair rather than obscure his view for even a moment by walking in front of him.

Adams opened his remarks—part of his annual message to Congress, a precursor to today's State of the Union address—by celebrating the relocation of the federal government to the new Federal district and to the Capitol, which, he acknowledged, still needed a bit of work:

> I congratulate the people of the United States on the assembling of Congress at the permanent seat of their Government, and I congratulate you, gentlemen, on the prospect of a residence not to be changed. Although there is cause to apprehend that accommodations are not now so complete as might be wished, yet there is great reason to believe that this inconvenience will cease with the present session.

Fittingly, Adams—in the political fight of his life as he skirmished with foreign governments and squashed domestic partisan dissent—reminded the Congress of its larger responsibilities to the nation and urged them to be worthy of the man whose name would be forever associated with the capital city:

> May this territory be the residence of virtue and happiness! In this city may that piety and virtue, that wisdom and magnanimity, that constancy and self-government, which adorned the great character whose name it bears be forever held in veneration! Here and throughout our country may simple manners, pure morals, and true religion flourish forever![26]

Still, even in a magnanimous mood, Adams wasn't above a bit of political partisanship. Following the death of commissioner Gustavus Scott on Christmas Day 1800, Adams—who had learned only a week earlier of his defeat in the contentious election of 1800—shoehorned in the appointment of his own nephew William Cranch as a replacement commissioner. With his lame-duck appointment, Adams was deliberately denying the incoming administration the opportunity to fill the position—a move that was sure to grate on the next president.

Exactly who that president might be, however, was a matter that would be determined by the House of Representatives as its members stared down the nation's first real Constitutional crisis. While the election of 1800 had seen John Adams lose the presidency definitively on electoral votes, there was no firm winner, as both Thomas Jefferson and Aaron Burr received seventy-three electoral votes apiece while Adams trailed with sixty-five, narrowly edging out a fourth contender, Charles Cotesworth Pinkney, who had sixty-four. With no clear guidance from the Constitution on what to do in the event of a tie, the House of Representatives ad-libbed, gathering in its cramped new chamber on the top floor of the Capitol in February 1801 to select the winner. Each of the sixteen state Congressional delegations were permitted to cast a single vote for president until one candidate earned the support of a majority of nine states or more. For a week, the states remained deadlocked until finally, on February 17—after thirty-five rounds of voting and plenty of political horse-trading—Thomas Jefferson was elected as the nation's third president with Burr, who had finished second, as his vice president.

Fifteen days later, on March 4, 1801, President-elect Jefferson left his rooms at Conrad and McMunn's boardinghouse on New Jersey Avenue in southeast Washington, D.C., and made the short walk north to the Capitol for his inauguration—the first to take place in the building as well as the first time in American government that power would transfer peacefully to a different political party. Taking to the crowded floor of the Senate—where, only months earlier, he had presided as vice president—Jefferson was administered the oath of office by Chief Justice John Marshall. In his first remarks as president, Jefferson assured a packed gallery of spectators that the American government was more resilient than mere politics.

"[E]very difference of opinion is not a difference of principle," Jefferson said warmly, informing the members of the warring political parties—especially the losers—that there were to be no hard feelings. "We are all Republicans," said Jefferson, "[and] we are all Federalists."[27] It was a sentiment that impressed the journalist Margaret Bayard Smith, who later wrote to her sister in awe:

> I have this morning witnessed one of the most interesting scenes, a free people can ever witness. The changes of administration, which in every government and in every age have most generally been epochs of confusion, villainy, and bloodshed, in this our happy country take place without any species of distraction, or disorder.[28]

For now.

Knowing as he did of Jefferson's roles in lobbying for the Potomac site for the Federal city and in selecting the winning designs for the Capitol, Thornton likely had high hopes for the new administration. He excitedly anticipated a return to the enthusiasm for the project that had been lacking under President Adams.

It would not take long for Thornton to be disappointed in the Jefferson administration.

A strident believer in a lean and limited federal government, Jefferson favored a smaller Federal district, with fewer federal employees and none of the kind of opulent monuments—including Thornton's current pet project, the Capitol crypt for the corpse of George Washington and its marble monument—that had been favored by L'Enfant and others. While he wouldn't resolve the issue once and for all, Jefferson dismissed the idea of entombing the first president in the Capitol as too monarchical, too much like enshrining sovereigns in Westminster Abbey or boy kings beneath pyramids. Without quite nodding enthusiastically along with Jefferson, the Congress would nonetheless continue to delay making any decisions about the final resting place of the first president.

Despite Jefferson's diplomatic words at his inaugural speech, politics also came into play. The three-man commission that had been in place since the Washington administration to oversee the District and the

Capitol was now derided as a Federalist contrivance—and Adams's last-minute appointment of his nephew William Cranch hadn't done a thing to convince critics that the commission was anything other than purely political. When Congress approved legislation in late February 1801 to formally place the District of Columbia under the jurisdiction of the Congress—permitting residents of the Federal city to establish their own municipal government while ceding most of its authority to the Congress[29]—Jefferson used the reorganization as an opportunity to remove the Federalist William Cranch and replace him with the more conservative Tristram Dalton.

Yet, even as their membership shifted, the commissioners were unanimous in their response to the demands from the cramped House of Representatives, whose officials wanted a larger space to call their own—especially as the results of the 1800 census meant that when the Congress reconvened in 1802, its ranks would swell from 106 to 141, with the addition of thirty-five new Congressional districts. Of the sixteen current states, New York's population had grown the fastest, earning seven new seats while Pennsylvania gained five and Virginia three. Ohio, with its single vote, would be admitted to the Union in 1803, bringing the total number of House seats to 142. The House wanted its own dedicated chamber as quickly as possible.

It was not an unreasonable request. As directed by President Washington and reiterated by Adams, Hoban had hustled to ensure that at least one wing of the Capitol was finished and ready in time for occupancy by the Congress in 1800—and he had completed the job capably, providing an elegant but lone two-story structure that the two chambers had shared ever since. House members, who found themselves crammed into a room designated for a library—large, to be certain, but not close to large enough—were understanding but losing patience. Where was the soaring central rotunda with its noble dome that Washington had enthused about? And when could they expect to see construction begin on their own wing just south of that rotunda, where Hoban and the commissioners had promised them a House chamber large enough to comfortably contain the nation's premier legislative body?

All good questions—and although the commissioners had very little money available for construction of a brand-new and permanent chamber, they nevertheless tried to provide some answers. In the spring of 1801, they tasked Hoban with designing a temporary House chamber to be erected on the current foundations of the missing south wing, which had gone mostly unused since being laid—in some places badly—by Hallet in 1796. At the moment, the footprint of the south wing was little more than a large rectangle surrounding a central ellipse—the ghostly stone outline of Thornton's intended shape of the new House chamber. Hoban decided to use those elliptical footings for his temporary structure and quickly completed drawings for a large oval-shaped wooden building that he estimated could be built speedily and, better yet, cheaply, spitballing costs of about $5,600. Until he had the funding to build a permanent House chamber, it would have to do.

With the commissioners in his corner, Jefferson—ever the aspiring architect—was now free to approve and oversee any work being done at the Capitol without any interference or second opinions. On June 1, 1801, the new president enthusiastically signed off on Hoban's proposed temporary structure, leaving it to the Congress to appropriate funding for building it. Before the end of the month, the Congress contracted with architects and surveyors William Lovering and William Dyer, who completed the temporary wing on time, and under budget, before the end of the year.[30]

And what a structure it was: an enormous, ninety-foot-long elliptical room that had a three-row observation gallery encircling the upper floor and that was connected to the Senate wing by a long, covered wooden passageway 145 feet long. It might have looked impressive, but it was poorly built and even more poorly ventilated; Lovering and Dyer had completed the work in less than seven months, and their haste was obvious in the final structure. Airflow was so poor that Congressmen often complained of the "suffocating feeling of the air in the Hall."[31]

Members would soon come to refer to it as "the Oven," not only as a commentary on its stifling heat and dead air but also as a nod to the building's profile, which resembled a Dutch oven—or at least a Dutch oven with its circular outer walls propped up at regular intervals by wooden braces. "The House of Representatives sat in some peril of their lives," noted one historian, "for had not the walls been strongly shored up from without, the structure would have crumbled to pieces."[32] Still, no matter how hot and rickety—and perhaps unsafe—it might have been, the members of the House finally had a place of their own.

And from the new chamber early in the summer of 1802, the House of Representatives would concur with the recommendation of Thomas Jefferson to dissolve the oversight commission entirely—a bit of bloody-knuckled political payback to the Adams administration. The elimination of the commission made Thornton nervous; a love of entertaining and a fondness for expensive horses meant he still needed regular income from a steady job, and he immediately started searching for a new position, mentioning his connection with George Washington wherever he could. But politics had changed in the Federal city; the original Founding Father's name didn't carry the weight it used to. Thornton found doors closed in his face.

To his likely surprise, he found a benefactor in Thomas Jefferson—the president's quibble had been with the former administration, not with Thornton—who appointed him as the first commissioner of the newly established Patent Office. It was a job with a regular though not extravagant salary and a position that Thornton, with his dilettantish leanings and wide range of interests, was well suited for and took seriously—he would review nearly every patent submitted to his offices personally and eventually quadrupled the number of patents awarded each year. Thornton would also become friendly with Jefferson and dine regularly at the President's House, where he likely continued to remind Jefferson, and anyone who would listen, of George Washington's grand vision for the Capitol—and how much that vision overlapped with Thornton's own. Despite his change in occupation, Thornton was hoping Jefferson would still give him some sway over the Capitol.

Jefferson, however, had other plans. With the commission dissolved, Jefferson personally appointed Thomas Munroe, who had served as a clerk to the commission, as the new superintendent tasked with overseeing the entire City of Washington, though he made it quite clear that Munroe's authority did not extend to the Capitol building. Instead, Jefferson intended for all decisions regarding the Capitol to run through his office—or at least through his chosen designee and right-hand man. Jefferson liked Hoban, who had overseen the work at the Capitol without any real conflict or drama—but now that Jefferson was taking a more hands-on approach to the design and construction of the Capitol, he was looking for a true collaborator—and that wasn't Hoban. Jefferson thanked Hoban for his service at the Capitol, dismissed him without prejudice, and replaced him with the man he thought was a better fit for his own architectural sensibilities: a talented though prickly thirty-eight-year-old architect named Benjamin Henry Latrobe.

The British-born Latrobe had been formally educated in architecture, so his bona fides for the job as the next Architect of the Capitol—or surveyor of public buildings, as the position was presently called—were undeniable. Jefferson had first come across Latrobe six years earlier in Fredericksburg, Virginia, where the architect—who had designed the state penitentiary in Virginia and the Bank of Pennsylvania in Philadelphia, both to considerable acclaim—had impressed the then vice president with his detailed accounting of the installation of canals near Charlottesville.

It was easy to see how Jefferson had been captivated by Latrobe; the man was a charmer, overflowing with confidence—and, at times, an inflated sense of self—and at six foot two, he could go from studious to smoldering just by dramatically removing his round-rimmed eyeglasses. Later, when Jefferson was considering the construction of covered dry docks on the Potomac, Latrobe again mesmerized him with passionate discourse that included lengthy monologues on the quality of limestone, the construction of arches, and "the domestic manners of Paris."[33] When it came time to select the next Architect of the Capitol, then, Jefferson felt sure he had found his man.

On March 6, 1803, Jefferson wrote to Latrobe to formally offer him the job, sweetening the deal by informing him that the Congress—which had grown exhausted by the delays in completing the building—had finally agreed to appropriate federal funding to finish the project, allocating $50,000 for the south wing, though still providing no money to build the central rotunda and dome. Latrobe accepted the job and was in Washington, D.C., by April, ready to focus on tearing down the sweltering Oven and replacing it with a proper and permanent House of Representatives.

Shortly after Latrobe's arrival, Jefferson pulled the architect aside and asked him to also make a frank appraisal of the condition of the north wing, which was already showing signs of wear, including flaking plaster, rotting floors, and a persistently leaky roof. After inspecting the north wing, Latrobe was alarmed; in his view, the entire building had been constructed with poor materials and in such a ramshackle manner that there was nothing to do but gut the building and start again. Jefferson privately agreed with that assessment but advised against proceeding with any work in the Senate wing until the new wing for the House of Representatives was completed.

But Latrobe didn't feel much better about Thornton's crude floor plans for the House wing, which essentially depicted the interior as not much more than a cavernous warehouse with a huge, oval-shaped meeting room at its center. Latrobe appealed to the president to let him redesign the interiors—but Jefferson, while sympathetic, reminded the architect that George Washington had personally signed off on Thornton's designs, and thus Latrobe was obligated to stick to them. However, Jefferson agreed that if structural integrity became an issue, Latrobe would have some leeway to deviate from Thornton's plans.

Still, Latrobe was determined to leave his fingerprints on the Capitol, hoping to make the new House chamber in his own image—and, if given the chance, the Senate chambers as well. In a long report to the Congress, Latrobe was hypercritical of Thornton's proposed designs for the House chamber, stridently questioning many of the first architect's decisions on room sizes, lighting, and locations of stairways and doorways, calling some of his choices "useless if not absurd."[34] Latrobe was also openly scornful of Thornton both as a draftsman and as a project manager, derisively referring to him as the "stupid genius" whom he personally blamed for the shoddy work in the Capitol's north wing. That was probably an unfair charge to lob solely at Thornton—the north wing had been overseen and constructed by many hands, not just his—but that was fine with Latrobe, who was also happy to lump previous architects and overseers into a club he sneeringly dismissed as "charlatans in architecture."[35]

While Latrobe titled his report "A Private Letter," it was anything but after being reproduced roundly in newspapers and pamphlets—and Thornton immediately and rightly saw Latrobe as a threat to his own legacy as Washington's handpicked designer and architect. Thornton pled his case publicly as well, defending his artistic and architectural visions and reminding Latrobe, and the Congress, that most of his decisions regarding room size and location had been approved by three presidents. It was little wonder, then, that when Latrobe asked Thornton for more detailed drawings or floor plans for the House wing to the south, Thornton—as had L'Enfant and Hallet when similarly cornered—refused to provide any.

As Thornton seethed, Latrobe set to work tearing down the Oven, which sent the House of Representatives back to their large room in the north wing, which was still designated for the future Library of Congress. At the same time, Latrobe, already planning improvements to the south wing, was carving more usable space for committee rooms out of Thornton's open-floor plan by raising the House chamber one story to what Latrobe would call "the principal floor." He would also alter the shape of the chamber from an ellipse to a hippodrome—essentially an oval with its long sides flattened, similar in shape to a modern racetrack.

They were changes that were certain to set off the older architect—though by this point, the relationship between the Latrobe and Thornton had grown so noxious that Jefferson, hoping for a truce, summoned both to the President's House. When that meeting failed to produce any peace, the president next directed Latrobe to send him revised drawings of his plans for the south wing, "retaining as much as possible the features of that adopted by General Washington."[36] Thornton had clearly made his point—Jefferson had taken his side—but he would begin to grouse harder and louder anyway, eventually airing his complaints about Latrobe in haughty articles and letters published in the newspapers.

At Jefferson's urging, Latrobe eventually tried ignoring Thornton's attacks—and succeeded in doing so, mainly because he spent most of his time with his wife and family away from the Federal city. As a side hustle, Latrobe was also doing business in Pennsylvania and Delaware, where he maintained private employment for the Chesapeake and Delaware Canal. That meant, as some annoyed Congressmen pointed out, that Latrobe was often supervising the Capitol project from a hundred fifty miles away.

While that was true, Latrobe had chosen a talented young Englishman named John Lenthall to serve as his "clerk of works" overseeing the work at the Capitol and generally act as his right-hand man and liaison with both Jefferson and the Congress. Lenthall was a good choice for both roles; he was a skilled architect who understood the importance of keeping careful records and detailed inventories that he could regularly place in front of influential but still skeptical Congressmen as they deliberated on funding for the project.

But even with Lenthall managing day-to-day operations, progress was slow—and part of the sluggish pace was due to Latrobe himself. While he had lost the fight with Thornton over the basic layout of the building, Latrobe was nonetheless determined to impress with his taste in interior design. What this meant in practice was that no detail was too small for his attention, and he wasn't going to skimp on the quality of any of the materials he chose to use. When Jefferson, still trying to keep costs down, suggested surrounding the House chamber with columns carved from wood rather than stone, a horrified Latrobe pushed back. Privately, he fumed to Lenthall that "[t]he wooden column idea is one with which I never will have anything to do. On that you may rely. I will give up my office sooner than build a temple of disgrace to myself and Mr. Jefferson."[37]

Artistic disagreements with Jefferson aside, Latrobe—like George Washington—understood that there was an inherent symbolism in the building at the center of the new government and that it deserved to be built for the ages. As far as Latrobe was concerned, the Capitol—like the new republic itself—should be constructed only from the strongest and sturdiest of materials.

Even as brick- and stonework slowly went up for the exterior of the new House wing—a mirror image of its Senate counterpart just across the empty space where the central rotunda and dome *still* weren't standing—the Capitol was fast becoming a tourist attraction, mostly for nosy visitors who wanted to peek at its construction. And its location, when pointed out to visitors, was no longer "up on Jenkins Hill"; rather, they were now directed "up to *Capitol Hill.*"

While Jefferson had been using the term casually in his correspondence since 1793, the name had recently crept into everyday use, showing up in newspaper articles and local advertisements.[38] The capital city, too, was becoming more of a destination, especially as the arrival of the diplomatic corps gave the city a more worldly and urbane atmosphere. Not everyone was impressed. Irish poet Thomas Moore thought Washington was, at best, an "embryo capital . . . where fancy sees squares in morasses, obelisks in trees . . . with shrines unbuilt and heroes yet unborn."[39]

Jefferson, however, surveyed the young city with approval, designating it "a pleasant country-residence . . . furnishing a plain and substantially good society."[40] Such enthusiasm didn't make it any easier to navigate the unfinished roads; one visitor noted that Pennsylvania Avenue—envisioned as the city's grand thoroughfare connecting the President's House to the Capitol—was mostly a narrow road hacked through bushes and brambles. Latrobe's own son described it as "a ditch, often filled with stagnant water. . . . [I]n dry weather the avenue was all dust; in wet weather, all mud."[41]

Through the wet and the weather, Latrobe worked slowly but steadily—and sometimes remotely—engaging Lenthall to help squeeze another $110,000 out of an increasingly impatient Congress by promising the money would at last be enough to complete the House wing—an empty promise, as it turned out, and one that would do little to endear the architect to the Congress. But with Jefferson encouraging the architect to hire as many carpenters and plasterers as he could—"[p]rice must not be regarded," Jefferson told Latrobe in words he would come to regret[42]—Latrobe could do one thing inside the House wing that Hoban hadn't had the money to do during his work on the Senate side: decorate it. And he had big plans, imagining decorative columns—made of stone, not wood—topped by ornate capitals and a House chamber adorned with a gigantic eagle carved into the frieze. On the chamber's outer edges, he wanted huge statues representing Agriculture, Art, Science, and Commerce looking benevolently down on the Congress and, behind the chair of the Speaker of the House, an enormous statue of Liberty.

Latrobe was a first-rate draftsman—he could draw the decorative capitals he envisioned beautifully—but he wasn't a sculptor; what was needed, then, was a craftsman skilled in stone and marble. Unfortunately, no American sculptor met the high expectations of either Latrobe or Jefferson—the best of the candidates, William Rush of Philadelphia, worked primarily in wood, not stone. If Latrobe wanted a classically trained sculptor skilled in stone or marble, he was going to have to look for one in Europe.[43]

At Jefferson's urging, Latrobe sought recommendations from Philip Mazzei, a longtime friend and business associate of the president who was now residing in Pisa. Latrobe asked Mazzei to recruit two Italian sculptors—preferably one to work in stone, one in marble—and send them to the United States as quickly as possible with all expenses paid by the United States government. On September 12, 1805, Mazzei wrote to Jefferson to inform him that he had found two young sculptors, Giuseppe Franzoni and his brother-in-law, Giovanni Andrei, "superior to the work they are required for, and remarkable for good moral and excellent temper."[44] Mazzei's word was good enough for Latrobe; Franzoni and Andrei were immediately dispatched to the Federal city.

In early 1806, the two sculptors arrived in Washington, where Latrobe promptly put Franzoni to work on the gigantic eagle he envisioned for the House chamber while assigning Andrei the more detailed, smaller decorative touches on walls and ceilings. There were problems almost immediately; Andrei, while talented, was a putterer—"the slowest hand ever I saw," sighed Latrobe[45]—and Franzoni was struggling with his eagle, which Latrobe thought looked too Roman and not at all like the American bald eagle he had envisioned. Searching for proper references for the young Italian, Latrobe wrote to the American painter Charles Willson Peale in Philadelphia and asked for drawings of the head and claws of a bald eagle. Peale promptly sent his drawings, along with an unexpected prize, a taxidermized bald eagle head. With this most useful reference on hand, Latrobe was happy with Franzoni's next try, a gorgeous bald eagle with a fourteen-foot wingspan carved into the frieze above the nearly twenty-seven-foot-high columns circling the House chamber. "I seem to see even now the Speaker's chair, with its rich surroundings, and the great stone eagle with outspread wings projecting from the frieze," recalled Latrobe's son years later, "as though it were hovering over and protecting those below."[46]

Franzoni's next assignment was the statue Latrobe wanted to place at the center of the chamber, just behind the Speaker's chair—a nearly nine-foot-high sculpture of a seated Lady Liberty with an eagle at her left hand. Once again, Latrobe was unhappy with Franzoni's early model, which caused him such headaches that he complained to Lenthall that "Lady Liberty . . . seldom behaves much like a Lady."[47] After multiple revisions, Franzoni would eventually get it right, finally unveiling a giant plaster model of Liberty, who had an eagle at her side and who was holding a rolled copy of the Constitution in her right hand and a liberty cap in her left. An impressed Latrobe said it was "excellent work and does Franzoni credit."[48] It was the first statue of Liberty to be formally displayed in the young country.

Latrobe had designed a striking interior for the Congress to occupy; now he just needed to make sure members could see once they were inside it. Latrobe was a stickler for adequate lighting; he always thought carefully about the way the sun would strike the Capitol at different times of day, and drew up room plans to ensure he could make the best use of natural daylight to illuminate his interiors. But in this matter, too, President Jefferson had strong opinions and insisted that the chamber be lit by skylights inset in the domed ceiling of the House chamber in a manner similar to the skylights he had seen in the Halle aux blés in Paris.

Latrobe could see only problems with that approach, from waterproofing to concerns that the sun beating down on the windows would make the chamber too hot. Latrobe delicately suggested lighting the room instead with an architectural lantern—a raised rooftop structure with glass windows that let light stream from all sides, but at more indirect angles. Latrobe tried to convince Jefferson that skylights were impractical and prone to excessive condensation—"What shall I do when the condensed vapor showers down upon the heads of the members [of Congress] from 100 skylights?" he asked.[49] But the persistent president insisted. Latrobe complied. Once built, the skylights dripped with condensation and blinded Congressmen with direct sunlight. Latrobe had been right.

Such disagreements, however, were thankfully rare, and both Jefferson and Latrobe were proud of the work on the south wing. Latrobe thanked the president for supporting him in his insistence on using only the best materials and hiring the best artists and craftsmen. "The works already created are the monuments of your judgment and your zeal and of your taste," Latrobe told Jefferson deferentially.[50] The president himself was effusive in his praise of Latrobe and their work together and finally understood that the investment was worth it. "I think that [the Capitol] when finished will be a durable and honorable monument of our infant republic," wrote Jefferson, "and will bear favorable comparison with the remains of the same kind of the ancient republics of Greece & Rome."[51]

Honorable it would be. Durable, it would not.

On October 26, 1807, President Jefferson called the Congress into session to debate the matter of America's continued neutrality in the Napoleonic Wars. Of special concern was the increasingly aggressive behavior of Great Britain, which had begun stopping American ships to force American seamen into serving on British vessels in their fight against the French. Members of Congress, who had been cooped up in the library space in the north wing since the razing of the Oven four years earlier, were anxious to take up the discussion in their new chamber. Latrobe wrote that their watching the building being slowly constructed had "created a very great impatience in all members to occupy their new Hall at the next session."[52]

While Latrobe had overpromised on the readiness of the chamber for the past several years, the arrival and installation of the glass for Jefferson's beloved skylights in August meant the new House chamber was finally ready for occupancy by autumn 1807, just in time for the debate on American neutrality. As members filed into their new space, Latrobe felt certain both the Congress and the public would be impressed with his work, though he worried that any descriptions in the newspapers would fail to do it justice. "No one who has not seen the Hall of Congress can . . . understand exactly the effect and appearance of the room," he fretted.[53]

The press nevertheless did its best, with the editor of the *National Intelligencer* hailing the chamber as "the handsomest room in the world occupied by a deliberative body." The *Washington Federalist*, meanwhile, conceded that while the space was attractive, it was so large that voices echoed loudly during floor debates, making it impossible to hear anything; another newspaper, the *True American and Commercial Advertiser* of Philadelphia, characterized the acoustics as "floating reverberations."[54] Latrobe bristled at such criticism, but privately agreed that the acoustics garbled "with equal impartiality the speeches of the eloquent, [and] the reveries of the stupid."[55] As a solution, Latrobe agreed to hang heavy crimson drapes between the enormous columns encircling the chamber to soak up the echo—and even he had to admit he was pleased with the elegant look they gave the chamber, calling it "most pleasing."

But the chamber's elegant look was also expensive. When Latrobe submitted his annual report to Congress in early 1808, he noted almost too casually that he had exceeded his budget by more than $35,000—an overcharge that Congressman John Randolph railed was "illegal and unjustifiable."[56] Latrobe was flummoxed by the response and hurt when the Congress asked for a formal investigation into the costs for the new structure. In Latrobe's mind, ensuring the House wing was completed quickly and safely had been an act of patriotism—and besides, hadn't the president himself insisted that "[p]rice must not be regarded"?

The House would ultimately determine that Latrobe's overages were acceptable and would provide federal funding to cover the deficit. Publicly, the architect had been vindicated; privately, however, his relationship with Jefferson was souring. Writing to Latrobe from Monticello, Jefferson—who spent most his life perpetually in debt—had the nerve to lecture the architect for being careless with federal funding:

> The lesson of last year has been a serious one, it has done you great injury & has much been felt by myself—it was so contrary to the principles of our Government, which makes the representatives of the people the sole arbiters of the public expense, and do not permit any work to be forced on them on a larger scale than their judgment deems adopted to the circumstances of the Nation.[57]

A frustrated Latrobe offered to resign; Jefferson, while still insisting he had never suggested money was no object, refused to even consider it. Latrobe would stay, but his reputation would be permanently sullied by the accusations of wastefulness.

With work on the House wing mostly complete—it still required some decorative detail and minor structural work—Latrobe could now train his focus on the Senate wing to the north. Because of its cracking plaster and rotten beams, Latrobe told the Congress that "[t]he present chamber cannot be considered as altogether safe."[58] But rather than replace the rotten floors and repair the sagging roof, Latrobe proposed to completely rebuild the interior within the existing exterior walls, using sturdy masonry and stone arches for structural support instead of wooden beams.

With the approval of the Congress, Latrobe began work on the first phase of the project by tearing out the entire eastern portion of the building. He concentrated on boosting the Senate chamber up from the ground floor to the first and—as he had done in the House wing—creating a new ground-floor space for hearing rooms and offices for clerks. Using the existing semicircular footprint, Latrobe planned to add directly beneath the new Senate chamber a dedicated meeting space for the Supreme Court, which had been holding its sessions in a spare committee room. While the repairs to its chamber were underway, the ever-patient members of the Senate continued to carry out their business in one of the small committee rooms on the first floor of the north wing.

The reliable Lenthall was assigned the task of overseeing construction of the new ground floor while Latrobe set to work with Franzoni fine-tuning the interior. Once again, no detail was too small to escape Latrobe's attention. To support the weight of the interior vaults he was constructing by the east entrance, Latrobe installed six new columns carved from the sandstone still being shipped in regularly from the Aquia Creek site. But rather than top his columns with capitals carved in the traditional Corinthian style—which often featured sculpted acanthus leaves spreading upward—Latrobe created his own uniquely American order of architecture.

In a stunning series of drawings provided to Franzoni, Latrobe sketched a set of capitals carved to resemble not acanthus but rather several ears of maize standing on their ends and tied together with rope, with their husks pulled open far enough to reveal the delicate kernels within. It was a distinctly American design—flint corn was a crop cultivated by Native Americans—and Franzoni beautifully translated Latrobe's drawings into a sculpted model that so pleased Latrobe that he proudly had it delivered to Jefferson to use as a stand for his sundial in his gardens at Monticello. Jefferson, too, loved it, and Latrobe seemed surprised to find that members of Congress did as well. "This Capital . . . obtained me more applause from the Members of Congress than all the Works of Magnitude, of difficulty & of splendor that surround them," he told Jefferson somewhat incredulously. He also noted that admiring Congressmen were already referring to his work as the "Corn Cob Capitals"—"whether for the sake of alliteration, I cannot tell," Latrobe reported with a shrug.[59]

If Latrobe was slowly winning admirers in the Congress, there was one person who remained unimpressed by him. William Thornton—still smarting from Latrobe's criticism of his work on the Senate wing and annoyed by his rival's tinkering with the floor plans of the House wing—had taken their disagreement public, insulting and taunting Latrobe in the pages of the *Washington Federalist*, a local newspaper. Thornton poked fun at the statues and decorative sculpture in the new House chamber, likening Franzoni's majestic eagle to a mere goose and questioning Latrobe's preference for lighting the chamber with a lantern—a raw spot, given Latrobe's disagreements with Jefferson, that likely irritated the architect even more than Thornton might have realized.

Thornton also made a number of odd accusations—among them the curious charges that Latrobe was neither English nor an actual architect—and claimed that George Washington himself had told him that when it came to Latrobe, "I can place no confidence in him whatsoever." Latrobe fired back, telling Thornton he considered his observations "too ignorant, vain, and despicable for argumentative refutation"—and back and forth they went until April 1808, when Latrobe finally sued Thornton for libel, asking for $10,000 in damages plus court costs. (The case would eventually be settled in 1813 in Latrobe's favor, with the architect settling for the public victory and, with his point made, waiving any out-of-pocket damages from Thornton beyond one cent plus court fees.)[60]

Still, it was clear Thornton had struck a nerve—and, in some cases, had hit the mark. When a Latrobe-designed arch in the Treasury Building collapsed during a hard freeze, Thornton couldn't resist tweaking Latrobe in a bit of verse as a "planner of grand steps and walls, / This falling arch-maker, this blunder roof gilder."[61] In his private correspondence with Lenthall, Latrobe could only shrug off the smear. "I am sorry the arches have fallen," he wrote, "but I have had these accidents before on a larger scale and must therefore grin and bear it."[62]

Latrobe's grin would fade shortly. As he continued with the drawings for the north wing, Latrobe designed a graceful semicircular chamber for the Supreme Court, with a domed ceiling supported by nine vaults radiating from the head of the chamber like the spokes of an umbrella. In executing this plan, however, Lenthall chose to modify Latrobe's design, using cheaper and simpler annular vaults at the outer edges of the space. Latrobe grumbled but approved Lenthall's modified plan, deferring to his foreman's expertise in overseeing similar vaulting in the south wing.

It would be a fatal error. In late July, work began on Lenthall's modified vaults, which were constructed on top of wooden frames to keep the structure in place for the two months it would take for the masonry to adequately set and dry. On Friday, September 16, 1808, Lenthall and a work crew began carefully removing the framework from the vaulting; the following Monday, as the last support was slowly removed, the ceiling above cracked and groaned under its own weight. Alarmed workers dove for the doorways as Lenthall's vaults failed, and the domed ceiling collapsed in a hail of bricks and mortar. Miraculously, there would be only one fatality: John Lenthall, who was crushed to death beneath more than a ton of debris.[63]

There were cries of conspiracy and whispers that the project had been vandalized by Federalists bitter over its growing costs. Latrobe, however, dismissed the rumors, assumed all responsibility for the accident, and publicly mourned the loss of his colleague. "[H]e was by all those who had known him long as much loved as respected," Latrobe wrote in the pages of the *National Intelligencer.* "His loss to the public will not be easy to repair."[64] A later urban legend would claim that with his dying breath, Lenthall placed a curse on the Capitol building[65]—which is unlikely, as he was already dead by the time his body was found in the rubble of the collapsed courtroom and there would have been no one around to hear his dying words. Conspiracy theories and ghost stories aside, however, John Lenthall's death is the first recorded fatality to have taken place inside the Capitol building. It would not be the last.

Latrobe would have the courtroom rebuilt using his original design—though, slightly spooked by Lenthall's fate, he would incorporate another row of supporting vaults to provide additional strength—and work would continue steadily on the north wing for the next year. Latrobe assured legislators that the both the Senate and the Supreme Court chambers would be ready by early 1810 and managed to persuade Congress to provide him with $15,000 to complete the vaulting in the courtroom and to furnish and decorate the Senate chamber. The appropriation would also cover the costs of reconfiguring the covered wooden passageway connecting the north and south wings in order to allow entry to each building on the first floor, where the House and Senate chambers were now located, rather than on the ground level.

This time, Latrobe was as good as his word; by February 1810, both the Senate and the Supreme Court could finally move into their respective new chambers. The Supreme Court—which for the past year had impatiently conducted its business out of Long's Tavern just east of the Capitol—happily moved into its formal semicircular space on the ground floor. Meanwhile, the Senate took its place in the similarly shaped chamber one story above; Latrobe, awed by the surgical theaters he had seen in Paris, would always be convinced that a semicircular room with a half-domed ceiling was the ideal—and most dramatic—shape for a legislative chamber.

Like its counterpart in the House wing, the Senate chamber was dramatic and impressive, though its smaller size—it was then serving only thirty-four Senators, compared with 142 members of the House—gave the space a more elegant intimacy. With mahogany desks arranged in a semicircle facing the throne-like chair and desk of the vice president—another decorative touch carefully designed by Latrobe—the Senate deliberately resembled an indoor amphitheater, which made it easy, at least in theory, to hear any speakers whether they stood at the front of the room or at the rear. Here, too, however, Latrobe found it necessary to hang heavy drapery to soak up some of the echo in the room.

He also had Franzoni sculpt statues similar to those in the House chamber, putting the young man to work on oversized figures representing the Arts, Commerce, Agriculture, Science, the Military, and Civilian Government. With funding slowing to a trickle, however, most of the work would remain unfinished. But with the eastern half of the north wing now mostly complete—and the Congress seemingly satisfied with Latrobe's work—the architect boldly approached the Congress for the funds necessary to begin work on the *other* half of the structure, which, Latrobe pointed out, was still filled with rotting timbers, sagging floors, and drooping ceilings.

Latrobe also had big plans for the eventual completion of the building, for which he turned in beautiful sketches of the Capitol, depicting its center section capped by a low dome reminiscent of the one beloved by Washington but—in a likely jab at Thornton—slightly revised and elevated on a central platform. He also envisioned an entrance to the building from a gatehouse at the lowest part of the western slope of Capitol Hill and a series of terraces and balconies built into the hillside to give visitors a panoramic view of the young city as it stretched out toward the Potomac.

But with a potential war with England looming on the horizon, a depressed economy, and American ports closed by embargo to foreign commerce, the Congress was not inclined to be generous with continued funding. Latrobe's appeal was rejected outright by appropriators who noted that such a request was "not deemed prudent at *this* time."[66] Instead, Latrobe would only be given enough money—about a third of what he had asked for—to finish off the Senate chambers and to complete any other unfinished work in the eastern half of the wing. And that would be it.

Latrobe fumed over what he regarded as pure Congressional stinginess, which, he felt certain, would blemish his reputation. Rather than having the noble domed structure he had regularly and enthusiastically described to lawmakers for a decade, the Capitol of 1810 would be made up of only two elegantly designed three-story buildings—one for the House, the other for the Senate and the Supreme Court—perched on the edge of Capitol Hill. Where there should have been a central structure topped by a low dome, there was only an open space about fifty yards wide through which had been constructed a covered wooden walkway that protected Congressmen and Senators from the elements as they moved between the two buildings. It was hardly the soaring structure Latrobe had envisioned when he had taken the job as architect seven years earlier.

And yet, as expected, Congress adjourned in March 1811 without approving any further funding for the Capitol. All work stopped, and Latrobe was informed that, as of July 1, 1811, his services would no longer be required. Congress agreed to pay Latrobe the last part of his salary, providing a final paycheck of $1,811 to the man they now referred to publicly as the "late surveyor." That one hurt.

While he had lost the support of the Congress, Latrobe still had an admirer in Thomas Jefferson, who had retired to Monticello after serving two terms as president and handing the keys to the President's House over to President James Madison. Jefferson had continued to follow Latrobe's progress—and frustrations—from a hundred miles away, and Latrobe definitely had his sympathies. "With respect to yourself, the little disquietudes from individuals not chosen for their taste in works of art, will be sunk into oblivion, while the [House of] Representative[s] chamber will remain a durable monument of your talent as an architect," Jefferson wrote reassuringly.[67] He also made clear he understood

Latrobe's disappointment in leaving the central portion of the building unfinished. "I shall live in the hope that the day will come when an opportunity will be given you of finishing the Middle building in a style worthy of the two wings," Jefferson told Latrobe warmly, "and worthy of the finest temple dedicated to the sovereignty of the people."[68]

Meanwhile, the administration of President James Madison was content to keep Latrobe at arm's length, mostly for reasons having to do with the bottom line. When Congressman Henry Clay complained about the condition of the floor in the House chamber and appealed to Latrobe for assistance, Madison refused to allow the architect to carry out the necessary repairs. Latrobe complained that he was the victim of a whispering campaign, which was likely true, but it was also clear that earlier charges of fiscal carelessness had damaged his reputation for good. "[President Madison] said at once, that I was so unpopular, and such strong prejudices existed against me, that he could not venture ever to employ me," Latrobe wrote bitterly to a business associate, "that I was thought extravagant, a waster of public money, and all the rest of the Trash."[69]

It's likely, too, that Madison's focus was elsewhere. Over the past five years, the American economy had soured under British and French restrictions on American imports and exports, and neither diplomacy nor legislation had done much to improve economic conditions or relations abroad. Further, a land-hungry Congress, in an early incarnation of Manifest Destiny, was intent on expanding north into Canada and as far west as the Mississippi River—and didn't care if it drove the British on the western frontier right into the Mississippi's muddy waters. Meanwhile, the British Royal Navy continued its habit of impressing American sailors into service, even as British ships and soldiers deliberately interfered with American trade with the French.

On June 1, 1812, President Madison put American complaints into writing, detailing the nation's grievances with Great Britain in a message to Congress, and warning that "the conduct of her government presents a series of acts hostile to the United States as an independent and neutral nation."[70] Two weeks later, on June 18, the United States formally declared war on Great Britain—the first such declaration in the young nation's history. Madison had deferentially pointed to the Constitutionally defined role of the legislative branch in declaring war, noting that he felt assured "that the decision will be worthy [of] the enlightened and patriotic councils of a virtuous, a free, and a powerful nation."

But the vote in the Congress would be close—the closest vote for a declaration of war in American history, in fact—passing the House seventy-nine to forty-nine and surviving in the Senate on a vote of nineteen to thirteen. "The period has now arrived, when the United States must support their character and station among the Nations of the Earth," thundered Congressman John Calhoun of South Carolina, "or submit to the most shameful degradation."[71]

In 1812, America was officially at war—and two years later, on the evening of August 24, 1814, British troops would march into Washington, D.C., occupy the very chamber from which Calhoun had spoken, and leave the United States Capitol in flames. As Latrobe sighed later, "The labor[s] of 10 Years of my life were destroyed in one night."[72]

By 1810, the Capitol was made up of only the House wing (seen at left) and the Senate wing (on the right), connected by a central covered wooden walkway. Much to the frustration of Architect of the Capitol Benjamin Latrobe, a lack of funding would keep him from completing the building's planned domed center section. When British Rear Admiral George Cockburn directed soldiers to torch the Capitol in August 1814, even some of his own men were "horrified at the order to burn the elegant Houses of [Congress]."

CHAPTER 3

A Melancholy Spectacle

1814–1817

The war was going badly.

Since the declaration of war on Great Britain in June 1812, American troops had been repulsed by the British at nearly every turn. By 1813, the British Army had taken Detroit and blown back a major American offensive at Queenston Heights in Upper Canada; meanwhile, the Royal Navy swaggered in the Chesapeake Bay, striking towns and settlements along the coastline in a nautical reign of terror that kept the Americans guessing.

And no American was more perplexed, it seemed, than John Armstrong, President Madison's secretary of war. Armstrong assured the president that while the British might threaten or even strike Baltimore near the head of Chesapeake Bay, they would never move on the American capital, forty miles to its southwest. "[T]hey certainly will not come here [to Washington, D.C.]; what the devil will they do here?" the secretary wrote. Baltimore, he informed the president, "is of so much more consequence"[1]—and thus, Armstrong counseled against a dedicated defense of Washington, D.C.

Still, the news, as Madison received it in the President's House, wasn't all bad. In late April 1813, U.S. forces slipped into Canada and occupied York—now modern-day Toronto—and set fire to the legislative hall and governor's house as they abandoned the settlement on April 30—deliberate acts of arson that humiliated and outraged the

British. In September, nine vessels of the U.S. Navy defeated six British ships on Lake Erie, with American Commander Oliver Perry assuring Major General William Henry Harrison, "We have met the enemy, and they are ours."

But the British, Madison knew, were mostly preoccupied; much of their attention was still focused on fighting the French under Napoleon. As Representative John Randolph had presciently cautioned the Congress in 1812, there would come a time when "[Napoleon] will cease to distract the world." Once that happened, he warned, "the Capitol will be in ruin."

In April 1814, with the armies of seven nations closing in, Napoleon admitted defeat—at least temporarily—and slunk off to exile on the isle of Elba. With their right arm now freed from the European continent, British troops turned their attention, and a curled fist, toward the United States, where their former colonies were conducting an active and messy war.

At a cabinet meeting on July 1, a cautious President Madison ordered the creation of a new Tenth Military District encompassing Baltimore and Washington, D.C., and put the somewhat unsteady Brigadier General William Winder—only just recently released from his capture at the Battle of Stoney Creek in Ontario—in charge of defending the Federal city. Despite the newly assigned militia, Secretary Armstrong remained unimpressed. One district militia commander reported Armstrong "generally treating with indifference, at least, if not levity, the idea of an attack by the enemy."[2]

British Vice Admiral Sir Alexander Cochran would make Armstrong regret his indifference. Still smarting from the "disgraceful outrages" and the burning of public buildings committed by American troops in Canada, Cochran believed Washington deserved to be "either destroyed or laid under contribution"[3]—and in mid-August, he approved the plan devised by his second-in-command, Rear Admiral Sir George Cockburn, to launch what he saw as a much-deserved attack on the American capital.

As part of the strategy, Cockburn would sail a fleet up the Patuxent River, which wriggled up the Maryland shore roughly midway between the Chesapeake Bay and the Potomac. With both Baltimore and Washington in easy marching distance of his ships, Cockburn suspected he could keep the Americans curious but unclear on which of the two cities was the real target.

On August 19, 1814, Cockburn docked his fleet at the sleepy town of Benedict, Maryland, a little more than twenty-five miles from the mouth of the Patuxent as it emptied into the Chesapeake and about fifty miles southeast of Washington. From there, a force of more than four thousand British troops under the command of Major General Robert Ross came ashore and began their steady march northwest, getting the better of American troops in several skirmishes along the way and spooking residents of Washington, D.C., badly enough that many government offices began packing up papers and preparing to evacuate the city.

Around noon on Wednesday, August 24, Ross and his troops arrived at the town of Bladensburg, Maryland, barely across Washington's northeastern border and just on the other side of a skinny section of the Potomac's Eastern Branch as it snaked its way up through Prince George's County. The Capitol building itself was practically within sight, only slightly more than five miles away to the southwest. Standing between Ross and his prize, however, was Madison's makeshift militia under the command of the shaky General Winder. Also present—incredibly and rather stupidly—was President Madison himself. With Secretary of State James Monroe scouting the area in advance, the president had come riding from the capital that morning to assess the situation.

It was chaos. Ross's troops swarmed across the bridge spanning the Eastern Branch, aiming straight for the District; Winder responded by throwing his own troops against them but shouted confusing and conflicting orders, resulting in a lack of cover fire that left many troops exposed and on the run. American soldiers scattered under the explosive red blast of the British Congreve rockets—notable more for their terrifying noise than their accuracy—while elsewhere troops from both sides engaged in hand-to-hand combat, clanging into one another with cutlasses and hand pikes. The American forces slightly outnumbered the British, but Winder chose to play defense—and with Madison watching in disbelief, Ross's troops swarmed down the main country road, heading for the District. Winder retreated in the same direction, backing his men through the trees and sprinting toward Capitol Hill.

For a moment, there was talk of making a stand at the Capitol by using the building itself as a makeshift fortress—but Winder's troops were in disarray, and most of them had already retreated through the District, then dispersed through Georgetown and into the Maryland countryside. Winder let them go, a decision that stunned his officers. "I could not, nor would not, believe that the city was to be given up without a fight," one American colonel reported incredulously as he sadly led his men out of the city, feeling "sorrow, grief and indignation."[4] President Madison made his way back to the President's House; then he escaped from Washington on horseback and eventually crossed into safety in northern Virginia under cover of darkness. The American militia, meanwhile, had been routed and scattered.

By evening, a victorious Ross and a resplendent Cockburn, riding a white horse and wearing a gold-laced hat and epaulettes, arrived on Capitol Hill with a small group of officers and guards. The Capitol building in front of them—still just two elegant, slightly rectangular buildings connected by a covered wooden walkway where the domed center section was supposed to be—was undefended and dark. To their left, they could see the glow of fires from the Navy Yard, where Commodore Thomas Tingey had been ordered by the secretary of the Navy to destroy the fleet docked on the Potomac rather than risk American ships falling into the hands of the British. Watching the Navy Yard burn, Cockburn intended to consign the Capitol to a similar fate.

With Cockburn leading the way, British troops stormed through the eastern entrance to the south wing, serving the House of Representatives. As they pushed their way into the House chamber, the junior officers were stunned by the beauty of Latrobe's design and handiwork. Even by torchlight, the House chamber seemed, as one British lieutenant remembered, of "monarchical splendor."[5] The heavy crimson drapes that Latrobe had carefully hung to soak up echoing voices in the chamber swayed lightly in the spaces between the enormous Corinthian columns. Rows of mahogany desks, abandoned as members had fled the building, followed the curved contours of the room, reflecting the flicker of torches in their dark polished wood. At the south end of the chamber, from over the canopied chair of the Speaker, Giuseppe Franzoni's statue of Liberty looked down on the invaders disapprovingly, as did the noble eagle he had so carefully carved, after multiple tries, into the frieze.

Cockburn scarcely seemed to notice. With his boots still caked with mud, the Englishman clumped up into the Speaker's mahogany chair and shouted into the chamber, as if calling the question before a session of Congress, "Shall this harbor of Yankee democracy be burned? All for it will say Aye!"[6] Even as some junior officers cheered, Captain Harry Smith, who had fought in the Napoleonic Wars in the South of France, was appalled at what Cockburn was asking his men to do. "I had no objection to burn[ing] arsenals, dockyards, frigates building, stores, barracks, etc.," Smith wrote later, "but . . . we were horrified at the order to burn the elegant Houses of [Congress]."[7]

At first, troops blasted several rounds of Congreve rockets into the domed ceiling, hoping to ignite the pinewood—but Latrobe's roof, covered with sheet iron, held firm and failed to catch fire. More determined now, Cockburn's men began breaking up the chamber's mahogany furniture, piling it into the center of the chamber along with any books or papers they could find. Then they pulled down a few of the enormous drapes, wadded them up, and tucked them into the pile. Finally, a Congreve rocket was broken open to empty its explosive powder onto the heap. As another officer lamented that it was a "pity to burn anything so beautiful,"[8] a torch was hurled onto the pile, which immediately caught fire. As Cockburn and his men backed out of the chamber, the room was already engulfed in flames.

Cockburn's men were having better luck in the north wing, where a similarly growing bonfire in the center of the Senate floor could be fed not only with broken-up furniture from the chamber but also with the books and other papers from the Library of Congress directly across the hall. Unlike in the House chamber, Latrobe had been permitted to upgrade only half of the wing with stone vaulting, leaving the western half unfinished and constructed mostly of timber, which caught fire so quickly and burned so hot that Cockburn's officers beat a hasty retreat out of the north wing with little time to set any additional fires.

Just across Rock Creek, less than five miles away, John McElroy, the bookkeeper for Georgetown College, spotted the Capitol in flames and noted as part of his daily record for August 24, 1814: "This evening about dark the British arrived in W[ashington] C[ity], fired the Capitol about 9:06 [p.m.]."[9] Later that evening, Ross would lead his troops down Pennsylvania Avenue to put the torch to the President's House as well as to structures housing the Treasury and the Department of War.

The fires would burn for much of the night; at one a.m., a government auditor fleeing the city with Treasury Secretary George Campbell noted that the flames of the capital were still "most dismally and most distinctly visible" from twenty-five miles north of the city.[10] Even farther away, one Baltimore resident reported seeing the glow of flames forty-five miles to the southwest, writing ominously, "We only know from the light during the night that the city was on fire."[11] Fortunately, a heavy, and unexpected, two-hour downpour on the afternoon of Thursday, August 25—"the most tremendous thunderstorm I had ever witnessed," wrote Navy clerk Mordecai Booth—would put out the fires for good.

But the rainstorm came too late to save the buildings. In less than twenty-four hours, twenty-one years of work at the Capitol—overseen by four architects and costing more than a half million dollars—had been gutted by the flames of British invaders. While the exterior walls of both buildings were mostly intact—surprising those who came to Capitol Hill to gawk at the damage and did not expect to see the buildings standing—the surfaces were streaked with dark black scorching where flames had licked out the windows. Interior walls had crumbled under the intense heat, ceilings had collapsed, and the House chamber, where Cockburn and his troops had started their fiery rampage, was simply gone. The wooden pathway between the buildings had burned away, too, while in the Senate chambers the marble pillars had buckled and dissolved in the flames. "A most magnificent ruin," Latrobe said sadly.

If some Americans were concerned that letting a foreign invader overrun and burn their capital city made them an international laughingstock, there was at least one who thought the British had overplayed their hand. "In the end, the transaction has helped rather than hurt us," wrote Thomas Jefferson to the Marquis de Lafayette, "by arousing the general indignation of our country, and marking to the world of Europe the vandalism and brutal character of the English Government. It has merely served to immortalize their infamy."[12]

To the British, it was simply payback for American atrocities in Canada that had left the capitol building at York in flames. "As just retribution," wrote Sir George Prévost, who had served as the governor-general of Canada, "the proud capital at Washington has experienced a similar fate."[13] But even the British newspapers were having a tough time falling in line with that argument. "Willingly would we throw a veil of oblivion over our transactions at Washington," wrote the editors of the *London Statesman*. "The Cossacks spared Paris, but we spared not the capital of America."[14]

Addressing the Congress less than a month after the burning of

Washington, President Madison assailed the "barbarous policy" of the British invaders and promised that "[they] will find [their] transient success, which interrupted for a moment only the ordinary public business at the seat of Government, no compensation for the loss of character with the world." He assured his fellow citizens that the American spirit remained unbroken and promised that the British would suffer "disaster and expulsion."[15] In fact, the war would end mostly with a thud and in a stalemate; by the end of the year, both the United States and England would have diplomats in Belgium negotiating a successful end to the war before signing the Treaty of Ghent on December 24, 1814.

In foreign affairs, Madison might have had things under control, but in domestic matters, he had a mutiny on his hands. With Washington, D.C., still in ruins and the House and Senate essentially homeless, Congress was deliberating whether Washington should be abandoned and a new capital city constructed somewhere else. Among the most vocal advocates of relocation was Senator Eligius Fromentin of Louisiana, who argued strenuously against remaining in the Federal city, which he saw as little more than a muddy frontier town that had now been burned beyond any hope of repair. "[W]hat, in the present state of things, are our prospects for the future?" he asked his colleagues rhetorically—then answered his own question. "Awful indeed. How many ages must elapse before this chaos is likely to assume anything like a describable shape?"[16]

Given the condition of the city, it was hard even for its defenders to deny Fromentin's grim outlook. The Capitol and the President's House were little more than charred shells, while the Navy Yard and the Departments of War and the Treasury had been burned to the ground. Once the damage was surveyed, rebuilding seemed not only impossible but also impossibly expensive. Even the pragmatic Daniel Webster shrugged that it was perhaps time to move the capital back to Philadelphia.

James Madison, however, was in no mood to dredge up the quarrels of 1790 that had led to the political horse-trading that had finally settled the Federal city on the banks of the Potomac. Madison intended to keep it there and hoped to slow the momentum of the relocation crowd by suggesting that "accommodations should be provided for the meeting of Congress" at a convenient site in Washington.[17] Once settled into this convenient but temporary location, the Congress could debate the issue more deliberately and, Madison hoped, much more slowly, giving pro-Washington advocates the opportunity to make their case.

The site Madison selected to serve as the nation's provisional capitol was Blodgett's Hotel near Seventh Street NW and E Street NW, only a little more than a half mile from the President's House. The building had never actually served as a hotel; born in the early 1790s of a failed scheme by businessman Samuel Blodget to encourage investment in the new Federal city, the James Hoban–designed structure had subsequently taken nearly two decades to complete and was now one of the largest buildings in the city. For several years, it had housed a local theater company, and, since 1810, it had served as home to the Post Office Department and Thornton's U.S. Patent Office. During the burning of Washington in August, in fact, it had been Thornton who had personally pled with British soldiers to spare his offices from the torch, even—as he often told it—dramatically throwing his own body across the door and daring the officers to "fire away, and let the charge pass through my body."[18]

The Congress formally assembled at Blodgett's for the first time on September 19, 1814. While Latrobe had been consulted to help make the space more functional, it was a tight fit. "[Blodgett's] was three stories high," Madison's enslaved servant Paul Jennings recalled, "[but] both Houses of Congress managed to get along, notwithstanding that it had to accommodate the Patent-office, City and General Post-office, committee rooms, and what was left of the Congressional Library."[19] It didn't take long for Senator Richard Stockton of New Jersey to crabbily assert they were meeting in rooms "not large enough to furnish a seat for each member, when all are present, although every spot, up to the fire-place and windows, is occupied."[20]

Cramped quarters aside, Blodgett's Hotel had the distinction of serving as the U.S. Capitol for nearly fifteen months, from September 1814 to December 1815. Modern visitors wishing to pay their respects to the temporary capitol will be disappointed, however, as Blodgett's burned down in December 1836. Today, the site is occupied by the Hotel Monaco.

Debate over the fate of the capital—and the Capitol—continued throughout the fall and winter of 1814 and early 1815. Cost was a major topic of discussion, with estimates for rebuilding the Capitol coming in at a little more than $787,000, a price tag that some argued was too high. "Provide for filling the ranks of your Army," railed Senator Fromentin, "[i]nstead of borrowing money for building costly edifices." But if Washington had to remain the capital, Fromentin suggested building Congress a "large, convenient, and unadorned house" in Georgetown.[21]

Fortunately, the reliable Thomas Munroe, still serving as superintendent of the City of Washington, reported to the Congress that he'd had the damaged buildings carefully examined by a group of architects and master builders, all of whom reported with confidence that "the walls of the President's House and both wings of the Capitol, with some inconsiderable repairs, will be safe and sufficient to rebuild on."[22] The Congress was eventually persuaded that constructing on the existing foundations and incorporating some of the standing walls would make the rebuilding much cheaper than investing in completely new structures.

It is perhaps no surprise that private interests also influenced the debate. Many supporters of keeping the capital in Washington argued repeatedly that countless financiers, including foreign bankers in America-friendly places like Holland, had purchased land in the nation's capital as sound investments—and they warned that any relocation would be a sign of bad faith to shareholders. Local property owners, too, were concerned that their own purchases in and around the capital region would be worthless if Congress and the government moved out—and so, in an effort reminiscent of the Compromise of 1790, they offered to make a deal.

"Mr. John Law, a large property owner about the Capitol, fearing it would not be rebuilt, got up a subscription and built a large brick building . . . and offered it to Congress for their use, till the Capitol should be re-built," Paul Jennings reported later. Law and several other investors proposed paying for the construction of a sturdy brick building directly across the street from the still charred Capitol to be used as a headquarters for the House and Senate—in effect, a new, albeit temporary, capitol—while the Capitol itself was being rebuilt and repaired. The gesture was apparently enough to resolve the question of relocating the seat of government. "This coaxed them back," wrote Jennings, "though strong efforts were made to move the seat of government North; but the Southern members kept it here."[23]

When the matter was finally put to a vote in February 1815 "after much zealous debate," the Congress—for now still in its uncomfortable quarters in Blodgett's Hotel—chose to keep the capital in D.C. and rebuild the Capitol building on its current site.

Now all that was needed was an architect to supervise the project.

Benjamin Latrobe was depressed.

He'd been angry when he'd skulked out of Washington, D.C., three years earlier. Following his curt dismissal by the Congress, he had fumed to a friend that he was glad to be "[b]idding an eternal adieu to the malice, backbiting, and slander, trickery, fraud & hypocrisy, lofty pretentions & scanty means . . . & five thousand other nuisances that constitute the very essence of this community."[24] And yet things had gone badly since then. He'd accepted a position working for Robert Fulton in Pittsburgh, where he speculated in the steamboat business as an agent of the Ohio Steamboat Company. But now Latrobe's friendship with Fulton was fracturing as their mutual business was failing, and Latrobe found himself nearly broke. He desperately needed a job.

He'd heard rumblings that there might be a need for an architect to attend to the rebuilding of the Capitol but figured he had little chance if the decision was left to the president of the United States. "Mr. Madison will never employ me again, I am told," he groaned to a friend in September 1814. "All I can do is to lie by and wait. If called upon, I will give all my talents & industry. . . . Perhaps Congress will call on me."[25]

To Latrobe's likely dismay, the matter seemed very much in the hands of Madison, who in March 1815 turned the management of the new federal buildings over to a new commission made up of the well-connected former New York Congressman John Van Ness, the equally well-connected Marylander Tench Ringgold, and the even better-connected onetime Virginia Congressman Richard Bland Lee. But despite the broad range of skills of this formidable trifecta, none of them knew a thing about architecture—their talents were better suited for managing the funding and keeping the project on schedule. They needed an architect.

Finding the right architect to oversee the reconstruction of the President's House was no problem—the reliable James Hoban was brought back to oversee the repairing and rebuilding of the structure he'd designed and spent eight years on supervising its construction. But reappointing Latrobe up at the Capitol wasn't going to be so easy or popular; Latrobe had left the project under a cloud and was generally disliked in the administration—and by the commissioners. Van Ness, in fact, had publicly, though anonymously, dressed down Latrobe in the newspapers in 1809 for overspending on the Capitol ("whenever an appropriation is to be expended," Van Ness said of Latrobe, "there you are").[26] But the commission also understood that no one knew the Capitol better than Benjamin Latrobe. Despite their dislike of the estranged architect, it was clear Latrobe was the man for the job.

Meanwhile, Latrobe's wife, Mary, watching her husband spiral into despair, had been pleading Latrobe's case to anyone in D.C. who would listen, including by sending impassioned letters to President Madison and his wife. Several weeks later, as Latrobe "reclined in a deep depression in an easy chair"—one of the few chairs the Latrobes had left after selling most of their furniture for money—Mary handed him a packet embossed with a waxy presidential seal. To Latrobe's shock, Madison—at the urging of the commission and with the nudging of Mrs. Latrobe—had formally offered him the job as the Architect of the Capitol. When his wife informed him of her efforts on his behalf, Latrobe sagged in her arms and wept.[27]

For reasons unknown, Latrobe waited nearly a month before reporting for duty in D.C.—a move that got him off to a bad start with the commissioners—and he was put under contract on April 18, 1815. Despite his late arrival, Latrobe was all business and immediately toured the grounds of the charred Capitol with Commissioners Ringgold and Van Ness. It was a "melancholy spectacle," he noted sadly.[28] "In the House of Representatives, the devastation has been dreadful," he recorded in a letter to Thomas Jefferson. The fire in the chamber had burned so intensely—over 2,700 degrees—that the glass in Jefferson's beloved skylights had simply melted. "I have now lumps [of glass] weighing many pounds run into a mass," Latrobe told Jefferson. The sandstone columns had calcinated and collapsed under the extreme heat, as had many of the interior stone walls and nearly all the sculptures. "I believe no known material could have withstood the effects of so sudden and intense a heat," Latrobe wrote.[29]

Over in the Senate wing, the western half of the building—the side Latrobe had not shored up with stone vaulting—was mostly gone, especially as the Library of Congress with its collection of books was one of the most flammable parts of the entire Capitol compound. But while the columns in the Senate chamber had decayed and collapsed in a manner similar to those in the House, most of the stone vaulting Latrobe had installed there and in the Supreme Court chamber remained standing. The stone stairwells and lobbies were mostly intact, too—the British had passed through them so quickly to escape the rapidly growing flames that they hadn't had time to put them to the torch—and to Latrobe's delight, his corncob capitals had been entirely spared.

The building was in bad shape but—as Munroe's teams of experts had rightly assessed—not irreparable. "The mischief is much more easily repaired than would appear at first sight," wrote Latrobe—though, looking at the wreckage, he determined that a complete rebuilding of the south wing and the western half of the north wing would be required. But he was surprisingly pragmatic about it. "The only fact that I regret deeply," he wrote, "is the destruction of our national Records. Everything else money can replace."[30]

Well . . . money plus time—and predictably, Latrobe immediately overpromised on his deadlines. While he rightly warned the commissioners that "*rapid* building is *bad* building,"[31] he still assured them that the Congress would be able to move into a completed Capitol by December 1816, a little more than a year and a half away. Still, Latrobe had reason to believe he would make his self-imposed deadline. Within weeks of arriving in Washington, he had assembled his main work crew and appointed the efficient Shadrach Davis, a former clerk at the Navy Yard, as his own clerk of the works. His foreman of carpenters was Leonard Harbaugh, who had supervised most of the carpentry at the President's House, and his foreman of stonecutters was the invaluable George Blagden, who had overseen most of the stonework carried out at the quarries and on the lawn of the Capitol.

Latrobe also had the foresight to reengage Giovanni Andrei, the slow but talented sculptor who had carved the impressive capitals that had topped the columns in the House chamber. In the race to make his deadline, Latrobe opted not to replace most of the sculptures that had been lost to the flames in the House chamber—that would have taken too much time. Instead, he would concentrate on beautifying his basic infrastructure, and he had plans for gorgeous columns in both the House and the Senate chambers. Envisioning elegant marble columns placed along the outer edges of each chamber, Latrobe immediately dispatched Giovanni Andrei to Carrara, Italy, to purchase the statuary marble needed for the new capitals for his columns, directing Andrei to find the best materials available at the most reasonable prices—a very American directive—and to sculpt the capitals in Italy and ship them back to Washington as quickly as possible. Latrobe estimated that, between the House and Senate chambers, he'd need thirty of them. Given Andrei's proclivity for a leisurely pace, all Latrobe could do was hope for the best.

Next, Latrobe set to work drawing up new floor plans. While he intended to work within the existing footprint of the building and stick with Thornton's exteriors, he was anxious to improve the House chamber. While Latrobe had always considered the House chamber as it had finally been constructed and decorated in 1807 to have been *his* design, he had always chafed at being pressured to work with Thornton's oval-shaped layout for the floor of the House. Given the opportunity to start again, then, Latrobe was determined to overhaul the House chamber—particularly when it came to addressing the room's famously terrible acoustics and problematic lighting—regardless of what Thornton, or President Madison, might have had to say about it.

The first and most major change he proposed was altering the layout of the room from racetrack-shaped to a semicircle, similar to the format of both the Senate and the Supreme Court chambers. And now that Jefferson was no longer in power and able to insist on the installation of troublesome and leaky skylights, Latrobe could finally light the room using the rooftop lantern he had argued for all along. "All complaint against insufficient light will be at once and forever removed," he boasted.[32]

Latrobe drew up the appropriate plans and submitted them to Madison, who gave the amended floor plan and improved lighting structure his approval. The slight shift in the design, however, quickly came to the attention of William Thornton, who wrote frantically to Thomas Jefferson to argue that altering the House floor from an oval to a semicircle differed too much from his own vision—and to ask if Madison himself hadn't instructed Latrobe to stick to the plan approved by George Washington. Jefferson—who had likely come to appreciate that the acoustics of the Senate's semicircular chamber were superior to those of the cavernous House chamber—quietly pocketed the letter without comment and, in deference to Madison, did nothing. Thornton's wife, Anna Maria, would later complain that her husband was being constantly undermined and deliberately denied the credit he deserved as the Capitol's first visionary. "Even of this honor they wish to deprive him," she lamented, "by attributing the plan to Hadfield, Latrobe . . . anybody but him!"[33]

At the close of the 1815 building season, things were off to a good start in both wings. Much of the exterior had been scrubbed of smoke damage—as well as of graffiti reading "James Madison is a rascal, a coward and a fool"[34]—and clean blocks had been placed around windows and doors where the stone had been stained black with soot. Temporary roofing had been installed, and in the north wing, Latrobe had nearly completed the stone vaults for the Senate committee rooms that would be located beneath the Library of Congress.

Meanwhile, just across the street from the Capitol, the temporary brick capitol building promised to the Congress by John Law and his group of investors was ready for occupation. Built in the sturdy Federal style of the age, it was uncharismatic, but also much less cramped than their quarters in Blodgett's Hotel, with adequate space for members to debate and for committees to meet. Madison informed the Congress that the government would cover the rent for the building at a discounted rate "until the Capitol is in a state of readiness for the reception of the Congress."[35] The Congress would meet in the building—which the locals would eventually come to call the Old Brick Capitol—for the first time on December 13, 1815, with no real idea of when they would be moving back into the building across the street. The work, it seemed, was progressing at an agonizingly slow rate.

Things were about to slow down even more. Even as Latrobe had work underway in the north wing, the Senate itself suddenly submitted a request asking Latrobe if it would be possible to enlarge their chambers to accommodate the new members who were likely to join in the coming years as new states were added in the Midwest—Indiana was poised to join the Union in late 1816—and in the South. Latrobe likely groaned; the Senate chamber was largely structurally intact, but giving the Senators what they were asking for was going to require him to take down most of the existing vaults in the Senate and Supreme Court chambers, move a staircase, and build an entirely new ceiling. Costs would go up, and Latrobe was certain the Congress would find a way to blame him for it.

Yet Latrobe dutifully informed the Senate that, yes, it *was* possible to expand the chamber within the existing footprint, and, after some head-scratching, he drew up plans that kept the chamber's semicircular shape, with its flat side against the eastern wall, while increasing its diameter from sixty to seventy-five feet. By the end of 1816, there would be nineeen states with thirty-eight Senators; and Latrobe estimated his chamber would have enough room to accommodate at least forty-eight Senators from twenty-four states. He also added new meeting rooms for Senate committees, mostly by taking the large space on the top floor previously occupied by the Library of Congress and dividing it up into eight good-sized rooms. That meant the library was going to have to be relocated—and Latrobe, who already had grand plans for it, envisioned it taking up several large, elegant rooms in the western portion of the still unbuilt center section.

But when Latrobe submitted his plans for the new Senate wing—along with his idea to move the library to the center section—the commissioners immediately had questions. Namely, they wanted to know if space could be made for the Library of Congress back in the north wing—at least for now—rather than waiting for completion of the still unbuilt center section.

The commission had good reason to ask the question. In the weeks following the burning of the Capitol and the destruction of the Library of Congress, Thomas Jefferson—disgusted by "the vandalism of our enemy . . . [and] the destruction of the public library with the noble edifice in which it was deposited"[36]—had offered to sell his own books to the Congress to replace the nearly three thousand volumes that had been lost to the fire. "You know my collection," Jefferson wrote to an acquaintance, the newspaper publisher Samuel Harrison Smith. "I have been 50 years making it, and have spared no pains, opportunity, or expense to make it what it is."[37] An enthusiastic collector of books—particularly "everything which related to America, and indeed whatever was rare and valuable in every science"[38]—Jefferson had acquired nearly sixty-five hundred volumes for his library at Monticello, making it the largest private collection in the United States. He thought it would make an ideal foundation on which to rebuild the Library of Congress.

Jefferson's motives weren't purely patriotic; he also needed the money. With several creditors at the door with their hands out, Jefferson left it to the Congress to determine a fair price for acquiring his collection, with the stipulation that it was an all-or-nothing deal—Congress had to take either his entire collection or none of it. While most in Congress were enthusiastic about the acquisition, some questioned Jefferson's tastes. During the debate to authorize funding to purchase Jefferson's books, Cyrus King, a rookie Representative from Massachusetts, complained that Jefferson's collection contained "irreligious and immoral books" of French philosophy and that the funding would be better spent on "purposes more indispensable than the purchase of a library."[39]

Supporters pushed back strenuously, though the final bill passed with only a slim majority, eighty-one to seventy-one—a margin that stunned some observers. "The next generation . . . will blush at the objections made in the Congress to the purchase of Mr. Jefferson's library," sniffed the editors of the *American Register.*[40] With passage of the bill, the Congress agreed to pay Jefferson $23,950, from which Jefferson promptly handed over $15,370 to his creditors. In a public investment worth about a half million dollars today, the Congress acquired 6,487 books, immediately doubling the number of volumes that had been held by the Library of Congress before the fire. As his bookcases were carted away from Monticello toward the capital, Jefferson noted with pride that "an interesting treasure is added to [Washington, D.C.], now become the depository of unquestionably the choicest collection of books in the U.S."[41] At the moment, however, there was still no permanent place to store that choice collection—and thus, the commissioners were hoping to find at least a temporary home for Jefferson's books in the Capitol's north wing.

But under Latrobe's current plan, the newly acquired library would remain packed away for an indeterminate amount of time until the Capitol's center section was completed. While Latrobe understood the need for a home for the library, he didn't want to risk the Congress getting too comfortable with any temporary space—that might make them less inclined to move it later, and he would have to rethink his plans for an elegant library space as a showpiece of the center section. Rather than cede his committee rooms, then, Latrobe agreed to set up a temporary space for the Library of Congress in one of the most inconvenient and uncomfortable locations possible: the cramped, low-ceilinged attic rooms of the north wing. When the time came to relocate the library, Latrobe felt certain that members of Congress would be aching—almost literally—to move it into its new and larger space in the center section.

With work proceeding at a surprisingly quick pace in the north wing—especially given all the tearing down and putting up that Latrobe had to do to enlarge the Senate chamber—the commissioners were now concerned that Latrobe was neglecting the House chamber. He was urged to get back to work on the south wing as quickly as possible. But the architect had his reasons for the perceived foot-dragging: he still lacked the stone needed to construct the enormous columns he wanted in both chambers.

Latrobe's plan for both wings of the Capitol, he told his sister, was to "restore them infinitely more splendidly than they existed before the invasion of the Goths."[42] It was a matter of message as much as architectural design—knock the United States down, and it would only build back better than before. The sandstone from which the original columns had been carved, he informed the Congress, was unworthy of the Capitol, as it had not been "of a texture fit for the finer works of buildings."[43]

Instead of sandstone columns, Latrobe envisioned lining both chambers in the new Capitol with columns made of a stronger and more impressive material such as marble—and if such a material could be found in the United States, that was even better. But so far, he hadn't found anything to inspire him. "For the columns, and for various other parts of the House of Representatives, no free-stone that could be admitted has been discovered," he wrote.[44] That would change in March 1816 when Latrobe took a marble mason named John Hartnett with him to explore the quarries and rock outcroppings along the banks of the Potomac just upriver from Washington in search of the ideal stone. Latrobe wasn't certain exactly what he was looking for, but the moment he spotted a large supply of beautiful dark rock near White's Ferry, Maryland, about forty miles upriver, he immediately knew he had found it.

Latrobe would initially describe the stone as "very hard but beautiful marble" and eventually christen it "Potomac marble." What Latrobe had found wasn't technically marble but breccia, which is a melting pot of materials, mostly irregularly shaped colored pebbles suspended in a cement matrix—in this case, it was a dark gray matrix flecked with red, green, black, and white stones. And in this particular section of Montgomery County, Maryland, breccia was everywhere; local farmers who dragged the junk rock out of the soil called it "an incumbrance to agriculture."[45] But Latrobe had a vision for it and believed that once it was properly cut and polished, it would "answer every expectation that was formed, not only of its beauty, but of its capacity to furnish columns of any length."[46]

The stone also had the advantage of being located close to a series of canals that the Potowmack Canal Company had completed in 1802. Mirroring the curves of the Potomac River, the canals with their accompanying locks made the waterway more easily navigable, especially at a point about halfway between White's Ferry and Washington where, even today, the Potomac drops more than seventy feet in less than a mile as it tumbles over a series of rapids and waterfalls known as Great Falls. But even with the canals in place to avoid the falls, conditions often had to be near perfect to successfully steer boats through the route's skinny sluices and bypasses; for much of the year, the water level simply wasn't high enough to let a boat get through. Only after the spring rains had sufficiently raised the level of the river could boats more freely navigate the canals and locks—and even then, the convenience would last for only about fifty days each year. If Latrobe was going to move the Potomac marble at White's Ferry down to D.C., timing was going to be everything.

For now, Latrobe arranged to contract with Hartnett to oversee the quarry and produce the columns he would need at a cost of about $1,550 per completed column. But Hartnett would prove to be a dawdler as well as a bad project manager—"the difficulties and expenses attending an enterprise of this kind proved to be greater than had been calculated on," Congress was told diplomatically.[47] Latrobe's columns would be slow to make it downriver. And Latrobe was certain he would be blamed for it.

As the walls continued going up on Capitol Hill, Madison decided in April 1816 that the most efficient management of the Capitol project was to place its oversight in the hands of a single administrator officially designated as the "commissioner of public buildings." Latrobe badly wanted the job and appealed personally to Madison, trying to make his case by informing the president how shabbily he'd been treated by the current commissioners, calling them "the most villainous board of Commissioners that ever had the power of tormenting in their heads."[48] Unswayed by Latrobe's uncompelling argument, Madison instead appointed Samuel Lane, an old friend of Secretary of State James Monroe and a veteran of the War of 1812, in which he'd been shot through the thigh and left with a nearly useless arm. Latrobe grumbled but was initially gracious, calling Lane "a gentleman of honor and feeling."[49] The goodwill wouldn't last long.

With Lane in place, he was also in the way—and Latrobe would now have no direct engagement with the president or Congress. Instead, he was to report directly to Lane, who would not only serve as his intermediary but also determine what information made it to the chief executive for his counsel in the first place. Lane was a model of military efficiency, and he expected the same from Latrobe, asking him to provide weekly reports with detailed information including the costs of materials, number of workers, and salaries being paid. He also made it clear to the architect that he was expected to maintain regular hours in Washington without disappearing to Baltimore or Philadelphia for any side gigs. When Lane spelled out his expectations in writing and mailed them to Latrobe, the architect huffily returned the package with a note reading "The enclosed has been sent by mistake to my address."[50] It was not a good start.

And yet Latrobe would continue to labor diligently, if unhappily, putting some of his best work into the details of both wings. One of his memorable flourishes would be just outside the Senate chamber where a large stairway had collapsed during the fire, resulting in its removal to another location. That left behind a circular open space that Latrobe would turn into a tall, skinny rotunda topped by a dome with an oculus at its center to let in light and air—essentially an ornamental ventilation shaft. As a finishing touch, Latrobe had the dome supported by a colonnade of sixteen columns, each topped with a capital carved to resemble tobacco leaves and flowers—another of Latrobe's uniquely American architectural conversation pieces. Visitors to the Small Senate Rotunda today need only look up toward the space's central chandelier, installed in 1965, to see that Latrobe's tobacco capitals are still there, beautifully detailed with gold, turquoise, and red paint.

One floor directly beneath the Senate was Latrobe's rebuilt Supreme Court, which had been similarly enlarged to mirror the dimensions of the Senate chamber overhead. Latrobe had proportionally scaled up the supportive vaulting necessary to support the floor above as well as the unusual umbrella-spoked ceiling, spanning it outward into a three-bay arcade. And this time, Latrobe, taking no chances of the ceiling collapsing under its own weight, shored up the room with sturdy piers.

The architect also wanted a sculpted relief of Justice to adorn the front wall of the court, a job he would normally have handed over to his master sculptor, Giuseppe Franzoni. Unfortunately, the sculptor had died in April 1815 at age thirty-five. Fortunately, the commissioners, before their disbandment, had had the foresight to recruit Franzoni's equally talented younger brother, a six-foot-four twenty-seven-year-old named Carlo, to replace him. Carlo was brought to Washington in 1816 and immediately put to work by Latrobe on producing a figure of Justice for the nation's highest court.

Franzoni's final product, completed the next year, wasn't a statue but rather a plaster relief of three figures that were placed in a semicircular lunette just over the court's main entrance, where it faced the justices as they presided over the chamber. In his allegorical group of figures,

Franzoni depicted a winged figure of Genius seated at the left, pointing to a document in his lap clearly labeled "The Constitution of the U.S." On the right, an American eagle perched atop a stack of law books turns its head to look back at Justice, who sits almost casually at center. With her right arm leaning on her unsheathed sword and her left upraised to hold a scale, Franzoni's Justice gazes deferentially over her shoulder at the Constitution. Curiously and notably, Franzoni chose not to depict Justice as blindfolded—a rare portrayal of the figure. Perhaps the sculptor hoped to convey that Justice viewed the Constitution with absolute clarity—and thus the highest court would always dispense justice in her favor. Whatever the intention, Franzoni would never explain his artistic decision, and his clear-eyed Justice—along with a similar figure on the Capitol's East Front—remains an anomaly among most sculpted versions of the figure.[51] She remains on the wall of the Old Supreme Court Chamber to this day, one of the oldest of the original works of art in the Capitol.

Commissioner Lane, however, wasn't going to ask Franzoni to explain his reasons for an unmasked figure of Justice; he was an accountant, not an art critic. He was much more interested in knowing how much money Latrobe planned to spend on finishing the building. Perpetually annoyed, Latrobe refused to answer the question and deflected by informing Lane that he had only one draftsman working for him—and thus didn't have "the means of making the necessary drawings"[52] to determine overall costs. "Our commissioner [Lane] is extremely weak and ignorant," he fumed.[53] Their relationship was deteriorating rapidly.

It was at this point that the Congress intervened and asked Latrobe for a detailed timeline for the completion of the building. Work on both the House and the Senate wings was proceeding slowly, neither wing had a roof—and no progress had been made at all on the center section. Further, in the opinion of the Congress, Latrobe seemed to be spending too much time fussing with small details—like sculpture and other decorations—rather than taking care of basic infrastructure needs, like moving into place the Potomac marble columns that were needed to support the ceiling and roof of each chamber safely.

A contrite Latrobe informed the Congress—through Lane—that he could really only guess how much more time it was going to take to finish the project . . . and he *guessed* that the Capitol might be ready for the Congress to occupy by December 1818—a bad guess, as it would turn out. "As to the Capitol, it goes on but slowly," he confessed privately. Partly the delay was due to Hartnett's plodding work out at the Potomac marble quarry in White's Ferry, where inexperienced and often inebriated work crews had already ruined more than eighty tons of marble. Without his marble and his columns, Latrobe couldn't finish either chamber. He pled with irritated members of Congress to be patient. He promised them it would be worth the wait.

The election of 1816 was never really in question. James Madison, honoring the precedent set by George Washington and Thomas Jefferson, opted to step down after serving two terms as president, leaving the office wide-open for a new slate of candidates to fight over. Madison's preferred candidate, James Monroe, would be the eventual nominee for the Democratic-Republicans, while the Federalists would only half-heartedly and informally field as their nominee New York Senator Rufus King, who had already run two unsuccessful campaigns for the vice presidency. Despite King's bona fides—he was a signer of the Constitution and he had served as the minister to the Court of St. James's in the Adams administration—the lack of enthusiasm among Federalists probably doomed his campaign before it could even begin. Monroe would win in a landslide, taking sixteen of nineteen states, including King's home state. King's loss would hasten the slide of the Federalist Party toward its eventual extinction in 1824.

There was some controversy over where exactly to administer the oath of office. With the Capitol still incomplete, Monroe was prepared to take his oath in the Old Brick Capitol across the street—but the House and Senate were bickering over which chamber would host the ceremony. Once it was agreed that the swearing in would take place in the House chamber, members next squabbled over the chairs that would be used for seating, with Speaker of the House Henry Clay refusing to allow Senators to bring their red chairs from the Senate chamber into the House chamber because the "black ones [in the House] were more becoming."[54]

With neither side budging, the ceremony was eventually moved outdoors—without chairs—and held directly in front of the building. On a beautiful March 4, 1817, in front of a crowd of eight thousand spectators and with temperatures hovering around 50 degrees, James Monroe became the first American president to be inaugurated outside the Capitol—or at least *a* capitol—rather than within it, a tradition that continues to this day.

Latrobe thought highly of Monroe. He was looking forward to developing a relationship with the president, likely seeing the Virginia colonel as the politician most inclined to embrace Jefferson's collaborative approach to design and construction and Madison's relative deference to the opinions of the architect. Monroe would certainly take a more hands-on approach to working with Latrobe but not always in a way that Latrobe might have hoped—for Monroe was interested not in architecture but in order. "Monroe," as Latrobe's first biographer, Talbot Hamlin, put it, "was a coldly efficient executive."[55]

For Monroe, completing the Capitol was going to be a priority in his administration—so much so that he spent part of his inauguration day with Latrobe and master stonecutter George Blagden discussing the viability of Potomac marble as a suitable building material. At that meeting, Blagden informed the president that it was his opinion that Potomac marble was too unstable even to be polished—that the rock would crumble when it was shaped and sanded—and that columns would collapse under their own weight well before a heavy domed ceiling could be placed atop them. Latrobe, in peril of losing his elegant stone, could insist only that Blagden was wrong.

Monroe had a decision to make—and Latrobe was pushing him to make it. Genuinely concerned about the stability of the columns—and the safety of the Congressmen who would be seated in their shadow—Monroe appointed an informal advisory board consisting of Latrobe and two trusted engineers, Lieutenant Colonel George Bomford of the Army Ordnance Department and General Joseph Swift of the Army Corps of Engineers, for guidance. "It is important to me to know whether these columns, regarding . . . the quality of the marble of which they are composed, will support such an immense weight," the president wrote.[56]

On March 25, as Washington was drenched by an early-spring rainstorm, Monroe climbed into a carriage at the President's House, joined by Colonel Bomford and General Swift, and slogged over muddy roads to White's Ferry so the three of them could personally examine the quarries. Bomford and Swift were quickly impressed; not only was the stone beautiful, but much of it was already exposed, making it easy to quarry and transport on the nearby canals. The engineers were also confident that the stone was indeed strong enough to carry the weight of a ceiling. To Latrobe's likely relief, Monroe was sufficiently reassured, and he signed off on the use of the Potomac marble.

One problem remained, however: John Hartnett's laissez-faire management of the site. As directed by the president himself, the government immediately purchased and took over the quarry and installed Robert Leckie, a much more experienced quarrier, as the manager of the quarrying process. Hartnett, meanwhile, was moved down to Washington, where he would oversee the shaping and polishing of the quarried stone once it arrived on Capitol Hill—a job that relied more on artistic sensibilities than on day-to-day administrative acumen.

Monroe had also retained a holdover from the Madison administration, keeping Samuel Lane as his commissioner of public buildings. The veteran administrator was placed in charge of ensuring that the White's Ferry site—situated as it was "in a county where no accommodations could be had for workmen"[57]—could become entirely self-sufficient. Lane was to "provide tools, lumber, nails, spikes and provisions," wrote Monroe, "[and] cause sheds to be erected for the workmen, for cooking and as store houses."[58] Lane followed Monroe's orders to the letter and soon had the quarry at White's Ferry humming with efficiency—or at least as much efficiency as a quarry could offer.

Given its hardness, Potomac marble was much more difficult to quarry than the softer sandstone downriver at Aquia, and it required a completely different method of extraction. Instead of chipping grooves in the stone as excavators did with sandstone, a quarrying team had first to drill a series of deep holes, only a foot or so apart, that marked the line where the rock was to be split away from the main body of stone. In an era before power tools, drilling was a strenuous, sometimes bone-breaking exercise that required a team of several men working in perfect sync. The drilling mechanism itself, known a star drill, was an iron rod about as thick as a good-sized thumb, with a star-shaped pointed tip. With the star drill held in place by a member of the crew known as the "shaker," two or sometimes three men slinging sledgehammers—called the "jacks"—would pound the drill into the rock, with each swing by the jacks coming perilously close to the head and hands of the shaker, kneeling at their feet.

After each hammer strike, the shaker would give the star drill a quick quarter turn—the so-called shake—which drove the drill deeper into the rock with every crack of the hammer. A good crew could work only so fast, however, as the shaker had to stop the hammering at regular intervals, withdraw the drill, then remove the rock and dust left behind in the hole by the drill's rotating tip. As the hole got deeper, the shaker would use a long, narrow spoon to scoop out the dust—or, at times, pour water down the hole to flood out dirt and small bits of stone. At this pace, an efficient team could drill out about sixty inches of rock in a day.

Once the row of holes was drilled, wedges would be inserted into each one and pounded down until the rock cracked along the seam, essentially cleaving the Potomac marble away from the rock face. From there, the raw stone would be moved to a flat-bottomed boat to be taken downriver and through the finicky canals at Great Falls. Some boats could be as large as seventy feet long and nine feet wide, with a crew of four to steer, row, and serve as lookout. At that size, some boats, after being loaded with nearly a ton or more of rock, sat so low in the water that they were unable to float if the river dropped below a certain level. Patience, and a good deal of luck, was required to move downriver.

Once the stone was delivered to the grounds of the Capitol—towed or rolled uphill from the docks at the base of Seventh Street—it was placed in the care of a skilled crew of masons led by Hartnett to be shaped and polished, using woolen cloths to rub the stone with sand, emery, and putty.[59] While Latrobe had initially hoped that columns could be cut from a single piece of marble, most would end up being built out of seven or eight marble "drums" stacked and cemented together at their joints. Cutting, moving, carving, and shaping the columns in this way was heavy, hot, and highly detailed work, but Latrobe was delighted with the results. After the first Potomac marble drums were finished and prepared for stacking and cementing in April, he could barely contain his excitement as he looked at their sparkling gray-green surfaces polished to a reflective sheen. "I have never seen anything so beautifully magnificent," Latrobe wrote to Jefferson. "Even the most clamorous opposers of their introduction are now silenced. When the columns are in their places, they will be a lasting proof of the firmness of the character of the present President of the U. States."[60]

All that was missing now were the capitals to be placed on top of each column—and to Latrobe's surprise, Andrei suddenly showed up unannounced in June 1817, returning from Italy with all the needed capitals, which had been carved beautifully from the finest Italian marble. He was a year late, which didn't matter much, given the slow rate at which marble was being imported from White's Ferry. He had also brought with him several talented Italian artists—including Francisco Iardella, a talented carver, and the moody sculptor Giuseppe Valaperti—to help Franzoni and him with the decorative work at the Capitol.

Every now and then, work could be slowed by a bad batch of stone. At one point, Lane explained to the Congress how several large blocks of Potomac marble that had been "quarried with great expense of time and labor . . . would often turn out to be full of dry veins, and in working would fall to pieces."[61] Given the time, labor, and breakage, the cost of each column would slowly creep upward from the $1,550 originally budgeted by Latrobe to nearly $5,000. And once again, Latrobe was certain he would be blamed.

Still, so long as Latrobe and Lane kept providing Monroe with regular updates—and regular financial reports—Monroe was inclined to keep providing the architect with the support and materials he needed. When Latrobe continued to complain about not having the help he needed to draft architectural drawings, Monroe provided him with additional staff to assist with the work. The president would very much remain the "foreman in chief," constantly prodding Lane, Latrobe, and their work crews to work faster and more efficiently, even as he continued to support Latrobe financially and logistically.

From time to time, however, Monroe would involve himself in architectural decisions—much to the dismay of Latrobe, who felt the president would never take his side, despite Monroe supporting him over Blagden in the matter of the Potomac marble. In the summer, Monroe, with an eye on speed, cost, and safety, suggested that the domed roof over the chamber of the House of Representatives be constructed of wood instead of brick covered by plaster as Latrobe had suggested. Aghast at the very idea, the architect appealed to his fellow advisory board members, Swift and Bomford. "A wooden dome is altogether unworthy of the marble columns," Latrobe contended, and pointed out that a wooden dome would eventually rot and need to be replaced much sooner than a dome constructed of brick. Swift and Bomford, however, were inclined to support the president, arguing that a dome made of lighter materials would keep the public, and the Congress, from worrying about the roof or vaults collapsing.

If Latrobe missed the subtle reference to the collapse of the vault and ceiling in the Supreme Court chamber that had killed John Lenthall nearly a decade earlier, Blagden, in his written reply to the president, was slightly more direct. In a deferential letter to Monroe, the stonemason mentioned that he knew from "terrible experience" the risks associated with stone vaults and heavy ceilings. The Capitol was already heavy enough, wrote Blagden, and was putting considerable strain on the supporting arches in the basement—which, he claimed, could be heard groaning under the weight of the building. "Why . . . this rush?" Blagden asked the president. "Why give an additional weight of nearly 500 tons to these arches?"[62] The counsel of Blagden, Swift, and Bomford prevailed; Monroe directed Latrobe to construct the domed ceiling of the House of Representatives out of wood.

Furious and feeling slightly humiliated, Latrobe again considered resigning, informing Lane that in his opinion "the public could do very well without [me]."[63] But Latrobe stayed. And Monroe would get his wooden ceiling.

With the additional draftsmen that Monroe had provided, Latrobe could at last put on paper his plans for the rest of the Capitol. That included providing sketches and floor plans for the still unrealized center section connecting the two wings and detailed drawings of the sculpture he wanted in the House chamber.

In the center section, Latrobe still planned to install the Library of

Congress. The library envisioned by Latrobe would extend more than a hundred feet beyond the wings of the building and have two stories of bookshelves and elegant galleries and tall windows looking west toward the slowly growing City of Washington.

Beneath the center dome—Washington's beloved center dome—Latrobe was less certain of his plans. He knew what he *didn't* want; some members of Congress were pushing for Latrobe to pack the center section with offices and other meeting spaces. But Latrobe was holding out for a magnificent open space dramatically lit by sunlight coming in from the dome above; on his drawings, he labeled it as the "Grand Vestibule, Hall of inauguration, of impeachment, and of all public occasions."[64] It was also going to be an art gallery, although in this case the art wasn't going to be statues or sculpture designed or commissioned by Latrobe; instead, the art was being brought to him: four enormous paintings depicting key events in America's history—at least up to that point in time—that Latrobe was being asked to display prominently.

At the moment, however, the paintings—like nearly everything else in the Capitol—weren't finished; most, in fact, hadn't even been started. In February 1817, the Congress had agreed to commission four large pieces by the sixty-year-old American artist John Trumbull, who specialized in paintings of the Revolutionary era. Trumbull painted partly from experience—he had been a solider in the Revolutionary War and had served as an aide-de-camp to George Washington—but he was also a stickler about painting from life; in 1786, for a miniature he had painted of the signers of the Declaration of Independence,[65] Trumbull had personally visited thirty-six of the fifty-six signers to capture their images, even traveling to Paris to paint Jefferson. "He has spared no pains in obtaining from life, the likenesses of those characters," an impressed George Washington, the subject of several portraits, had remarked.[66]

Typically, the Congress quibbled over precisely how much to pay Trumbull for his four paintings, eventually settling on $32,000[67]—an amount that Trumbull, who was running a struggling art studio in New York, was happy to receive. The Congress was going to get a lot for its money; initially, Trumbull had planned on making his paintings six feet tall by nine feet wide, but then James Madison took the artist aside. "Consider, sir, the vast size of the apartment in which these works are to be placed," counseled Madison, ". . . paintings of the size which you proposed will be lost in such a space."[68] Trumbull would double the size of his canvases to a spectacular twelve by eighteen feet, allowing him to paint nearly life-sized figures.

Over the next seven years, Trumbull would produce four magnificent paintings depicting major moments in America's battle for independence—*The Declaration of Independence*, *Surrender of General Burgoyne*, *Surrender of Lord Cornwallis*, and *General George Washington Resigning His Commission*—but for now, he had barely started on his painting of the signers of the Declaration of Independence, which he intended to base on his 1786 miniature. Latrobe began sending Trumbull drawings and descriptions of various ways to display his art in the grand vestibule, telling the artist he was "honored in having my Walls destined to support your paintings."[69] As always, no detail would be too small for Latrobe's attention, and Trumbull and he corresponded regularly over the ideal height for hanging artwork and whether the art should be displayed flat in a frame or carefully stretched to follow the curve of the walls. No decisions were made.

At the same time that he was discussing paintings for the center vestibule with Trumbull, Latrobe was talking with Carlo Franzoni about plans to adorn the House chamber with ornamental sculpture. Rather than re-create the sculpture that had been lost in the fire, Latrobe planned to decorate the chamber with entirely new pieces. Given the semicircular layout of the new chamber, Latrobe, in an act of deliberate symbolism, intended to place above the main entrance an elegant sculpted *Car of History*, in which Clio, the Greek muse of history, would be depicted in her winged chariot recording the events transpiring in the chamber beneath her. Latrobe provided Franzoni with a guiding sketch that the sculptor improved upon in execution, mostly by depicting Clio standing in her car, rather than sitting, and sculpting Clio's robes as slightly billowing behind her, giving her, and the chariot, a dramatic sense of moving through time.

Meanwhile, over the Speaker's chair, where there had once stood Giuseppe Franzoni's statue of Liberty, Latrobe wanted another representation of Liberty; this time he worked with the Italian sculptor Enrico Causici on an updated model. In Causici's hands, Liberty, standing more than thirteen feet high, was posed confidently with her left hand on her hip and her right hand waving the Constitution in front of an attentive American eagle; to her left, a serpent, as the symbol of wisdom, curls around a short column.

With Franzoni and Causici at work on the decorative sculpture and Hartnett's crew polishing and assembling marble columns as fast as they could, Latrobe was beginning to feel confident that he could complete the Capitol in a timely manner. But "timely" was a matter of opinion only—and James Monroe was running out of patience.

In July 1817, the locks in the canals at one of the lower falls in the Potomac collapsed. "[They] have fallen in, beyond the power of Art to restore them," Latrobe groaned in a letter to Thomas Jefferson.[70] Delivery of the Potomac marble slowed to a crawl as the raw stone was offloaded at Little Falls and put onto wagons to be hauled to Capitol Hill, about ten miles away. Delays in delivering the marble also meant delays in completing both chambers—having on hand *some* columns wasn't going to be enough to hold up the ceilings; Latrobe needed *all* of them.

As the summer heat began to stifle Washington, President Monroe announced he was going to take a three-month tour of New England, going directly to the heart of rival Federalist territory, prompting a Federalist journalist to dub the Monroe administration one that embodied a new "Era of Good Feelings," with American optimism soaring in the decade after the War of 1812. Monroe made it clear to both Lane and Latrobe that when he returned from his three-month tour, he expected to see the Capitol ready for occupancy—and failure, the president stressed, would mean the dismissal of Lane or Latrobe or both. Latrobe felt he was being set up—so much for good feelings. Why else had Lane promised the president that the Capitol would be ready to be occupied by the end of the year? Yet Latrobe had tried to manage Monroe's expectations, explaining to the president that if all went well, the building *might* be ready by December 1818, another year away. But Monroe was tired of explanations and excuses—and tired of continuing to pay rent on the Old Brick Capitol. It was time to bring the Congress home for good.

But without his Potomac marble, nothing was going to be finished anytime soon—and when Monroe returned from New England, very little had been done. "On his arrival, the President, misled by I don't know who, expected the Capitol to be finished," Latrobe told Trumbull, directing his scorn at Lane. "Of course he was disappointed."[71] That was putting it mildly; Latrobe's first biographer described Monroe's reaction as "a towering rage."[72] In a tight-lipped message to Congress, the disappointed Monroe informed them that "the Capitol is not yet in a state to receive you"—but perhaps remembering Latrobe's own guesstimate, he stipulated, "There is good cause to presume that the two wings . . . will be prepared for that purpose at the next session."[73] There was still no word on completing the center section and its dome.

Monroe immediately tasked a new commission with looking into delays at the Capitol. The president's commission dutifully compiled reams of detailed information as they watched Latrobe's work crews count lumber and bricks, weigh lime and sand, and determine how many blocks of Potomac marble remained to be quarried. The general consensus seemed to be that Latrobe was to blame for the slow pace of work, with some suggesting that the architect had been distracted by his side trips to Baltimore to work on that city's Basilica—a gorgeous building that still stands as a testament to Latrobe's taste and skill. Latrobe tartly responded with raw data, pointing out that he had been away from the city for only thirty-seven days over twenty-nine months. But the grumbling would grow only louder, and Latrobe, in his correspondence with Trumbull, lamented that he was dealing with "a very angry President."[74]

At times, Lane, too, seemed determined to push Latrobe's buttons, ordering premade marble fireplace mantels from London without notifying the architect, who was stunned when the shipment arrived. Even more frustrating for Latrobe, Lane, citing "inefficiency," personally fired Latrobe's clerk of the works, Shadrach Davis, and installed in Davis's place his own man, Captain Peter Lenox, who had occupied a similar position down at the President's House. Latrobe protested—he considered Lenox a show-off—but Lane was unmoved, informing the architect that he had made the decision to replace Davis simply to speed up construction. "Knowing my duties, I Shall scrupulously perform them," Lane wrote haughtily to Latrobe. "All I ask of you is attention to your own."[75]

Latrobe's nerves were fraying, and his confidence was shaken. He was also nearly broke as he continued digging his way out of old debts in Pittsburgh and fell behind on his rent in Washington. As one acquaintance wrote, "Latrobe has many enemies; his great fault is in being poor."[76] With Lane maneuvering against him and a president who seemed perpetually annoyed with him, Latrobe was already on the verge of despair when word came from New Orleans that his eldest son, Henry, who was in that city working on a water project, had died of yellow fever at the age of twenty-five.

Latrobe sank into dark depression. He continued to blame Lane for his sagging public reputation, seething in a letter to Thomas Jefferson, "The present commissioner, Colonel Lane, has from the first week, treated me as his clerk, & certainly not with the delicacy with which I treat my mechanics."[77] Lane admitted that the architect could make him angry and insisted that Latrobe, after storming out of one of their meetings, make "immediate concessions for leaving him in a rage, [or] he would look for another Architect."[78] At that point, President Monroe decided he'd had enough. On November 20, 1817, both men were summoned to the President's House—only just recently readied for occupation after three years of repairs and reconstruction overseen by Hoban—for a frank conversation.

Things didn't go well. As the discussion between Latrobe and Lane grew from heated to antagonistic, Lane condescendingly reprimanded Latrobe in front of the president. The architect angrily leapt at Lane—who was several inches shorter than Latrobe and hampered by a useless arm—and shook him violently. "Were you not a cripple I would shake you to atoms, you poor contemptible wretch," Latrobe snarled—then, with his voice rising, shouted into Lane's face, "Am I to be dictated to by you?"

A stunned James Monroe could only look on in disbelief. Finally, he asked Latrobe incredulously, "Do you know who I am, Sir?"

Latrobe slowly released Lane. "Yes, I do," the architect responded blankly. "And I ask your pardon."[79]

Latrobe submitted his letter of resignation the next day. "My situation as architect of the Capitol has become such as to leave me no choice, but between resignation and the sacrifice of all my self-respect," Latrobe wrote to Monroe.[80] As a final humiliation, Latrobe's resignation was accepted not by Monroe but by Lane, who wrote back to the architect asking that he send Peter Lenox "all the books, plans, instruments, etc., belonging to the public in your possession."[81] Latrobe, unlike most of the architects before him, would dutifully hand over all his materials and all the drawings he had completed—including detailed plans of the still unbuilt center section—and contritely apologize to the president for them "not being as perfect as I wish."[82]

Despite the micromanaging of Samuel Lane and the disapproving glares of James Monroe, Latrobe left the Capitol in respectable shape. The House and Senate chambers were nearly complete—but until the rest of the Potomac marble could be quarried, shaped, and polished, both wings would remain unfinished and uncovered. Latrobe had also designed and completed a magnificent Supreme Court chamber and directed the work for much of the still unfinished decorative sculpture in the House chamber.

Latrobe left Washington, D.C., in late 1817 as a beaten man. Within two weeks of his resignation, he would file for bankruptcy and again sell nearly everything he owned to appease his creditors; even then, he was briefly imprisoned for debt in January 1818. On his release, he stayed for a short time in Baltimore to oversee completion of the cathedral, then moved on to New Orleans to continue the work his son had started on bringing drinking water to the city. On September 3, 1820, Latrobe, like his son before him, would die in New Orleans of yellow fever. He was fifty-six years old.

Despite his often prickly personality and easily bruised ego, Latrobe's taste, talent, and eye for architectural detail had an undeniable influence on the Capitol. While Latrobe, for the most part, obeyed his marching orders and stuck to Thornton's basic plans, he shaped the building in significant ways that reflected his own style and preferences, from the configuration of the chambers to his choice of construction materials. Partly, too, he had an undeniable sense of drama, which he expressed by funneling visitors of his era into the main chambers up grand stairways and through majestic domed lobbies—all still in place today, though many guests simply pass through them without ever looking up to admire Latrobe's corncob or tobacco capitals. His flair for the dramatic still informs any renovations or additions to the Capitol to this day, from his designs for the Rotunda to his insistence on using quality building materials.

Even as Latrobe rode sadly out of Washington in 1817, President Monroe knew that, despite his quirks, Latrobe's considerable talents would be missed—indeed, he would be nearly irreplaceable. "Mr. Latrobe is a great loss," Monroe wrote to Senator Harrison Otis, "and it will require two persons to supply his place."[83]

CAPITOL, 1828, EAST FRONT.
From a sketch by Charles Bulfinch

In the years after the Capitol's burning by the British in 1814, architect Charles Bulfinch would oversee most of its reconstruction, finally completing the building in 1828. As designed by Bulfinch, the new center section had an east entrance fronted with a portico accessible by a long flight of stairs and topped by a dome that Bulfinch considered too "lofty" and ungainly but that President James Monroe enthusiastically endorsed.

CHAPTER 4

Solidity to Grandeur

1817–1828

Even before Benjamin Latrobe's assault on Commissioner Samuel Lane and meltdown in front of President James Monroe, the buzz in Washington for much of 1817 was that Latrobe was already in trouble. As early as September, two months before Latrobe's confrontation with Lane, William Lee—an auditor in the Treasury Department and a confidant of Monroe—confessed that he was "very sorry for Latrobe, who is an amiable man, possesses genius, and has a large family, but in addition to the President's not being satisfied with him, there is an unaccountable and I think unjust prejudice against him by many members of the Government, Senate, and Congress."[1]

Monroe, too, had already grown frustrated with Latrobe, and even before Latrobe's abrupt resignation following his outburst at the President's House, Monroe was casually searching for his possible replacement. Several months earlier, during his summer tour of New England, the president had been impressed by the treatment he'd received in Boston, where a committee of local selectmen had hosted a week of receptions, celebrations, and dinners—including a parade in which Monroe had cut a magnificent and very presidential figure astride a stunning white charger as he rode all two and a half miles of the parade route. Chairing the reception committee was a fifty-four-year-old architect named Charles Bulfinch, who had been educated at Harvard—in mathematics, not architecture—and who, like William Thornton, was a self-taught architect who had learned and honed his craft mostly by doing. And he had done a lot. Since winning the commission to design the Massachusetts State House—an elegant Federal-style building that had been completed in 1798—he had become Boston's premiere architect, designing and managing the construction of countless churches, theaters, hospitals, and private residences, and overseeing repairs or improvements at Harvard, Faneuil Hall, and the Old North Church.

As chairman of the board of selectmen and thus the de facto mayor of Boston, Bulfinch had been at Monroe's side for the entire week, and the two men chatted amiably through church services, lectures, tours, even a dinner at Harvard attended by eighty-one-year-old former President John Adams. Monroe was captivated by the genial Bulfinch, not only with his obvious talents as an architect—his work was simple but tasteful—but also with his calm demeanor, his gentlemanly manners, and his New England pedigree. Indeed, there was very little pretense about Bulfinch; even in looks, there was something mildly reassuring about the man, with his soft, doe-like eyes, prominent nose, and mouth set in a slight smile. And while Bulfinch had worn a traditional wig as a younger man, he now went about with his balding head exposed, his slightly wild hair combed long in back. He seemed to be a man who was truly comfortable in his own skin. In late summer 1817 as Monroe returned to Washington and grumbled about Latrobe's still unfinished Capitol, he might have wondered how the project would have been proceeding under the management of an architect who was much less driven by ego and drama.

As Latrobe began imploding in the fall of 1817, friends of Bulfinch began informally promoting him to the president for the position of Architect of the Capitol, with William Lee as the Bostonian's most vocal cheerleader. "While the President was here, you were mentioned in case Latrobe should be forced to retire," Lee wrote to Bulfinch after a visit with Monroe.[2] Lee didn't think it would take much to push Latrobe out the door—but Bulfinch was a decent man who wasn't inclined to force anyone out of a job. "I have always endeavored to avoid unpleasant competition with others," he told Lee gently. "I should much regret to be an instrument of depriving a man of undoubted talents of an employment which places him at the head of his profession, and which is necessary to his family's support."[3]

However, after Latrobe's resignation in November, Lee wrote excitedly to the president, convinced Bulfinch could now be wooed to Washington. Monroe would say only that he was working on it; in correspondence with Massachusetts Senator Harrison Otis, who was also pushing for Bulfinch, Monroe responded tersely: "Sir, we are looking to him."[4] But Bulfinch wasn't going to be easy to get. He was an active and well-liked member of his community as well as a dedicated public servant who had served as the chair of the Boston board of selectmen for the last nineteen years. Resigning his position and leaving his wide circle of friends was going to be tough. "I was well established," Bulfinch wrote later, "and [was] a numerous and respectable acquaintance."[5]

Further, as a father of seven children—including five boys ranging in age from eight to seventeen years old—Bulfinch was slightly nervous about educational and cultural opportunities available in Washington compared with New England, where several of his older sons had already attended the prestigious Phillips Exeter Academy and Harvard. (His son Thomas, who had graduated from Harvard in 1814, would be responsible for *Bulfinch's Mythology* and make Greek, Roman, and Arthurian lore more accessible to generations of high school students.)

But for all his refinement and skill, Bulfinch—like Latrobe before him—was terrible with money. His position as a selectman was prestigious but didn't pay; Bulfinch—again like Latrobe—relied mostly on architectural side jobs for income. Even then, while Bulfinch was a respected architect, he wasn't always a financially successful one. In 1796, he had gone bankrupt; fifteen years later, his continued debts had landed him in jail for a month. A decent salary was bound to catch his attention. In December 1817, after further prodding by Otis and Lee—and likely a nudge from newly appointed Secretary of State John Quincy Adams—Monroe finally offered Bulfinch the security of a full-time job that paid an annual salary of $2,500—a decent, though not luxurious, income. But Bulfinch, very much in need of steady pay, decided it was enough.[6]

While Bulfinch had the job—after all, Monroe's word was all that was really needed—he didn't want there to be even the whiff of a rumor that he had pushed out Latrobe. "I declined making any application that might lead to Mr. Latrobe's removal," Bulfinch wrote later, "but before the end of the year disagreements between him and the Commissioner became so serious that he determined to resign." Once Latrobe was officially out, Bulfinch formally applied for the position by submitting his paperwork to the president through John Quincy Adams, a fellow son of Massachusetts. "And by return of post," reported Bulfinch, "received notice from him of my appointment."[7]

Bulfinch was officially hired as the new Architect of the Capitol on January 8, 1818. With his son Thomas escorting him, he departed promptly for Washington—a move that already distinguished him from Latrobe, who had dawdled for weeks before reporting for duty. Bulfinch was pleasantly surprised by the capital city; while one visitor of the era complained that Washington still resembled nothing more than "a watering place,"[8] Bulfinch could see its potential, both good and bad. "The place is new but the society, especially in the winter, is such as has grown up in older capitals, and has been accustomed to all the refinements and elegancies—and I fear the extravagances and dissipation—of established cities."[9] He was more certain than ever that coming to this place had been the right decision. "One is immediately convinced that a great city must here grow up," he wrote to his wife.[10]

The Bulfinches dutifully reported to the President's House, where Monroe greeted them warmly, stressed that completion of the Capitol was a priority of his administration, and encouraged the architect to confer with him regularly. The following morning, after paying a respectful call on John Quincy Adams, Bulfinch headed for Capitol Hill to meet Commissioner Lane—despite Monroe's open-door policy, Bulfinch would still report to an intermediary. Then he moved into his office in the Capitol, a large room sparsely furnished but stocked with plenty of drawing paper and drafting instruments.

In addition to inheriting Lane as a supervisor, Bulfinch was expected to maintain the same regular office hours of ten a.m. to three p.m. that had been imposed on Latrobe. He was also assigned Latrobe's clerk, Peter Lenox. However, unlike Latrobe, who had nearly resigned over the appointment of Lenox, Bulfinch liked the clerk immediately and was grateful to have an experienced hand to show him around the grounds and explain operations at the Capitol. At the moment, the site was still just "two stone edifices—the wings of the Congress hall"[11]—but the place was buzzing with activity, with most of the hundred twenty workmen on the site cutting, shaping, and polishing the Potomac marble columns still waiting to be put in place.

Next, Lane turned over to Bulfinch all of Latrobe's architectural plans, which included not only drawings of the completed House and Senate wings, but also Latrobe's vision—such as it was—for the central section, which still didn't exist beyond some foundational stones. Bulfinch was captivated, almost intimidated, by Latrobe's beautifully detailed drawings. "At the first view of these drawings, my courage almost failed me," Bulfinch wrote. "They are beautifully executed, and the design is in the boldest style."[12] The longer he pored over the plans, however, and the more he walked the two wings, Bulfinch could see "certain faults enough in Latrobe's designs to justify the opposition to him." Offending Bulfinch's architectural sensibilities the most were Latrobe's stairways, which Bulfinch found "crowded, and not easy of access," as well as some of his hallways, which were "intricate and dark." Overall, he thought the finished version of the Capitol, at least as imagined by Latrobe, had "a somber appearance."[13]

Still, after making a careful assessment of the work that had been done on the building so far, Bulfinch was inclined to be complimentary of his predecessor. "Great progress has been made toward rebuilding the north and south wings," Bulfinch reported to the Congress, and assured them that he had every intention of finishing the wings "according to the designs already adopted, and on the foundations already made."[14] There would be plenty of time for Bulfinch to flex his own creative muscles and express his own architectural preferences—including straighter hallways and wider stairways—when he turned his attention to designing the central section. For now his job was to stick to Latrobe's plans, be a good engineer and foreman, and keep his own ego out of the way.

Still, he was bound to make Latrobe bristle from time to time; it was Bulfinch's skill as an engineer that would bring him into his first conflict with his predecessor. From a purely aesthetic standpoint, Latrobe had never liked the look of multiple chimneys sticking up at random from the roof of the Capitol. He had cleverly tried to solve the problem in the Senate wing by routing all the chimneys through a stone cupola he wanted placed at the center of the domed ceiling in the Senate chambers. On paper, it was an elegant solution, and Bulfinch thought it was a brilliant idea. "I felt perfect confidence in Mr. Latrobe's genius as an architect, and his acknowledged skill as an engineer," Bulfinch reported later, and thus "gave direction to the workmen to proceed strictly according to their orders from him."[15]

But as Bulfinch's work crew finally moved the completed Senate cupola into place, the entire ceiling structure suddenly creaked and shifted; Latrobe had—perhaps predictably—installed an arch that was of insufficient strength to carry the enormous weight of the cupola. "The workmen left it in alarm and considered it very hazardous," reported Bulfinch.[16] In his report to Congress, Bulfinch noted matter-of-factly that it was "dangerous to trust the arch to bear the weight" and he had redesigned the entire support structure without complaint. That was all too much for Latrobe, who read Bulfinch's report and felt obligated to fire back with the long public pamphlet *Vindication of His Professional Skill*, in which he explained that he deserved none of the blame because the cupola, while built according to his specifications, had been constructed without his supervision. Weirdly, he concluded by blaming stonemason George Blagden for disparaging him.

Latrobe's bruised ego aside, Bulfinch's first year on the job would be largely uneventful; Bulfinch was exactly the calm and organized presence the project needed. Not that there weren't problems; like with Latrobe before him, Bulfinch's progress was often slowed by the constant waiting for Potomac marble to be quarried and shipped from White's Ferry; even Lane admitted that the marble was a source of "perpetual anxiety and vexation."[17] Finally, on June 15, after weeks of agonizing waiting, the last load of Potomac marble left the quarry in Montgomery County and headed downriver to the Capitol.

Despite Bulfinch's efficient management, neither chamber was going to be ready to receive the Congress by the end of 1818. Congress would remain in the Old Brick Capitol, watching as crews worked slowly and steadily on the building across the street. In November, members of the Committee on Public Buildings and Grounds toured the site and gave Bulfinch a great deal of credit for all that had been accomplished during the year, even as they expressed disappointment that the Congress couldn't yet move in. Lane assured them that their new chambers would be ready in twelve months, just in time for the *next* Congress—a promise that Bulfinch appeared to be capable of keeping. And for once, members of Congress seemed to understand that ensuring the building was finished safely and satisfactorily was going to take time—the benefit of the doubt they had never once given Latrobe. But Bulfinch was seen as a levelheaded realist who had earned their confidence; indeed, before the end of the year, he informed the Congress, "The columns of Potomac marble of the Representatives room have been repaired and set in their places."[18] Visible progress was being made; that was all they could ask.

So much progress, in fact, that the Supreme Court—which had been operating out of a nearby tavern—could move into its chamber beneath Latrobe's umbrella-spoked ceiling in time for its February 1819 session. Franzoni's sculpted plaster relief of the unblindfolded Justice was already in place above the entrance, watching and waiting. From his seat at the head of the chamber, Chief Justice John Marshall would preside over a busy court for the next sixteen years, issuing landmark decisions like *McCulloch v. Maryland*, which recognized Congress's authority to "make all laws which shall be necessary and proper"—a concept that to this day countless conservatives have never forgiven him for validating. Marshall would also write that slavery "is contrary to the law of nature" while consistently ruling in favor of enslavers like himself. Justice's over-the-shoulder glance at the Constitution might have been a look of utter disappointment.

By the summer of 1819, Latrobe had the House chamber nearly finished; the Potomac marble columns had finally been carefully set into place, which allowed for completion of the chamber's domed ceiling. As Monroe had requested, it was made of smooth wood that had been carefully painted, at Bulfinch's instruction, to look like a coffered dome made of stone—that is, as if it were a stone ceiling inset with sunken panels. Despite the convincing effect, the ceiling would wreak havoc with the room's acoustics, making House debates—once again—a cacophony of noise. The echo would be so famously terrible that even Thornton would check in to razz the architect, admonishing both Bulfinch and Latrobe for abandoning the elliptical chamber that Thornton had championed more than two decades ago.

So awful were the acoustics, in fact, that a House committee would later be appointed to determine how they might be improved. The committee would propose various solutions, from stretching a canvas lid across the ceiling to dampen the echo (which it did, but it also made it impossible to hear the Speaker of the House) to installing wooden panels between each marble pillar (which was inefficient and ugly). A slightly flummoxed Bulfinch finally suggested installing a glass ceiling over the entire room, just above the level of galleries, to reduce echo while still ensuring the room could be lit by the rooftop lantern. This approach, too, was rejected by the House. Latrobe's previous approach to the problem—hanging drapes between the columns to soak up the echo—didn't work much better, resulting in muddied voices. Until a more satisfactory solution was found, Congress would have to learn to deal with the chamber's problematic acoustics.

As the House ceiling was being painted, Bulfinch oversaw the completion and installation of the sculpture that had been underway in the final months of Latrobe's tenure. Over the central door to the chamber went Carlo Franzoni's very impressive *Car of History*, with finely detailed work—including a profile of George Washington engraved into the side of the car just below Clio's foot—barely visible from the floor below. Simon Willard, a noted clockmaker from just outside Boston, would install the clock that has been set into the chariot's wheel since 1837; the finished statue is still in the original House chamber today, passing time and passing judgment. Franzoni himself, however, never saw his work put into place; in May 1819, he was startled by a doorbell and dropped dead of a heart attack.

Directly across from Franzoni's *Car of History*, in a niche above the Speaker's chair, went Enrico Causici's thirteen-foot-high statue of Liberty—the one flanked by an eagle and a serpent—still made only of plaster and never cast in marble. On the frieze directly below Causici's Liberty, the Italian artist Giuseppe Valaperti had sculpted a stern-looking American eagle leaning slightly forward, with its wings outspread almost like a cape, giving it an appearance of standing on tiptoe. It was a strange enough look that it caused some sniggering among Capitol visitors—and Valaperti was allegedly so distraught at the response that he later went missing mysteriously and was rumored to have committed suicide.

With the Potomac marble columns ready to install, the Senate chamber, too, was nearing completion. As directed by Latrobe and completed by Bulfinch, the columns in each chamber varied slightly and were executed in dignified styles—there would be no playful corncob capitals in the chambers. In the House wing, the columns were executed in the Corinthian order, with their capitals carved to resemble acanthus leaves; in the Senate, the columns were consistent with the Ionic order, topped with simple scrollwork capitals.

To perhaps no one's surprise, Thornton had strong feelings about the Potomac marble columns, taking particular umbrage at Bulfinch spacing them around the House chamber in a manner Thornton considered "sickening."[19] But where Latrobe might have responded to Thornton's charges with a haughty pamphlet or letter to an editor, Bulfinch again shrugged off the criticism and said nothing. "Architects expect criticism," Bulfinch said later, "and must learn to bear it patiently."[20]

Just as he had done in the House chamber, Bulfinch had closely followed Latrobe's plans for the Senate. The updated Senate chamber wasn't quite as striking as the one that had been torched by the British, but with its upscaled size, it seemed more commanding and statesmanlike—a place where the people's business could be conducted with the gravitas it deserved. Bulfinch did his best to give the room some elegance and intimacy by bringing in gorgeous mahogany tables, chairs, and desks—supplied by New York cabinetmaker Thomas Constantine under a noncompete contract issued by Vice President Daniel Tompkins—and brass fixtures as well as an enormous, ornate chandelier that burned enough whale oil to keep the room lit for hours.

Unlike their House colleagues, Senators would have no ornate marble timepiece watching over their chamber. Instead, they would rely on the same clock that had been in their chambers in the Old Brick Capitol—one that, in its own way, was no less elegant than the House's *Car of History*. The clock had initially been ordered in 1815 by Senator David Daggett of Connecticut, who asked Philadelphia clockmaker Thomas Voigt to provide a "good and handsome" timepiece for the chamber. Voigt had done exactly that, shipping an eleven-foot mahogany clock topped by a fearless-looking carved eagle with its beak agape and arrows clutched in its talons; on the front was an embossed shield with seventeen stars and seventeen stripes.

For reasons still unknown—and even though the face of the clock is printed with "Thomas Voigt, Philadelphia"—the clock would come to be known as the "Ohio Clock." Some have speculated that the seventeen stars visible on the carved shield acknowledged Ohio's entry into the Union as the seventeenth state, though at the time Daggett ordered the clock there were already eighteen states—and Ohio had been a state for twelve years. Thomas Voigt would remain inscrutable, never explaining the meaning behind the seventeen stars on the shield. The clock, still standing in the Capitol, is referred to as the Ohio Clock to this day.

Like its counterpart in the House, the domed ceiling over the Senate was also made from wood—Latrobe had lost that argument to Monroe as well; but it was covered at Bulfinch's direction with painted plaster to give it a more stonelike appearance. And as in the House chamber, the acoustics were awful. Heavy red draperies were hung between the columns to mute the echoes bouncing from the wooden ceiling—but the Senate, like the House, would continue to be known for its bad acoustics.

Famously terrible acoustics aside, however, Bulfinch completed the bulk of the work on the north and south wings of the Capitol by early December 1819. As Lane had promised, the Capitol was ready for occupancy—and President Monroe was delighted. "The public buildings being advanced to a stage to afford accommodation for Congress, I offer you my sincere congratulations upon the recommencement of your duties in the Capitol," the president said proudly to the Congress in his annual address.[21] In early December 1819—almost exactly four years since they had taken their seats in the Old Brick Capitol—both the House and the Senate convened in their newly restored chambers.

Once abandoned, the reliable, if crowded, Old Brick Capitol would go on to serve as a private school and then as a boardinghouse; one of its most famous boarders—the Southern demagogue, former vice president, and, at the time, sitting U.S. Senator John Calhoun—would die of tuberculosis in the building in 1850. During the U.S. Civil War, with more space made available by the addition of a new wing, the sturdy brick structure would be repurposed as a federal prison that was the site for the detention of a number of notable prisoners, including Dr. Samuel Mudd, Mary Surratt, and several others involved in the assassination of President Abraham Lincoln. In the years following the war, the former capitol would be converted into private row houses before finally being acquired and demolished by the federal government in 1929 to clear the way for construction of another major federal building. That building, finally completed in 1935, is home to the Supreme Court of the United States.

With the House and Senate wings mostly completed—and completed almost entirely according to Latrobe's vision—Bulfinch could now turn his attention to the incomplete center section. Apart from some scattered stone foundations, the central portion existed only on paper, in one version or another, in some of Latrobe's plans and in a few of Thornton's original drawings. Bulfinch would have considerable latitude in designing and executing the center section as well as its eastern and western entrances to reflect his own style and preferences as an architect. There was one design element of the center section, however, that would always be nonnegotiable: George Washington's beloved dome.

In early 1818, when he had been on the job for only a week, Bulfinch had been asked to come up with both a plan and a timeline for completing the center section, its entrances, and its all-important dome. Out of respect, Bulfinch called on Thornton—now living on F Street NW less than two blocks from the President's House—to discuss any plans the first architect might have had for the center section, which

Thornton had initially imagined as a "grand vestibule." Bulfinch quickly regretted the courtesy call; Thornton spent most of their time complaining about all the changes that others—but mostly Latrobe—had made to the Capitol. Bulfinch left shaking his head in awe; Thornton, Bulfinch reported to his wife, was "a very singular character . . . very dedicated to finding fault with Latrobe for the changes."[22] But Bulfinch's charm offensive had worked; Thornton was impressed with the new architect and would stay mostly out of his way.

In his Capitol office, Bulfinch unrolled Latrobe's plans to carefully study exactly what his predecessor had had in mind for the Capitol's centerpiece. On most of Latrobe's detailed plans for the center section, the Library of Congress took up the entirety of the western side—but rather than keeping the western face of the center section even with the House and Senate wings, Latrobe had pushed the section out more than a hundred feet. This westward extension provided plenty of space for the library and for much-needed committee meeting rooms—and, more important, it ensured that neither the library nor the committee rooms encroached into the space beneath the center dome where Latrobe had placed the large central rotunda.

Bulfinch was intrigued by Latrobe's plans—and, as always, impressed by his predecessor's ability to draw. While he was under no obligation to follow them, Bulfinch *did* agree with Latrobe—and with Thornton—that there absolutely must be a large and impressive rotunda; in this, the three architects were united. To Bulfinch, the Rotunda was more than just a meeting space for official business; the Rotunda was a grand entry to the halls of Congress to its north and south and one of the first spaces visitors would encounter when they arrived from the east or west entrances. It needed elegance and drama and a scale worthy of the rest of the building—and the republic.

Still, some in the Congress argued that a cavernous space beneath the dome, no matter how majestic, was a waste of perfectly usable interior real estate. Some suggested Bulfinch fill it with two stories of meeting rooms instead. Chewing over the recommendation, Bulfinch briefly considered dedicating the main floor to meeting rooms and placing on the level above it a picture gallery where John Trumbull's paintings would be displayed. Bulfinch even floated that idea past Trumbull—a friend of more than twenty years—only to have the painter recoil in near revulsion. "I should be deeply mortified if, after having devoted my life to recording the great events of the Revolution, my paintings, when finished, should be placed in a disadvantageous light," wrote Trumbull. "In truth, my dear friend, it would paralyze my exertions."[23] Trumbull much preferred a "great central circular room" for his art.[24] So did Bulfinch—but he had to make sure he proceeded in a way that still followed the directive of Congress to provide adequate meeting spaces.

Bulfinch would, for the most part, work within the building's existing foundations, sliding his new center section neatly between Latrobe's House and Senate wings. When it came to providing the much-needed space for meeting rooms and offices, however . . . well, Bulfinch could certainly appreciate what his predecessor had been *trying* to do. Latrobe had proposed pushing the center section out toward the west and down the slope of Capitol Hill to protect the space for the Rotunda, changing the footprint from mostly rectangular to a T-shape. It was an approach that made sense—at least on paper. But pushing the West Face of the center section out another hundred feet was going to be a logistical nightmare. Given the downward grade of Capitol Hill—which quickly dropped away from the building's west side—pushing the center section of the building out toward the west was going to require tearing out some of the existing foundation and moving several tons of soil to shore up the hill to support the building's weight with its new footprint.

Bulfinch thought he had a better solution for creating the new and needed space: rather than pushing the building *out*, Bulfinch proposed pushing it *down* by digging deep enough into the soil and rock of Capitol Hill that the bottom floor for the center section would be one story lower than the ground floors of the north and south wings—essentially creating an inverted four-story central structure flanked by the existing three-story House and Senate wings. Bulfinch would still need to extend the western face of the new center section slightly beyond the existing foundations—but with the addition of the new lower level, he would pick up enough square footage so that his western extension, while some thirty-five feet shorter than the one proposed by Latrobe, provided enough space for forty meeting rooms compared to Latrobe's twenty-four. This structural change would still give the Capitol a T-shaped footprint, with the top crossbar running north and south and its stem extending out—though not too far out—into the west-facing slope of Capitol Hill. To keep things tidy on the west face, Bulfinch also abandoned a templelike entrance that Latrobe had poked out from the west side, instead placing his entrance flush with the face of the building.

The only remaining problem was purely aesthetic rather than structural. Given the slope of the hill, the bottom floor of the new central wing would now be exposed as the hill dropped away—as if the building were dangling its legs out over the western slope. This would give the Capitol the appearance of being four stories when viewed from the west, but only three stories when seen from the east. Bulfinch devised a novel solution in the name of visual symmetry: he asked his masons to finish the face of the bottom story on the exposed west side with a dark Boston granite rather than the lighter freestone from Aquia used on the rest of the exterior. Trumbull applauded his old friend's creative solution. "[T]he necessity of the case justifies the novelty," the painter said warmly.[25]

President Monroe, too, was pleased with the plan. Bulfinch had managed to keep what worked in both Thornton's and Latrobe's plans—a central domed section flanked by identical House and Senate wings would always be the building's defining template—and to discard what didn't, like Latrobe's just slightly too bulky, extended western front. Impressed, the president gave the plan his stamp of approval and agreed to an appropriation of $100,000 for Bulfinch to get started.

Bulfinch's crew worked steadily through the spring of 1818, hauling away the old foundation stones, which had been in place since Hadfield had laid them in 1795, and digging down far enough in the west side of Capitol Hill to lay a new and deeper foundation. On August 24, 1818, exactly four years since the burning of the Capitol, Bulfinch and Lane presided over a low-key laying of the cornerstone for the new center section of the building, then provided food and drinks for the work crew afterward. The *National Intelligencer* couldn't let the occasion pass without noting that the stone had been laid "on the anniversary of that day, on which a barbarous enemy here made war upon the arts, upon literature, and upon civilized laws."[26]

By the time the cold weather arrived, Bulfinch proudly informed the Congress that the foundations had been laid for the new section, with sturdy stone arches locked into place. On the bottom floor of the central section, Bulfinch had his crew installing forty stout Doric columns—smooth-sided columns topped with flat square capitals—strong enough to carry the enormous weight of the Rotunda and dome that were to be constructed above. But Bulfinch's basement was more than just vital structural support; it was also a dramatic space, due to Bulfinch's careful placement of his gigantic columns—made of dignified sandstone, not flashy Potomac marble, which was reserved for the House and Senate chambers—in two concentric circles. The space was often designated on maps as the "lower rotunda," but with its sandstone floors, slightly low ceiling, and circles of columns, it would be more commonly referred to as the Crypt.

By Bulfinch's estimate, it was going to take two million bricks and six hundred tons of sandstone and roofing materials to complete the Rotunda and dome. The quarry at Aquia was slowly continuing to produce most of the sandstone for the building, some of which had already started cracking. Bulfinch found that the best way to repair and strengthen the cracked stone was to paint it white—which, to his delight, gave the stone an almost marble-like appearance. This unexpected benefit would also help speed up construction; rather than looking carefully through the quarried sandstone to find perfectly unblemished pieces, Bulfinch could now use *any* stones, since he planned on painting all of it white—a practice that would be used extensively throughout the Capitol. To this day, in many places in the Capitol, careful eyes can spot plain Virginia sandstone disguised as fine Italian marble.

During Bulfinch's courtesy call on Thornton, the old architect, apart from loudly griping about Latrobe, had repeatedly stressed just how important the dome was to the look of the building, and reminded Bulfinch that George Washington himself had been its biggest fan. (Thornton would never tire of dropping Washington's name, despite the great man being dead for nearly two decades.) But Bulfinch didn't need reminding or encouraging; he was really *good* at domes. In fact, he had constructed one of the first domes on any public building in the United States when he placed one atop the Massachusetts State House, which he had designed back in 1787.

For the Capitol, Bulfinch was planning to place the dome atop a low "drum"—a round platform just high enough to elevate the dome so it wouldn't be obstructed by the parapet lining the roof's outer edges. Latrobe had similarly planned for a drum to ensure that even a low dome, like the one favored by Washington, would be fully visible. Next, Bulfinch created several drawings of the Capitol with domes of varying heights and profiles from which President Monroe and key Congressmen could choose a final design. Some sketches featured low domes, such as the button-like dome preferred by Washington and Thornton, while other drawings depicted domes that swelled elegantly upward in a half circle or—in a worst-case version that Bulfinch had drawn solely for contrast and comparison—arched seventy feet above the roof like a gigantic inverted teacup, instantly doubling the height of the Capitol and throwing off the balance of the building.

To present the options to the president and members of Congress, Bulfinch chose to provide not only his drawings but also several three-dimensional models showing the Capitol with domes of varying sizes. To a person, they all agreed that the dome preferred by Washington "was *too low*," Bulfinch recalled later—but to his shock, they also agreed that that the largest dome was the one they liked best. The dome "of a greater height than the one I should have preferred" had won the day, Bulfinch said.[27] He would never be a fan of the seventy-foot dome, which, when completed, would resemble a knit winter cap placed atop the building. Thornton would publicly howl at the design, guffawing that the tall dome in the middle, flanked by the shorter lanterns letting in light over the House and Senate chambers, looked like a tea set.

Once again, Bulfinch ignored Thornton's public derision and instead focused his attention on the Rotunda—or "rotundo," as he frequently called it in his correspondence. Given the soaring height of the new dome, which would tower 145 feet above the ground, Bulfinch was now unhappy with the unbalanced proportions of the interior space beneath it. More to his tastes were the tidy and classical proportions of the Pantheon in Rome—where the enclosed space is as tall as it is wide—and so Bulfinch would fudge the proportions of his rotunda by constructing an interior dome to enclose the space at a height matching the circular floor's diameter. "In the rotunda, a bold simplicity has been studied, suitable to a great central entrance," wrote Bulfinch with a near-audible sigh of relief. "The room is 96 feet in diameter, and of the same height."[28]

Looking up from the inside, then, visitors wouldn't be staring at the underside of the seventy-foot exterior dome; instead, they would be looking up into a smaller dome tucked just beneath the too large outer one, with an oculus at the center to let light and air stream in from above. The exterior dome itself would be made of wood—Bulfinch wanted to use fireproof brick, but he had been rebuffed by a parsimonious Congress. Then the outer surface of the dome would be coated with copper, topped with a round skylight twenty-four feet in diameter "intended to admit light into the great Rotunda,"[29] and surrounded by a balustrade to give it a more finished appearance.[30] Congress, and the president, loved the look of it, believing that, as Bulfinch put it, "there was something bold and picturesque in a *lofty dome.*"[31] Lofty or not, Bulfinch still hated it. He would continue to try, without success, to convince his superiors to let him scale the dome back to what he considered a better-proportioned size even as the one he detested was being built.

"The principal labor of the season has been devoted to raising the dome of the center," Bulfinch reported to the Congress in late 1822—and indeed, the interior dome would be completed before the end of the year, while the exterior dome would be missing only its outside copper coating. Bulfinch continued to loathe the scale of the outer dome, but he was delighted with the neat proportions of the inner Rotunda, though there was still one feature of the space that gnawed at his sense of order: cut into the center of the Rotunda floor was a large circular opening about ten feet in diameter, looking down into the Crypt below.

It was another quirky architectural detail that had been inflicted on his design sense by Thornton, who had reminded Bulfinch that the Capitol was still intended to be the final resting place of George Washington. And so Bulfinch had stuck with Thornton's plan for a hole in the center of the Rotunda floor through which visitors might view a statue of Washington in the chamber directly below. However, while the lower rotunda would always be casually referred to as the Crypt, it was never intended for Washington to be interred there; instead, Bulfinch would construct a smaller compartment at the building's lowest level, in a small vaulted space directly beneath the Crypt, to serve as the potential final resting place for George and Martha Washington. He would leave it to the Congress to work out the details.[32]

Bulfinch also reported that the westward projection of the center section was mostly finished and that the exterior western face of the building "exhibits the appearance it is intended to retain." The interior committee rooms in the basement were also nearly ready for use, though plaster was still drying throughout most of the space. Still missing, however, was any sign of the center section's eastern portico, which would serve as the Capitol's main entrance. Despite the lack of a formal entrance, Bulfinch was proud of what had been accomplished over the last twelve months, and he finished his report by generously lauding the "cheerful and unremitted exertions of the workmen." He then signed off with the same modesty and optimism that continued to endear him to a normally fed-up and impatient Congress: "I sincerely hope that the effects of our joint efforts will meet the approbation of the President of the United States, and the Representatives of the Nation."[33]

Bulfinch's only real disagreement with his Congressional overseers had come earlier in the spring, following the death of Commissioner Samuel Lane. Monroe had appointed Lane's clerk, Joseph Elgar, to fill the post—and Elgar, feeling pressure from Congress to keep costs down, had notified Bulfinch that it was his "painful duty" to inform him that his salary was being reduced by $500 annually.[34] A flabbergasted Bulfinch appealed that decision directly to Secretary of State John Quincy Adams, arguing that the $2,500 salary was an implied contract that had been an "inducement for quitting a place where I was well established" and that any change in his already "prudent and economical" lifestyle would be "irksome and humiliating."[35] Adams pled Bulfinch's case to President Monroe, who referred the question to Attorney General William Wirt, who sided with Bulfinch. Bulfinch's annual pay would remain at $2,500; meanwhile, the Congress—after a close reading of the Residence Act of 1790 that led legislators to decide Elgar's responsibilities were "less arduous than they formerly were"[36]—would reduce Elgar's salary by $500.

Bulfinch spent 1823 completing work on the Library of Congress, which would end up being one of the most highly regarded spaces of the Bulfinch era. By taking up most of the top two floors of the west side of the center section, Bulfinch constructed a library large enough to contain forty thousand books—nearly seven times more than the Library of Congress owned at that time, giving the collection adequate space to grow. On the main floor, he constructed deep, shelf-lined alcoves overlooked by shallower alcoves on the balcony level. In an arched ceiling spanning nearly the entire length of the library from south to north—about ninety feet—Bulfinch inset three large circular skylights to ensure plenty of light for daytime reading. Finally, in the western wall were four high arched windows providing spectacular views of the Federal city, the Potomac, and the flickering lantern lights of Alexandria on the Virginia side of the river.

Bulfinch would finish the room with comfortable sofas, chairs, and writing tables, keeping it warm in the winter with elegant iron stoves instead of fireplaces, ensuring the room could be heated without the open fires that were so dangerous to books and papers. It was a space that invited lingering and lounging, whether visitors were reading a newspaper on a sofa, nestled in one of the deep alcoves, or gazing out the tall windows at the still mostly rural city. The *National Intelligencer* would later call it "the most beautiful apartment in the building," applauding Bulfinch for architecture that "displays a great deal of taste."[37] The library was open only to members of Congress and certain government officials; in a town with few lending libraries or literary salons, the Library of Congress and its "most beautiful apartment" would for now remain inaccessible to the public.

The library was also inaccessible to *everyone* from the west side of the building, as Bulfinch had chosen to install no doors in the western face of the center section, even as he had also abandoned Latrobe's plans for a temple entrance to the building at the base of the western slope of Capitol Hill. Latrobe's ambitious drawings aside, the west side of the building was never really considered for a showcase entrance into the Capitol; starting with Thornton's earliest drawings, it was always the east side that presented the more formal point of entry. In Thornton's 1793 concept, the entrance to the building was through an eastern portico at ground level—which made sense, given that in Thornton's original plan both chambers of Congress had been located on the ground floor. However, when Latrobe moved each chamber up one floor, he then added to the eastern front a wide set of steps leading up to what was now considered the main level. There guests would be welcomed into the building through a stylish column-lined portico that ran the width of the center section and was topped with a decorative triangular pediment.

Bulfinch liked elements of plans by both architects but ultimately decided Latrobe's design was more suitably grand and worthy of the scale of the building. Sticking to his practice of adopting design elements that worked while discarding those that didn't, Bulfinch quietly abandoned Thornton's understated ground floor entry as the main entrance in favor of the majestic staircase envisioned by Latrobe that brought visitors directly into the central Rotunda on the building's main level. More than two hundred years later, it's easy to see that Bulfinch made the right decision; the building's grand central staircase, portico, and triangular pediment—expanded from Latrobe's original vision—still give the approach to the Capitol a heart-thumping sense of drama. Walking up those steps toward the building's main entrance is surely as exciting today as it must have been in Bulfinch's time.

But Latrobe's design was also more expensive, especially as his plan required not just a grand stairway but also twice the number of marble columns as Thornton's did. Oddly, Commissioner Elgar, who had been quick to reduce Bulfinch's salary in the name of economy, in this case willingly increased costs by deciding that all twenty-four columns needed for the portico were to be shaped from single blocks of stone rather than assembled from drums as was standard practice. Stonecutter George Blagden, however, thought that was a bad idea—because stone of that size would be easily cracked, causing him "fear as respects the strength and durability."[38] Outranked by Elgar, Blagden merely urged the rock cutters at Aquia to select their stone carefully, even if it slowed the quarrying process.

The first three large pieces of stone were quarried in late 1823 and sent upriver to be off-loaded at the Navy Yard. "They are taken from the wharf, without the aid of horses, upon a strong carriage, with a hundred men pulling," reported one journalist. The raw columns would be pulled from the wharf to Blagden's workshop, just over a mile away, up on the lawn of the Capitol, where the arrival of each column would be greeted by loud cheers along with celebratory drinking. Blagden and his team of masons would then shape and polish the rough stone into the columns needed for the portico. Meanwhile, Giovanni Andrei had his team carving the twenty-four ornate Corinthian capitals that would be placed atop the columns, a detailed process that required about six months of work to complete each one. Fortunately, Andrei's team could work on more than one at a time.

Even with the deliberately slow pace, both Bulfinch and Elgar were pleased with the work—and so were their House overseers. The Committee on Public Buildings reported that they "[found] reasons to be highly gratified" and praised Bulfinch for "the style of the workmanship . . . giving solidity to grandeur."[39] But Bulfinch and Elgar also knew that the Congress was not going to be inclined to wait indefinitely. Fortunately, while progress on the exterior portico was slow—by late 1824, only thirteen of the portico's twenty-four columns had been moved into place—the interior of the Capitol would be nearly complete by the end of the year.

Of all interior spaces in the Capitol, perhaps none would be as awe-inspiring as the Rotunda. At seven thousand square feet, it was not only the largest room in the Capitol but one of the largest rooms anywhere in the United States. (The sheer size, in fact, baffled some, including an editor for the *New-York Statesman* who thought it "one of the grandest domes in the world, but I cannot learn that any use is to be made of it," especially as there was nowhere to sit.)[40]

Bulfinch had used pilasters—ornamental columns carved directly onto the surface of the wall—to divide the circular walls into twelve sections; in the sections at the four points of the compass were doors leading into the Senate (north), the House (south), the Library of Congress (west), and out onto the main portico entrance (east). Between the doors were large rectangular niches for displaying paintings, with four of them already reserved for John Trumbull's now completed work. At the moment, Trumbull had his paintings hanging in various locations around the Capitol while he waited for the walls of the Rotunda to finish drying.

Encircling the room forty-eight feet above the floor, as if supported by the pilasters, was an entablature carved with wreaths ("apparently in honor of the subjects of national history to be exhibited below," Bulfinch suggested), and, above that, the inner dome soaring gracefully upward toward a round skylight to let in light from the opening in the outer dome directly above. Latrobe had wanted to include thirty-foot niches in the walls for statues, but Bulfinch disregarded that part of his plans, preferring to leave the space free of overlarge statues while also making the walls more structurally sound. Various carvings, frescoes, and plaques would eventually decorate the walls of the Rotunda, but Bulfinch purposely kept the room relatively simple and dignified—an entirely appropriate space to serve as the gateway to the American experiment.

As Bulfinch kept his crew busy on the Capitol's exterior in the early months of 1825, most of the nation's attention was focused on what was happening inside on the floor of the Congress, where the outcome of the election of 1824—in a replay of the election of 1800—would be decided by the House of Representatives. James Monroe, after an easy reelection in 1820, had continued the tradition of serving only two terms by opting out of the election of 1824, leading to an electoral free-for-all in which four candidates spread out the votes sufficiently that even the highest vote getter—a Tennessee Senator and hero of the War of 1812 named Andrew Jackson—failed to achieve a majority in either the popular or the electoral vote.

Operating under procedures set out under the Twelfth Amendment—ratified in 1804 to clarify the process for electing the president and vice president—the House, with each state delegation casting a single vote, quickly elected as president the candidate from Massachusetts and sitting secretary of state, John Quincy Adams. Jackson was stunned—and seething. Fuming that the election had been stolen—the result of a backroom "corrupt bargain" between Adams and another presidential candidate, Speaker of the House Henry Clay—a steaming-mad Jackson swore to spend the next four years riling up opposition to the Adams administration while vowing revenge and ginning up support for another run for president in 1828. The Era of Good Feelings had come to a definitive end.

Meanwhile, the lame-duck Monroe—who had spent his first day in office as president with Latrobe dickering over Potomac marble—would spend some of his last days consulting with Bulfinch and Commissioner of Public Buildings Joseph Elgar about decorative sculpture for the triangular pediment directly above the eastern entrance to the Capitol. "The ornaments for the Pediment of the Capitol has [*sic*] been a subject of various consideration for some time past," wrote Elgar.[41] Both Bulfinch and Monroe understood that the ornamentation over the Capitol's main entrance was more than just decorative sculpture; it was also a statement on American ideals. But Monroe, knowing the clock was ticking, offered no opinions on the design—and on his way out the door of the President's House, he simply punted the question to a national competition similar to the one that had brought in the designs for the Capitol itself, all the way down to a $500 prize for the winner.

This particular competition, however, was doomed to failure, mostly because the contest as printed specified only the dimensions of the pediment without providing any suggestions on preferred designs or subjects to fill it. Bulfinch was disappointed in most of the submissions anyway. "About 30 persons presented 36 designs," he reported to his son Thomas, "some well and others badly executed."[42] The real problem, as Elgar explained to newly elected President John Quincy Adams, was that lawmaking wasn't a terribly inspiring subject. "A building dedicated to purposes of Legislation presents a new field to the artist," wrote Elgar. While Elgar hoped one or two artists might rise to the occasion, he told the president that so far "they have not done so."[43]

Adams was shrewd enough to read between the lines of Elgar's explanation and decided to involve himself directly in the planning and design of the pediment. Advising him in the matter would be an informal committee made up of Elgar and Bulfinch plus the always opinionated William Thornton and the Italian sculptor Luigi Persico, who the year before had impressed Adams with his bust of Lafayette unveiled during the Frenchman's tour of the United States. After considerable discussion and consultation, Persico turned in a rough sketch for a design featuring at the center "a personification of the United States standing on a throne" flanked by a blindfolded figure of Justice on her right and Hercules, as a symbol of strength, on her left. Filling the corners of the pediment were figures representing Peace and Plenty.

Adams hated it. Not only was the pediment too crowded with figures, but he made it clear to Bulfinch that there were to be no "triumphal cars and emblems of Victory . . . [nor any] heathen mythology."[44] To unclutter the design, the president asked for the removal of Peace and Plenty from the corners and proposed putting the figure of America on a pedestal—not a *throne!*—inscribed with the effective dates of the Declaration of Independence and the U.S. Constitution. Finally, he suggested reworking the figure of Hercules into the personification of Hope standing upon an anchor. With this positioning of figures, Adams intended for the work to represent

> the American Union founded on the Declaration of Independence and consummated by the organization of the General Government under the Federal Constitution, supported by Justice in the past, and relying upon Hope in Providence for the future.[45]

That kind of artistic analysis was a lot to ask of Capitol visitors craning their necks to look at the pediment. While Adams told Bulfinch he felt certain that this triptych of figures would convey "the duties of the Nation or its Legislators . . . in an obvious and intelligible manner,"[46] he also directed that there be an "appropriate inscription . . . [to] explain the meaning and the moral to dull comprehensions."[47]

As executed by Persico, the figures sculpted in sandstone for the final ornamentation—officially designated as *The Genius of America*—would stand more than nine feet high and be posed at the center of a triangular pediment eighty-one feet long.[48] America, with her arm on a shield emblazoned with "USA" and a stern-looking eagle at her feet, points to her right at the figure of unblindfolded Justice—yet another figure of Justice with her eyes uncovered in the Capitol—who holds a scale in her left hand and the Constitution in her right. To America's left, Hope leans on an anchor with her right arm upraised, beckoning optimistically toward America. When the piece was finally installed in 1828, there would be no inscription anywhere to explain it, leading to wild guesses in later guidebooks about the precise meaning being conveyed by the interaction of its figures.[49] Even Bulfinch, in a letter to his son, garbled Adams's intent, explaining it as "while we cultivate Justice, we may hope for success."[50] Just another dull comprehension, apparently.

When Congress convened in early December 1825, the Rotunda walls, which were still slightly wet, had large rectangular niches awaiting

Trumbull's paintings. To keep the cold of the Washington winter at bay, fires blazed in some of the more than hundred twenty fireplaces in the building. Without an open flame, Bulfinch's well-designed stoves in the Library of Congress kept the space one of the most comfortable in the building—but even the precautions the architect had taken to safely warm the room couldn't save the library from human carelessness.

On December 22, 1825, at eleven p.m., as Massachusetts Congressman Edward Everett and his wife left a party, the thirty-one-year-old chairman of the House Committee on the Library looked up toward the Capitol and spotted lights flickering in the library windows. Concerned, he ran to the building and sought the help of a policeman there on patrol. The policeman didn't have a key to unlock the library door, but he assured Everett everything was in order and sent the concerned Congressman on his way.

Almost immediately after Everett's departure, however, several other policemen noticed a bright light glowing in the library windows and tracked down George Watterson, the librarian of Congress, who *did* have a key. Opening the doors, they found a fire roaring in one of the upper galleries, threatening to spread to the wooden ceiling and then likely over to the enormous central wooden dome. Watterson clanged a bell in the work yard, hoping to attract the fire department, and eventually roused not only firefighters but also Everett and Representatives Sam Houston of Tennessee and Daniel Webster of Massachusetts, all of whom helped put out the blaze before it could spread beyond the library.

An investigation revealed that the fire had been started by a candle that had been left burning in the upper gallery—and to the likely relief of both Watterson and Everett, damage to the library's collection of books was minimal. Firemen had managed to remove many books while fighting the flames, and most of the books that had been destroyed were duplicates. Apart from some water and smoke damage, the most expensive loss was a carpet valued at $1,000. Bulfinch, too, was relieved; he had been, as his wife informed their sons, "concerned and anxious"—

especially "as he is very reasonably proud of that room."[51] Congress briefly considered directing Bulfinch to fireproof the existing library, then decided against the considerable expense—a cost-saving measure that would come to have disastrous consequences.

Still, the fire got Congress and Bulfinch thinking about other flammable hazards in the building, with Bulfinch focusing mostly on the dark cellars beneath the north and south wings, where firewood and fuel were stored to keep the Capitol's fireplaces, furnaces, and heating stoves well stocked. There, all it would have taken was a candle or lantern dropped by a worker tasked with fetching armloads of firewood, and the entire building would erupt in flames. A concerned Bulfinch quickly presented the Congress with a proposal to construct a terrace at a good distance from the western face of the central section; it would run nearly the length of the building and enclose a pair of courtyards in the space between it and the Capitol building. The terrace would be large enough to accommodate storage for wood, coal, and fuel—anything that needed to be accessible and close to the Capitol but not *too* close, like twelve brand-new privies for the House and six for the Senate. The latter detail helped sweeten the proposal for the Congress, which eventually appropriated $99,000 to execute the plan.

Besides the safer storage space, the terrace would also serve an aesthetic purpose, concealing the basement level that Bulfinch had already attempted to hide by facing it with dark granite. Bulfinch also partially obscured the terrace walls with a sloping grassy berm that camouflaged the basement floor even further. Atop the terrace, Bulfinch created a walkway accessible from patios at the north and south ends of the Capitol. He did so by laying Seneca paving stones, quarried in Maryland, across the terrace roof and installing iron railings to keep walkers from falling into the courtyards below. Eventually, Bulfinch would install a door in the western front and connect the entrance to the terrace with a short bridge so visitors could enter and exit through the library. The effect, as Bulfinch's wife recorded it, was "much commended."[52]

While no one would be injured by leaping into the courtyards, the western terrace wouldn't be completed without a major tragedy. In late spring 1826, an embankment near an exposed foundation wall collapsed, killing the invaluable master stonecutter George Blagden. "A severe loss," Commissioner Elgar wrote in his year-end report to President Adams. He praised the mason, who had been on the Capitol project since 1794, for "possessing in a high degree the science, and practical knowledge of his profession" as well as for the "precision, and fidelity, which he carried into all relations of life."[53]

By spring of 1827, it was finished.

It had been thirty-four years since William Thornton had submitted the winning drawing that had established the Capitol's basic look—a domed center section flanked by matching wings housing each body of Congress. Later that same year, George Washington had personally laid the cornerstone of the building on the edge of heavily wooded Jenkins Hill. In the wake of unreliable funding, delayed supplies, and no small amount of backbiting and political bickering, the first usable version of the Capitol was the lone Senate wing, which Thornton and his work crews had rushed so something—anything—was ready for the Congress to occupy when it moved from Philadelphia to Washington in 1800. Fourteen years later, the next working version of the building—the freestanding House and Senate wings connected only by a wooden walkway—was left in flames by Admiral Cockburn and his invading British troops. After which, architect Benjamin Latrobe would essentially have to start all over again.

Since that time, progress had been slow, with work often occurring in fits and starts, as Latrobe and then Bulfinch had been subject to pressures and work conditions—including agonizing waits for quarried stone from White's Ferry and Aquia; inclement weather; the arched eyebrow of an impatient chief executive; and the whims of an unpredictable and, at times, tightfisted Congress—that were sometimes, though not always, beyond their control. From Thornton's first drawings to the impressive structure with the copper dome now gleaming on the banks of the Potomac, the project had chewed up and spit out at least four different architects, with only Bulfinch still standing; claimed at least two lives; sparked very public disagreements; prompted at least one court case; and, ultimately, cost about $2 million.[54]

Bulfinch had kept with Thornton's basic design as well as with Latrobe's basic architectural look, ensuring that the new center section blended seamlessly with the old House and Senate wings. Unlike some architects, Bulfinch had resisted the urge to put his own flourishes on the building. He had finished the wings with low domed roofs supported inside by columns of Potomac marble and topped by lanterns that let sunlight into each inner legislative chamber.

And with the new center section in place, visitors no longer had to enter through the muddy ground floor entrances of each wing; instead, they could bound up the elegant central steps on the East Front, cross the covered portico—soon to be crowned with the triangular pediment featuring Persico's *Genius of America*—and enter the soaring, shady Rotunda as the first stop on their way to either chamber. On the back of the building, the center section now jutted slightly west and over the slope of Capitol Hill, providing a dedicated space for the rapidly growing Library of Congress as well as for much-needed meeting rooms.

Squatting atop the building was the one feature that George Washington had been adamant about and had not lived to see: a dome. It was not the button-sized dome of Thornton's original drawing, but rather the taller, "lofty" one admired by James Monroe and foisted by the president on Bulfinch, who still thought it oddly proportioned. Topped with its copper dome, the Capitol was 145 feet tall at its highest point, making it one of the largest structures in the region—and one worthy of the aspirations of the growing nation.

While the basic structure was complete, there was work left to be done. Out on the eastern portico, Persico's sculpture was still missing from the pediment; it would finally be installed in 1828 to great fanfare and constant misinterpretation. Meanwhile, the well-regarded Italian sculptor Antonio Capellano had been hired to create a sandstone relief showing George Washington being crowned by Fame and Peace for placement directly over the main door at the top of the grand eastern steps. From there, the first president would stonily nod approval to visitors as they passed through the east entrance and stepped into the Rotunda.

In the Rotunda, too, ornamental details were being finished, including four sculpted relief panels featuring scenes from America's colonial past, all of which seemed to feature Native Americans being conquered, killed, or demeaned.[55] Representative Henry Wise of Virginia pointed out acidly that the story told by the four panels was one of "the old world coming to the new, and the new welcoming the old, and giving it corn; but in the next was the representative of a treaty in which the white man cheated the Indian! . . . A pretty faithful history of our dealing with the native tribes!"[56]

It was all a bit much for Representative Tristam Burges of Rhode Island, too. Staring at the cramped and grisly depiction of Daniel Boone knife fighting with a Native American—with the two figures literally grappling on the body of a fallen Native warrior—Burges observed that it "very truly represented our dealing with the Indians, for we had not left them even a space to die upon." A 1907 guide to the Capitol referred to the panels as "disgraceful disfigurements of the room."[57] Two hundred years after their placement, the controversial panels are still in place in the Rotunda.[58]

Less controversial were John Trumbull's four paintings, which were finally on display in the niches Bulfinch had designated for the artist's work, though Trumbull was less than happy with conditions in the Rotunda. "I found the grand room finished indeed," he wrote, "but so very damp that I felt great reluctance in placing [the paintings] there." Trumbull demanded that Bulfinch close the hole at the center of the floor, which, he said, let in air that was "equally damp and cold as the weather in the open square."[59] Bulfinch quietly disregarded the artist's suggestion.

Bulfinch, meanwhile, had focused his attention on the landscaping of the Capitol grounds, requesting the funding necessary to complete the stone and iron fencing surrounding all 22.5 acres; that infrastructure had been put in place largely to keep out wandering livestock. The architect also asked Congress to install several gates and stone guardhouses to provide access to the grounds on the western and eastern sides, but the increasingly stingy Congress pared down the request to just two gates and guardhouses on the west side alone.

Over the next year, Bulfinch would continue to ask for the money necessary to finish off the fine details he thought the building needed before he would truly consider it completed; eventually, he submitted an estimate for a little more than $60,000.[60] For some requests—such as construction of a new visitor gallery for the Senate and funds to reconfigure a staircase accessing the House chamber—he would be successful; for others, such as his guardhouses, there would be significant pushback or flat-out refusal. Some Congressmen complained that the building seemed to be *always* under construction—indeed, for members like Senator Elias Kane of Illinois and Representative Thomas Moore of Kentucky, who had been born *after* the laying of the Capitol's cornerstone in 1793, the Capitol had literally been a work in progress for their entire lives. Others cynically suggested that the building might never be completed so long as there were full-time employees—like Bulfinch—whose livelihoods, they insinuated, depended on incorporating just one more change to the building.

Perhaps sensing his days were numbered, Bulfinch kept his head down and kept working. Over the objections of Congress, who feared a climate-controlled Capitol would attract vagrants and loiterers, the architect installed stoves in the Crypt to carry much-needed heat into the Rotunda just above. However, when cold air moving through the Rotunda and Crypt continued to frustrate his efforts to keep the space warm, Bulfinch finally supported Trumbull's request to seal the hole in the Rotunda's floor and completed the task in 1828.

Delighted, the artist promptly hurried to Washington to check on his canvases, only to discover that the damp air in the chamber had, as he feared, caused the backs of the paintings to mildew. At Trumbull's direction, vents were cut into the Rotunda walls directly behind the paintings, and a sludge of melted beeswax and turpentine was spread across the backs of the canvases to preserve and protect them from mold. Finally, the four paintings were stretched across boards drilled with hundreds of tiny holes to keep air circulating and prevent any further damage. Once the enormous paintings were back on display in their niches, Trumbull installed curtains that could be drawn in front of them to protect them from dust. The artist found the new conditions more than satisfactory and was thrilled that Bulfinch and he had managed to find a way to keep his paintings "perfectly and permanently secured against the deleterious effects of dampness."[61]

Bulfinch's tenure as Architect of the Capitol would come to an end—at least on paper—when his position was officially abolished by an act of Congress on May 2, 1828. But if Congress thought the Capitol was complete, Bulfinch didn't—and so he simply kept reporting for work every day, continuing to oversee construction and submitting more requests for funding to finish projects or maintain work that had already been completed. Eventually, on June 25, 1829—more than a year after Congress had handed the architect his walking papers—Elgar informed Bulfinch in a tight-lipped letter that "the office of Architect of the Capitol will terminate with the present month."[62] Bulfinch and his wife would linger in Washington for another year, but the Bulfinch era was officially over.

As Bulfinch left Washington by stagecoach to return to Boston in

1830, he looked back on his time in the capital city without regrets. "[We are] leaving friends who appear sincerely attached to us, and a place which has given us a pleasant and respectable home for 12 years," he wrote, "and where we leave memorials of us which we hope will long endure."[63] Twelve years earlier, the Boston architect had arrived in Washington to find a Capitol gutted and scorched by British fire; now, as he boarded the stagecoach in Baltimore, he left behind a finished building comfortably accommodating the House, Senate, Library of Congress, and Supreme Court.

It had been an era with relatively little drama or disagreement; unlike his predecessors, Bulfinch would leave his post admired and esteemed and with his public and professional reputations intact. He had dutifully honored the basics of Thornton's template and stuck with Latrobe's layout largely without ego or complaint, modifying or improvising only as needed. He would leave his mark mostly on the center section with the Library of Congress he was so proud of and an impressive Rotunda, which would likely have exceeded even Latrobe's expectations. And while Bulfinch would never be pleased with the dome, he had given the Capitol a distinctive silhouette and an elegant look that would be admired, sketched, etched, painted, even photographed for reproduction on postcards, sheet music, calendars, and dinnerware. For the next twenty-five years, the building would remain largely unchanged—and become, as Bulfinch had hoped, a memorial that would long endure.

Taken in 1846, one of the first known photographs of the U.S. Capitol features the building as completed by Architect of the Capitol Charles Bulfinch in 1828. It would remain largely unchanged until the 1850s.

CHAPTER 5

A Magnificent Palace

1828–1850

On Tuesday, April 15, 1828, the private secretary for President John Quincy Adams arrived at the Capitol to deliver official messages from the president to the chambers of the House and Senate. This messenger was no run-of-the-mill presidential appointee; Adams had engaged to serve as his personal secretary a dashing twenty-four-year-old aspiring lawyer named John Adams II, the sitting president's own son and the grandson of the second president of the United States—a most distinguished pedigree.

As secretary to the president, Adams delivered messages to Congressional leaders in person as part of his regular routine, and the young man was as familiar with the Capitol's often labyrinthian layout as he was with his route home. On this particular Tuesday, Adams delivered his first message to the chamber of the House of Representatives, then exited through the circular lobby just off the north entrance to the House floor. From there, walking stick in hand, he entered the Rotunda through its southern door and headed for the entrance to the Senate wing directly across from him in the cavernous space beneath the dome.

The Rotunda, as usual, was noisy and bustling. Members of Congress passed through the area on their way to confer in committee rooms or to head to the floor for debate. Merchants loitered at the curved perimeter of the space, waiting for just the right opportunity to pull their Senator or Congressman into one of the small side nooks to engage in a bit of lobbying as they pled their cases for particular bills or issues. Along the walls, visitors lounged on benches, some directly beneath Trumbull's enormous paintings, while journalists could often be spotted near the doors, listening in on conversations for some political intel they might publish in their papers. As Adams crossed the Rotunda toward the north door, one of those journalists—Russell Jarvis, the thirty-seven-year-old editor of the fiercely anti-Adams daily newspaper *United States Telegraph*—was waiting for him.

Jarvis was only a recent convert to the anti-Adams cause; years earlier, in fact, he had been an active Adams supporter, serving as editor of the pro-Adams newspaper *Boston Patriot* and even sitting on the committee of delegates that had nominated Adams for the presidency in 1824. When his support for the president failed to result in a political appointment, however, the disgruntled Jarvis had been easily swayed—some would say riled up—by the fiery rhetoric of Adams's opponent, Andrew Jackson, and his charges of a stolen election. From the editorial seat of the *Telegraph*, then, Jarvis had turned his newspaper into one of the nation's most aggressive pro-Jackson mouthpieces. He was determined to do whatever it took to elevate Jackson to the presidency—even if it meant stirring up some anti-Adams controversy with a manufactured grievance.

Jarvis would later insist that the president's secretary had had it coming; two weeks earlier, at a public reception at the President's House, Jarvis claimed John Adams II had insulted his wife. Adams hadn't,[1] but Jarvis, craving salacious headlines—and ideally the gratitude of Jackson—publicly challenged the president's son to a duel. Knowing full well that the younger Adams, like his father, found the practice and protocols of the duello barbaric and slightly baffling, Jarvis felt certain Adams would refuse to rise to any actual confrontation. The *Telegraph* could then call out Adams as a coward, thus smearing the sitting president simply for being kinship-adjacent to his own son. At the same time, Jarvis intended to make it clear that Jackson—a notorious duelist and hothead who had killed at least one challenger and still had a bullet lodged in his own chest—would *never* have allowed such a personal affront to stand.

As Jarvis suspected, Adams had refused to take the bait. According to the rules of the duel, then, when the challenged party refused to settle the matter on the dueling grounds, the aggrieved party was permitted the satisfaction of assaulting their opponent without warning anywhere they might choose.

Jarvis chose Tuesday, April 15, 1828, in the Rotunda as his opportunity to settle the score with the president's son—and to gain some political points with Jackson.

Stepping toward Adams as he crossed the Rotunda, Jarvis grabbed the young man's nose and pulled it, then slapped him hard across the face—"with an open hand," horrified witnesses reported later—and attempted to wrestle away Adams's walking stick. To Jarvis's likely surprise, Adams fought back aggressively; then Jarvis—his point made, but with his hands fuller than he had perhaps anticipated—turned to stride haughtily away. Adams, now brandishing his walking stick overhead like a weapon, shouted and ran after him, but before the two men could tangle, they were pulled apart by several Congressmen. As Jarvis was dragged away by Maryland Representative Clement Dorsey, he taunted Adams, shouting, "You know my name! You know my place of residence!" Jarvis was practically daring the president's son to continue their fight beyond the walls of the Capitol.[2]

But by bringing his fight inside the Capitol building in the first place, Jarvis had overplayed his hand. While President John Quincy Adams roared that his son had been "waylaid and assaulted," he also suggested in a formal letter to the Congress that this was more than merely a slap in the face of his son or the Adams administration. By assaulting the president's personal secretary as he conducted official business with the House and Senate—and in the Capitol no less—Jarvis had disparaged the entire legislative branch and tainted the people's building. Secretary of State Henry Clay—the only member of the Adams administration with any experience in dueling—warned, "The act is of a most dangerous character. . . . It tends to introduce assassination into the Capitol."[3] Such a dangerous precedent, wrote Adams, demanded that Congress reassert its authority and preserve the sanctity of the Capitol—a clever pivot that shifted the burden of reputation salvaging off the back of his son and onto the shoulders of the Congress. At the very least, Adams suggested that the Congress boost security in the Capitol building to prevent any such clashes from happening again.

The response from Congress was a near-audible yawn. The Congress of 1828 was comprised heavily of members who opposed the Adams administration, and as Clay noted privately to the president, "It is indeed too probable that in the present disposition of both houses of Congress they may do nothing to remedy the evil." But even a Congress hostile to the president had to concede that Adams had made a good point about standing up for the reputation of the institution and preserving the integrity of the Capitol. After some hemming and hawing, the Congress finally agreed to investigate the scuffle in the Rotunda and appointed a seven-member committee composed mostly of members who were inclined to play down the severity of Jarvis's assault and lay down political cover for Andrew Jackson.

As the committee looked half-heartedly into the incident, Jackson's supporters very publicly snickered at "the pulling of the Prince's nose" and insisted that the younger Adams—referred to derisively in the pages of the *Telegraph* as "the Royal puppy"—deserved the treatment he had received at the hands of Jarvis. But as the committee continued its work and public sentiment began to tilt toward the younger Adams—who was finally recognized as a victim of an actual assault—Jackson's supporters stopped their swaggering and asserted instead that their own investigation was being over-publicized and politicized. The true objective of the committee, they now argued, stepping on their own narrative, was to damage Jackson's looming campaign for president—or, barring that, to deflect attention away from another Congressional investigation that was certain to embarrass the Adams administration. They promised to make the findings of that inquiry public as quickly as possible. (There were no such findings, as there would never be such an investigation.)

The committee's final report, issued in late May, conceded that Adams had indeed been assaulted by Jarvis in the Rotunda—though the committee wouldn't state unequivocally whether Adams had been slapped or nose-pulled—and further agreed that such behavior was beneath the dignity of the House of Representatives. But as Clay had predicted, the Jackson-friendly Congress declined to pursue the case any further, eventually tabling a motion to formally reprimand Jarvis.

Congress did, however, grudgingly agree with President Adams that more security was needed for the Capitol and on May 2, 1828, established the United States Capitol Police—then, as now, the only federal law enforcement agency appointed by, and under the direction of, the United States Congress. Initially, the United States Capitol Police consisted of a captain and three patrolmen; today, more than two thousand Capitol police protect the Capitol, its compound, its surrounding neighborhoods, and, most important, its members.[4]

As Adams had crossed the Rotunda in April 1828, however, only a single guard had been on duty when Jarvis committed the building's first major act of politically motivated violence—one carried out in the name of a presidential candidate. Seven months later, that candidate, Andrew Jackson—running at the head of a newly consolidated Democratic ticket against the National Republican candidate and sitting president, John Quincy Adams—was elected president of the United States. This time, the contest wasn't even close. Jackson executed a masterful campaign based on personality rather than on policy—stymieing the more cerebral Adams—and presented himself to the voters as a man of the people who would stand up to the elites, especially the old patrician families of Massachusetts and the gentry of Virginia, who had run things for far too long. It was a message that seemed to resonate with voters, and Jackson would end up winning 55 percent of the popular vote and handily carrying fifteen of the nation's twenty-four states.

Because Jackson was a populist candidate, it was little surprise that his inauguration on March 4, 1829, was seen as nothing short of An Event; public interest in seeing Old Hickory live and in person was so great that it quickly became clear it would be impossible to administer the oath of office to Jackson within the confines of the House chamber. Instead, the ceremony was brought outside to the Capitol's eastern portico, making Jackson the first president to be sworn in on the Capitol's eastern steps—a tradition that, weather permitting, would be embraced by every U.S. president until 1981, when the ceremony would be moved to the building's western side. There on the east steps, Jackson was sworn in by Chief Justice John Marshall in front of a crowd of more than twenty thousand cheering spectators. "Thousands and thousands of people, without distinction of rank, collected in an immense mass round the Capitol," marveled one spectator.[5] It was a site that moved Francis Scott Key—who knew a thing or two about being stirred by spectacle—to enthuse, "It is beautiful; it is sublime!"[6]

It was easy to spot Jackson in the crowd—he was one of the few who hadn't shown up wearing a hat. One person who would not be seen in the throng, however, was John Quincy Adams. The entire campaign of 1828 had left a bad taste in his mouth—not least because of the humiliation of having his own vice president, John Calhoun, abandon him to become Jackson's running mate—so Adams had quietly departed Washington before Jackson's inauguration. He remained concerned enough about Jackson's policies to return to public life in 1830 and actively, though usually unsuccessfully, counter the Jackson administration as an elected member of Congress. His tenure as a Congressman from Massachusetts would last longer than Jackson's two terms as president, as Adams would be reelected eight times over the next eighteen years. John Adams II, however, would die in 1834 at age thirty-one, succumbing to alcoholism.

Unlike John Quincy Adams, who had directly involved himself in a number of decisions involving the Capitol during his presidency, Andrew Jackson would take a much more hands-off approach to its management. The building itself was finished and would remain basically unmodified for decades, though there was still some work underway to complete the landscaping and western terraces. But even without any requested renovations or improvements on the books, a building as large as the Capitol still needed constant attention, whether there was plaster to be repaired, windows to be replaced, or new fireplace mantels to be installed. But after the termination of the position of Architect of the Capitol in 1828, neither Jackson nor the Congress was inclined to appoint a new full-time architect to oversee even the smallest of maintenance needs. Instead, the Capitol was just one of the many public structures in Washington placed under the jurisdiction of the commissioner of public buildings, a post Jackson had filled with a competent project manager, Major William Noland, who was more than happy to rely on local contractors to perform any work that needed to be done.

At the Capitol, the local relied upon the most was a forty-nine-year-old South Carolina–born architect named Robert Mills, who had studied under both Hoban and Latrobe and made his name designing mainly churches and prisons. But Mills's role would largely be that of a consultant—"architect to aid in forming the plans," as Jackson put it. The actual oversight of projects was left to a versatile master carpenter and all-around handyman named Pringle Slight, who had first been hired by Bulfinch in 1825 to complete the copper work on the Capitol's center dome.

The in-demand Mills, meanwhile, was continuing to pick up commissions in and around D.C. regularly, and in Baltimore, he had recently overseen the completion of a monument to George Washington that he had designed back in 1815—a massive hundred-eighty-foot Doric column with an interior stairway providing visitors with access to the top and a view of the surrounding neighborhood. Mills's structure was the only public monument to Washington anywhere in the United States, giving Baltimore—as James Buchanan, president of the site's board of directors, put it—"the glory of being the first to erect a monument of gratitude to the father and benefactor of our country."[7]

It wasn't lost on the Congress that they had been beaten to the punch on an assignment they'd been postponing since 1799, when Thornton had envisioned the Capitol as a burial site for George and Martha Washington to be marked by a marble monument to the first president. Bulfinch, sticking with Thornton's vision, had left a vaulted space beneath the lower rotunda to serve as the president's final resting place, but he had deferred the specific planning—and the spending—back to the Congress.

Now, with Washington's hundredth birthday in February 1832 looming on the horizon—and somewhat embarrassed by their own inactivity—the Congress was again engaged with the matter. "When we look around for the statue, the monument, the mausoleum they had ordered [in 1799]," Congressman Leonard Jarvis of Maine reminded his House colleagues, "it is not to be seen."[8] And so detailed plans and cost estimates for a presidential tomb were requested of Robert Brown, who had taken over as the Capitol's chief stonemason following the death of George Blagden. Brown submitted plans for a brick mausoleum in the space directly below the Crypt; it would be secured by a strong iron gate with an even stronger iron lock, accessible from the basement level. Brown's plan was approved and the space beneath the Crypt was prepared.

The marble monument itself, however, was still a point of considerable contention. In his original plans for the Federal city, Pierre L'Enfant had envisioned a gigantic statue of Washington on horseback situated in an outdoor space where it would be visible from both the Capitol and the President's House. Thornton, however, had insisted on a monument inside the Capitol, ideally erected in the center of the Crypt directly over the presidential tomb and visible through a circular opening in the floor of the main Rotunda—an aperture that Bulfinch, at the urging of artist John Trumbull, had sealed shut with matching stone in 1828.

Mills, trying to circumvent the question of the marble monument entirely, proposed unsealing the opening in the floor of the Rotunda, then cutting another hole in the floor in the center of the Crypt. That way, visitors could peer straight down from the Rotunda all the way into the mausoleum two stories below, where the sarcophagus containing the bodies of the Washingtons would be respectfully on display.

With just days to go before Washington's centennial birthday, a special Congressional committee wrote to Washington's heirs to remind them that Martha Washington had agreed in 1799 to have the bodies of both her husband and herself interred at the Capitol. At the same time, the committee laid before the Congress a formal resolution asking John A. Washington II, the president's grandnephew and the current proprietor of Mount Vernon, "for the body of George Washington, to be removed and deposited in the Capitol, at Washington City, in conformity with resolutions of Congress of the 24th December 1799."[9]

But despite the goodwill and Martha Washington's prior endorsement, not everyone was so enthusiastic. When the committee's resolution was presented to the Congress for a vote, several Senators voted against it, reminding their colleagues that the president himself had specified he was to be buried at Mount Vernon; in the House, meanwhile, the Virginia delegation objected strenuously to the possible removal of their state's most famous son from his preferred burial site.

Still, things appeared to be going according to plan until John A. Washington II replied from Mount Vernon with a firm no. In a polite but tight-lipped letter to the Congress, Washington informed the committee that if the matter were left up to him—and it was in the end—the president would remain buried at Mount Vernon, just as he had requested, "in perfect tranquility, surrounded by . . . other endeared members of the family," he wrote. "I hope Congress will do justice to the motives which seem to me to require that I should not consent to their separation."[10] That settled the issue for good. George Washington would remain at Mount Vernon. The tomb that had been prepared for him in the guts of the Capitol would remain empty. Today, in the center of the Crypt, where Thornton and others had intended for the monument to stand, the floor is marked instead with a white star not only designating the center of the Capitol building, but also defining the District of Columbia's prime meridian—the starting point from which the city is divided into its four quadrants. One level directly below the Crypt, the small space intended to entomb the Washingtons is now mostly empty. To date, no one has been buried or entombed in the Capitol.

With nothing to show for the first president's centennial birthday—no tomb, no marble monument, not even a commemorative painting—Congress sought a consolation prize of sorts. A resolution was swiftly approved instructing President Jackson to commission twenty-seven-year-old sculptor Horatio Greenough of Massachusetts—who had recently executed acclaimed lifelike busts of James Fenimore Cooper and the Marquis de Lafayette—to sculpt a marble statue of Washington for placement in the center of the Capitol Rotunda.

The only specific directions given to the artist were that he should execute "in marble, a full length pedestrian statue of Washington"—meaning it should not depict the president on horseback—and that he should copy the head from the statue of Washington in the Virginia state capitol by sculptor Jean-Antoine Houdon, who had based his version on a life mask of the president.[11] The rest was left to Greenough's personal taste and discretion. Essayist Ralph Waldo Emerson, familiar with Greenough's work, promised Congress it would be delighted with the final sculpture, assuring them that Greenough was "a superior man, ardent and eloquent."[12]

Greenough spent the next eight years working on his statue, which he completed in Italy before shipping it to the United States in 1841—nine years after the presidential centennial, but better late than never. Weighing twelve tons, Greenough's *George Washington* was off-loaded at a pier at the Navy Yard and heaved by a crew of workmen up the stairs of the Capitol's eastern portico, where—to their dismay—they found the doors into the building were too narrow for the statue to pass through. Only after removing the doors and cutting away some of the masonry could the statue finally be pushed through the opening and into the Rotunda, where it was placed on a wooden platform to be ready for its ceremonial unveiling in December.

Anticipating the statue's enormous weight, Mills had reinforced the Rotunda floor with support beams in the Crypt, shoring up the stone surface beneath the ten-foot opening that had been refilled by Bulfinch, which left it as the weakest spot in the floor. Greenough, however, didn't want his statue in the center of the space—he wanted it moved just off-center toward the western door leading to the Library of Congress, where the light would fall on the statue at what he thought was a more dramatic and appropriate angle. But Congress dismissed that suggestion outright, with Henry Clay arguing that a grand statue of Washington belonged at the center of the room, where it would symbolize "the center of the Union—the offspring, the creation of his mind of his labors."[13] The statue would stay in the middle of the Rotunda.

The placement and the lighting would be the least of Greenough's problems. When the statue was formally unveiled on December 1, 1841, in a small ceremony with President John Tyler in attendance, the crowd was stunned to see what appeared to be a mostly naked president. Greenough had chosen to depict Washington in neoclassical style, with the president wearing a loosely draped toga—exposing a bare and lightly muscled upper body—and Roman sandals while seated on an ornate chair. With his right hand, Washington points skyward—toward God and divine providence—as he presents a sheathed sword with his left, reverently handing power back to the people. On the back of Washington's chair, Greenough had helpfully parsed his intention with a clumsy Latin phrase roughly translated as "Horatio Greenough made this image as a great example of freedom, which will not survive without freedom itself."

Greenough's symbolic intent aside, many were aghast at his artistic license. "The man does not live, and never lived, who saw Washington without his shirt,"[14] gasped Congressman Henry Wise of Virginia, who also took issue with Greenough's "bad Latin written in Italy."[15] Bulfinch, describing the statue in a letter to his son, thought Washington looked as if he were "entering or leaving a bath" and suggested the statue "be placed in the Parthenon with other great naked men."[16]

Not everyone hated it. The arts-loving American diplomat Alexander Everett hailed it as "a grand work" and took to the newspapers to inform detractors that "the more the subject is weighed, the more these objections will be found to lose their force."[17] In other words, "Get used to it." Ralph Waldo Emerson, meanwhile, felt Greenough had executed Washington brilliantly, in a style "simple & grand, nobly draped below & nobler nude above."[18] However, the English novelist Charles Dickens, visiting the Capitol in 1842, wasn't so sure. Washington, he thought, looked "rather strained,"[19] but he diplomatically blamed the poor lighting.

Greenough was convinced that, when the public and critics were given time and the chance to *Get used to it*, his Washington would be hailed as a masterpiece—and insisted it just had to be displayed correctly. The sculptor continued to plead with the Congress to scoot the statue just slightly away from the Rotunda's center—or, barring that, to display it prominently in the sunlight out on the Capitol's busy western lawn.

At this point, the Congress was more than willing to accommodate Greenough's request to relocate what they now regarded as a presidential eyesore. Funding was approved to move Washington to a less visible spot on the *east* lawn—a deliberate jab at Greenough, who had requested the west side. The scantily clad president was placed on a granite pedestal in a small, enclosed garden facing the Capitol. After sitting stoically in rain, snow, and baking sun for six decades, Washington was finally carted off to the Smithsonian in 1908; it was the first work of art to be removed from the Capitol for offending public sensibilities.

In 1964, Greenough's Washington—sometimes referred to as *Enthroned Washington*—went on public display on the opening day of the Smithsonian's National Museum of American History. He remains there, on the second floor near the escalators and restrooms, greeting museum guests in his underwear.

As the centennial birthday of George Washington came and went in 1832, the Congress—which had mostly failed in its efforts to commemorate the occasion in a timely manner—now seemed determined to ensure that the first president's image would be *everywhere.* At nearly the same time the Congress was commissioning a sculpture of George Washington from Greenough for placement in the Rotunda, the Senate was negotiating with the prolific American portrait painter Rembrandt Peale to purchase his 1824 painting *Patriae Pater*—Latin for "Father of His Country"—which depicted a stern and slightly grizzled-looking Washington visible through an illustrated stone "porthole." The Senate eventually agreed to acquire the portrait from Peale for $2,000 and hung it in the office used by the vice president, just off the floor of the Senate, before moving it into the Senate chamber in 1835.

The House, determined not to be outdone, commissioned a full-length painting of the first president by the respected New York artist John Vanderlyn, who was given the flexibility to paint the president as he pleased so long as he based the head and face on Gilbert Stuart's already iconic portraits of Washington. Unlike Greenough, Vanderlyn would portray the president wearing traditional eighteenth-century attire and looking almost as if he had been painted on the same day, and in the same room, as Stuart's 1796 full-length portrait. Both Peale's and Vanderlyn's paintings still hang in the Capitol, with Peale's portrait still in the Old Senate Chamber while Vanderlyn's has been moved to the new House chamber.

Apart from images of Washington, there was still the matter of filling the four remaining niches in the Rotunda with counterpart pieces to Trumbull's quartet of Revolutionary War–era paintings. By a joint resolution approved on June 23, 1836, a Congressional committee was appointed to "contract with one or more competent American artists for the execution of four historical pictures." And what a contract it was, with each of the four artists being paid $10,000 for twelve-foot-by-eighteen-foot paintings featuring a subject of their own choosing.

Virginia artist John Gadsby Chapman, who had studied landscape and portrait painting in Italy, created the *Baptism of Pocahontas*—a tableau featuring the daughter of the Algonkian chief converting to Christianity to marry colonist John Rolfe—while New Yorker Robert W. Weir, an instructor of drawing at West Point, painted the *Embarkation of the Pilgrims* depicting the Pilgrims in prayer before their journey to North America with the exultation "God with us" noticeably daubed onto a sail. Henry Inman—noted for his portraits but less so for his landscapes—was at work on a painting featuring Daniel Boone when he died suddenly at age forty-four; William H. Powell, a student of Inman's, would pick up the contract and eventually turn in the brightly colored canvas *Discovery of the Mississippi by De Soto*, with Native leaders skeptically extending a peace pipe to well-armed Spanish interlopers. The fourth contract was awarded to the dependable but slow John Vanderlyn, who would take five years to complete his *Landing of Columbus*, in which a reverential Columbus claims the New World for his Spanish patrons as Natives watch warily from the edge of a forest.

Visitors to the Capitol now as then have noted that the four paintings depict—or at least imply—a conquest of Indigenous people. But perhaps no work in the Capitol would do so as blatantly, or as offensively, as a set of complementary sculptures created in the 1830s by Horatio Greenough—the reveal of his controversial statue of the bare-chested Washington was still at least five years away—and Luigi Persico for prominent placement on either side of the Capitol's eastern staircase leading up to the building's main entrance.

Both Persico and Greenough would propose and complete works that reflected the concept of Manifest Destiny, the American expansionist ideology *en vogue* in the era. It was a concept that aggressively invoked the nation's preordained right to expand its boundaries into occupied—and, as many saw it, unenlightened—territories, justifying America's violent westward expansion into lands occupied by Indigenous people. Although the term "Manifest Destiny" didn't become popular until 1845, the Jackson administration embraced its dogma, enforced it through the enactment of policies like the Indian Removal Act of 1830, and celebrated it through works of art like Greenough's and Persico's staircase sculptures.

And so, on the south side of the Capitol's eastern steps stood Persico's fifteen-foot marble sculpture *Discovery of America*, featuring Columbus striding purposefully forward, a globe held triumphantly overhead in his right hand, as a Native woman turns to regard the conqueror in deferential awe—a clear message that Native people must yield to domination by civilization. Directly across from it on the steps' northern side, Greenough's *Rescue* depicted an American frontiersman grappling with a much smaller ax-wielding Indian who is threatening the frontiersman's wife and child. Greenough left no doubt as to his artistic intent. "I have endeavored to convey the idea of the triumph of the whites over the savage tribes," he wrote, "at the same time that it illustrates the dangers of peopling the country."[20]

Public sentiment, and public policy, would evolve over time, and demands for the removal of both *Discovery of America* and *Rescue* would intensify with each passing decade. By the 1930s, a House joint resolution would recommend that the particularly offensive *Rescue* be "ground into dust and scattered to the four winds, that no more remembrance may be perpetuated of our barbaric past"; two years later, the House called for replacing *Rescue* with "a statue of one of the great Indian leaders famous in American history." In 1958, with the Capitol under renovation, both *Discovery* and *Rescue* were quietly removed and put into storage—which makes Horatio Greenough the only artist to have *two* objectionable works removed from the Capitol.

Perhaps fittingly, *Rescue* would shatter when it was accidentally dropped by a crane during a relocation in 1976. Today, the fragmented remains of Greenough's *Rescue* along with Persico's *Discovery* are held in storage by the Smithsonian. While the spaces where each sculpture once stood remain empty, new and more appropriate images of Native people now grace other areas of the Capitol complex today, including dignified statues of Po'Pay, Sakakawea, Sequoyah, and King Kamehameha I.

In 1832, Andrew Jackson was handily reelected to a second term as president. He secured 54 percent of the popular vote and won in an electoral landslide by taking sixteen of twenty-four states. Internal bickering in the Jackson cabinet—especially over issues involving nullification, the ability of states to ignore federal law—had so strained Jackson's relationship with his own vice president that he had replaced the fiery Southerner Calhoun on the ticket with the cunning New Yorker Martin Van Buren, a decision that didn't cost Jackson a single state.

There was snow on the ground as Jackson approached the Capitol grounds on the morning of March 4, 1833. It was a bone-chilling 29 degrees that morning—too cold, it was decided, to hold the swearing-in ceremony outside, especially given the sixty-five-year-old Jackson's declining health. Instead, Jackson and Van Buren would be hustled into the chamber of the House of Representatives, where each would be sworn in by Chief Justice John Marshall, presiding over his ninth presidential inauguration, a record that stands to this day. Jackson would deliver thoughtful though little quoted inaugural remarks promising to balance his support for states' rights with the need for a strong central government but vowing above all to protect the "integrity of the union."

It was a promise that was getting increasingly hard to keep. Throughout his second term, Jackson would find himself actively opposed by states' rights/proslavery Congressmen who thought Jackson was too enamored with a strong central government; some had even broken away from Jackson's Democratic Party to rally behind Calhoun to create a small but vocal alternate party, the Nullifiers, who believed in the rights of states to overturn federal law and supported their own presidential candidate against Jackson in 1832. While mostly confined to the South Carolina delegation, the Nullifiers could count several vocal and well-placed firebrands among their ranks, including Congressman Francis Wilkinson Pickens, who encouraged states to reject all federal authority, and Congressman Warren Davis, an enslaver and the former chair of the House Judiciary Committee.

Two years later, Davis died at age forty-one—and on Friday, January 30, 1835, as Jackson left the funeral service for Davis in the House chamber, the Capitol would become the site of what the *New-York Evening Post* would call "the most audacious outrage ever attempted in this country"[21]: the first assassination attempt against a sitting American president.

Jackson, now sixty-seven, was truly looking like *Old* Hickory, white-haired and somewhat frail—and as he left the House chamber and crossed through the Rotunda that afternoon, he leaned heavily on a cane while Treasury Secretary Levi Woodbury gently took his other arm. A crowd had gathered on the eastern portico, just beyond the Rotunda's eastern entrance, and as Jackson stepped out into the brisk winter air, there was a hum of excitement at the sight of the president.

At that moment, Richard Lawrence, a thirty-five-year-old unemployed housepainter,[22] emerged from behind one of the portico's large Corinthian columns, drew a small pistol, and fired directly at Jackson, only eight feet away. The gun sparked and flashed loudly but never fired a bullet. "The explosion of the cap was so loud that many persons thought the pistol had fired," recalled Senator Thomas Hart Benton of Missouri.[23] Most in the crowd thought Jackson had surely been shot.

As bystanders surged forward in confusion, Lawrence raised his left hand, where he was holding another loaded derringer. But that gun, too, misfired with a dramatic spark and loud bang and never discharged its bullet either—and at that moment, Jackson, with the nerve and fury that had made him the hero of the Battle of New Orleans, rushed the would-be assassin and began beating him with his cane. Woodbury, who only moments before had been propping up the president, now struggled to pull him off Lawrence, who was quickly wrestled to the ground and restrained by several bystanders, including Tennessee Congressman Davy Crockett.[24]

The hot-tempered Jackson immediately smelled a conspiracy, baselessly blaming his political enemies—most often Senator George Poindexter of Mississippi, who was disliked by both Jackson and Van Buren—for putting Lawrence up to the act. "This man has been hired by that damned rascal Poindexter to assassinate me," Jackson shouted as he was dragged off Lawrence and hustled away to the safety of the President's House.[25] Once back at home, however, he continued to rant against Poindexter and others late into the evening, a performance that rattled visiting diplomat Nathaniel Niles, who was alarmed that the president would accuse a political rival of murder without any evidence. "The President may have private enemies like any other man, but it must not be believed that mere party hostility can lead to such results," Niles wrote. "If it be so it is all over with us—our system cannot be preserved, nor, indeed, is it worth preserving."[26]

While local newspapers, too, would quickly get in on the conspiracy business—even Vice President Van Buren was accused of a cover-up—Lawrence never had been, and never would be, part of any secret scheme; he was mentally ill. Brought to a speedy trial and prosecuted by District Attorney Francis Scott Key, Lawrence insisted that he was the rightful heir to the throne of England—other times he claimed to be Richard III—and that Jackson, in his opposition to the charter for the Second Bank of the United States, had deliberately prevented him from receiving the money he needed to pay for his English estate. In the courtroom, he spent most of his time talking over his lawyers or laughing to himself. It was little wonder the jury deliberated only five minutes before reaching a verdict of not guilty by reason of insanity. Richard Lawrence, the first would-be presidential assassin in U.S. history, would spend the rest of his life in asylums and die in Washington, D.C., at the Government Hospital for the Insane—later St. Elizabeths Hospital—at the age of sixty-one.

Andrew Jackson, meanwhile, would see his reputation only further enhanced—at least among his most zealous supporters—by the failed assassination attempt. In 1935, experts at the Smithsonian examined Lawrence's pistols; finding both to be in perfect working condition, the analysts determined that the cold and damp January weather had likely caused the derringers to misfire—and that the likelihood of *both* guns misfiring was a staggering 125,000 to 1. Jacksonian supporters saw the inexplicable double misfire as proof that "Providence has ever guarded the life of the man who has been destined to preserve and raise his country's glory."[27]

In an era before radio, film, or television, the Congress of the nineteenth century was a reliable source of both news and entertainment, with newspapers regularly, sometimes breathlessly, following its proceedings and often publishing lengthy debates verbatim. To accommodate crowds, the visitor galleries in both the House and the Senate chambers were expanded in the 1830s—and they were regularly filled to capacity. The English novelist Charles Dickens, touring the United States in 1842, found the House of Representatives to be "beautiful and spacious" and noted that women particularly enjoyed the spectacle, treating it like theater. "They sit in the front rows," wrote Dickens, "and come in and go out as at a play or concert."[28]

Another renowned observer of the Congress was the French writer and historian Alexis de Tocqueville, who had visited the United States in the 1830s and laid down his impressions of the young nation in his seminal 1835 work of political theory, *Democracy in America*. Tocqueville had been captivated by the Capitol building, calling it "a magnificent palace"—though he noted with disdain that "[the Americans] have given it the pompous name of *the Capitol*."[29] He was much less impressed with the Congress, whose members he thought engaged too often in "petty minutia" and grandstanding. "The consequence is that the debates of that great assembly are frequently vague and perplexed," Tocqueville wrote, "and that they seem rather to drag their slow length along than to advance towards a distinct object."[30]

Tocqueville, however, was in the minority; most visitors to D.C. thought the Congress was the best show in town—as well as one of the noisiest. With office space in the Capitol complex at a premium, very few members of Congress had private workspaces; for most members, then, their desk on the floor of the House or Senate chamber *was* their official Congressional office.[31] From their desks, members took care not only of official business but of many of their personal affairs as well, whether writing letters, eating and drinking, reading the newspapers, or carrying on loud discussions—and all usually while the Congress was in session. The buzz of conversation, along with the terrible acoustics, gave the chamber a constant dull hum that made it nearly impossible to hear much of anything. The real work would get done in the much quieter committee rooms, which were closed to the public and stocked with whiskey and cigars.

And nearly everyone, it seemed, chewed—and spit—tobacco. "The headquarters of tobacco-tinctured saliva," Charles Dickens wrote of the Federal city; it was a habit he found "offensive and sickening." He was particularly repulsed by the House and the Senate chambers, where members of Congress, attempting to spit in the general direction of any of the spittoons placed strategically around the rooms, had notoriously bad aim, sullying the otherwise "handsomely carpeted" floors instead. "I strongly recommend all strangers not to look at the floor," Dickens wrote, practically dry heaving, "and if they happen to drop anything, though it be their purse, not to pick it up with an ungloved hand on any account."[32]

And still, the crowds loved every minute of it. Spit-stained carpets notwithstanding, spectators lingered in the galleries for hours to catch a glimpse of—and maybe a speech from—some of the most famous figures of the era. Visitors to the House might spot former President John Quincy Adams, called "Old Man Eloquent" and so respected that when he rose to speak, the normally rowdy House floor would grow almost reverentially quiet. Adams would continue his principled and often lonely opposition to slavery through five presidencies—he would be one of only fourteen House members to oppose the Mexican-American War in 1846 on the grounds that it would expand slavery in the West—and he would remain at his desk even as his voice weakened and his health failed.

In 1848, the eighty-year-old Adams would suffer a cerebral hemorrhage just after casting a vote at his desk—a loud and emphatic *No!* on a resolution honoring officers who served in the Mexican-American War—and he would be carried to the Speaker's Room, just off the floor of the House. Two days later, on February 23, 1848, with his wife, Louisa, at his side, Adams would pass away in the same room—the first and only president to die in the Capitol, giving rise to another of the Capitol's ghost stories; some visitors to the old House chamber still claim to hear his *No!* echoing off the walls.

It was the Senate, however, that was truly stacked with political rock stars like Henry Clay, Daniel Webster, John Calhoun, and Thomas Hart Benton. If there was even a rumor that one of these marquee members was going to speak, the galleries would be packed, making an already hot Senate chamber even stuffier. Sweaty spectators were admonished against putting their feet up on the railings in the galleries to keep the dirt and stones from falling off their boots and onto the heads of Senators below.

Sometimes heated floor debates could erupt into actual fighting—much to the delight of onlookers. In September 1841, Representatives Edward Stanly of North Carolina and Henry Wise of Virginia, after listening to a clerk read President Tyler's veto message on a banking bill, began arguing loudly and insulting each other, spurring Wise to punch Stanly. With the gallery roaring its approval, "nearly all the members"[33] on the floor rushed into the brawl, recalled chief House clerk Benjamin Brown French, and began throwing punches—a free-for-all that the official House record diplomatically described as "great heat and confusion arising"—until the Speaker of the House finally restored order.[34]

Dueling, too, remained a very real problem, with members regularly threatening to take disagreements outside to be settled with pistols. In an age when many Congressmen openly carried guns—and thought nothing of brandishing them—such challenges to one's honor were more than just talk; during one particularly heated committee hearing in 1840, the chairman threatened to kill a witness, prompting a standoff in which the chair and another member stood with their hands on their pistols, each daring the other to make the first move. And the waving of weapons wasn't always confined just to members; in 1830, James Watson Webb, editor of the *New York Courier and Enquirer*, assaulted rival editor Duff Green of the *United States Telegraph* on the eastern steps of the Capitol, backing down only when Green stuck a cocked pistol in his face.

If each chamber seemed to be rowdier and packed with more members than ever . . . it's because both chambers were. When Bulfinch had started his work on the design and construction on the refurbished Capitol in early 1818, there were twenty states in the Union, which meant accommodating forty Senators and 185 Congressmen. By the time Bulfinch completed his work in 1828, the nation had added another four states, which put eight more Senators in the north chamber and twenty-eight more Congressmen in the House chamber to the south. By the late 1830s, following the admission of Arkansas and Michigan, there were twenty-six states, requiring fifty-two Senators and 242 Representatives—and as new desks were brought in and aisles narrowed, members literally found themselves tripping over one another.

The House would pick up some breathing room in 1842, when the 1840 census triggered a reapportionment that would actually reduce the total number of House seats by nineteen, but that total slowly climbed again with each passing election. In 1843, there was enough concern about the diminishing space that Congress approved a resolution asking for plans "for a room or apartment in the Capitol, or to be added thereto, for the better accommodation of the sittings of the House of Representatives."[35] There would be some discussion of extending the House into a new wing attached at the south end of the building, but no action was taken.

The famously terrible acoustics in the House chamber would soon convince Congress to revisit the issue of space. The floor of the House was already a din of debates and conversations that, when coupled with the chamber's awful acoustics, so bewildered the Speaker of the House that he often couldn't tell who had sought recognition, causing him to gawk around in some confusion until he located the member seeking the floor. ("It is an elegant chamber to look at," Dickens reported, "but a singularly bad one for all purposes of hearing.")[36] Brainstorming for solutions, the resourceful Robert Mills tried everything from reconfiguring the seating—even turning everyone around to face the rear of the chamber—to adding wooden partitions between the Potomac marble pillars in an effort to contain voices. Nothing worked. The room was restored to its prior configuration and complaints only continued.

More than a few members—eyeing the gorgeous space occupied by the Library of Congress, including its dramatic westward view of Washington—suggested the House of Representatives and the library simply swap places. That suggestion was enough to pique the interest of New York Congressman Zadock Pratt, chair of the House Committee on Public Buildings and Grounds, who in 1844 brought in architect William Strickland of Philadelphia to advise the committee on the feasibility of moving the Congress into the library's space.

Ultimately, Strickland and the committee recommended against the idea and threw up their hands at any further suggestions on how to modify the acoustics in the current House chamber. Instead, the committee recommended starting over by constructing a completely new House wing—one with much better thought-out acoustics—just south of the current House chamber. To ensure the symmetry of the building, the committee also proposed a similar extension of the Senate wing to the north.

Pratt's committee also pointed out several other problems with inadequate space beyond just the House chamber. For one thing, the number of working committees far exceeded the forty committee rooms Bulfinch had cleverly carved out of the western extension. The Library of Congress, too, was rapidly outgrowing its space—if a new House wing was ever constructed, the committee recommended moving the library into the House's old chamber. The Supreme Court, too, had outgrown its space and was spilling books and papers out into the surrounding hallways. Mostly, there just never seemed to be enough room in which to *put* anything; even the mausoleum intended for the remains of George and Martha Washington had become a storage space for junk no one wanted to throw away, filling up with broken furniture and old lamps. Pratt's committee pled for recommendations on expanding the Capitol; once again, no one offered anything very helpful. Part of the problem was that there was still no Architect of the Capitol who might have been tasked with exploring these questions. In 1845, newly elected President James

K. Polk chose to continue to leave the position empty, opting instead to appoint a new commissioner of public buildings, replacing the reliable William Noland with the merely competent Charles Douglas.

Not every committee was complaining about a lack of space. In February 1838, the House Commerce Committee had ceded space in its committee room to the inventor Samuel F. B. Morse, who was tinkering with a device that would change the way the world communicated. Morse was well-known to the Congress more as an artist than as an inventor; in 1822, he had spent four months working out of a room just off the House floor to complete an enormous painting depicting the Congress meeting in an evening session. With a careful eye for the details of the chamber, from the Potomac marble pillars to the statue of Clio overlooking the proceedings, Morse's *House of Representatives* was an accurate depiction of the House in action and a piece that was well-regarded by critics but had failed to resonate with the public or earn him any money. Its poor public reception had partly convinced him to start looking elsewhere to earn a living.

Now, sixteen years later, the resourceful Morse was working to improve the cumbersome electric telegraph. It was a device that Morse hadn't invented but one that he felt he could most certainly refine to make it more reliable and efficient as well as capable of transmitting across great distances—without loss of signal—using just a single wire rather than the bulky twenty-plus wires required under the present design. Hoping for financial support from Congress, Morse had convinced Representative F. O. J. Smith of Maine, chairman of the House Commerce Committee, to let him demonstrate to the Congress and several members of President Van Buren's cabinet how well his improvements to the device worked.

Only a month earlier, Morse had carried out a slightly more ambitious demonstration in Morristown, New Jersey, cramming a building at the Speedwell Ironworks full of more than two miles of wire over which he had transmitted—in a language of his own devising later to be called "Morse code"—the rather uninspired message "A patient waiter is no loser."[37] After watching Morse explain the mechanics of his upgrades to the House Commerce Committee, Chairman Smith excitedly recommended a $30,000 appropriation—more than $1 million today—for Morse to extend the reach of his improved telegraph. It was a suggestion the Congress ignored for the moment.

But Morse would keep asking, coming back again in 1842 with a much more impressive demonstration. This time, Morse would run his single-wire line nearly the length of the Capitol, stretching it across the building from the House Commerce Committee room in the south wing to the meeting room for the Senate Committee on Naval Affairs in the north end, and transmitting practical if mundane messages like "Mr. Brown of Indiana is here."[38] But it was enough to convince the Congress to approve the $30,000 that Smith—who not at all coincidentally had signed on as Morse's business partner after leaving Congress in 1839—had recommended for the project four years earlier, giving Morse the opportunity to run a line from Washington, D.C., to Baltimore, some forty miles away.

In late April 1844, Morse installed a small workshop in a first-floor committee room directly across from the Supreme Court chamber. It would take him several weeks to set up his telegraph and to ensure the wire running from the Capitol remained firmly connected to the line he had strung on poles alongside the tracks of the Baltimore & Ohio Railroad. He would test the line over a shorter distance on May 1, when his partner Alfred Vail, stationed in Annapolis Junction, Maryland—a little more than halfway to Baltimore—transmitted the latest news out of the Whig Party convention in Baltimore, informing the capital that the party had nominated Henry Clay as its candidate for president. So far, so good—and on May 24, 1844, Morse, his nerves sufficiently steeled, was finally ready to officially open the Washington–Baltimore line.

Morse summoned a group of observers to the committee room[39] to watch him send his first message, which would be transmitted from the

Capitol building to the Mount Clare train station in Baltimore, forty miles away, where Alfred Vail was standing by to receive it.[40] A little after eleven a.m., the fifty-three-year-old Morse sent a message suggested to him by Annie Ellsworth, the teenage daughter of his friend Henry L. Ellsworth, the commissioner of patents. He solemnly tapped out the biblical verse from Numbers 23:23: *WHAT HATH GOD WROUGHT.*

Vail received the message—"before the lapse of half a minute," gasped the *Baltimore Patriot & Commercial Gazette*[41]—and wasted no time firing back his response: "What is the news from Washington?" Morse and Vail had made their point; information from a great distance away could be transmitted clearly and nearly instantaneously. "Time and space has been completely annihilated," the *Baltimore Sun* reported in awe.[42] Within a year, the Senate would install a telegraph office in its own press gallery and transmit news from the Capitol to remote communities—and remote *voters*—in a matter of moments, instead of days.

Morse wasn't the only visionary bringing technological marvels before the Congress in hopes of securing federal funding. "It was not an uncommon thing for inventors of all kinds of outlandish and impractical machines to hang around the Capitol buttonholing every senator and member they could meet," Senate doorkeeper Isaac Bassett said later.[43] One of the slickest was James Crutchett, who had created a system for producing and delivering gas lighting and hoped to convince the Congress to let him bring his expertise to the Capitol. Crutchett, who lived on North Capitol Street just within sight of the Capitol, had gained some local repute for installing gaslight streetlamps in his Capitol Hill neighborhood; a delighted press had applauded his "incomparably beautiful and splendid lights."[44]

The display was enough to get Crutchett a meeting with the Congress to make his case—and the Congress, dazzled by the smooth-talking Crutchett, awarded him a $17,500 contract to provide gas lighting in the Capitol without their considering any other proposals or vetting Crutchett himself. Crutchett also had timing on his side, for the

Congress was in the market for new ways to light the interior of the Capitol more reliably than with marble fireplaces and oil lamps and chandeliers. Several years earlier, House members had gotten a scare when the seven-thousand-pound glass chandelier hanging in the House chamber—a bulky structure that became even heavier when weighed down with the whale oil that kept its lamps burning—had crashed to the floor. No one had been hurt—and only some furniture was damaged—but for the safety, and sanity, of the Congress, it was clearly time to look into new lighting technology.

Using a system of his own invention—while Crutchett was a shameless self-promoter, his science was surprisingly sound—Crutchett pumped gas from a small room in the Capitol's subbasement into gas lines he had installed in the House and Senate chambers and a few surrounding rooms. The enormous oil-burning lights were removed from each chamber and replaced with decorative and much less weighty gas-burning chandeliers and sconces. Senator John Fairfield of Maine was impressed. "The Senate chamber was lighted up last evening with gas, and looked splendidly," he reported to his wife. "The light proceeds from a lot of chandeliers suspended in the center and quite up to the ceiling. The above makes light enough to write by and read the finest print in my part of the chamber."[45]

Fairfield was far less dazzled, however, by Crutchett's elaborate system for lighting the interior of the Rotunda. On top of the dome, Crutchett erected a ninety-two-foot-high white pine mast on which he mounted an enormous iron-and-glass lantern nearly twenty feet high and six feet in diameter.[46] When lit, the lantern's light would shine down through the dome's center oculus and into the Rotunda, where Crutchett used a series of mirrors and reflectors to direct the light into the farther reaches of the space. It was a clever system and highly visible from the outside—the light could be seen for miles, a deliberate bit of advertising for Crutchett's services—but it didn't work very well inside the dome, where it lit mostly the top part of the Rotunda, leaving things dark at floor level. "Crutchett's big light on the dome of the Capitol I don't think much of," wrote Fairfield when the lights were turned on in November 1847. "It affords a tolerable light immediately about the Capitol but the light is not extended so far as had been anticipated."[47]

Public opinion was divided as well. "One of the most splendid and beautiful spectacles we ever beheld," gushed the *Washington Union*,[48] while the *New York Daily Herald* called it a "bird-killing eyesore."[49] Seven months after making its D.C. debut, Crutchett's lantern—and the entire ugly structure—would be dismantled, mostly out of concern that the swaying of the lantern would eventually cause structural damage in the dome. Crutchett had also proved to be an unreliable businessman and collaborator and would be dismissed, though the rest of his infrastructure—the gas lines, chandeliers, and sconces—would remain in place. His contract to provide lighting would be taken over by a group of investors headed by chief House clerk Benjamin B. French, who would create the Washington Gas Light Company—the utility company still serving more than a million customers in Washington, D.C.

Along with upgraded lighting came improvements to another amenity, as Congress began the process of bringing water into the Capitol. After tapping into a spring three miles from the building, engineers left it to gravity to move the water downhill in newly laid pipes, sending it flowing into reservoirs at the Capitol to be piped into various places in the building. Those locations included the Capitol's restaurant in the basement—where oysters, veal, mutton, and green turtle soup were served daily—and a public drinking fountain mostly hidden between two staircases but so beautifully designed by Mills that one visitor tut-tutted that it was too pretty to keep hidden away.

Despite the new conveniences, many members of Congress were still finding the Capitol too uncomfortable, too loud, and too crowded. In 1848, after conducting a mostly successful war against Mexico—the very war that John Quincy Adams had futilely recommended against waging—the United States found itself in possession of more than half a million new square miles in the American West, with every acre potentially part of a brand-new state, each requiring new Senators and members of Congress. It would be up to the Congress to determine the terms and conditions under which new states might enter the Union, including whether slavery would be permitted—and in 1850, Henry Clay would take the lead in trying to construct compromise legislation to appease both sides of the slavery issue dividing the nation.

While he was an enslaver himself, Clay acknowledged that the practice was a "great evil . . . the darkest spot in the map of our country." It was a principled position, but one unpopular enough in the South that it had likely kept the presidency out of Clay's reach each of the five times he either ran or sought the nomination ("I'd rather be right than be president," Clay had remarked at the time).[50] Clay's solution—the so-called Compromise of 1850, which was little more than kicking the can down the road toward a civil war at this point—was to admit California as a free state while leaving the status of the territories of New Mexico and Utah to be determined by popular sovereignty. Regardless of the terms under which new states were admitted, it was clear that the Capitol, in its current condition, was going to need more space for new members of the House and Senate.

Mills, in consultation with the members of the Committee on Public Buildings and Grounds, began circulating architectural drawings depicting the Capitol with spacious matching extensions on the north and south ends. Mills's revised layout would require some shuffling around, as the House and Senate would be asked to scoot over into their respective new extensions, the Library of Congress would be given most of the center section, and the Supreme Court would move into the space formerly occupied by the Senate.

Mills was delighted to find the Senate was supportive of the proposed changes. The House, however, was not. With an eye on costs—and doubts about the feasibility of constructing on the sloping western side of Capitol Hill—the House suggested picking up the space by extending the building's eastern front instead. With the House and Senate in disagreement, there seemed to be only one logical solution to resolve the issue once and for all.

It was time for another contest.

Architect Thomas U. Walter won the national contest soliciting proposals to expand the Capitol to accommodate the rapidly growing House and Senate. President Millard Fillmore approved Walter's design, which attached the extensions, seen at far left and far right, directly to Bulfinch's existing Capitol. Walter would quickly come to realize that Bulfinch's copper dome was too small—and definitely not grand enough—for the enlarged structure.

CHAPTER 6

One Harmonious Structure

1850–1854

The May 28, 1850, report from the Committee on Public Buildings was brutally frank.

Working with consulting architect Robert Mills, the committee had assessed the current workspaces within the Capitol building—and it didn't have much good to say. As Senator Robert M. T. Hunter of Virginia reported to his colleagues, the current Senate chamber "is already too small for the present number of senators. . . . Nor does it afford sufficient accommodation for spectators." The Supreme Court, meanwhile, "requires a larger and more comfortable apartment," while the current space for the Library of Congress "is insufficient for the books which have been accumulated." But it was the House chamber that drew the harshest criticism. "[B]esides being too small," reported Hunter, "[it] has been proved by experience to be unfit for purposes of deliberation."[1]

That particular finding came as no surprise to members of the House of Representatives. As Delaware Representative John Houston stood to speak in favor of the report, the *Congressional Globe* pointed out that he was "scarcely heard in the confusion of the Hall." When William Richardson of Illinois took the floor to debate Houston, the *Globe* noted editorially that "it was not possible to hear." However, the stenographer had no trouble hearing South Carolina Congressman Joseph Woodward as he stood to lament how the acoustics of the chamber often made the House "an unmannerly hall" and noted dryly that "a stranger would suppose . . . there was not a man in the nation . . . who knew that there was in nature such a science as acoustics."[2]

In their report, Mills and the committee recommended extending the Capitol by placing new freestanding buildings, each measuring a hundred feet by two hundred feet, about sixty feet from the north and south ends of the current Capitol, creating what Mills called a "spacious court" between the old Capitol and each new addition. Mills also seemed prepared for complaints about the acoustics, devoting several pages in the committee report to reminding the Congress of his own résumé in order to assure them that he had "had occasion to examine into the laws which govern sound at an early day in my professional practice" and to inform them that he had written several papers on acoustics and designed a number of churches "favorable to the voice and the ear."[3]

Debate continued for several fractious and unproductive weeks, with neither the House nor the Senate able to agree on much of anything. The House, in fact, suggested extending the center section even farther out to the east to make new space rather than adding the two new structures—but there was also debate on how much everything should cost and even over whether the Capitol should be expanded at all. Lewis Cass, the sleepy-eyed Senator from Michigan, made clear that while he "[knew] nothing as to the merits of the several plans proposed," he intended to vote in favor of something—*anything*—to be done. "I think this to be the very worst building on the face of the earth for the purposes to which it is devoted," Cass complained. "You can scarcely hear in this [Senate] Chamber, and in the House you cannot hear at all."[4] As if making his point, debate in the House broke down into incomprehension. "I cannot hear a word the gentleman says," Representative Woodward finally told a colleague tartly as Congress moved to take up the bill. "Not one word, sir."[5]

Congress finally resolved the issue on September 25 by punting the entire matter to the executive branch. Legislators inserted into the Civil and Diplomatic Appropriations bill language deferring to the president of the United States for the final decision and providing $100,000 "to be expended under his direction, by such architect as he may appoint to execute the same."[6] At the same time, the Congress, wanting to ensure the president had plenty of options to consider, approved language authorizing the Committee on Public Buildings "to invite plans, accompanied by estimates, for the extension of the Capitol, and to allow a premium of $500 for the plan."[7] Once again, when it came time for a major artistic decision regarding the Capitol, the Congress would turn to the people.

The ad began appearing in regional newspapers on September 30, 1850, though its wording—similar to the phrasing in earlier contests—was deliberately vague. "The committee do not desire to prescribe any condition that may restrain the free exercise of architectural taste and judgement," read the announcement in the District's *Daily Republic*; however, the committee did ask that applicants "preserve the general symmetry of the entire structure." The notice also specified that the Congress was considering plans to extend the Capitol either with new wings "to be placed on the north and south of the present building," as the Senate preferred, or "by the erection of a separate and distinct building" to the east, as preferred by the House. Applicants could submit plans for one option or both.[8]

Thirteen architects submitted entries, though some professional architects blanched at the very idea of participating in a contest for their services. "Presenting competition plans as such a mode of doing business is not agreeable to my views and feelings as a professional man," sniffed Richard Upjohn, a well-respected designer of Gothic Revival–style churches who very much wanted the job of Architect of the Capitol but refused to submit an entry.[9] Upjohn's eye-rolling aside, both professional and aspiring architects had come a long way since the days of the 1792 competition; there would be no out-of-proportion weather vanes mounted on the roof or interiors that didn't match the exteriors. Entrants approached the competition seriously and competently, and the committee treated the entries respectfully, putting all the submitted plans on display in the Library of Congress and in various committee rooms in December 1850 so members could examine the drawings up close.

Most entrants submitted two sets of drawings, providing the committee with both of the requested looks—that is, one version with extensions at the north and south ends and another with a single addition to the east. While all submitted designs had their differences, the entries focusing on the new eastern building varied widely and sometimes wildly. Most proposed a large freestanding structure that mirrored the neoclassical architecture of the original Capitol. The hardworking Robert Mills, hoping to impress President Millard Fillmore into appointing him the official Architect of the Capitol, submitted an entry with a "duplicate Capitol" that was set three hundred feet east of the original building and that connected back to the main Capitol via a huge warehouse-like structure containing the Library of Congress—or if the committee didn't like that, he would create between the two buildings a walled-in courtyard with an enormous monument to the American Revolution at its open center.

Another plan, submitted by Philadelphia architect Thomas U. Walter, was more elegant: it proposed the construction of an enormous House-Senate complex to the east, with its entrance replicating the Capitol's existing eastern front. From the outside, it resembled an enormous square compound with the Capitol's main dome at its rear; inside, Walter enclosed a bustling interior—think today's indoor malls—with a grand, high-ceilinged promenade running the length of the building. In Walter's dramatic vision, visitors would enter the Capitol through the new eastern entrance, proceed down the promenade through the new addition, and end up in the Rotunda of the old Capitol, where light would stream in from the dome over their heads.

As impressive and dramatic as the submitted designs might be, the committee was unable to decide on any single plan and instead divided the prize money among four entrants, including Mills and Walter. The committee then asked Mills to take the four winning entries and turn them into a series of hybrid drawings, incorporating the best elements of each. Mills dutifully did as instructed and submitted a final set of drawings to committee member Jefferson Davis in February 1851. Mills turned in a well thought-out floor plan with extensions on the north and south ends that were connected directly to the old Capitol rather than separated from it by breezeways. Completely missing, however, was any sign of a new structure to the Capitol's east—a deliberate omission that was certain to raise eyebrows among House members.

With his extensive knowledge of the Capitol grounds, Mills had cleverly pushed the two new wings slightly forward on the north and south ends of the building rather than centering them. That positioning kept their foundations mostly away from the steep slope of Capitol Hill to the west, reducing construction costs—a feature he thought the Congress would appreciate. He also placed the House and Senate chambers themselves in the eastern half of each new wing, with windows—but no doors—facing out onto the busy east lawn. That meant there would be no direct eastern access to the wings; instead, visitors would enter the House wing through a new portico on the south face and the Senate wing from a new portico in the north end.

As for his exterior, Mills integrated the extensions seamlessly with the old Capitol in the same neoclassical style—though after adding small domed turrets on top of each new wing to let in light, he decided to balance the look of the entire structure by slightly heightening the center dome, plunking on top of Bulfinch's copper dome a small cap supported by a circle of columns.

The drawings were a lot of extra work for Mills, who must have thought things were looking good for his appointment by the president as the new Architect of the Capitol—while Mills had been calling himself that for years, there had been no official architect since the departure of Bulfinch in 1829. It couldn't be denied that Mills had the credentials; besides his oversight of the Capitol, he had designed several other important buildings around the Federal city, including the Treasury Building, the Patent Office, and the General Post Office—all still part of Washington's urban landscape. And out on a muddy piece of land about half a mile in front of the President's House—a wide-open public space that was already being called the Mall—construction was underway on what would be Mills's most iconic contribution not just to the Washington, D.C., skyline but to the national psyche: the Washington Monument. In 1814, Mills had won a competition in Baltimore to design the nation's first monument to the first president; in 1836, he had won the contest for a similar monument in the nation's capital. Clearly, Mills seemed to have a knack for giving the people what they wanted—and he had been serving as a superintendent and overseer at the Capitol for a long time. He felt certain the job was his.

But other architects were also converging on Washington to make their case for the highly coveted appointment. None would do so more skillfully—and, at times, brazenly—than Thomas Walter, whose drawing of the new eastern building with its elegant interior promenade had impressed House members and made his entry a favorite. "A gentleman of great practical experience," enthused the Congress—and with good reason.[10]

Born in Philadelphia on September 4, 1804, Thomas Ustick Walter had been studying architectural drawing and design since the age of fifteen, when he put himself under the tutelage of William Strickland, Philadelphia's most noted architect and civil engineer and a former student of Benjamin Latrobe. At age twenty-eight, Walter made a name for himself—and cemented his reputation as something of a boy wonder—when his entry in the competition to design Girard College in Philadelphia, executed boldly in Greek Revival style, was selected over several high-profile entries, including one submitted by his mentor, Strickland. That project led to other lucrative and often exotic commissions—there were railroads in South America and a port in Venezuela—before Walter finally settled into a regular work routine designing churches, private homes, and public buildings. Walter was good and in demand; in 1850 alone, he had designed seventeen houses, twelve churches, five schools, and two hotels.[11] But as a recently remarried widower with twelve children—including two under the age of three—Walter didn't want just commissions; he wanted the security provided by a full-time federal post.

In early October 1850, Walter left Philadelphia for Washington and began meeting with key Senators and Congressmen—including members of the Committee on Public Buildings—to get a better idea of what they did and didn't like about the different proposals for expanding the Capitol. As a founding member of the American Institute of Architects, Walter had well-placed contacts in the city that he used to great advantage, eventually securing an introduction to President Millard Fillmore.

The president was more than willing to provide Walter with his opinion. For one thing, the president didn't like the House and Senate chambers out in the eastern ends of the new wings; he worried that when the windows were open, the noise and dust from the Capitol's east lawn would have a detrimental effect on the ability of the Congress to carry out the people's business. Some House members—notably Richard Stanton of Kentucky, the chair of the Committee on Public Buildings—continued to push for connecting a large building to the Capitol's eastern front, like the first design Walter had submitted; they complained that under the north-south extension plan, the House and Senate chambers would be too far apart and it would be impossible to get from one to the other without having to wind one's way through most of the Capitol complex. The Senate, meanwhile, refused to budge from its preference for putting the extensions on the north and south ends of the current Capitol building.

Walter carefully listened to all of the differing opinions, then drew and redrew his sheaf of plans to reflect the comments of legislators and—more important—the president, who would be making the final decision. For months, Walter sketched revisions of the eastern extension, along with new interpretations of the north and south wings, which he circulated to Congress and Fillmore before revising again and again. Not even the death of one of his daughters from illness could distract Walter from his mission; within days of burying his child, he was back in Washington to meet with Fillmore.

On June 10, 1851, President Fillmore officially appointed Thomas U. Walter as the newest Architect of the Capitol—or, more specifically, the "Architect of the United States Capitol Extension," an odd check on the new position's authority—at an annual salary of $4,500, about $180,000 today. It was generous enough for Walter to live in the capital in relative comfort, and he promptly returned to Philadelphia to fetch his family and move them into a boardinghouse in Washington while he looked for a permanent residence. Mills was bitterly disappointed to learn that Walter was the president's choice; he still believed his longtime association with the Capitol made him the best man for the job. But at age sixty-nine, Mills might have been seen as too old to oversee a project that could take a decade to complete; Walter, at forty-six, had stamina on his side.

In his months of meetings with Fillmore, Walter had also proven that he had the talent and the disposition for the job. The same day the president announced Walter's hiring, he signed off on the architect's plan to expand the Capitol by adding to its north and south ends—in this instance, Walter had demonstrated some much-appreciated flexibility by moving away from his own plan for an eastern addition to give the president and the Senate their preferred north-south layout. Politically, too, Fillmore had made a shrewd decision in his selection of Walter, choosing the architect preferred by the House while asking him to execute a floor plan favored by the Senate.

At the president's suggestion, Walter had centered the long sides of the new rectangular wings on the north and south ends of Bulfinch's completed Capitol building, and then connected each back to the original structure via an enclosed corridor. Fillmore had further asked that legislative chambers in both extensions be relocated to the west sides of the buildings, rather than the east, so members could look out over Capitol Hill as it sloped down toward the gatehouses, which allowed entrance to the Capitol complex. This configuration would not only put the chambers on the quieter sides of the buildings but also make room for entrances in the eastern faces of the new extensions. Doing so would give the Capitol symmetry in triplicate, as the south, central, and north sections would each be accessible in their east faces by wide stairs leading up to covered porticos capped by triangular pediments.

The president also endorsed Walter's basic exterior design, which continued with the same neoclassical style initiated by Thornton—and carefully sustained by Latrobe and Bulfinch—which ensured that the new wings wouldn't look stitched on. Extending away from the eastern porticos and stairways of each new wing, then, would be colonnades wrapped around the sides of the new extensions and lined with more than a hundred columns of marble. Walter explained that "the exterior is designed to correspond in its principal features to that of the present [old] building," giving it the appearance of "one harmonious structure."[12] And where it wasn't harmonious, Walter would retrofit things—proposing, for example, to paint the stone on Bulfinch's original building to match the white marble he planned to use for the exterior walls of the extensions.

Paralyzed by its inability to make any decisions about the expansion of the Capitol, Congress had essentially ceded its oversight authority for the building to the president—and Fillmore had made the most of it, selecting the architect and approving the building's new footprint and profile. But Fillmore, now free of Congressional interference, then took the controversial step of having Walter report directly to the secretary of the interior, head of a department created only two years earlier, rather than to the commissioner of public buildings and grounds—a change that nudged the architect out from under Congressional oversight and more directly under the authority of the executive branch.

That new chain of command didn't sit well with the current commissioner of public buildings, William Easby, who complained that his authority was being deliberately undermined—which it likely was. Congress, however, merely shrugged, likely knowing that any funding Fillmore or Walter might need still had to be approved by both the House and the Senate. Until then, they were happy to have the Fillmore administration be responsible for the day-to-day management of the project. That was fine with Fillmore, who—showing an unexpected flair for the dramatic—announced the date when the cornerstone for the new additions would be laid and the official beginning of the project would be kicked off with considerable pomp, circumstance, and fireworks.

The Fourth of July.

Friday, July 4, 1851, was a beautiful day in Washington, D.C., warm but not too humid, and the morning sky was sparkling clear as Walter stood on Capitol Hill and scanned the city to the west. "The day was ushered in by salutes of artillery from different points of the city," reported the *Weekly National Intelligencer*, "and, as the glorious sun gilded our tallest spires and shed a lustre on the dome of the Capitol, it was welcomed by a display of National Flags and the rings of bells from the various churches and engine houses."[13]

For President Fillmore, the first order of business for the day was a presentation at the Washington Monument, which had been under construction since 1848. Even as Fillmore was politely applauding the "beautiful block of marble" that was being placed ceremonially at the monument, thousands of visitors were pouring into the city from the surrounding counties, hustling to Capitol Hill to secure a place on the east plaza. Not only was there a cornerstone-laying ceremony to watch, but Daniel Webster—the former distinguished Senator from New Hampshire who was President Fillmore's secretary of state and still the nation's foremost orator—was scheduled to give closing remarks from the steps of the eastern portico. It was a show not to be missed.

Shortly before noon, President Fillmore entered the Capitol grounds through the north gate, flanked by a crowd that included members of his cabinet, military officers, and Walter Lenox, mayor of Washington, D.C.—and, coincidentally, the son of Peter Lenox, the clerk whose appointment more than three decades earlier had nearly driven Benjamin Latrobe to hand in his resignation. Fillmore wasn't a Mason, but out of deference to tradition, he had agreed to let the cornerstone, located at the northeast corner of the new House wing, be laid in the Masonic fashion. As part of the ceremony, Walter—who was more Baptist than Mason—placed in the "specially fashioned" granite cornerstone a sealed jar containing coins and newspapers of the era. As Walter stepped away, Grand Master Benjamin French—the former clerk of the House—sealed the cornerstone with the same trowel that President George Washington had used in a similar ceremony in 1793.

As a hush fell over the crowd, Webster stepped forward onto a platform extending from the eastern steps. Webster was sixty-nine, but his voice was still as powerful as ever, even as years of chronic alcoholism were destroying his liver and shortening his life—he would be dead fifteen months later. But on this July 4, Webster spoke forcefully for nearly two hours to his "fellow-citizens" as he enthused on American principles and outlined a brief history of the United States. As one of the leading advocates of the Compromise of 1850, Webster understood the very real concern that the nation could be wrenched apart by the issue of slavery. But he assured his audience that—in his opinion at least—secession was still "the greatest of all improbabilities."

> Fellow-citizens, take courage; be of good cheer. . . . We shall live, and not die. . . . The ill-omened sounds of fanaticism will be hushed; the ghastly spectres of Secession and Disunion will disappear, and the enemies of united constitutional liberty, if

> their hatred cannot be appeased, may prepare to sear their eyeballs as they behold the steady flight of the American Eagle, on his burnished wings, for years and years to come.[14]

It was soaring rhetoric but doomed optimism, as the nation was continuing to plod toward secession and a civil war that would begin a decade later. Concluding his remarks, Webster stirred the crowd with a rousing call for unity and faith in an everlasting republic:

> And all here assembled . . . unite in sincere and fervent prayers that this [cornerstone] and the walls and arches, the domes and towers, the columns and entablatures now to be erected over it, may endure forever! God save the United States of America![15]

Webster's remarks were met with thunderous applause and another appreciative blast of artillery from the north end of the Capitol. That night, fireworks lit up the skies over the Mall, illuminating the President's House in flashes of red, white, and blue.

As he settled into his new job, Walter hired Samuel Strong, a well-connected New York builder, as his superintendent of construction. From Walter's offices on A Street—just a brisk walk across the street from the Capitol—Strong and he began to divide the project into a series of tasks that could be put out for bids to contractors: mostly for doing the granite and marble work but also for providing construction materials like bricks, lumber, scaffolding, sand, and cement. It was a reasonable approach to getting things done efficiently but one that would cause Walter considerable distress and eventually splatter his spotless reputation with mud.

With the laying of the ceremonial cornerstone behind them, work crews began laying the foundations for the new wings in early August 1851. The plunging slope of Capitol Hill was an immediate challenge; while foundations on the east side of the additions needed to be dug down only fifteen feet to find solid strata, on the west side, Walter's crew had to go nearly forty feet down and remove more than fifty thousand cubic yards of earth to reach bedrock strong enough to support the footings for the extensions. The procedure was expensive, proving that Mills had been absolutely right about the costs when he had proposed moving the extensions forward, away from the slope of the hill; as a result, much of the funding Congress had appropriated was quickly eaten up. But since moving Walter's post over to the auspices of the executive branch, Fillmore had been treating the Capitol expansion as his own project and was doing little consulting with the Congress on their own building. Fillmore also tended to defer to Walter on most of the details without going to the Congress for approval—an executive strategy that would also come back to plague Walter.

But Walter was doing his job with great care and due diligence—there was good reason he had been one of the most in-demand architects in the region—and Fillmore was right to trust the architect's eye for detail. "I consider it desirable that all the marble from both buildings should come from the same quarry, so as to ensure a uniformity of color," Walter wrote to the president in September[16]—and he would visit the quarries personally to make certain not only that the marble was of the best quality but also that there would be enough of it. Walter eventually contracted with quarries in Lee, Massachusetts, to provide marble for the exterior of the buildings, and in Cockeysville, Maryland, for the marble that would be used for the more than one hundred columns surrounding the new extensions.

However, a malicious whispering campaign by unsuccessful contractors had some in Congress watching skeptically as dirt was being moved, foundations were being laid, and the initial appropriation of $100,000 was being whittled away. There was grumbling about deliberately slow work and—despite Walter's fastidious bookkeeping—veiled accusations about Walter's authority to draw down federal funding. "That money has been under the control of the architect himself, who has drawn it out of the Treasury himself," complained Pennsylvania Congressman John McNair, who loathed President Fillmore and delighted in roadblocking any project backed by the administration. "It has been expended; how, we know not."[17] When funding ran out at the end of 1851, Congressman Richard Stanton, a vocal supporter of Walter, pressed immediately for another appropriation. He ran squarely into opposition from McNair and others.

Squabbles regarding the quality of the work broke out on the floor, with several members questioning whether Walter really knew what he was doing, and a special committee—chaired by the continually carping John McNair—was appointed to scrutinize Walter's work and his architectural drawings. After examining the foundations for only a few minutes, one partisan declared that the work was "dreadful";[18] meanwhile, McNair proclaimed to the Congress that another architect—whom he wouldn't name—had looked at the foundation and "declared to me . . . that he would venture his life the building would fall down if built upon it."[19]

That was it for Stanton, who accused McNair of acting on nothing more than the baseless accusations of a disgruntled contractor. "You can delay, embarrass, and ruin the work, by listening to the idle clamor of the ignorant and the envious," warned Stanton, "but such a course will be more discreditable to you than to the President, the architect he has employed, or any one acting under them." He cautioned Congress that the Capitol would never be completed "if the work and the plans are changed and modified by the action of special committees, raised at the instance of every stupid fellow who imagines that he sees a brick awry, or some small crevice not perfectly puttied up."[20]

As a compromise, Stanton permitted the site to be examined by what he considered a neutral and reputable party, the U.S. Army Corps of Topographical Engineers, who closely inspected the work and submitted a report vindicating Walter and his team. "The character of the work and the mode of construction we consider excellent," reported the Army engineers. "We respectfully, therefore, submit it as our opinion, that the existing foundations are sufficient for their purpose."[21]

Meanwhile, the Senate, likely trying to reassert some degree of Congressional oversight, approved a resolution asking the president to "communicate . . . any plan which may have been adopted for the extension of the Capitol." That request demanded a detailed accounting of expenditures, copies of contracts, and—one of the most important matters—"what, if any, plan of construction has been adopted, with reference to the principles of acoustics."[22] The matter was settled—at least for the moment—and $500,000 was appropriated so work could continue.

On the morning of Christmas Eve 1851, John W. Jones, captain of the Capitol Police, jiggled the handles of the locked doors of the Library of Congress as part of his regular patrol of the building. He continued on his route through the Capitol, and two hours later—nearing eight a.m.—he had circled back again to the entrance of the library, where he jiggled the handles again—and was certain he smelled smoke. Oddly, Jones didn't have a key to the library—it was 1825 all over again—but rather than waste valuable time calling for the librarian of Congress, Jones instead broke the door down. Books, shelves, and reading tables in the northern end of the library were on fire. For a moment, Jones thought the fire looked manageable—but breaking in the door had also let in a sudden whoosh of oxygen, which sent the flames roaring up the walls to the ceiling and out onto the roof, threatening Bulfinch's copper-coated but still very wooden dome.[23]

Captain Jones dispatched a messenger to call for help; several fire departments around the city responded, dragging their fire engines up the stairs of the eastern portico and into the Rotunda to train their hoses on the flames. Hampered by cold temperatures that often froze the water in their hoses, firefighters battled the flames for more than a day before the fire was eventually extinguished. But Bulfinch's gorgeous library, the space he was proudest of in the entire building, had been gutted, leaving an empty, cavernous space burned right down to its interior brick walls.

There had been plenty of fuel to feed the fire; since 1846, when President James K. Polk had signed legislation authorizing the Library of Congress to receive "one copy of every copyrighted book, map, chart, musical composition, print, cut, or engraving,"[24] the shelves in the library had begun filling at an alarming rate. Lost in the Christmas Eve fire were thirty-five thousand of the library's fifty-five thousand books, including about two-thirds of the books that had been purchased from Thomas Jefferson—the very soul of the library's collection. Also lost was a bronze bust of George Washington, a statue of Thomas Jefferson, and original portraits of the first five presidents by painter Gilbert Stuart. "A considerable portion of this loss is highly irreparable," the *Washington Union* reported sadly, "and will be deeply felt by the country."[25]

Librarian of Congress John Silva Meehan was heartbroken—and confused. He had strict rules about open flames in the library and couldn't imagine what had been the cause of such a devastating fire. After a thorough investigation, Walter found a flaw in a chimney flue running up between the wooden framing in one of the alcoves—and when a fire had been lit in a committee room below the library, sparks had blown through a small hole in the flue and set fire to the library's interior wooden beams. "No human forethought or vigilance could, under the circumstances, have prevented the catastrophe," Walter reassured the librarian.[26]

Meehan was fortunate to have an ally in the Congress in Senator

James Alfred Pearce of Maryland, chairman of the Joint Library Committee, who promised to champion funding for rebuilding the library and restocking it with new books. Suddenly, Walter had another major project in the Capitol to design and supervise.

While Bulfinch had argued in vain for the funding needed to rebuild the library out of fireproof materials after the 1825 fire, Walter found the current Congress more receptive—especially when Walter impressed them with plans for rebuilding the entire library completely out of cast iron, which had been greatly improved and strengthened as a building material over the last half century. Unlike stone or marble, iron could be shaped by molds and mass-produced. It was also easier and cheaper to move than marble or stone, and it could be painted, noted Walter, "to give depth and effect." Under Walter's unique design, there would be three stories of iron floors, ornately decorated iron galleries, bookshelves, and alcoves, and an iron ceiling—the very first in the United States made with iron trusses suspending thin iron plates. Even the main doors would be made of iron, though Walter promised they would be painted to look as if they were made of mahogany.

Walter assured Chairman Pearce and the Congress that all the work could be done for $72,500—an estimate he overshot by $20,000 during construction. When his request for additional funds went before the Congress in 1852, some House members snarkily questioned Walter's ability to do basic math; in the Senate, skeptical Senators wondered aloud how any single space could cost nearly $100,000—about $4 million today. Still, Walter would get his money and complete work by July 1, 1853. Shortly thereafter, it was visited by British scientist Sir Charles Lyell, who declared the new library to be "the most beautiful room in the world."[27]

Few would have argued with Lyell. When the public was given its first look at the new library on August 23, 1853, the response from the media was a collective gasp of awe. "[V]ery beautiful—I might almost say gorgeous," wrote the near-giddy correspondent from the *Raleigh Register*.[28]

Everything in the galleries was made of ornate cast iron, from the pillars and the latticework to the trusses and the stairs. Large ornamental scrolls at the ceiling were carved with iron grapes and ears of corn. In the iron ceiling—painted to resemble brown marble—were eight skylights, each glazed with tinted glass that scattered diamonds of colored light throughout the library, where they glinted off the gold leaf highlights painted on railings and bookcases.

"The first impression as you look up and around is one of unalloyed pleasure," wrote a correspondent from the *New Orleans Crescent*, who noted that the room was so ornately finished, so "splendidly . . . painted and gilded," that it was hard to believe everything was made from iron.[29] It was an impressive space, both structurally and artistically, as well as more functional than before; thanks to Walter's careful reconfiguring of the alcoves, no ladders were needed to reach the top shelves, which were already filling up with the flood of books, maps, charts, and sheet music that regularly flowed into the librarian's office. The correspondent for the *Crescent* nodded approvingly. "The books can be reached," he wrote.[30]

Flush with new funding from the Congress—and ignoring objections from naysayers like McNair—Walter continued work on the extensions steadily and free from drama. By the end of 1851, he was able to report that all foundations had been laid, the cellars of both extensions were finished, and the vaulting work—reminiscent of Latrobe's preferred style of building—was in place and ready to support the basement floors. Walter was now showing members his plans for the new and grandly decorated House and Senate chambers, which had all the modern conveniences: each was lit by natural light coming in from the western windows during the day and by gas lamps at night, and each was heated by boilers running hot water through pipes, "making open fires unnecessary," Walter explained. In general, members of Congress liked Walter—

he looked like a character from a Gothic romance novel, approachably handsome with a large mop of white hair stacked high on his head—and it was easy for them to get caught up in his enthusiasm. Members were anxious to move into their new space; most put their trust in him to get the building constructed quickly and safely.

But not everyone was a fan. William Easby, the commissioner of public buildings, was still angry about Walter's appointment as architect and his seeming lack of accountability to the legislative branch. As far as Easby was concerned, only he—and not Walter—had the official imprimatur of the Congress behind him; Walter was acting as an independent agent of the executive branch spending a Congressional appropriation without Congressional oversight or approval. Easby therefore made no objection when a Congressional committee introduced legislation to make the commissioner of public buildings the disbursing agent of funds for any public building projects—a proposal that, if passed, would have put Walter under Easby's thumb.

Another thorn in Walter's side was Senator Solon Borland, a brooding and generally disliked member, even back in his home state of Arkansas. Borland had been one of those who had complained the loudest about the strength of the foundations for the extensions, and he regularly took to the floor to question any expenditures for the Capitol while baselessly criticizing Walter's ability to manage the project. "We are legislating in the dark," Borland complained—a comment that drew a rebuke from Public Buildings and Grounds Committee member Robert Hunter. "We are legislating with precisely such information as we have with regard to all other appropriations," Hunter shot back.[31]

In the summer of 1852, Easby formally flung charges of fraud at Walter, accusing him of using federal funding to purchase flawed marble and ignoring shoddy workmanship. They were charges the brooding Borland was more than happy to investigate, especially as he had just been appointed to a special committee chaired by Senator Sam Houston of Texas to investigate "abuse, bribery or fraud . . . in obtaining or granting [government] contracts."[32] For the rest of the summer and into autumn, Houston and Borland hauled more than three dozen witnesses before their committee and eventually uncovered some minor discrepancies, including the odd charge that some of the foundations were "unnecessarily strong."[33] The most damaging finding involved Walter's superintendent, Samuel Strong, who was discovered to have a fiscal interest in one of the contracts that had been awarded for providing bricks for the project—a charge with enough merit that Strong resigned in late 1852.

Walter aggressively defended himself, submitting 123 handwritten pages to the committee, along with copies of his immaculately kept records. Walter effectively exposed Easby as a resentful bully with any number of axes to grind; Walter's careful paper trail also revealed that Easby's son had at one point tried to sell inferior stone to Strong, who had promptly shown the young man the door. To no one's surprise, Borland was unswayed, and on March 22, 1853, the committee issued a 216-page report concluding that "public funds had been spent wastefully and should be put under the control of another official"[34]—a black mark on Walter's reputation and the precise recommendation that Easby was hoping to hear.

When the committee report landed on the president's desk, however, it was picked up and thumbed through not by Millard Fillmore but by a new president, Franklin Pierce, who had taken office only two weeks earlier. Pierce had been a lackluster and mostly reluctant candidate—he had run, as one Pierce biographer put it, one of "the least exciting campaigns in presidential history"[35]—and he had been buoyed into office largely by disinterested voters in an era of relative peace after the tumultuous years that had led to the Compromise of 1850. While his résumé was lengthy and diverse—lawyer, Congressman, Senator, veteran, alcoholic—Pierce was an inexperienced, if mostly inoffensive, chief executive. Though disciplined—he had delivered his inaugural remarks from memory rather than reading them—he would preside over a laissez-faire administration, leaning heavily on the guidance of his cabinet.

One of the most trusted members of that cabinet would be his secretary of war, Jefferson Davis, whom Pierce had plucked from the Congress and placed in his cabinet at the height of Borland's probe into Walter's management of the Capitol. With Davis likely whispering in his ear, Pierce issued on March 23, 1853, an executive order responding to the committee's recommendation that oversight of the Capitol be moved to "another official," uprooting it from its home within the Department of the Interior and placing it under the jurisdiction of Davis's Department of War.

Easby was stunned; he had been certain Pierce would have no choice but to return oversight of the Capitol to Easby's office of the commissioner of public buildings. But the president defended the decision with a straight face, pointing out that the Capitol compound would be best served by placing it within the realm of a qualified neutral party like the Army Corps of Engineers, which had already proven itself to be an acceptable mediator during the squabble over the depth of the foundations.

Critics argued, probably rightly, that it was odd to put a civilian project under the control of the military—but mostly the project was being put under the watchful eye of Jefferson Davis, who knew and cared more about the fate of the Capitol than perhaps anyone else in Washington. It was Davis who had helped guide the Capitol extensions from Mills's preliminary drawings through the contest phase and now to the stone-and-marble structure Walter was slowly erecting on Capitol Hill. Gone was any semblance of Congressional oversight; under the new chain of command, Secretary of War Jefferson Davis—and Jefferson Davis alone—was in charge. And his first decision was to appoint a new superintendent for the project from within the ranks of the War Department, tapping thirty-six-year-old M. C. Meigs, a captain in the Army Corp of Engineers, as engineer in charge.

Montgomery Cunningham Meigs was born in Augusta, Georgia, in 1816 into a wealthy and well-connected family; his father was a respected obstetrician and his grandfather a Yale-educated academic who had once served as president of the University of Georgia. As a teenager, Meigs had studied at the Franklin Institute in Philadelphia and briefly attended the University of Pennsylvania before transferring to West Point at age sixteen to pursue his true passion: engineering. After graduating in 1836, Meigs spent the next decade helping with the mapping of the Mississippi River—giving him an opportunity to share a canoe and a cabin with the brilliant young lieutenant Robert E. Lee—and then pushed farther west to oversee the design and construction of several forts needed to support troops engaged in the war with Mexico. Meigs was well-liked, relatively well-connected, and a really good engineer.

In 1852, his wife and he were dispatched to Washington, D.C., where Meigs was tasked by the Congress with the important job of surveying and overseeing the construction of the Washington Aqueduct. It was an ambitious project that had been inspired partly by the 1851 fire in the Library of Congress, which had highlighted a need for better and quicker access to water in the Federal district—especially on Capitol Hill, where water still arrived mostly from springs and small creeks. But Meigs was also moved by the idea of bringing clean—or at least cleaner—water from the Potomac River to some of the poorest parts of the Federal city, where filthy drinking water currently brought death and disease. Meigs so impressed the Congress with his thoroughness—his first report to Congress ran fifty-five pages and contained an overview of water systems in New York, Paris, and ancient Rome—that his boss, Secretary of War Jefferson Davis, assigned him as the superintendent for two other major projects, both of which had been designed by architect Thomas U. Walter: expansions of the Post Office near the White House and the new extensions on the U.S. Capitol.

Meigs was a great organizer, a gifted engineer, and a capable though still aspiring architect—an ambition that would eventually cause friction with Walter. There would be no such chafing between Meigs and Davis, however; both had similar tastes in design and materials, and each believed that buildings could be both functional *and* beautiful—a sentiment that had not necessarily been shared by the Fillmore administration, which favored simplicity in the name of frugality. Not so the Pierce administration—and definitely not on Jefferson Davis's watch.

Davis wanted the Capitol building to reflect favorably on the nation—and the administration. In the Pierce administration, only the best artists and craftsmen would be employed, and only the finest materials would be used. With Davis and Meigs in charge, interiors wouldn't be finished with sandstone painted white to *resemble* marble; they'd be made of *actual* marble.

As the second Army officer to get his hands on the Capitol—the first was L'Enfant, who had also been a captain in the Corps of Engineers—Meigs was accustomed to following orders. One of his first came from Davis, who told him that when it came to staffing needs, he was "fully empowered to make such changes in the present administration as you may deem necessary."[36] Walter, still smarting from the findings of Borland and the committee, was uncertain whether he'd be retained as Architect of the Capitol under the new administration. But Meigs assured Walter the job was still his; Meigs knew a smear campaign when he saw one. And to Walter's surprise—and likely delight—he also suddenly found himself free of both Senator Solon Borland, whom Pierce appointed as ambassador to Nicaragua, and Commissioner of Public Buildings William Easby, who had been replaced by the president with former House clerk Benjamin B. French. Two of Walter's main adversaries were suddenly off his back.

But Walter now found his flank attacked by an unlikely new antagonist: the still disgruntled Robert Mills. As the Fillmore administration wound down, Mills, with the support of twenty Senators and seventeen Representatives, had petitioned the president to "return" him to the position of Architect of the Capitol—a position he had never actually held—and demanded Walter be removed. Fillmore had ignored Mills, recognizing the swagger was all a bluff.

Mills would change his tone with the Pierce administration; at this point, Mills needed a job and was prepared to beg for it. Disappointed that Pierce had passed him over for the post of commissioner of public buildings, he appealed to Jefferson Davis for *any* position, suggesting he would even work for Walter as a clerk. Davis forwarded Mills's request to Meigs, who dismissed the former superintendent curtly. "As a draftsman, Mr. Mills was tried in the Engineers office," wrote Meigs, "and not found qualified."[37] Mills would retire in despair and die in Washington two years later, on March 3, 1855, at age seventy-three without ever seeing the completed Capitol. And the Washington Monument he had so proudly designed was still a stone stump on the Mall. It would not be finished for another thirty years.

Meigs and Walter worked together well, at least at first. Walter was happy to turn details like invoicing, supply ordering, and payroll over to Meigs—and Meigs *excelled* at details. Meigs approached his job with military discipline, which Walter appreciated; no detail would be too small for Meigs's attention. He would read up on ventilation, art, and decoration and visit auditoriums and other music halls around the country to study their acoustics. He obsessively counted the number of bricks laid at the Capitol each day and made sure to buy as many bricks as he could from brickyards in Baltimore, Philadelphia, and New York City so the supply would never run out. For his part, Walter was delighted to let Meigs and Davis worry about the bookkeeping; after the brutal 1852 he'd had at the hands of Borland and Easby, he'd spend most of 1853 keeping his head down.

But Meigs also had an ego; like some others before him, he was itching to get his hands on the Capitol. As a devoted and lifelong military officer, Meigs had watched with distress—and some jealously—as many of his West Point colleagues had left the Army and gone on to lucrative careers in the private sector. Meigs was willing to forfeit money in exchange for legacy, but he didn't intend to go down in history as the executor of someone else's architectural plan; instead, he wanted credit as one of the building's designers.

He made his first move in May 1853 as he unrolled Walter's floor plans and suggested to the architect that perhaps the House and Senate chambers might be relocated to different spots within their respective future wings. In the current plan, each chamber was situated against the western end of its new addition. While that placement gave each chamber plenty of natural light from the tall western windows facing the Mall, Meigs pointed out a fatal flaw: the present floor plan had members of Congress entering their respective chambers through a single interior door connected to a busy public hallway where they were certain to be harassed on their way to the floor by lobbyists and reporters.

Instead, Meigs recommended placing each chamber in the *center* of its respective wing and surrounding each chamber with cloakrooms, lobbies, and hallways that could be closed off to the public, providing members with an unobstructed route to their respective chambers. This relocation would also allow for public galleries to surround the chambers on all four sides; one floor up, the galleries would be accessible by what Meigs envisioned as grand marble staircases.

Walter had to admit that Meigs had a good point—and had proposed a good solution—but cautioned that moving the chambers to the center of the building meant there would be no windows, which meant no natural light and little natural circulation or ventilation. As Walter drew up the new floor plans, he mentioned to Meigs that to execute them would require some major feats of engineering.

Fortunately, Captain Meigs considered himself a major engineer. Creating a completely controlled environment—one for which he would determine the lighting, circulation, acoustics, and ventilation—appealed to Meigs's sense of order and his inclination for control. He would make his first mark on the Capitol by giving members of the House and the Senate the perfectly lit, well-ventilated, acoustically sound chambers that each wanted and needed. Trusting in Meigs's ability to make it all work, Jefferson Davis and President Pierce signed off on the new floor plan.

Walter would draw and redraw and draw some more, trying to ground some of Meigs's aspirations in three-dimensional reality. At the center of the new south wing, Walter would create a House chamber 137 feet long, 92 feet wide, and 30 feet high, giving it floor space enough for three hundred desks arranged in a semicircle facing a central marble rostrum—plenty of room for the 233 Representatives currently seated in the Thirty-second Congress. On the Senate side, the chamber was smaller—112 feet by 82—but that was more than enough space for the current roster of sixty-two Senators. Each chamber was surrounded by committee rooms and conference rooms; on the Senate side, there were various suites, including an office for the vice president. Walter and Meigs had also designed ceilings constructed of iron and glass—and here Meigs would literally sign his work by having his name cast on every one of the iron beams that formed the trusses of the roof. Walter could only shake his head in amusement, joking to his wife that he was certain Meigs would eventually "order old Vulcan to stamp his name on the thunderbolts."[38]

Meigs would show some restraint on the exterior, however, asking only for decorative pediments above the main entrances to the new north and south wings, which would now be east-facing porticos mirroring the one on the center section. Walter had deliberately left each triangular space blank in his drawings, preferring not to pull the focus away from the central pediment designed by John Quincy Adams and carved by Persico almost three decades earlier. But Meigs—and Davis—wanted the exterior entrances to the new wings to reflect the growing dignity and grandeur of the young nation; Meigs envisioned elaborate sculpture in each pediment—better sculpture than Persico's, he hoped, as he'd never been a fan—as well as ornately carved bronze doors opening off the porticos and into the new wings. Walter wouldn't even be asked for his input; Meigs immediately began searching for sculptors—ideally *American* sculptors—to design and complete the work.

For the pediments, Meigs approached two American artists residing in Italy: a Vermont-born neoclassical sculptor named Hiram Powers, who was living in Florence, and Thomas Crawford, a New Yorker residing in Rome. Powers, the better-known name, dismissed Meigs outright, citing a lack of time. Meigs had better luck with Crawford, who was regarded as America's up-and-coming sculptor after designing a majestic equestrian statue of George Washington for the public square in Richmond, Virginia. (One wonders why he wasn't asked to execute a similar statue of Washington for the Capitol after Greenough and the bathtub-Washington disaster.) With Powers taking himself out of consideration for the job, Meigs would award the commission for the design of the Senate pediment to Crawford; the House pediment would have to wait.

Meigs would dictate to Crawford his vision for the pediment on the north wing, asking for a piece reflecting westward expansion on the American continent. "In our history of the struggle between civilized man and the savage, between the cultivated and the wild nature, are certainly to be found themes worthy of the artist and capable of appealing to the feelings of all classes," Meigs wrote Crawford in 1853.[39] Using the latest technology—photography—Crawford sent Meigs photos from Rome of the sketches for his proposed models, which Meigs then showed to Davis for his eventual approval.

Persico's central pediment, with its three figures, looked downright anemic when compared with Crawford's *thirteen* sprawling across the sixty feet of the Senate wing's pediment. Similarly to in Persico's composition, a figure of America stands at the center of Crawford's work, which he titled *Progress of Civilization*. In her right hand, Crawford's

America holds wreaths of laurel and oak, symbolizing civic and military glory, as she stands before a rising sun and with an eagle at her left. On her head is a liberty cap, the traditional symbol of freed enslaved laborers—and only here did Jefferson Davis, an enslaver who understood full well the symbolism and its implications, raise any objection. "He says it is the sign of a freedman," Meigs wrote Crawford, "and that we were always free, not freemen, not slaves just released."[40] Crawford, however, dismissed Davis's complaint. The cap would stay on the figure in the Senate pediment—but Crawford would not be as successful dismissing a later, similar complaint from Davis.

The pediment would also feature, to America's right, the victors in the new nation's march into the nineteenth century: a soldier in the act of drawing his sword; a seated merchant with his hand resting on a globe; a group of schoolchildren and their nattily dressed instructor; and finally, a mechanic, his sleeves still rolled up as he lounges against a large gear. To America's left, however, the tableau becomes bleaker: a woodsman in shirtsleeves hacks away at a tree with an ax, frightening a coiled snake. Beyond him, a young Native boy with his dog glances back over his shoulder toward the woodsman as the boy's father, a muscled chief in a headdress, sits with his head in his hands in resignation—"left alone," as one journalist described it, "the solitary off-shoot of a mighty race."[41] Completing the arrangement of figures, a beautiful Native woman cuddles her child close to her breast as her feet rest ominously on a grave. It was a composition consistent with Meigs's insistence that the work reflect "the progress of civilization and the decay of the Indian race."[42]

Crawford's models were diligently reproduced by sculptors on the grounds of the Capitol—in marble taken from the quarries in Lee, Massachusetts—and were clearly designed by an artist who was used to having his work closely inspected from every angle. When Crawford's Senate pediment was cleaned in 2016, it was discovered that every figure had been intricately sculpted in three dimensions; even the parts of the figures that couldn't be seen from the ground were sculpted in great detail, all the way down to a readable geometry lesson etched into the schoolmaster's scroll. It was also found that Crawford had included a bit of deliberate political commentary in his sculpture, inserting an inscription near the foot of the merchant reading "$28,000,000"—the exact amount of the Treasury's surplus in 1853 at a time when Crawford and other artists were scraping for federal funding to subsidize American arts.

Crawford's *Progress of Civilization* would finally be installed in 1863 to considerable acclaim and some journalistic hyperbole. "[H]is work will be welcomed in America, as something similar to the triumphant feelings of national gratification, with which the early Florentines hailed the uncovering of Michelangelo's immortal statues in the Medicean chapel of San Lorenzo," gushed the editor of the New York magazine *The Crayon*.[43] Naturally, Meigs took credit for its success, saying he would "esteem myself fortunate in having been the means of causing such an example of American skill to be executed."[44] Crawford's pediment remains over the entrance to the Senate wing to this day, a reminder of America's obsession with Manifest Destiny at any cost, but also one of the few works of art on the subject in the Capitol that attempts to portray the anguish of doomed Indigenous people.

Crawford's work was so satisfactory, in fact, that he was next given the commission to design the fourteen-foot-high bronze double doors for the east portico entrances of both the House and the Senate wings. Using as his model Walter's designs, which even Meigs had to admit were "good and magnificent," Crawford chose to illustrate the House doors with key moments in the American Revolution on a series of eight panels—four in each door—showing events such as the Battle of Lexington, the first public reading of the Declaration of Independence, and George Washington delivering his farewell address to his staff. The doors in the Senate's eastern portico were even more George Washington–centric, with six panels depicting major events associated with the first president, from the Battle of Yorktown to his inauguration as president.

Unfortunately, as he was completing the doors in Rome in 1856, Crawford began to experience problems with his eyes and was unable to continue sculpting. With his vision deteriorating, he sought treatment in London, where he died of brain cancer in October 1857 at age forty-three, leaving the unfinished bronze doors to be completed by sculptor W. H. Rinehart. The doors for the Senate would be hung in place in the east portico of the Senate wing in 1868, directly beneath the figures of Justice and History that Crawford had also modeled more than a decade earlier.

The House doors, however, would take a more circuitous route to their destination. The models for the doors would ship from Italy in 1867, but a lack of funding for casting the doors in bronze meant the models would be stored in the Crypt of the Capitol—and temporary wooden doors would remain in place on the House's east portico—until money was available. The doors remained oddly out of sight and out of mind for nearly forty years until they were finally cast in bronze by a Massachusetts artist in 1903. During their formal installation ceremony in August 1905, a snapped cable sent one of the fourteen-foot-tall doors crashing to the ground, breaking it into three pieces. The repaired doors would finally be hung to great acclaim in October 1905, nearly fifty years after Crawford had drawn his first sketches. Meigs, who in 1905 had been dead for thirteen years, was no longer around to claim credit for them.

It was steaming hot and humid in Washington in July 1854. "Intensely hot," Meigs wrote in his journal, noting that work had mostly stopped at the Capitol while waiting for the heat to break. Among the workers who remained, some collapsed from heatstroke, a situation that was met with annoyance rather than compassion by Meigs. When work on the new wings eventually continued, Meigs remained obsessed with the bricklaying, even tracking in his journal how many bricks were being laid per second.

For his part, Walter continued to quietly visit the marble quarries and oversee the workmen carving the capitals for the marble pillars. However, the previously cordial relationship between him and Meigs was beginning to fray. The two bickered over the design and materials for window frames and doorframes, for example, with Walter—as directed years earlier by the penny-pinching Fillmore—arguing for wooden frames even as Meigs haughtily overrode the decision in favor of iron. Later, after Walter okayed the use of fused marble drums to craft the more than one hundred exterior columns, Meigs vetoed the approval and ordered that each be cut from a single piece instead. It was with annoyance—though some amusement—that Walter groaned that Meigs "keeps after me with whips and spurs from morning to night."[45]

For much of the time, Meigs would find himself—as Walter had in 1852—harangued by members of Congress, led mostly by Representative Richard Stanton, a former ally turned adversary. After losing the chair of the Joint Committee on Public Buildings and Grounds to Senator James Bayard Jr. of Delaware, Stanton seemed determined to make a pest of himself and quickly secured a seat on the Select Committee on Military Superintendence, in which he spent much of the year inquiring why the Capitol had been placed under the authority of the military. "I have no patience with those who assert that Army officers are better qualified for these places than other men," Stanton huffed to his Senate colleagues. "The history of the country, the experience of the Government, our own reason, teaches us that is not so."[46]

As Congress took up yet another funding request for the extensions, Stanton regularly rushed to the House floor to question at length every decision made by Meigs, accusing the military engineer of overstepping his authority and overriding Walter, the civilian architect, on issues relating to architecture. There was some truth to the assertions. Meigs *had* largely sidelined Walter, using his direct access to Secretary Davis to downgrade the architect to little more than a staff member. Even more egregious, Meigs regarded himself as an arm of the executive branch and rarely kept the Congress informed of what he was doing—Meigs, complained Stanton, had "little respect for the will of Congress."[47] It was a habit that did not endear Meigs to legislators.

Fortunately, Congress felt better about Walter—and Chairman Bayard was a particularly vocal fan. He was tired of listening to members nitpick the decisions about the Capitol that had been made. "Are they architects?" Bayard asked his colleagues. "Can they tell what are the difficulties to be encountered?"[48] But even as others continued to rail against Meigs and the military, Walter wasn't willing to pile on; he *liked* working with military men, with their attention to recordkeeping and details—"I have enough to do without such trouble," said Walter.[49] He much preferred having Meigs handle the minutiae—including the counting of bricks—while he focused solely on architecture. He might have been scuffling with Meigs, but in general, Walter believed the engineer was "composed of good stuff, and I shall stand by him through thick and thin."[50] Still, the stalled funding request—now boosted to $750,000—eventually sailed through the Congress almost entirely on Walter's reputation alone.

But if Walter was standing by Meigs, the engineer wasn't inclined to return the favor; when summoned by Davis for a frank conversation about the architect and whether to continue his employment on the Capitol project, Meigs saw the one-on-one as an ideal opportunity to polish his own reputation at the expense of Walter's. According to Meigs, who very likely embellished the conversation in his favor:

> [Davis] said that he had always thought that my reputation would be injured by Walter's presence; that he would get . . . credit that really belonged to me. . . . The building under Walter was imperfect and would have been a failure. I had totally changed it in all its most important parts, and to me would appropriately belong the credit of success, while if Walter remained with the title of architect, to him

> would go, if he could grasp it, the credit which really should be mine.[51]

Certainly, to Meigs, the work mattered—his projects would be impeccably completed—but credit would always seem to matter just as much. In his private journal, Meigs insisted that his response to Davis had been magnanimous—that he had explained that while *he* had done most of the work on the Capitol, "I knew that I should not from the people get all I deserved." But rather than give the appearance of having pushed Walter out in a fit of jealousy, he told Secretary Davis that "for my own reputation, I thought it better that Walter should remain." He was also certain that Walter would never appreciate all that Meigs had done for him. "He would not feel grateful, for I said pretty frankly what I thought of him, as ungrateful, unjust, disposed to grasp what does not belong to him," Meigs wrote acidly. "Yet, he owed his position to my determination to do right and to my influence with the Secretary."[52] Meigs's ego was setting him on a collision course with Walter; a face-off seemed imminent.

And yet Walter still seemed content to do the work needed to ground the engineer's vision in reality and to quietly carry out Meigs's orders. On some long afternoons, Walter would oversee the marble work being completed on the grounds of the Capitol to Meigs's specifications; other times, he would be dispatched regularly to deal with inquiries from Representative Stanton, to whom Meigs was openly and derisively referring as "my enemy."[53] But with Meigs preoccupied mostly with the building's interior—especially the ventilation and heating of the chambers—Walter was continuing to consider and sketch improvements to the exterior. Lately, he had completed a drawing of the exterior of the Capitol with a major change that was so striking that even the normally unreceptive Meigs made a note of it.

"Mr. Walter," Meigs reported in his journal, "has made a sketch for a new dome."[54]

This detailed drawing, by draftsman August Schoenborn, reflected Walter's desire for a new dome that he felt was better proportioned for the building after the addition of its new extensions. After spotting similar drawings hanging in Walter's offices, an enthusiastic Congress approved construction of the new dome without any real idea of its costs.

CHAPTER 7

A Very Perfect Thing

1854–1856

Thomas U. Walter had strong opinions on domes.

In 1838, shortly after he completed his work on Philadelphia's Girard College, the college's building committee sent Walter on an all-expenses-paid tour of England, France, and Italy, where he was expected to look to European architecture as an inspiration for campus improvements in Pennsylvania. While the then thirty-four-year-old Walter eagerly soaked up all the sights, taking careful notes and making detailed sketches, he found himself fascinated by domes—especially those soaring over St. Peter's Basilica in Rome, St. Paul's Cathedral in London, and the Pantheon in Paris.

Of the three, he was the least impressed by St. Peter's Basilica—then, as now, the tallest dome in world, and perhaps the one with the most distinguished pedigree, as it was designed by Michelangelo following his appointment as *capomaestro* to the St. Peter's project in 1547. Despite its noble origins, Walter thought St. Peter's to be of "very little architectural merit" and pointed out in his journals the dome's "many faults in the minutia of its design." St. Paul's, too, failed to impress him as an overall structure—"a confused effect" was the best he could muster about architect Christopher Wren's 1710 baroque masterwork. But its dome? "A most agreeable effect . . . that affords repose to the eye,"

Walter wrote. He particularly admired Wren's decision to cap the dome's circle of supporting columns—its colonnade—with a continuous and relatively clean entablature, a touch that gave the dome a sense of calm and grandeur, in contrast to the "incongruous" building beneath it.[1]

But it was the dome crowning the Pantheon in Paris that stirred his architectural imagination and enthusiasm. A neoclassical structure designed by Jacques-Germain Soufflot in 1755 to honor notable French citizens, the Pantheon, Walter was convinced, was "the most beautiful specimen of Architecture in Paris."[2] Similar to St. Paul's, the dome had a colonnade that was capped by an unbroken entablature and that rested on a large circular base—a drum—and it was topped by a tall lantern. It was the clean look that Walter admired—but it was Soufflot's interior that truly captivated him.

Soufflot's dome was actually *three* domes, each one fitting within the other like nesting dolls. Inside the building, visitors looked up into the interior of the first dome, which had a large oculus at its apex. Through this oculus could be seen the ceiling of the second dome, which was decorated with a fresco depicting the apotheosis of St. Genevieve painted by the French artist Antoine-Jean Gros. Encasing both was the third and outer dome, topped with a tall lantern that let in enough sunlight to strikingly illuminate Gros's mural. An impressed Walter carefully drew a cross section of Soufflot's structure in his notebook and filed it away with his papers, likely never expecting that an 1838 sketch of a monument to French nationalism would inspire his own shrine to the American experiment in 1854.

As he appraised the Capitol's proposed new silhouette, Walter was certain that Bulfinch's dome was unworthy of the building growing beneath it. The copper plating covering Bulfinch's wooden dome no longer gleamed in the sunlight, having long since faded to a dull green patina. And while Bulfinch had groaned in 1822 when President Monroe had opted for the largest possible dome, it was clear, as the work was progressing on the new north and south wings, that even Monroe's oversized dome was now too small for and out of proportion with the rest of the growing structure. "It is well known that the present dome is entirely too low to preserve the symmetry of the building when the extensions are completed," agreed Congressman Richard Stanton, who cautioned his House colleagues that leaving Bulfinch's dome on the Capitol "will give it a squatty appearance."[3]

Walter's new dome was going to be anything but squatty. Spreading out his old notebooks for inspiration, Walter began sketching. As early as June 1854, Meigs noted in his diary that the architect was at work designing a new dome, grudgingly admitting that it was "generally good" even as he nitpicked that "it will want a good deal of studying to make it as good as it ought to be."[4] Walter continued at his drawing table throughout the summer, stopping only long enough to move the offices Meigs and he shared on A Street over to three empty rooms in the new House wing destined for the Committee on Agriculture. Neither their new rooms nor the House extension was complete—Meigs had to put temporary wooden planking down over the dirt floor. But Meigs wanted to be in the middle of everything, where he could oversee the ongoing construction and be that much closer to the Congress. Walter, barely looking up from his work, could only complain about the dust and wood shavings that littered the floors and covered his drawing table.

By late autumn, Walter had produced on a piece of paper seven feet long a highly detailed and enormous drawing depicting the Capitol with its new north and south wings in place and its central section capped not by Bulfinch's inverted teacup, but by a soaring, magnificent neoclassical dome. Walter's tall and ellipsoidal dome was crowned with a lantern—and, perched atop the lantern, a statue of some sort. Upholding the dome were two colonnades tightly scrunched together and capped with relatively clean entablatures that encircled the lower half of the structure like a baroque exoskeleton—and all rested on an unfussy, unadorned drum. As a final touch, Walter couldn't resist drawing the lawn of the East Front of the building filled with people, with detailed sketches of couples strolling the grounds or lounging on benches and top-hatted men on horseback, some in carriages, and still others clustered in conversation. Walter's bustling crowd not only helped give an idea of the building's scale but added an energy and a sense of what the finished building would look like as a real structure and as a focal point of the Washington, D.C., community.

Walter's dome might have been classical in design, but he intended for it to be constructed with the most modern materials possible by building it not from stone or marble but with iron. It was cheap and easy to work with; it could be mass-produced—with each piece exactly like others as needed; and it weighed significantly less than stone or marble. That would allow Walter to build a lighter, larger, and more ornate dome worthy of the proportions, and prominence, of the finished Capitol.

It would also mean the dome was fireproof; more than a few members of Congress shared Walter's concern that apart from being an eyesore, Bulfinch's old wooden dome had also become a fire hazard. "There is not a shanty within a hundred miles of this city which is such a complete tinder box as is this Capitol," harrumphed Pennsylvania Congressman Joseph Chandler.[5] Walter's gorgeous 1851 redesign and rebuilding of the Library of Congress in fireproof cast iron had won him praise from the Congress and the public—but as far as Walter was concerned, that earlier success had merely been a test run for this much larger and much more ambitious project. This new dome, he declared, was "magnificent" and "of such proportions as to throw all other domes in the shade."[6]

Those who saw Walter's drawing tended to agree. By winter, his seven-foot illustration hung in the offices he and Meigs shared in the Capitol—and when Congress returned to work in December 1854, members who passed by their offices were immediately drawn to the architect's exciting vision for the finished building. At times, Meigs would bring members into the office to discuss his plans for his own decorations in the halls and stairways, only to find their attention focused on Walter's dome instead. When Massachusetts Congressman Samuel Crocker and several other members paid Meigs a visit in early December and oohed and aahed over the dome, Meigs downplayed Walter's contribution and told Crocker the current expansion didn't actually include the large dome depicted in Walter's drawing. Meigs suggested it might be "a thing to be done sometime hereafter and as separate from the Capitol extension."

Intrigued, Crocker asked—"jokingly," Meigs thought—how much it would cost to add Walter's new dome to the current extension project. "I told them I had not made any estimate, though supposed $200,000," Meigs wrote. "I said if they saw fit to order it, I should be proud and glad to build it myself."[7] Crocker was immediately on board. "Let's have it done!" the Congressman said excitedly, but Meigs couldn't muster much enthusiasm. "This is a joke," Meigs wrote privately, "and probably will lead to nothing."[8]

Only Crocker wasn't joking. Walter knew he had astonished his audience with his dome—"every member of Congress who has seen it is enthusiastically in its favor," he wrote—and even normally tight-fisted Congressional appropriators seemed ready to untie the purse strings to give Walter whatever funding he needed to make his dome a reality. "[It] will cost half a million at least," Walter thought—more than double the $200,000 price tag Meigs had spitballed for Crocker.[9] But for the moment, the price of the dome didn't seem to matter—an enthusiastic Congress was ready to rush an appropriations bill to the floor to pay for it. And now that it was clear Congress wanted to move forward with a more majestic dome, Meigs wanted it to be seen as *his* project, not Walter's. "I wish to have the credit and the pleasure of building this dome," Meigs wrote in his journal.[10] "If I can get the appropriation to go on and build this great dome over the rotunda of the Capitol, I should be much pleased and gratified as if it were for myself."[11]

During the final weeks of 1854, then, the ambitious superintendent was busy sketching his own version of a tall dome, which he hoped would be favored by Congress over Walter's drawing; that would make the project entirely his from concept to execution. "I think the sketch I have made is a better outline than the one Mr. Walter and myself settled upon before," Meigs boasted in his diary, "and I wish to have something to do with this design myself."[12] But the reception of Meigs's proposed dome was mixed; while one visitor praised Meigs's design as "superior in richness" to Walter's, another preferred Walter's version, dismissing Meigs's dome as merely "tall."[13]

It was Walter who suggested that the two of them submit both sets of drawings to the Congress to let that body decide which it preferred. Walter likely believed his dome was superior and would prevail in any head-to-head competition; Meigs, however, sulked, complaining that the only possible reason Walter's dome might be selected was because the architect had incorporated so many of Meigs's own suggestions into his drawing. "He followed my hints," Meigs groused, "yet, he would never allow that I had the least claim of any merit in this design." If Walter's design was chosen, Meigs was certain the architect would take all the credit. "[Walter] has assumed the whole merit," Meigs complained to his diary. "I am getting tired of it."[14]

In early February 1855, Congress began its debate on which dome it preferred—Walter's or Meigs's—as well as on how much funding it would provide for its construction. His annoyance with Walter aside, Meigs was actively lobbying Congress to approve an appropriation as quickly as possible; he excitedly guaranteed legislators that if they funded the project—*his* project—immediately and adequately, he could have the dome completed before the end of the year and maybe even by fall—a promise he had no realistic way of keeping.

Helping to manage the bill on the floor was Representative Richard Stanton, now in his final weeks in Congress after losing his bid for re-election in 1854. Stanton remained a generally reliable ally, despite his ongoing bickering with Meigs. But to Meigs's dismay, Stanton picked up in February 1855 almost exactly where he'd left off in the summer of 1854: by challenging the decision to move oversight of the Capitol to the Department of War. "Military architecture and engineering are totally different things from civil architecture and civil engineering," Stanton lectured his colleagues. "The building you propose to erect must have a civil architect."[15] Few members, however, expressed a similar concern.

After losing that argument, Stanton next tried to dampen military oversight by proposing that the project be explicitly placed under the authority of the Architect of the Capitol—a move that deliberately bypassed and undercut Meigs. When Meigs protested, Commissioner of Public Buildings Benjamin French suggested that the project be returned to *his* office—a proposition Meigs derisively compared to handing the project over to "Goths and Vandals."[16] Meigs's preferred alternative would eventually prevail; funding would flow into the Department of War and flow out only on the authority of Jefferson Davis—which, for all practical purposes, meant on the authority of Montgomery Meigs. Meigs had control of the purse strings; now all he needed for complete ownership—and credit—was for the Congress to choose his design for the dome over Walter's.

It wasn't going to happen. While Meigs had some members in his corner, most had been in awe of Walter's dramatic dome from the moment they first set eyes on it in the architect's office. "The architect of the building has designed a dome . . . which commends itself to my judgement," Stanton authoritatively announced on the floor. "All who have seen it say it is most beautiful and perfect."[17] The final bill, approved February 25, provided $100,000 for construction of the dome and specified that Meigs would oversee the construction of a dome of Walter's design. "I have no doubt he will make it a very perfect thing," added Stanton, to Meigs's likely annoyance.[18]

The $100,000 was a figure based on nothing more than a guess; apart from Walter's drawing and Meigs's offhand estimate, there had been no real analysis of the costs of materials or labor. The appropriations bill was submitted to President Pierce and signed on March 3, only a little more than ten weeks since Walter's drawing had first been spotted hanging in his office—a remarkably brisk pace for a legislative body. In their enthusiasm and haste, Congress had approved the funding with no questions asked—a far too disinterested approach that would come back to imperil the project.

Flush with funding, Meigs and Walter went to work immediately, with the architect heading for his drawing table in the Capitol to begin producing the detailed plans necessary for the actual construction of the dome. The first task at hand, however, was the removal of Bulfinch's wooden dome. For this job, Meigs found an unexpected assistant in the now sixty-five-year-old master carpenter Pringle Slight, who had been maintaining Bulfinch's wood-and-copper dome for more than twenty-five years—and whose familiarity with its construction meant he also knew the best way to take it down. In 1834, Slight had overseen the tricky installation of the dome's copper plating—a challenge he had addressed by designing and building ladders that followed the gentle curve of the dome. Now, two decades later, Slight recommended using the same ladders to remove the copper cladding in large pieces, which could then be sold for reuse—a demolition and rummage sale certain to appeal to the parsimonious Congress.

At the same time, Meigs would begin constructing the derricks and cranes necessary for removing the stone from the base of the old dome as well as for carrying the iron and other materials required for construction of the new one. For this, the ever-industrious Meigs proposed building a crane that would rise straight up from the center of the floor of the now dome-less Rotunda. By Meigs's estimates, he would need a crane capable of lifting loads as heavy as ten tons and raising them more than two hundred feet above the ground.

The West Point engineer could barely contain his excitement. "The mechanical details and process would be just the most agreeable study I could have," he wrote. "The cranes and cupolas and planning machines and the other tools necessary for [the dome's] construction would be a constant source of occupation and delight to me."

Here again, Pringle Slight would be a valuable resource when he reminded Meigs that, several decades ago, there had been a circular opening cut into the floor of the Capitol's Rotunda for the purpose of peering down into the never-completed tomb of George Washington. The opening had been carefully bricked closed in the late 1820s, but that meant the center of the Rotunda—exactly where Meigs wanted to place the footings of his crane—was the weakest part of the floor. To ensure his cranes were on steady footing, then, Meigs filled the Rotunda with wooden scaffolding constructed like a three-legged stool that straddled the covered opening and distributed the scaffolding's weight toward the outer walls rather than to the center of the Rotunda floor.

From this scaffolding rose a wooden derrick that sprouted straight up through the top of the Rotunda, now open to the sky with the removal of Bulfinch's dome. Once clear of the building, the derrick carried the mast and a boom, each eighty feet long, to lift the ironwork from the ground to the rooftop construction area with the help of several steam engines that Meigs had placed on the Capitol's roof. To power these engines, Meigs burned the wood salvaged from Bulfinch's dome. To no one's surprise, the wood burned up quickly; Bulfinch's dome had indeed, as Representative Chandler feared, been a "tinder box."

Even before a single square foot of the new dome had been constructed, Meigs's work on the derrick alone was already being regarded with awe and rightfully hailed as a major feat of engineering. In his December 3, 1855, report to Congress, Secretary of War Jefferson Davis lauded Meigs's massive and impressive machinery, saying such work reflected "the highest credit upon the capacity and skill . . . of the officer in charge of the work."[19] Meigs proudly called it "a beautiful machine."[20]

As Walter continued the architectural drawings for the dome, Meigs was doing more than just obsessing over the derricks; he was also positively consumed with the ventilation system that would be installed in both new legislative chambers. Meigs, with Walter's consultation and approval, had settled on the relatively new innovation of a forced-air system in which steam-powered fans sixteen feet in diameter blew air into the rooms. In the summer, this kept air circulating in the chambers, providing some relief from the stifling heat of the enclosed spaces; in the winter, air would pass over coils of pipes filled with hot water, thus fanning heated air into the cavernous rooms. Members of Congress signed off on the system, though few had any idea how it actually worked.

In the Congress, Stanton continued to question Meigs's skills as an engineer just enough to make some members uneasy; in the Senate, there was nervous laughter at the suggestion that an explosion in the ventilation system might take out both legislative bodies—and Michigan Senator Lewis Cass finally pled utter confusion. "The air is to be pumped up, or pumped down, by some kind of machine," Cass flailed, "nobody knows what."[21] Most put their faith in Meigs and, to a greater extent, Walter to make it work. Louisiana Congressman Miles Taylor, who was used to swampy humidity, thought any system was better than their current stifling accommodations. "I know that this Hall, though well lighted, is very poorly ventilated," Taylor said of the current House chamber, "and I trust that the new one will be better prepared to accommodate the members of the House."[22]

Unfortunately, the completed system, as installed by the New York firm of Nason & Dodge to Meigs's specifications, never worked quite as well in practice as it had promised to do on paper. While the rooms stayed mostly warm in the winter, each chamber was baking hot in the summer—especially as under Meigs's revised floor plan, the chambers were centrally located in the building with no windows to let in fresh air or encourage circulation. Members would be so miserable that there would be decades of legislative grumbling about redesigning or even relocating the chambers to a spot in the building that had exterior windows. The Senate chamber, complained New Hampshire Senator John P. Hale, "is the worst, the most inconvenient, uncomfortable, and unhealthy place that ever I was in in all my life."[23] Congress would swelter and sweat for the next seventy years; relief would eventually come with the installation of air-conditioning in the Capitol in 1928.

By early 1856, Walter was far enough along with his detailed drawings to finally provide his boss, Jefferson Davis, with a more informed estimate of the costs of building the dome. He assured Davis that "no *essential* alteration has been made . . . that could be considered as a departure from the original plan," but noted that he had modified some features, such as the top cupola, "so as to make it more graceful," and had slightly increased the height "so as to bring it into better proportion with the entire mass." While the final expense would depend on the market price of iron, Walter thought constructing the dome would cost $945,000—well beyond the $100,000 that had been appropriated by the Congress but remarkably close to what would be the actual final price tag of $1,047,271. And over the next decade, Meigs and he were going to have to beg and scrape for every penny.[24]

Walter had also turned his attention to the dome's interior. Inspired by the nesting domes Jacques-Germain Soufflot had constructed at the Pantheon, Walter, like Bulfinch before him, had plans for a similar kind of "double dome," which involved curving the walls of the Rotunda upward to create an inner dome nestled just inside the cast-iron outer dome. Visitors gazing up from the floor of the Rotunda would be staring through a central oculus in the inner dome and into the iron skeleton of the exterior dome. At its top was a large lantern that would allow in the sunlight that would shine down through the oculus like a spotlight onto the floor of the Rotunda more than two hundred feet below. Even Meigs approved of Walter's double dome, assuring the Congress that "the whole will form a fitting centre to this magnificent building, the very central meeting-point of a great nation."[25]

Meigs was less magnanimous, however, when it came to the dome's exterior. Perhaps still hoping the Congress might adopt his version of the dome, he made a point of hanging Walter's original and updated drawings side by side in the House Ways and Means Committee room so members could "judge for themselves" whether the money they were being asked to spend seemed worth it.[26] The revised drawings didn't change any minds—to most eyes, they didn't look all that different—but they did prompt new questions about the sheer size of the new dome and concerns about whether the round walls of the Rotunda, and the building's foundations itself, could withstand the dome's weight.

These questions were exactly the sort that Meigs excelled at answering. In an exhaustive response to Congress, the engineer confidently provided pages and pages of details about how much weight various kinds of brick and marble could bear before they crumbled. He also reminded members that the dome was to be constructed from iron, which weighed significantly less than marble or stone; each iron column going into place on the Capitol's dome weighed ten thousand pounds, he explained, while the same columns made from marble would have weighed twenty-three thousand pounds each. Thus the dome, despite its grandeur, was considerably lighter than it looked. Meigs put the weight of the finished dome at about fifteen million pounds, and after walking members thorough several more pages of elaborate math and physics, he assured them that "there can be no doubt of the sufficiency of the walls of the rotundo to support the dome."[27] As it turned out, the completed dome would weigh even less than Meigs's initial estimate, coming in at a lean 8,909,200 pounds.[28]

Now that it was clear the Congress was fine with, and even excited about, Walter's revised dome, Meigs misleadingly informed key lawmakers that the revised dome had actually been a group effort. "I consider that in whatever credit or responsibility there is to be attached to the work hereafter, we have to share," Meigs wrote to the chairman of the House Ways and Means Committee.[29] Privately, however, he seethed that, in his opinion, Walter had done nothing more than fob the task off on one of his master draftsmen, a twenty-eight-year-old German emigrant named August Schoenborn, who could translate Walter's detailed drawings of the exterior of the dome into beautifully intricate plans for its individual parts. "[Walter] wishes to have all the credit to himself, and he will always claim all the credit of all the design of the Capitol, plans and all, I suppose, hereafter," Meigs wrote in his diary, then stated again that "the design is quite as much, if not more, mine than his."[30]

While none of that was true, Meigs might have found some satisfaction in knowing there was one important part of the Capitol project over which he could rightly claim much of the credit: its astounding assortment of art, sculpture, and interesting details. Partly, this was due to the enthusiasm of the Pierce administration, which not only supported Meigs in his use of high-quality materials but also encouraged him to hire the finest artisans he could find to decorate the place with paintings and sculptures. As he did with nearly any project, Meigs took his assignment seriously, burying himself in books, papers, and reference materials. In August 1854, he visited the Astor Library in New York City to page through a collection of color prints of Raphael's paintings on the walls of the Vatican; he noted in his journal that "this . . . will give us ideas in decorating our lobbies."[31] On the same trip, he also visited a French bookstore, where he purchased an expensive volume reproducing the art from the Palace of Versailles; he paid particular attention to the ceiling frescoes and the placement of statues and sculptures.

If Meigs had his way, then, the Capitol was going to be more stunning than any European palace. And so he would become something like an American Medici, doling out federal funds to recruit and retain painters and sculptors to beautify his building. He was almost immediately inundated with samples from hungry artists eager for a government commission, and he found painters hovering in the doorway of his Capitol office, where they would ask for just a moment of his time. Most were rejected outright; Meigs was a tough audience, with exceptionally good taste and good instincts. Neither prior reputation nor glowing recommendations would be enough to guarantee an artist a spot in the Capitol—especially if Meigs detected even the slightest whiff of controversy.

Meigs was also willing to recruit the *best* artists—not just the best *American* artists—which would lead to bruised egos, whispered insinuations about Meigs's patriotism, and grumbling from some Congressmen who didn't want American dollars being funneled to foreigners. None of that seemed to matter to Meigs or to former New York Congressman and statesman Gouverneur Kemble, a close friend and associate of Meigs from their mutual involvement with the West Point Foundry. Knowing that Meigs was determined to have murals decorating the walls and ceilings of the extensions, Kemble advised Meigs to "get an artist who has studied more in Rome."[32] Meigs promised Kemble he would keep his eyes, and his office door, open.

As it turned out, exactly the right artist had presented himself to Meigs only two years earlier. In December 1854, the physician and sculptor Horatio Stone—another friend and associate who would influence Meigs—had stopped by Meigs's office in the Capitol, accompanied by an Italian fresco artist with flyaway hair and a scraggly beard. Meigs and the painter chatted briefly in "bad French," and Meigs agreed to give the artist a tryout of sorts by permitting him to paint "a small piece . . . on a piece of fresh wall, as a sample of what he could do." Meigs pointed to the space beneath a small arch at one end of his office and asked the painter for "an allegorical painting of agriculture, supposing that the room might be occupied by the Committee on Agriculture at some future day." The artist promised to complete a fresco in the space by spring 1855 and, satisfied, left with Stone.[33] The artist "spoke very confidently of his own skill," an impressed Meigs wrote later—though he was not impressed enough to remember the artist's name, merely writing in his diary that afternoon that he had been visited by "an Italian painter named—I forget."[34]

Meigs had just met Constantino Brumidi, a Roman-educated artist who, over the next quarter century, would provide the Capitol with some of its most beautiful and memorable art.

Even in the Capitol's messy, dome-less, and still unfinished state, Brumidi could see the building had potential, both as a structure and as a national symbol. "My one ambition and my daily prayer is that I may live long enough to make beautiful the Capitol of the one country on earth in which there is liberty,"[35] he wrote—and since catching Meigs's attention in his Capitol office, Brumidi was determined to prove to both Meigs and Walter that he was exactly the artist to do it.

Brumidi stood only five foot five, with an unkempt beard, messy hair, and a seemingly perpetual impish grin—Meigs later described him more memorably as "a lively old man with a very red nose"[36]—but his rumpled appearance belied a distinguished pedigree. Born and raised in Rome, Brumidi had trained at the city's most prestigious art school, the Accademia di San Luca, starting at age thirteen. He had quickly gained a reputation as a noted painter of frescoes in a realistic style—his figures often looked as if they could step right out of the surface they were painted on—and he had so impressed officials at the Vatican that he was asked to paint the chapel at the Palazzo Torlonia. That project, a nine-hundred-square-foot fresco completed at the palazzo, led to Brumidi being hired to paint the inside of the dome at the Church of the Madonna dell'Archetto; then, in 1847, at the age of forty-two, he was commissioned to paint a portrait of the new pope, Pius IX. Admirers compared his work favorably with "the great masters of the High Renaissance."[37]

Brumidi's life was upended starting in 1848, when revolution in the

Italian states sent Pius IX scurrying from Rome to Gaeta. In 1851, amid an era of political turmoil, Brumidi was arrested and jailed—mostly on trumped-up charges involving grand larceny and kidnapping—and he was ultimately sentenced to eighteen years in prison. Fortunately for Brumidi, Pius IX was eventually restored to Rome, where he granted the artist a full pardon. A free but wary Brumidi immediately fled the country, leaving behind his wife and two children—Brumidi would maintain a relationship with his daughter but would never see his wife and son again. He arrived in the United States on September 18, 1852. Since then, he had kicked around New York and Mexico, taking commissions for portraits, before arriving at the Capitol in 1854 and paying a visit to Captain Meigs.

Now, as he walked the corridors of the new extensions, looking at the lunettes and other spaces Meigs had deliberately left empty for decorating, Brumidi was in awe of just how beautiful the Capitol building was even without a single layer of ornamental paint. It couldn't be denied that Walter had vision and Meigs had taste; even in their still unfinished state, the new House and Senate chambers were stunning, with luxuriant glass and iron ceilings letting in plenty of natural light, and walls filled with nooks and niches for statues and large panels perfect for painting. Marble work over the doorways was carved with maple leaves and grape clusters. In the vestibules leading into each chamber, Walter had defined the passageways by lining them with majestic Corinthian columns supporting an ornate marble ceiling with stained glass panels. At the top of the columns were capitals designed by Walter to resemble tobacco, corn, and magnolia leaves—an homage to Latrobe's corncob and tobacco capitals, which still graced columns just outside the Old Senate Chamber. Always a stickler for detail, Meigs had ridden on horseback to a Maryland tobacco farm to bring back real leaves for Italian sculptor Francis Vincenti to use for reference.

There was an even more striking hallway on the ground floor of the new House extension: directly beneath the House chamber, the impressive "Hall of Columns" ran more than a hundred feet, nearly the entire length of the south wing, and supported a cast-iron ceiling. There, Walter had lined the hallway with twenty-eight Corinthian columns made from marble quarried in Lee, Massachusetts, and he topped them with capitals carved to resemble thistles, corn, magnolias, and tobacco—yet another bit of American order architecture inspired by Latrobe. "The form is very graceful and beautiful," wrote an impressed Meigs. "It does not much resemble any capital which I have ever seen."[38]

Each wing also featured grand public staircases with marble steps and railings, and enormous marble Corinthian columns and pilasters topped by bronze capitals. The staircases, which were wide and well lit by skylights, had more spaces for paintings and statuary. Window and door trim throughout the extension was made of cast iron—a matter Walter and Meigs had quarreled over before—and the hallways were hung with opulent gas-lit chandeliers that illuminated even more niches, spaces, and surfaces that Brumidi thought were practically *begging* for paint.

Looking down, Brumidi could see that Meigs and Walter had even paid careful attention to the floors. While Walter and Meigs had decided that the House and Senate chambers themselves would be carpeted—mostly to repress the echo—neither of them wanted to install the kind of plain marble or stone pavers that had covered the floors of the original Capitol. Instead, the floors of the extensions would be laid with colorful, ornately patterned encaustic tiles provided by Minton, Hollins and Company of Stoke-upon-Trent in Staffordshire, England; Meigs had found them through an advertisement in *The Engineer's Journal*.[39]

All through the fall of 1855, enormous wooden boxes of tiles, each weighing nearly eleven hundred pounds, were shipped from Liverpool to New York City, where they were transported by railroad to Washington, D.C., and off-loaded at the Capitol. And to anyone concerned that Meigs was sending federal funding to companies overseas, the engineer was more than happy to explain that the tiles were inlaid with colored clay rather than the colors simply being applied to the surface, so they were extremely durable and resistant to fading or wear when walked on—and thus a bargain for taxpayers over time.

Despite the tiles' durability, the foot traffic in the building—and the general muddiness of Washington, D.C.—was bound to make them dirty. Meigs anticipated the problem by laying a new water main beneath the building—all part of his overall plan to bring water to the District via the Washington Aqueduct—and then placing along the hallways several small, shallow closets, each about thirty inches high and containing a water spigot, a drain, and just barely enough space to fill a bucket for mopping the tile floors. The easier access to water would also be useful in the event of fire, a lesson Walter and Meigs had both learned from the ineffective firefighting in the Library of Congress in 1851. Mounted to the opening of each closet was a small, arched cast-iron door, complete with a convincing-looking knob and a lock, giving the tiny closets a somewhat fairy-tale-like appearance that still intrigues and delights Capitol visitors, who feel certain that either cats or gnomes dwell behind the doors.

In short, the building was magical—and Brumidi couldn't wait to get his hands on it.

He sincerely believed the Capitol was worthy of the high art that graced the walls of some of the noblest buildings of antiquity—and he was also quite certain he was just the man for the job. "The solid construction of this National Building required a superior style of decoration in real fresco," he wrote later, "like the palaces of Augustus and Nero, the Baths of Titus and Livia at Rome, and the admired relics of the painting at Herculaneum and Pompeii."[40]

While he could discuss with ease the paintings at Herculaneum and Pompeii, Brumidi was quickly learning about his adopted home as well. Since emigrating to the United States, he had become a devoted student of its history and its heroes, closely studying portraits of American presidents and other statesmen. He already had a special appreciation for the life and character of George Washington. For his "audition" for Meigs, he had been asked to decorate the walls of Meigs's Capitol office, which would eventually be occupied by the House Committee on Agriculture. Brumidi quickly completed a fresco called *Calling of Cincinnatus from the Plow* that featured the notable Roman warrior who was reluctant to leave his farm when summoned to lead his people. It was an appropriate image to decorate the walls of the Agriculture Committee, but it was also an apt metaphor for George Washington, another leader who had put down the plow and taken up the sword for a higher cause. Meigs understood the symbolism immediately—and loved it. "Brumidi is better for our work than any painter we have,"[41] enthused Meigs, who quickly hired the artist full time, putting him to work painting hallways and stairways in the new extensions and paying him $8 a day, the highest salary permitted for Capitol employees at that time.

Walter, too, thought Brumidi was brilliant and privately confessed that the disheveled artist was "the best living artist in fresco . . . [and] one of the most amiable, and excellent and unostentatious of men."[42] Publicly, however, Walter wasn't willing to be quite as generous; in his view, Brumidi was too closely associated with Meigs, as he decorated ceilings and stairwells at Meigs's bidding without ever once stopping to consult with Walter or ask for his opinion. In his official communications, then, Walter often lashed out at the artist, chipping away at Meigs's reputation by overtly questioning the quality of Brumidi's work, even going so far as to complain that some of the rooms painted by the artist "are so extravagantly decorated with crude and disharmonious colors that it is painful to remain in them."[43] But Walter's grievances weren't actually with Brumidi; they were with Meigs and his increasingly out-of-control ego as well as with his deliberate efforts to keep the architect in the dark and out of the loop. Brumidi, who had already done jail time for being on the wrong side of a political fight, simply kept his head down and kept painting.

Not all artistic suitors who approached Meigs would be as successful as Brumidi. In late 1855, the noted American sculptor Henry Kirke Brown came to Meigs with photographs of a piece he thought would be ideal to represent "American Industry" in the still empty pediment over the House's east portico. At its center, Brown's proposal featured a female figure of America flanked by various figures of American workers, which included a depiction of an enslaved laborer. Meigs rejected it immediately; while Meigs abhorred slavery, he warned the sculptor that the politics implicit in such a depiction were too dangerous—especially with a nation on the edge of fracturing over the very issue. Brown pushed back, telling Meigs that the prominent placement of an enslaved person in the pediment would force a national debate on the issue. But Meigs told Brown that while he thought his work was "truthful," it was also too controversial.[44]

Undeterred, Brown submitted several revisions, all of which were similarly rejected by Meigs. Meigs was going to do his best to protect his project from conflict—even when it sent a message he believed in. The pediment would remain empty until August 1916, when it would be filled by the noncontroversial *Apotheosis of Democracy* by Paul Wayland Bartlett.

Meigs would have more success with artist Thomas Crawford, who had already designed the impressive *Progress of Civilization* sculpture for the pediment over the Senate's east-facing portico. Meigs had found Crawford to be a good collaborator, and now he was personally assigning the artist the important task of providing the enormous bronze statue that would be placed on the tholus—essentially a ring of columns supporting a flat roof—at the very top of Walter's dome, nearly three hundred feet off the ground.

Walter's first drawings for the dome had included a very rough sketch of a figure at the dome's apex but provided no further details apart from the height of the statue—sixteen feet—and a vague suggestion that the figure should be holding a liberty cap on the end of a pole. But what Walter wanted didn't matter all that much to Meigs, who wrote to Crawford at his studio in Rome with some ideas of his own. In his correspondence, Meigs groused that he didn't want to top the dome with yet another statue of George Washington or an embodiment of America. The best options, he suggested, were allegorical figures like Liberty or Victory—and "Liberty, I fear," Meigs wrote, "is the best we can get."[45] Crawford translated that suggestion into a piece he called "Freedom Triumphant—in Peace and War," which depicted a female figure of Freedom crowned in laurels and wheat. Crawford stood her on a squatty pedestal and placed an olive branch in her left hand as she gently rested her right on a sheathed sword.

However, once Crawford received detailed drawings and measurements of the dome, he worried that his statue was too short and started over again. This time, he sculpted a taller, slightly more willowy figure, which he draped in classical dress. Then he placed a liberty cap encircled with stars on her head as well as a wreath, a shield, and a sheathed sword in her hands. Calling this updated version "Armed Liberty," he positioned her atop a taller, tapered pedestal inscribed with "*E pluribus unum*"—Latin for "out of many, one"—the traditional motto of the United States. He then took several photos of the latest piece and mailed them to Meigs for a look. Meigs liked what he saw but suspected that Jefferson Davis would once again object to the figure wearing a liberty cap, just as he had complained about the liberty cap Crawford had placed on the figure of America in the pediment crowning the Senate's eastern portico a year earlier.

Davis's response, then, was almost entirely predictable. "As to the cap, I can only say . . . that it seems to me its history renders it inappropriate to a people who were born free and would not be enslaved," he wrote to Meigs, and suggested instead that "armed Liberty wear a helmet."[46] While Meigs had ignored Davis's suggestion to remove the liberty cap from Crawford's figure of America in the Senate's pediment, when it came to the Capitol's crowning sculpture, Meigs was more inclined to give Davis his way. Crawford dutifully adjusted his design in response to Davis's criticisms, placing on Freedom's head instead a Roman helmet encircled with stars and crowned with an eagle's head and feathers. From the ground, the plumed helmet, with Freedom's long hair trailing out from under it, is often confused for a Native headdress—a deliberate bit of misdirection by Crawford, who admitted that the design for the helmet, and the figure's fur-trimmed robe, had been "suggested by the costume of our Indian tribes."[47]

Davis approved Crawford's amended design in April 1856, and the sculptor began the process of turning his small model into a full-sized clay figure—now simply called *Freedom* or, more formally, *Statue of Freedom*—to eventually be cast in plaster in five sections for easy shipment to the United States. Meanwhile, Crawford's revised proportions on his figure—his redesign had grown Freedom from sixteen feet tall to just over nineteen feet, with the statue standing on a pedestal eighteen feet high—meant that Walter would have to slightly modify the dome to accommodate the taller and heavier pedestal and statue. Walter's revision mostly involved squashing the top of the dome down somewhat, making it more circular than oval, a happy accident that gives the dome the sturdy and generally uniform profile that still defines its silhouette.

Despite Meigs's best efforts, work on the Capitol dome and extensions would never proceed rapidly enough to please the Congress. "We went home and returned, but we saw no dome," complained Ohio Congressman Edward Ball in the spring of 1856.[48] Annoyed, Ball began to question every one of Meigs's expenditures on the building, and he wondered aloud why the Congress was spending so much money on marble mantels and tiled floors in the Capitol when there were more important tasks to invest in, like clearing the mouth of the Mississippi River for easier navigation. Mostly, though, Ball was just unhappy with the unfinished dome, which Meigs, in his earlier enthusiasm, had promised would be completed quickly and cheaply. Meigs responded in writing in his typically thorough manner, swamping members with his meticulous bookkeeping, which accounted for every dollar and every delay. It was enough to sway Illinois Senator Stephen Douglas, who vowed to give Meigs whatever funding he needed to build the grandest dome in the world.

While more funding was appreciated, what Meigs most needed was time. By the autumn of 1856, the final stones supporting Bulfinch's dome were removed by Meigs's steam-powered cranes and hauled away in wagons. With Pringle Slight's invaluable help, Bulfinch's dome had been peeled cleanly off the Rotunda and the forty-eight feet of sandstone walls below it. That left an opening three hundred feet in circumference that exposed everything below it to the elements. With winter on the way and Congress returning to session in early December, Meigs would need to cover the open Rotunda. For a moment, he considered simply stretching canvas over the opening but thought better of it once he realized that anything dropped by laborers working high up inside the dome would likely punch right through a fabric covering. Instead, Meigs ordered the construction of a temporary wooden roof with an opening in the center just large enough to poke the derrick through. It was yet another task that fell to Pringle Slight and his work crew, which now included Slight's thirty-seven-year-old son, Robert.

Although Meigs and Walter were fighting a low-level feud, for the most part they gave an outward appearance of civility—so much so that Congressman Stanton publicly, and incorrectly, declared on the floor of the House that "there is no sort of conflict between the engineer and the architect."[49] The same, however, could not be said of members of Congress. As the nation continued to skid toward civil war, Senators and Representatives often visibly and violently skirmished in their respective chambers, brandishing pistols, waving canes, and drawing blood.

Slavery and whether it would be permitted in new states entering the Union continued to be the major topics of dissent—though tempers, it seemed, could fray over nearly anything. In April 1850, Senators Henry Foote of Mississippi and Thomas Hart Benton of Missouri squabbled loudly over the enforcement of a Senate rule by the presiding officer, Vice President Millard Fillmore. Benton found the rule disrespectful to the authority of the Senate. Benton and Foote quarreled fiercely, with Benton eventually growing so angry that he advanced up the center aisle toward the much smaller Foote, only to find the Mississippian pointing a cocked pistol directly at him.

Members jumped to their feet, some shouting to the chair to call for order, others appealing to the sergeant at arms to intervene. Wisconsin Senator Henry Dodge scuffled briefly with Benton, trying to push him away from Foote—but Benton dramatically threw open his coat to show that he was unarmed. "Let him fire!" Benton shouted. "Stand out of the way and let the assassin fire!"[50] Fillmore eventually got a chaotic Senate to agree to adjourn, even as one member complained that Benton and Foote should have taken their squabble to the street, and noted, "There is plenty of room *out* of the Senate."[51]

Such scuffles aside, the floor of the Senate would also be the site of the worst assault on a sitting member of Congress in the Capitol's history—and by another sitting member, no less.

Six years after the Benton-Foote skirmish, Congress was embroiled in the fallout from the passage of the Kansas-Nebraska Act of 1854, which had overturned the Missouri Compromise's ban on slavery above of the 36-degree-30-minute line of latitude—basically anywhere north of modern-day Arkansas and Oklahoma. Instead, the Kansas-Nebraska Act embraced the concept of popular sovereignty, which permitted new states to determine for themselves whether slavery would be legal. That law had quickly led to plenty of bickering in the Congress along North-South lines and—more seriously—to a state-level civil war in the Kansas territory between pro- and antislavery factions. Both sides clashed in such violent confrontations across the region that the new territory would come to be known as "Bleeding Kansas."

Kansas was still bleeding as the first session of the Thirty-fourth Congress opened in November 1855, with both the House and the Senate convening in their old chambers while they waited—some impatiently—for Meigs and his workers to put the finishing touches on the still incomplete extensions. As members took their seats, Southerners were already warning that if the North made any effort to prohibit slavery in the Kansas and Nebraska territories, "it would be the duty of the South to take possession of the Capitol."[52]

Northerners, however, made it equally clear that they were not going to be intimidated by such Southern saber-rattling. Over two sweltering days in May 1856, Charles Sumner, a fiery first-term antislavery Senator from Massachusetts, took to the floor of the Senate for nearly five hours as he argued for Kansas to enter the Union as a free state—a position likely to provoke the ire of Southerners. But Sumner made it about more than just Southern politics; he also made it personal. With the Senate visitor gallery packed and spectators hanging on his every word, Sumner called out by name several Senate colleagues, including Stephen Douglas of Illinois and Andrew Butler of South Carolina—both of whom, said Sumner, "have raised themselves to eminence . . . in championship of human wrongs."[53] Butler in particular, said Sumner, "has chosen a mistress to whom he has made his vows, and who, though ugly to others, is always lovely to him . . . the harlot Slavery."[54] Douglas, fuming, paced at the rear of the chamber and stage-whispered to a colleague, "[T]hat damn fool is going to get himself shot by some other damn fool."[55]

It seemed likely. When Sumner's comments boomeranged across the Capitol from the Senate to the House side, Southern members reacted with palpable anger and outrage. "Mr. Sumner ought to be knocked down and his face jumped into," declared Tennessee Representative Thomas Rivers.[56] But for one Southern Congressman—thirty-six-year-old Representative Preston Brooks of South Carolina—it was more than just a matter of honor. Brooks was related to Senator Butler—a first cousin once removed—and thus any insult Sumner might hurl at Butler was regarded as a slur against Brooks and his entire extended family. Brooks was determined to do something about it.

On May 22, Brooks rounded up fellow South Carolina Representative Laurence M. Keitt and Virginian Henry Edmundson; the three of them had spent the previous evening drinking together and plotting ways to teach Sumner a lesson. Together, they stalked out of the House chamber, passed through the Rotunda—likely stepping around Meigs's scaffolding as they did so—and entered the Senate chamber. The Senate, though it had adjourned for the day, was still buzzing with members and visitors, including several Congressmen and young women. Brooks, who preferred there be no ladies present when he confronted Sumner, pointed to one particularly attractive young woman and asked Senate clerk Joseph Nicholson, "Can't you manage to get her out?"[57]

Before Nicholson could answer, Brooks began striding deliberately up the center aisle toward Sumner, who was working at his desk, unaware the South Carolinian was bearing down on him. "You have libeled my state and slandered a relative," Brooks intoned as he approached the forty-five-year-old Senator, "and I am come to punish you for it."[58]

Sumner had barely enough time to look up before Brooks raised his thick, gold-handled walking stick and brought it swiftly and repeatedly down on Sumner's head, opening at least two large gashes in his scalp and cutting him nearly to the bone. Stunned and bleeding, Sumner tried to stand up, forgetting his heavy desk and chair were anchored to the floor; all he could do was hold his hands over his head in self-defense, trying weakly to protect himself as Brooks brutally brought his cane down on Sumner's head and shoulders again and again.

Sumner eventually untangled himself from his desk and staggered into the aisle with his shirt and coat soaked in blood. "He bellowed like a calf," Brooks boasted later.[59] He continued to beat Sumner as he crawled away, still warding off Brooks's blows. Several alarmed Senators rushed over to the fracas; one of them, Senator John Crittenden of Kentucky, leapt from his seat, shouting, "Don't kill him!" But Crittenden was held at bay by Keitt, who waved his own cane menacingly and screamed, "Let them alone, God damn you!" Brooks later recalled striking Sumner at least thirty times—"until I was satisfied," he said. The assault stopped only when Brooks's walking stick finally shattered into several pieces. As New York Congressman Ambrose Murray pulled Brooks off Sumner, the dazed Sumner weakly whispered, "I could not believe such a thing was possible," and lost consciousness.[60]

A special House committee investigated the attack and recommended expulsion for Brooks and "disapprobation" of Keitt.[61] While their colleagues voted against any form of punishment, both Brooks and Keitt resigned their seats in protest, with Brooks remaining defiant and unapologetic to the very end. As he skulked out of the Capitol to return to South Carolina, he warned the Congress of impending bloodshed. In a special election a month later, South Carolinians enthusiastically voted to send him back to Congress—and then again in the regular election in November.

While Southerners clearly supported Brooks and his actions—with many approvingly mailing him new walking sticks to replace the one he had broken by smashing it against Sumner's skull—there were some who thought his choice of venue was inappropriate and ungentlemanly. "All agree that if Brooks had beaten him anywhere but *on the head & in the Senate*, he would have but served him right," observed one Southern lady as she reported on the assault.[62] Regardless of Brooks's chosen setting, in the opinion of Southerners, both Sumner and the North deserved the pummeling; Brooks had not only preserved the reputation of his kin but also defended the honor of the entire South.

To the Northern press, there was nothing honorable about any of it. A Southern Congressman assaulting a Northern Senator in the building at the very heart of the American government was democratic thuggery and a sure sign that the South was willing to spread its brutality—including chattel slavery—beyond its current borders. Writing in the *New York Courier and Enquirer*, publisher James Webb asserted that "no reasonable man should doubt that the Slave power have unalterably determined to extend the area of their now merely *local* institution; and if possible, to render it *National*."[63]

William Cullen Bryant, the powerful editor of the respected *New-York Evening Post*, also feared that conflict was inevitable now that the South had degraded democracy by making violent confrontation rather than careful deliberation the language of the Senate. "The truth is, that the Pro-Slavery part which rules the Senate looks upon violence as the proper instrument of its designs. . . . [V]iolence has now found its way into the Senate chamber. . . . In short, violence is the order of the day," he wrote. He then warned readers they could likely no longer look to their institutions to save them. "It is idle to wait for what the Senate may do—the Senate will do nothing—it never does anything on such occasions," he wrote, and then finished with a portentous warning: "[T]he people must take the matter into their own hands."[64] The editors of the *Boston Atlas* were even more blunt. "We understand perfectly well," said the *Atlas*, "that nothing would give [Southerners] more exquisite pleasure than to kill us all."[65]

Brooks hadn't killed Sumner, but he had injured him badly enough that Sumner had difficulty eating and sleeping and was perpetually in pain for the rest of his life. He wouldn't return to his duties in the Senate for nearly three years. The entire assault had lasted only a minute—but neither Sumner nor the nation would ever be the same.

In May 1856, Brooks sent a clear message: the South was done talking. Violence was inevitable—and the soul of a nation was at stake. As the nation seemed to hold its breath, awaiting a national reckoning, the Capitol sat under the darkening skies of Washington, D.C., still unfinished and very much a work in progress—just like the United States itself.

The Capitol as it appeared on the day Abraham Lincoln was inaugurated in March 1861, with the derrick and cranes constructed by Montgomery Meigs jutting up from the floor of the Rotunda through the center of the unfinished dome. It looked, noted one Congressman, "as if a cannon ball had cut it off."

Tortola-born physician William Thornton was a self-taught architect who won the national competition to design the Capitol building. Considered the first architect of the Capitol, Thornton would struggle to work with Stephen Hallet—and others—on the building's construction and worried constantly about his reputation.

The National Gallery of Art, Andrew W. Mellon Collection

Responding to the 1792 contest searching for designs for the new Capitol building, architect Étienne Sulpice Hallet submitted this drawing, which came to be called the "fancy piece." It was the front runner until George Washington received William Thornton's simpler and more elegant design.

Library of Congress, Prints and Photographs Division

This watercolor by William Birch shows the Capitol as it looked when first occupied by Congress in 1800. Only the north wing had been completed in time, forcing both legislative bodies to cram themselves into a structure meant to contain only the Senate. Tradesmen can be seen in the foreground, cutting stones as work continued.

Library of Congress, Prints and Photographs Division

The formally educated architect Benjamin Henry Latrobe was selected by President Thomas Jefferson in 1803 to oversee construction of the Capitol building. Latrobe focused on designing the new House wing and a nearly complete renovation of the Senate wing before being dismissed in 1811. He'd be rehired by James Madison in 1814 to supervise the rebuilding of the Capitol after its burning by the British.

The White House Collection

With a flair for the dramatic and an eye for details, architect Benjamin Latrobe was determined to give the Capitol its own uniquely American architecture. The corn cob capitals he designed for the Senate wing enchanted senators in 1809 and still delight visitors to the Capitol today.

Architect of the Capitol

An etching of the Capitol from its west side as it appeared prior to its burning by the British. The Senate wing, on the left, and the House wing, on the right, were connected at the middle by a covered wooden walkway.

Library of Congress

Installed in the old House chamber in 1819 was sculptor Carlo Franzoni's stunning *Car of History*, featuring Clio, the Muse of History, in a winged chariot recording the events transpiring on the House floor beneath her. Congress moved to its current wing in 1857, but Clio is still in the old chamber—now National Statuary Hall—and still keeping her eye on Capitol visitors.

Architect of the Capitol

Charles Bulfinch was Boston's premier architect when he was hired by President James Monroe in 1818 to construct the Capitol's still-unfinished wings and missing center section. The no-nonsense Bulfinch would complete the building, and top it with a copper-plated dome, in 1828.

Architect of the Capitol

This dramatic 1822 painting by Samuel F. B. Morse depicts the House of Representatives working in the lamplight of an evening session in its new chambers, as begun by Latrobe and completed by Bulfinch. While the room was awe-inspiring, its acoustics were notoriously terrible.

The National Gallery of Art, Corcoran Collection (Museum Purchase, Gallery Fund)

The pediment over the Capitol's main east entrance was conceived by President John Quincy Adams and executed by sculptor Luigi Persico. Titled *The Genius of America*, the pediment features America with an eagle at center, Justice—without her blindfold—holding the Constitution on the left, and Hope, gesturing optimistically toward America, on the right. What it all meant, only Adams seemed to know. *The Genius of America* is still over the main entrance today.

Architect of the Capitol

Sculptor Horatio Greenough's twelve-ton statue of President George Washington was originally intended for placement in the Capitol Rotunda. After its disastrous unveiling in 1841—Bulfinch snickered that the bare-chested Washington looked as if he were "entering or leaving a bath"—the statue was unceremoniously relocated to the Capitol's east lawn, then carted off to the Smithsonian.

Smithsonian American Art Museum, Transfer from the U.S. Capitol

Philadelphia architect Thomas Ustick Walter's designs for extending the Capitol dazzled President Millard Fillmore, who appointed him architect of the Capitol in 1851. Walter, seen here in this 1859 photograph, would design the additions that still define the look of the building, including its House and Senate extensions, the Rotunda, and its iconic dome.

Library of Congress, Prints and Photographs Division

After multiple fires damaged the Library of Congress, housed in the Capitol's center section, Walter designed and constructed—in a speedy eighteen months—a new and magnificent library made mostly from painted cast iron. It was, said one visitor, "the most beautiful room in the world."

Library of Congress, Prints and Photographs Division

Captain Montgomery C. Meigs was an army engineer appointed by Secretary of War Jefferson Davis in 1853 to serve as superintendent of the Capitol. President Abraham Lincoln would promote Meigs to general and appoint him as quartermaster of the U.S. Army.

Library of Congress, Prints and Photographs Division

Thomas Crawford's pediment for the eastern entrance to the Senate extension shows the figure of America at center, with the victors in Manifest Destiny on the left and its victims on the right, including a Native chief who sits with his head in his hands and a woman with her feet on a grave. Crawford's pediment is one of the few works of art depicting Manifest Destiny in the Capitol that attempts to portray the anguish of doomed Indigenous people.

Architect of the Capitol

Thomas Crawford's majestic *Statue of Freedom* was actually a second draft, after Jefferson Davis objected to the figure wearing a liberty cap, typically associated with freed slaves. Crawford next outfitted the figure in a plumed Roman helmet and fur-lined robe, deliberately suggesting "the costume of our Indian tribes." The plaster model shown here would be cast in bronze by Philip Reid, an enslaved artisan.

Library of Congress, Prints and Photographs Division, photograph by Harris and Ewing

Construction of the dome continued through the Civil War, thanks largely to the New York–based foundry of Janes, Fowler & Kirtland, who ignored a stop-work order by Meigs and continued to raise the dome without pay. As Walter later noted, the firm ensured that "the sound of the hammer [never stopped] during all of our civil war troubles."

Library of Congress, Prints and Photographs Division

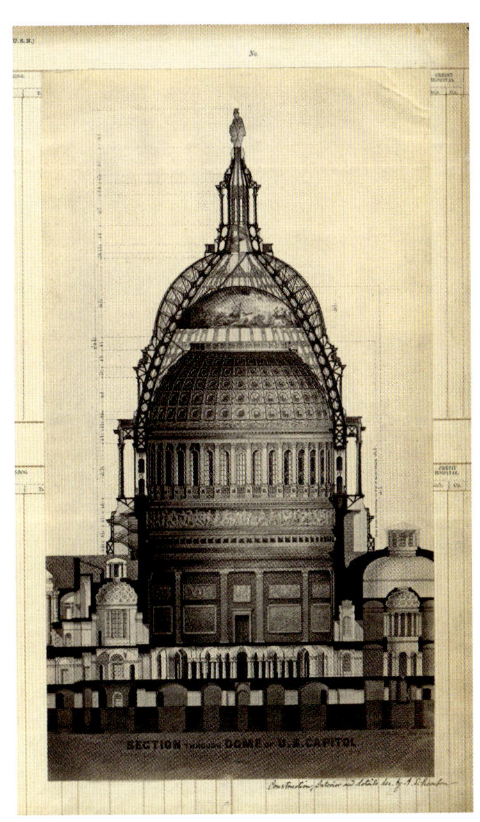

This detailed cross-section of Walter's double dome shows how the inner dome and Rotunda are nestled just inside the iron shell of the outer dome. The struts mounted to the outer wall of the Rotunda—serving as cantilevers to support the weight of the outer dome—are visible just below the window line. The cross-section also shows Constantino Brumidi's *The Apotheosis of Washington* mounted in the top of the outer dome, and the *Frieze of American History* winding its way around the Rotunda's midsection, just below the struts.

Library of Congress,
Prints and Photographs Division

Roman-born painter Constantino Brumidi was hailed as "the genius of the Capitol" for his gorgeous frescoes. Initially hired to paint committee rooms and hallways, Brumidi would be asked by Walter to provide the stunning *Apotheosis of Washington.* "My one ambition," wrote Brumidi, "is that I may live long enough to make beautiful the Capitol of the one country on earth in which there is liberty."

Library of Congress,
Prints and Photographs Division

Brumidi's gigantic mural *The Apotheosis of Washington* depicts the first president ascending to the heavens, flanked by Liberty and Victory, surrounded by maidens representing the original thirteen colonies, and encircled by six scenes representing American industries and ideals. The gigantic mural takes up more than 4,600 square feet and is visible through the oculus in the top of the inner dome, in a manner similar to the Pantheon in Paris.

Library of Congress,
Prints and Photographs Division

This photo, taken from the building's west side, captures the moment on December 2, 1863, when the final piece of Crawford's *Statue of Freedom* was bolted into place atop the dome, essentially completing construction of the Capitol.

Library of Congress,
Prints and Photographs Division

Following the resignation of Walter, the mild-mannered Edward Clark was appointed as architect of the Capitol by President Andrew Johnson—a position he would maintain for thirty-seven years and through nine presidencies. Clark's tenure would involve overseeing the landscaping and construction of the building's western terrace.

Library of Congress,
Prints and Photographs Division

Frederick Law Olmsted—shown here in 1858, around the time he was designing New York City's Central Park—was the preeminent landscape architect of the era, and the ideal artist to organize the unkempt grounds of the U.S. Capitol in 1873.

The New York Public Library, the Miriam and Ira D. Wallach Division of Art, Prints and Photographs

Olmsted's one-page landscaping plan made the Capitol itself the showpiece, ensuring the building looked striking from anywhere on the grounds.

Architect of the Capitol

This detail of the panel *William Penn and the Indians*—part of the three-hundred-foot *Frieze of American History* encircling the Rotunda—shows where artist Filippo Costaggini took over following Brumidi's death in 1880. Brumidi had completed as far as Penn's left shoe; Costaggini began by painting the three Native Americans on the right side of the panel. He would paint eight more scenes, but a miscalculation would still leave the frieze thirty-one feet short, and incomplete for another six decades.

Architect of the Capitol

A view of the west side of the Capitol, taken from the northwest, showing Olmsted's newly installed terrace encircling its base.

Library of Congress, Prints and Photographs Division

At the request of members of Congress, Elliott Woods installed an underground subway system connecting the new House and Senate office buildings with the Capitol across the street. At right is the subway as installed in 1916, a mid-century update at center, and today's sleeker enclosed train at bottom.

Library of Congress, Prints and Photographs Division, Harris and Ewing Photographs

Library of Congress, Prints and Photographs Division, *U.S. News & World Report Magazine* Collection

Architect of the Capitol

A bomb planted by German nationalist Erich Muenter rocked the Senate Reception Room in July 1915, leaving mirrors shattered, wood splintered, and the ceiling scorched. Muenter fled Washington, D.C., for New York, where he planted a similar bomb on a munitions ship and shot American financier J. P. Morgan Jr.

Library of Congress, Prints and Photographs Division

On March 1, 1854, four Puerto Rican nationalists fired more than thirty shots from the House gallery, wounding five congressmen on the House floor below. The most seriously wounded was Rep. Alvin Bentley, who is seen here being carried on a gurney down the steps of the Capitol as House page Bill Emerson screams at photographers.

United States Senate

Left: Pacifists protest on the central east steps of the Capitol in April 1917, just hours in advance of President Woodrow Wilson's address to a joint session of Congress seeking a declaration of war against Germany. That same day, Senator Henry Cabot Lodge assaulted a protestor just outside a Capitol committee room—the only known instance of a sitting member attacking a constituent in the building.

Library of Congress, Prints and Photographs Division, Harris and Ewing Photographs

In 1993, Crawford's *Statue of Freedom* was removed from the dome by helicopter and placed on the lawn of the Capitol for five months of restoration. She was ceremoniously returned to the top of the dome on October 23, 1993.

Library of Congress, Prints and Photographs Division, photograph by Carol M. Highsmith

Crawford's plaster cast for *Statue of Freedom* stands as the centerpiece of Emancipation Hall at the Capitol Visitor Center. Overflow statues from National Statuary Hall can be seen in the foreground. The visitor center provides visitors with an educational experience on the building, as well as a more rigorously controlled access.

Architect of the Capitol

Public Buildings and Grounds, was through waiting. Ball, who regularly railed against "profligate and wasteful expenditures"[1] in public projects, took to the House floor to remind his colleagues that Meigs had already promised that the dome would be completed in a year at a cost of $100,000—and in Ball's opinion, Meigs had little to show for it. The chairman suggested that it was time to move oversight of the Capitol project away from Meigs—and, indeed, away from the military altogether.

Meigs was mostly unconcerned with Ball's bluster; Meigs had allies in the Senate, including the influential Senators Lewis Cass and William Seward, who would likely oppose any effort to usurp his authority. He also had the support of the Department of War. Publicly, Meigs suggested that only his knowledge and skills as a military engineer were keeping things running as smoothly, quickly, and—as Ball must surely have appreciated—efficiently as they were. In addition, he pointed out that the modern machinery on the lawn kept work continuing almost nonstop through D.C.'s humid summers and freezing winters. The Congress rejected Ball's suggestion to remove the Capitol from Meigs's oversight—and, in a show of confidence in the engineer, appropriated not only more funding for the dome and the extension but also another $500,000 for Meigs to finish work on another pet project of his, the Washington Aqueduct. Meigs, with his ego somewhat placated, told the Congress he thought the work would likely take two more years.

But if Meigs was emboldened in this victory, he was also savvy enough to feel the political tide beginning to pull him slowly away from the shore and out to sea. President Franklin Pierce, hemorrhaging support from Democrats who found him both too weak and too strident on the issue of slavery, would not be renominated for the presidency in 1856. Instead, the party put up the relatively inoffensive James Buchanan, who soundly defeated Republican John C. Frémont and former president and Know-Nothing candidate Millard Fillmore in a three-way race.

With the departure of Pierce—and with him his secretary of war,

CHAPTER 8

A Beauty and Genuine Success

1856–1863

In early 1856, Meigs handed over the keys to the first few com rooms ready for occupancy in the new Senate extension. To the pointment of most Senators, their chambers weren't among th the moment, Meigs had six committee rooms finished on the we of the first floor; they would serve as the headquarters for th Court of Claims until the Senate could move into the new wing cally, Meigs was effusive about the completed spaces, proudly p out details like the Minton tiles on the floor and the cast-iron do window casings.

The Congress agreed that the new rooms were, indeed, gran both the Senate and the House were beginning to run out of p with Meigs and his seemingly endless empty promises. It w Meigs had his foremen and his workers busy; Pringle Slight team of forty-eight carpenters were still working on all the n doors, windows, and interior shutters, while out on the lawn, powered engines huffed and smoked as they kept Meigs's crane bricks to the rooftop, kept power drills and cutting saws roar kept marble turning for cutting and polishing. But progress w and it seemed that every year Meigs came back before the C hat in hand, to ask for more funding to complete the extens the dome.

Congressman Edward Ball of Ohio, chairman of the Com

Jefferson Davis—Meigs suddenly found himself with few friends in the administration. He could no longer lord the president's support over the heads of members of Congress or use his relationship with Davis as leverage in outmaneuvering architect Thomas U. Walter.

As Meigs scrambled to make progress on the extensions, Walter was just beginning his work on construction of the dome. Meigs's tripod footings and derrick were still in place in the Rotunda, extending up through Pringle Slight's temporary wooden covering. That was fine by Walter, as he could put Meigs's machinery to work hauling bricks from the lawn up onto the roof of the Capitol, where a team of masons began adding 26.5 feet of circular brick wall directly on top of the Rotunda's 48 feet of curved sandstone, just enough to push the Rotunda's walls up beyond the top of the Capitol's central section.

The walls of the Rotunda were now a messy hybrid of sandstone and brick—a problem Walter solved by hiding the interior face of the newly laid brick wall behind seventy-two ornamental cast-iron panels, leaving about eight feet of brick exposed above the paneling. Walter planned to cover up the remaining brick with art of some kind—perhaps a relief sculpture depicting the history of the United States. But those details would be worked out later; for now, Walter had a dome to build.

But there was a problem.

As originally drawn by Walter, the lowest level of his dome—a circular peristyle of thirty-six columns—would have been supported by a sturdy base placed directly on the roof of the Capitol, similar to the structural support provided for the dome at St. Paul's Cathedral, which Walter so admired. Doing the math, however, revealed to Walter that the Capitol's current roof and interior walls weren't sturdy enough to support the weight of the base, much less the entirety of the gigantic dome. A solution was going to require some careful engineering—meaning Walter had to consult with Meigs to find some way to evenly distribute the weight of the base and the dome. The answer? Some architectural sleight of hand.

At the suggestion of Meigs, Walter embedded thirty-six gigantic iron brackets, each weighing nearly 2.5 tons, into the outward-facing side of the Rotunda's new circular brick wall, then fanned the brackets out at regular intervals like spokes radiating from the outside of a wheel. For good measure, the brackets were bricked directly onto the wall, cementing them into its very structure. For even further stability, the wall was reinforced with iron hoops, so that the brackets were held tightly in place by a round ring of plate iron nearly two inches thick. Onto each of these brackets would then be mounted an iron column, creating the majestic lower peristyle of thirty-six columns encircling the bottom of the dome. Walter's peristyle, and his dome, wouldn't be resting directly on the bricks of the circular walls of the Rotunda, but rather on the iron brackets radiating from the walls and serving as cantilevers for the columns—and thus the dome—which eliminated the need for a load-bearing base.

To give the appearance that the dome was supported by a base on the roof of the Capitol, Walter planned to wrap the brackets in an iron skirt, concealing them from view, and then he would mold the skirt so that it resembled a circular drum. It was another bit of architectural misdirection, courtesy of Walter and Meigs; when you look up at the base of the dome today, you're still seeing their optical illusion at work. Very little, if any, of the dome's weight is carried by the drum you see at its base; it's hollow and mostly for show. The real work is being done by what you *don't* see: the thirty-six brackets mounted to the circular Rotunda walls just behind the iron facade of the faux drum.

The first tier of iron columns was manufactured by the Poole & Hunt Foundry and Machine Works in Baltimore, which regularly shipped each of the ten-thousand-pound columns to Washington by train for off-loading at the New Jersey Avenue Station about a block north of the Capitol. From there, they were moved by horse and cart up the incline of Capitol Hill and placed on the lawn of the Capitol building for assembly. Each iron column was twenty-seven feet high and hollow—both to reduce their weight and to allow the columns to be used as chimneys or drainpipes as needed—and as a cost-saving trick, the bases and capitals were simply slipped over the appropriate ends of the columns and screwed into place for safe and easy assembly before each completed column was hauled up to the peristyle.

Throughout the summer and fall of 1857, crowds regularly gathered on the lawn at the base of Capitol Hill to watch in awe as Meigs's lifting equipment slowly raised each column to its mounted bracket nearly a hundred thirty feet off the ground. Meigs, with justified pride, wrote in his annual report to Congress that it was "one of the most complicated and difficult works of engineering and architecture ever attempted."[2]

The House of Representatives officially occupied its new chambers on Wednesday, December 16, 1857, with Congressmen taking their seats at noon in front of a gallery stuffed with observers. The House floor, too, was packed; Walter had provided desks for each of the 237 members—two Congressmen had just been elected to represent the new state of Minnesota—so legislators had very little room to squeeze past one another on the floor. Few complained, however; the room was stunning to look at, and they literally had the best seats in the House to take it all in.

Meigs had placed the members' desks in semicircular rows facing the Speaker's rostrum at the front. Flanking the rostrum were life-sized portraits of George Washington, by the renowned American portrait artist John Vanderlyn, and the Marquis de Lafayette, by French artist Ary Scheffer, which Meigs had carefully removed from the old chamber and rehung in the new space. Painted on one of the enormous wall panels in the far-right corner, beyond the portrait of Lafayette, was a fresco only recently completed by Brumidi—the walls were barely dry—depicting Cornwallis surrendering to Washington. Brumidi, who had officially become an American citizen only a month earlier, inscribed the painting with "C. Brumidi Artist Citizen of the U.S."—a bit of palpable pride on the part of the artist and perhaps also an artistic thumbing of the nose at critics who complained that so much of the art in the U.S. Capitol had been put in the hands of a "foreigner."

Around the room were fifteen elegant doors through which Congressmen could enter the chamber; each was mounted in an iron frame with a clear glass transom above it and lit by bronze sconces with carved female figures holding glass globes enclosing gas-lit flames. While Carlo Franzoni's sculpture *Car of History*—which had watched over House proceedings since 1819 and kept its official time since 1837—remained in the old House chamber, Walter had designed a similarly impressive timepiece for placement over the new chamber's north central door; it featured graceful bronze figures of a backwoodsman and a Native American sculpted by Baltimore-based artist W. H. Rinehart.

The chamber was ready, presenting a gorgeous space to the Congress and the public even as, behind the scenes, Meigs and Walter continued to squabble over its acoustics, ventilation, and decorations. Walter snickered at the mixed reception to the decor—"a monstrous salon,"[3] complained former chief House clerk Benjamin B. French—and Meigs and he bickered openly during a committee hearing on the ventilation system, with Meigs doing little to endear himself to committee members by lecturing them on the science of aeration. Walter, noted Meigs with some delight, skulked out of the hearing in a "very violent" mood.[4]

And as always, Meigs agonized over who would get the credit for what he deemed a "most magnificent" chamber. He unjustly accused Walter of trying to "scratch my name from the records"[5] and repeatedly maneuvered to get the architect fired—or, barring that, plotted to smear his reputation. But with his own insecurity gnawing at him, Meigs eventually committed an unforgivable act of deception: he attempted to fabricate the official record in his favor by adding his name at the bottom of each page of Walter's original plans for the Capitol, which had been approved by President Franklin Pierce in 1853—and with which Meigs had had nothing to do. Meigs was planning to substitute the altered pages for the 1853 originals when Walter discovered the fraudulent documents and, fuming, alerted Secretary of War John Floyd of the ruse. Meigs, feigning innocence, called the accusations "preposterous"[6] and continued to insist to anyone who would listen, including President Buchanan, that Walter should be fired.

But no decision on Walter's fate would be forthcoming—not from the president, nor from the secretary of war, nor from the Congress, nor from anyone else—for there were bigger and more pressing issues to attend to than mediating a spat between Walter and Meigs.

On December 21, 1857, voters in the Kansas territory ratified the Lecompton Constitution—named for the town in which it had been drafted and signed—which protected slavery in the territory and created a bill of rights that excluded free Blacks. While Kansas voters had earlier elected a free-state majority to the Kansas House and Senate, free-state supporters had boycotted the Lecompton convention, resulting in a fraudulent election and the adoption of a proslavery document that didn't reflect the views and principles of most Kansans.

Nevertheless, in February 1858, President Buchanan—a supporter of enslavers' rights, which he believed were necessary to prevent Southern secession—submitted the Lecompton Constitution to the Congress and recommended it approve admission of Kansas to the Union as a slave state. "The President knows that the people of that territory are opposed to that Constitution, 5 to 1," thundered the editors of the Free-Soil newspaper the *Holmes County Republican*. "Justice has been violated there, frauds, outrages and murders have been committed."[7] It was perhaps little surprise that the resulting debate over the status of Kansas in the Congress would provoke not only an extended floor fight but also an actual brawl on the floor of the new chamber for the U.S. House of Representatives.

Led by proslavery members, the House took up the Kansas question on Friday, February 5, spending much of the day on detailed procedural votes—such as time-consuming motions excusing a member from voting or motions to adjourn. Antislavery members asked for the yeas and nays on each in the hope of bogging down the House and delaying resolution on the fate of Kansas. It was a slog, but members seemed willing to sit through it, chatting amiably throughout the day, with many at their desks eating dinner, smoking, spitting tobacco, and knocking out one vote after another until clerks were hoarse from calling the roll aloud. As the sun went down and the gaslights flared on in the chamber, one journalist noted that "the House is in good humor, but in great confusion" as each side waited for the other to give way.[8] By nine thirty p.m., antislavery Congressmen had so successfully gummed up the works that the Speaker informed the House it would take at least four hours to vote on all resolutions awaiting action. Members prepared for a long night.

Voting continued into the early hours of February 6, with exhausted legislators reclining on the tops of their desks or stretched across chairs, raising their heads just long enough to register their votes with the clerks; others, having managed to claim the sofas scattered around the edges of the chamber earlier in the evening, settled in for the anticipated long night of voting in relative comfort. More than a hundred spectators remained in the gallery, most sprawled out asleep on the bench seats and jerking awake only when the clerks read aloud the results of each roll call vote. A little before two a.m., however, nearly everyone sat up at the sound of Pennsylvania Republican Galusha Grow and South Carolina Democrat Laurence Keitt loudly shouting at each other.

Only moments earlier, Keitt—a notorious hothead who had been involved in the caning of Senator Charles Sumner—had taken umbrage at the Republican Grow's setting foot on the Democratic side of the House. Grow had crossed the aisle only to consult with Congressman John Hickman, a fellow Pennsylvanian who was sympathetic to the Free-Soil cause. To Keitt, that in itself was already offensive enough—the equivalent of allowing the enemy in behind allied lines. But when Grow, still standing on the Democratic side of the House, objected to a Democratic Congressman seeking recognition to speak—further delaying the already hours-long string of votes—Keitt lost his temper.

"If you are going to object, return to your own side of the House!" Kiett shouted at Grow. "You have no business over here, anyway!"[9]

"This is a free hall," Grow shot back, "and everybody has a right to be where he pleases."

Keitt jumped from his seat and moved down the aisle menacingly toward Grow. "I want to know what you mean by such an answer as that," Keitt snarled. As Grow defiantly repeated his remarks, Keitt seized him by the throat. "Sir," growled Keitt, "you are a damned Black Republican puppy!"

Grow—bearded, rangy, and known for his sometimes "bilious temperament"[10]—simply knocked Keitt's hand away. "Never mind what I am," he shot back. "No negro-driver shall crack his whip over me."[11] At that, Keitt's hand was again back at Grow's throat—and once more Grow knocked it aside, this time ramming his shoulder into Keitt and knocking him to the floor. "In an instant," reported the *Congressional Globe*, "the House was in the greatest possible confusion" as more than thirty members from both sides of the aisle immediately jumped into the fracas.

Two Wisconsin Republicans, John "Bowie Knife" Potter and Cadwallader Washburn, rushed up the aisle into a sea of Democrats, with Potter throwing punches indiscriminately. Owen Lovejoy, an Illinois abolitionist, and Lucius Lamar, a Mississippi enslaver, were in a shoving match—"pawing each other," Grow said later—and even Richard Mott, one of the body's known pacifists, jumped into the fray, swinging his fists hard enough to bloody his own knuckles, though "he afterward declared that he intervened in the interest of peace," Grow reported. Meanwhile, abolitionist Congressman John Covode grabbed the heavy spittoon from his desk and went running down the aisle looking to smash it over someone's head—then, thinking better of it, returned to his seat.

With the House in chaos, Speaker James Orr gaveled uselessly for order, then loudly instructed Adam Glossbrenner, a stocky Pennsylvanian serving as the body's sergeant at arms, to restore order or arrest the offending members. Glossbrenner dutifully grabbed the House mace—the silver-and-ebony ceremonial staff that symbolized the authority of the House of Representatives and that, under House protocol, was meant to restore order when presented before any unruly member. Glossbrenner boldly waded into the fray with the mace before him, trying to part the sea of pugnacious members by waving the House's symbolic sign of authority in their faces.

It was just then that Washburn noticed his older brother Illinois Congressman Elihu Washburne[12] tangling with another noted Democratic firebrand, the pro-secessionist Mississippian William Barksdale. Rushing to his brother's aid, the younger Washburn leapt for Barksdale, throwing a wild punch that glanced off Barksdale's forehead and knocked his dark wig onto the floor. Fighting suddenly stopped as all eyes went to the mortified Barksdale. With as much dignity as he could muster, the stocky Mississippian retrieved his hairpiece and placed it back on his head, inadvertently putting in on backward.

In that moment, said Grow, "[E]verybody nearby broke out in a loud guffaw," and order was quickly restored in the chamber. Keitt, still laid out on the floor after being hit by Grow, was helped to his feet and escorted to a side corridor where he could cool down. Around six thirty in the morning of Saturday, February 6, both Keitt and Grow took to the floor to publicly apologize to their colleagues for their conduct; shortly thereafter, Congress adjourned. They had been in session for more than nineteen straight hours.

Two months later, on April 10, 1858, the House and Senate agreed to admit Kansas to the Union as a slave state, but only if the proslavery Lecompton Constitution was ratified by Kansans by popular vote. Before the year was over, Kansans overwhelmingly rejected the Lecompton Constitution in favor of an antislavery platform. When Kansas entered the Union just over two years later in January 1861, it would do so as a free state. With that, the steady march toward civil war broke into a sprint.

Meigs and Walter were barely speaking to each other. In a snit, Meigs moved out of the Capitol office the two men shared and relocated to offices over a delivery company on A Street. Walter, glad to be free of the superintendent, headed for several comfortable rooms on the third floor of the Capitol's central section. Besides being closer to the work underway on the dome, the new rooms were also fireproof and lockable. Walter could now take comfort in the knowledge that his drawings were safe from fire as well as from further "mutilations" by Meigs.[13]

Walter also continued to engage in a whispering campaign against Meigs, complaining to Secretary Floyd and other influential Congressmen about Meigs's tastes in decor. Many members were inclined to agree; Virginia's Muscoe Garnett griped that the opulent art Meigs had commissioned had turned the House chamber into a "sarcophagus for the living"[14]—and he proposed prohibiting any further expenditures for art in the building unless approved by a commission of artists appointed by the president or Congress. For several weeks, members derided the art on the chamber walls directly in front of them or complained about the colors decorating the ceiling over their heads. Eventually, in June 1858, the Congress sent to President Buchanan a bill prohibiting funding from being spent on any new works of art unless approved by an art commission composed of three members appointed by the president.

Walter had won the day; in retaliation, Meigs fired one of Walter's best draftsmen. Things were getting petty.

And yet, even with Meigs and Walter clawing at each other, the work always continued. The iron columns of the dome's first colonnade were in place by summer, mounted firmly to their brackets on the Rotunda's outer wall. Working at heights was already presenting a problem for Meigs's workers—acrophobia was a very real issue—and construction had only just started; there were still more than a hundred fifty feet of dome remaining to be built. Meigs reported to the Congress that many in his crew were having difficulty standing upright as they scaled even the lowest parts of the new dome, slowing work down significantly.

Meigs also updated the Congress on work that was underway on a project that had been on the books since May 1855: a set of large bronze doors depicting the life of Christopher Columbus that Meigs had ordered from the American sculptor Randolph Rogers. Meigs had big plans for the Columbus doors, as he intended to use them at the main entrance to the center section, a showcase piece that visitors to the Capitol would pass through as they entered the Rotunda from the central east portico. Rogers, who had been modeling the doors in a workshop in Italy, promised Meigs that they were nearly complete and would soon be sent to an American foundry for casting and delivery.

Finally, Meigs informed the Congress that he had every intention of having the Senate's new chamber ready for them to occupy when the next session of Congress began in December 1858—but added testily that if the space wasn't ready, they should take it up with Walter. The architect, who was fed up with Meigs, was ready to resign. "I am under, probably, the most tyrannical, despotic, vain, and unscrupulous man the world ever saw," Walter complained to a Pennsylvania friend. "I have refused to speak to him for months past. . . . I am daily looking for his removal, and if it don't [*sic*] come soon, I shall go myself."[15]

However, the Congress—and particularly the Senate—wasn't interested in such ultimatums, nor did they care who was to blame for any delays on completing the dome or sculpting the fancy new bronze doors. At this point, they simply wanted their chamber finished. Running out of patience, the Senate—still conducting business in its old chambers in December 1858—passed a resolution insisting that its new hall be ready for occupancy by January 4, 1859.

Meigs, with the message received, worked all through Christmas 1858 and New Year's Day 1859, trying to make sure he could meet the Senate's own ultimatum, even moving his own desk into the chamber to serve as a center of operations as the space was completed. Over the week, Meigs stage-managed the installation of the carpets and arranged the desks and chairs from the old chamber in the familiar semicircular pattern facing the podium. As he had done with the House chamber, he personally checked the acoustics in the room and confirmed to his satisfaction that the ventilation system would keep members warm when they convened on January 4.

On the morning of January 3—a clear but chilly Monday—Meigs started his day at the Washington Aqueduct, still under construction but more and more operational every day. On this particular morning, Meigs opened a reservoir that would start water flowing to the grounds of the Capitol—a trip that would take several hours for the water to make as it filled the newly laid pipes en route to the Capitol. After opening the reservoir, a giddy Meigs returned home and took a carriage to Capitol Hill to continue his work inside the new Senate chamber. Around two thirty p.m., as he was still scooting desks around the Senate floor, he received word that the water was at last arriving at the Capitol building. Meigs headed for the Library of Congress in the Capitol's center section and looked out the tall western windows toward the enormous fountain he had constructed at the base of Capitol Hill. As Meigs watched, the fountain burbled to life, erupting into "a magnificent column of water" thirty feet high.[16]

Meigs was delighted—not only with the fountain but with what it symbolized. "This city will forever after have a sufficient supply of water for safety, health and comfort," Meigs wrote in his journal. "No more shall the houses of the poor burn in flames for want of the means to extinguish them. And the poor and the servant will now be relieved of the unhealthy labor of carrying water from the pumps through the snowed-up streets of winter."

Thanks to Montgomery C. Meigs, clean water had at last come to the Capitol—and to Washington, D.C.

Thomas Walter pushed his way into the Old Senate Chamber shortly after noon on January 4, 1859, just in time to hear the session's opening prayer. A crowd had gathered to watch the Senate solemnly vacate their old chamber and take possession of their new one; the onlookers not only filled the galleries of both chambers to capacity but also stood several deep along the hallways winding from the old chamber to the new extension. After conducting morning business and listening to Vice President John C. Breckinridge deliver what Meigs remembered as the "the most eloquent oration I ever heard,"[17] the United States Senate bid farewell to the elegant but cozy chamber that had served as its home since 1819. "This place, which has known us so long," said Senator John Crittenden of Kentucky solemnly, "is to know us no more forever as a Senate."[18]

With that, the entire Senate, led by Vice President Breckinridge, made its way in a dignified procession to its new chamber, where sixty-four desks, carefully arranged in a semicircle by Meigs, were awaiting members. Visitor galleries overlooked the chamber on all four of its sides, providing seating for six hundred, with separate seating areas for ladies, gentlemen, guests, staff, and diplomats. After the members had settled at their desks, the Senate chaplain led the body in another prayer, and the United States Senate officially began conducting business in its new home. It was a tasteful ceremony, a combination of reflection and celebration and one Walter thought "most beautiful and appropriate."

As beautiful as the ceremony was, the chamber itself was not overly decorated—and deliberately so. In the wake of the complaints about the decor in the House chamber—"I desire very much that kind of thing may be kept out of the Senate," groused Vermont Senator Jacob Collamer—the Senate chamber would be positively subdued. The overhead skylights, with their stained glass images depicting representations of Industry and Agriculture, were the most colorful part of the space. The walls, though tastefully divided into sections by pilasters and wall panels, were left plain, without any real decorations or paintings to be found; in fact, in 1884, the Senate would codify its artistic preferences by unanimously approving a policy specifying that "no paintings or portraits be placed upon the walls in the Senate chamber."[19]

The distaste for decorations and clutter even made it difficult to find just the right spot for the stately Ohio Clock, Thomas Voigt's reliable and already iconic eleven-foot mahogany clock, which had kept time in the old chamber since 1819. Isaac Bassett, a beloved assistant doorkeeper who had been serving as a Senate employee since 1831 when he was twelve years old, eventually scooted the clock to a spot just outside the south entrance to the chamber. It's still there today, usually in the background of countless Senatorial press conferences.

Apart from the ornamental skylights in the ceiling, then, the only real decor in the Senate, as decided by an 1886 resolution, would be busts of vice presidents—whose primary Senate duty is still to preside over the body and cast any needed tiebreaking votes. Today, tastefully displayed at regular intervals in niches in the chamber walls, busts of twenty of the first twenty-one vice presidents stare down toward the floor of the Senate;[20] the rest can be found in the second-floor corridors of the Senate wing, just outside the Senate chamber, their numbers slowly growing with each passing administration.

To the delight of members who had requested more opportunities for privacy, Walter and Meigs had provided cloakrooms directly behind the chamber, giving Senators space just off the floor to confer in private without interrupting or talking over floor debate. Compared with its House counterpart, the Senate chamber has a smaller footprint: the House chamber stretches to nearly thirteen thousand square feet while the Senate takes up just over nine thousand—and Walter had put the extra space surrounding the chamber to good use. As members came off the Senate floor, they would find their new wing filled with reception rooms, meeting rooms, and offices. Walter had even included a much-desired official space for the vice president's use just off the northeast corner of the Senate chamber—today, it's room S-214 on the second floor of the Capitol, accessible by crossing a private hallway that runs the length of the north side of the Senate chamber.

It was in this relatively modest room—it would be more sumptuously decorated by William McKinley's first vice president, Garret Hobart, in the late nineteenth century—that Ulysses S. Grant's ailing vice president, Henry Wilson, would die of complications from a stroke in November 1875. In 1881, Vice President Chester A. Arthur would take the oath of office in here after the assassination of President James Garfield. And in 1919, Vice President Thomas Marshall would sit at the room's enormous double-pedestal mahogany desk to sign the Constitutional amendment formally granting national suffrage to women.[21]

Walter had also taken to heart a suggestion made by George Washington nearly seventy years earlier, when the first president had requested a room in the Capitol "for the joint business of the President and the Senate."[22] Walter set aside an office for the president—designated as room S-216 on today's official maps of the Capitol—just off the northwest corner of the Senate chamber. Meigs had worked to ensure that the room would be worthy—at least in his determination—of the office of the chief executive. The floors were covered by the same sturdy Minton tiles that the engineer had so carefully selected for much of the new extensions, and he had asked Brumidi to paint the ceiling and the walls with his usual vibrant colors. The artist had responded with an Americanized version of a Vatican ceiling, with beautiful frescoes featuring notable figures like George Washington, Christopher Columbus, and Amerigo Vespucci as well as allegorical figures representing Executive Authority and Liberty. It was the closest the artist was going to get to having his work featured in the Senate chambers, where decorative painting had been banned by Congressional decree.

Starting with James Buchanan, presidents would regularly use the office to sign bills approved in the last moments of a Congressional session as well as to confer with Senators on their advise-and-consent duties for treaties or executive nominees. In 1965, long after presidents had opted to sign bills at the White House instead of in the Capitol, President Lyndon Johnson chose to sign the historic Voting Rights Act, prohibiting discrimination at the polls, in the President's Room.

Placed directly between these two rooms was a narrow, enclosed space, somewhat crowded with four majestic columns, that would come to be called the Marble Room because of its ceiling of veined Italian marble and walls of dark Tennessee marble. Originally intended as a stylish reception room to be used by the president or vice president to receive guests, the space served as a public meeting room—it would be occupied by suffragist protestors in 1896—and as a lounge before being formally taken over by the Senate in 1921. At that time, a new Senate rule officially designated the room as part of the Senate chamber, which made it accessible only to members and closed it off for good to the public and—for a while at least—even to spouses. The space, designated today as S-215, is still reserved for use only by Senators and their authorized guests.

Benjamin French, normally a cynic, admitted he liked the Senate's new chamber, though the room certainly had its share of problems. The flat glass skylight ceiling, while dramatic, tended to upset the room's acoustics, bouncing sounds straight down and making it difficult to hear debate. Any heavy rain on the skylight also echoed so loudly throughout the chamber that the Senate would often recess rather than try to talk over the din. And while Meigs noted proudly that "the air was pure,"[23]

French disagreed, saying the Senate chamber resembled nothing more than "a cellar ventilated by a furnace blower."[24]

Meigs's ventilation system aside, the new chamber was an overwhelming success both with the public and with the critics who mattered most: the members of the Senate. Walter proudly noted that as he mingled with members on that first day, "scores of Senators congratulated me—some who I did not know."[25] For once, Meigs didn't seem bothered that Walter was getting the credit he might have thought was rightly his; the engineer was too busy soaking up the accolades for his fountain at the base of Capitol Hill, now spraying a jet of water more than sixty feet into the air—a sight that the local newspapers had called "the most beautiful thing in Washington."[26]

Freedom had come at last to the Capitol—though really it was sheer good luck she ever made it at all.

Standing slightly more than nineteen feet tall and made from plaster, sculptor Thomas Crawford's *Statute of Freedom* had been disassembled into five pieces and packed into several large crates in Rome by Crawford's widow, following the artist's death in late 1857. In the spring of 1858, the crates had been loaded onto a small and shaky sailing vessel bound for the United States and had only just started on what would normally have been a two-month voyage when the ship sprang a leak and had to divert to Gibraltar for repairs. After being fixed, the ship set out once more, only to begin leaking again, this time taking on water so rapidly that the crew began throwing cargo overboard to lighten the ship—though fortunately none of the crates containing *Freedom* were given the heave-ho. The ship managed to limp to Bermuda, where the boat was dry-docked and its remaining cargo put in storage until new transportation could be arranged. With Meigs nervously tracking the statue's progress, half of the crates arrived in New York in December 1858, with the rest finally making it to Washington in March 1859.

That summer, Meigs had the crates containing the five sections of *Freedom* carefully unpacked in the old House chamber—at this point still used mostly for storage. There, they were so carefully and skillfully reassembled by an Italian sculptor that it was impossible to see the seams between the five sections. Even in plaster, the statue was heavy—so heavy, in fact, that Meigs worried it might collapse the floor. And so he would have the statue carted out to the eastern lawn of the Capitol, where it was displayed next to Horatio Greenough's enormous and unceremoniously abandoned statue of the shirtless George Washington. It was a temporary solution anyway; sometime over the next year, the plaster statue was due to be cast in bronze in preparation for its move to the top of the dome.

With the bulk of the work completed on the new extensions—or at least enough to keep the Congress happy—Walter turned his attention back to the dome, which he was constantly rethinking and revising. He had already adjusted the height and shape of the dome's exterior to accommodate Crawford's unexpectedly taller *Freedom* statue—and as he looked at the size of the plaster model on the east lawn, he was confident that had been the right decision. Now he was more closely studying the dome's interior, where he was still intending to carry out a double dome, nesting a slightly smaller dome just inside the larger exterior one, similar to the one constructed by architect Jacques-Germain Soufflot in the Pantheon in Paris. But as Walter considered the proportions of his own Capitol dome, he decided he was going to take Soufflot's work at the Pantheon even more to heart.

Walter decided that visitors would no longer look up from the floor of the Rotunda to peer through a high central oculus that simply opened onto the dome's external skeleton and top lantern. Instead, the architect had something much more dramatic in mind. In a manner similar to what Soufflot had done in Paris, Walter designed his domes so that visitors to the Capitol could look up through the inner oculus at an enormous painting on the inner surface of the outer dome depicting . . . well, Walter wasn't quite sure yet. But he knew he wanted it grand and inspiring and heroic, similar to Antoine-Jean Gros's fresco of the apotheosis of St. Genevieve, the patron saint of Paris, visible through the oculus in the Pantheon. It would also need to be big—big enough to be seen from the floor of the Rotunda a hundred eighty feet below.

Walter diligently drew up plans for the new double dome, sketching out the fresco that would be visible through the eye of the inner dome as well as a sculpted frieze depicting a history of the United States that he envisioned in the space just below the line where the dome met the Rotunda—the belt of still-exposed brick about eight feet high that ran around the full three-hundred-foot circumference of the Rotunda. Walter didn't bother informing Meigs of any of his changes or the artwork he was envisioning; instead, they were simply filed away in his Capitol office—a place Meigs stubbornly refused to set foot.

In fact, most of the work on the Capitol had ground to a halt that autumn for that very reason; to oversee work and bid out contracts, Meigs needed Walter's architectural drawings, which remained secured in Walter's office—and Meigs, his ego still smarting, had no intention of going to Walter's office to ask for them. As far as Meigs was concerned, he was Walter's supervisor—which wasn't true—and therefore, Walter should have brought the drawings to him. Walter had no intention of doing so—and, in fact, he intended to push Meigs's buttons in another way. As Walter put the finishing touches on his latest drawings of the dome, he submitted payment vouchers for his draftsmen to Meigs. Likely knowing that doing so would annoy Meigs, Walter signed his name with the title "Architect of the New Dome."

The signature had the desired effect; Meigs erupted in anger and refused to honor Walter's vouchers, informing the architect that he had *no idea* Walter had been given such a lofty title. Secretary of War Floyd, tiring of the squabbling, ordered Meigs to make the payments—but Meigs insisted he would do no such thing until the secretary of war himself produced the paperwork officially bestowing on Walter his new title. Meigs would eventually pay the vouchers, but Walter had clearly gotten under Meigs's skin—and Meigs was dangerously testing the patience of Secretary Floyd.

Meigs's ego—and his annoyance with Walter—would soon cost him his job. In November 1859, acting Secretary of War William Drinkard presented Meigs with several unpaid invoices from a contractor who had laid the granite at the new post office—another project on which Walter and Meigs were working in uneasy tandem as architect and supervising engineer. Meigs tartly explained to Drinkard that he hadn't paid those particular bills because he didn't have access to Walter's drawings of the post office and therefore had no way of knowing exactly how much granite had actually been required for the work. If Drinkard wanted to ensure the invoices were accurate, Meigs explained, he would need to check Walter's drawings himself.

Drinkard, keeping his temper in check, calmly instructed Meigs to simply *go to Walter's office*, look at the drawings, and pay the invoices. Meigs, perhaps feeling the acting secretary was being condescending, fired back a missive dripping with attitude. "I am as capable of understanding a written order of the Secretary of War as the chief clerk or the acting secretary," he wrote, pithily reminding Drinkard that he was merely the *acting* secretary of war.[27]

That was the end for Meigs. On November 1, 1859, citing "glaring insubordination," Secretary of War John B. Floyd relieved Montgomery C. Meigs of his duties as engineer in charge of the construction of the post office extensions and the U.S. Capitol, though he would still have oversight over his beloved aqueduct. Floyd replaced him with the less prickly Captain William B. Franklin from the U.S. Army Corps of Topographical Engineers.

Meigs would never quite see how his own stubbornness and ego had tripped him up with Floyd. In his private journal, he wrote angrily that he had "been foully wronged by this Secretary," but he was careful to note, "I have not sought revenge."[28]

The next day, he gathered his work crew in the newly finished Senate

Reception Room—a beautifully decorated space just east of the Senate chamber—and bid everyone farewell. "Strong men looked upon me with moistened eyes," wrote Meigs, who became so emotional that he couldn't read his own prepared remarks. After choking out his goodbyes, he exited the Capitol with his replacement, Captain Franklin, and led him on a tour of the Capitol grounds and the workshops. Then, wrote Meigs, "we drove home."[29]

With that, Montgomery Meigs was gone, officially off the Capitol project and out of Walter's way.

It wasn't the last Thomas Walter would see of him.

While Captain William Buel Franklin was new to the U.S. Capitol project, he was well acquainted with the United States Congress. His great-grandfather, the Pennsylvania architect Samuel Rhoads, had been a delegate to the First Continental Congress in 1774; his father, the noted lawyer Walter S. Franklin, had served as clerk of the House of Representatives from 1833 to 1838, primarily under Speaker James K. Polk. Politics, it seemed, was in Franklin's blood.

William Franklin's own talents and interests, however, took him not into politics but into the military—and after his appointment to the U.S. Military Academy by then Senator James Buchanan in 1839, Franklin had graduated first in his class and been recruited to join the elite Corps of Topographical Engineers, which was devoted to mapping and the construction of federal civil works. Following his service as a surveyor in the Great Lakes region and in the Rocky Mountains—as well as a brief stint serving in the Mexican-American War—Franklin arrived in Washington in 1857 to serve as the Army engineer secretary of the Light House Board, overseeing lighthouses along the Atlantic Seaboard. Two years later, with a reputation as an amenable mediator, Franklin found himself in charge of the U.S. Capitol.

Walter was delighted with the change in leadership. "He is kind, affable, gentlemanly, liberal in his views," Walter wrote after his first meeting with Franklin. "Our interview was cordial and perfectly agreeable and satisfactory in every particular—What a contrast with the scamp that preceded him!"[30] With Meigs out of the way, the drawings that had been stored away in Walter's office were suddenly readily available for review, which meant that invoices could be paid and work on the dome could continue.

At this point, much of the remaining work involved construction of the shell—the white iron pieces that formed the gentle curve of the dome. Janes, Beebe & Company, now operating as Janes, Fowler & Kirtland Company, had started the job, and was still under contract to provide much of the ironwork for the dome. The New York–based company suggested that it should be permitted to provide *all* of the remaining ironwork, explaining that the overall design and construction of the dome "is so dependent, the one part on the other, that it forms a whole that cannot well be divided."[31] The company proposed a reasonable price per pound of iron, and Walter, Captain Franklin, and Secretary Floyd were all inclined to accept it.

The only dissent came from Meigs—still in Washington, D.C., to oversee the aqueduct and still keeping an unofficial eye on the Capitol. Meigs rightly pointed out that it was likely illegal, and definitely unfair, to give Janes, Fowler & Kirtland Company such a contract without putting it up for bid. But opening the contract to competing offers meant delaying the work—and with Congress now grumbling about the unfinished dome gaping up at the skies over D.C., Franklin was anxious to finish it as quickly as possible. Walter managed to get Janes, Fowler & Kirtland Company to throw in the costs of the scaffolding and hoisting for the project, sweetening the deal enough to tamp down any possible opposition to the unconventional business arrangement. That was good enough for Secretary Floyd, who signed the contract with Janes on February 15, 1860.

With the engineer in his corner—a luxury Walter had rarely, if ever, had with Meigs—he worked closely with the Janes, Fowler & Kirtland crew, monitoring their progress and advocating for them with Franklin and others to ensure they had everything they needed to get the job done quickly and safely. Sometimes, that meant finger wagging and pleading with Janes to hire more workers when they seemed to be slowing down. "I sincerely wish you would *greatly* increase your force on the Dome," Walter wrote the company in early 1860, "—you are suffering in public estimation by the slowness with which the work goes on."[32]

The departure of Meigs had also removed a major impediment in the relationship between Walter and Brumidi, with Walter now going out of his way to publicly compliment the artist—something he had never dared do with Meigs around. And now Walter began talking with Brumidi about having the artist work on the gigantic painting that he had envisioned for the ceiling of the Rotunda, which would be visible through the central oculus. Walter explained that he had been inspired by Gros's *Apotheosis of St. Genevieve* at Soufflot's Pantheon, and that he wanted the subject to be the apotheosis of George Washington—literally the elevation of Washington to divinity or at least to an ideal. As far as Walter was concerned, Brumidi—who had painted several large frescoes while living in Italy—was the perfect artist for the job.

There was more. Walter also asked Brumidi to begin designing the frieze for the space he had left in the upper walls of the Rotunda. He imagined that in the eight-foot-tall "belt" encircling the Rotunda just below the dome, there might be a depiction of the history of the United States illustrated through a painted fresco that would give the illusion of being sculpted relief, which was just the kind of artistic magic at which Brumidi excelled. Brumidi prepared a sketch tracing America's history from Columbus through the Revolutionary War to what he considered the most important current major event: the California Gold Rush of the late 1840s. But a lack of funding—and the Civil War—would interrupt his progress; in fact, Brumidi wouldn't begin working on the frieze for another eighteen years.

Despite the progress being made on the extensions and the dome, Congress still found plenty to complain about. First, the Senate was upset about their new chamber's relatively poor lighting. Senator John Hale of New Hampshire went so far as to suggest that the Senate relocate to the three rooms just north of the chamber currently taken up by the Marble Room and the president's and vice president's offices, all of which had large windows in their north walls. There was a general nodding of heads that the chamber *could* stand to be better lit, but when Hale's proposal to reconfigure the three rooms across the hall was put to a vote, it received only nine votes in favor. The Senate preferred its more spacious, if inconsistently lit, chamber.

More successful was the motion by Senator Jesse D. Bright of Indiana, who offered an amendment to convert the Old Senate Chamber into a space for use by the Supreme Court and to turn the court's current chamber on the Capitol's lower level into a law library. After lengthy discussion about the potential costs of the project, the Senate eventually agreed to the recommendation on a vote of twenty-two to seventeen, officially giving the Supreme Court a new and slightly more spacious home.

And so, in what was now the Old Senate Chamber, the terraced floors that had elevated the three rows of Senators' desks would be replaced, the visitor gallery would be removed, and a long bench for the nine justices—a number that would fluctuate slightly over the next nine years—would replace the canopied rostrum at the front of the room formerly occupied by the vice president. Meanwhile, the court's rapidly growing law library was moved into what was now dubbed the Old Supreme Court Chamber, providing a quiet place to read and study in a space that might or might not have still been haunted by the ghost of poor John Lenthall. The court and the library would remain in their new locations in the Capitol from 1860 until 1935, when both moved into the new Supreme Court building, constructed directly across the street just east of the Capitol.

★★★

By June 1860, Captain Franklin was ready to remove Crawford's plaster *Statue of Freedom* from the east lawn and take it to the foundry owned by self-taught sculptor Clark Mills for casting in bronze. Mills's foundry, just inside the D.C. border near Bladensburg, Maryland, was regarded as the finest in the nation after his work on the gigantic equestrian statue of Andrew Jackson—the first bronze statue cast in the United States, which still sits at the center of Lafayette Square just north of the White House. For *Freedom*, Secretary Floyd agreed to have the federal government rent the foundry, pay Mills a monthly salary, and cover all expenses associated with its casting.

Part of those expenses was for services performed by a remarkable enslaved worker named Philip Reid, whom Mills had purchased in Charleston, South Carolina, when Reid "was quite a youth," recalled Mills. Observing him at work, the foundryman and sculptor could see that Reid had considerable skills he was willing to pay for, later writing that "because of his evident talent for the business in which your petitioner was engaged . . . [I] paid twelve hundred dollars for him."[33] Mills brought Reid to Washington with him in the late 1840s, when Reid was around thirty years old, and he relied heavily on Reid's services in casting, moving, and assembling the statue of Andrew Jackson for Lafayette Square. In 1860, Reid was still working in Mills's foundry, where he was the only enslaved laborer assigned to the big job of casting in bronze Crawford's *Statue of Freedom*.

Reid's skills and experience were invaluable and were put to good use almost immediately. To transport the statue required disassembling its five sections, but the sculptor who had put the plaster pieces together so tightly on their arrival at the Capitol that their seams were invisible now informed Mills that there would be an additional cost for him to take them apart. Waving off such artistic extortion, Reid figured out that if he suspended *Freedom* from a cable looped through a hook in her helmet, the statue would slowly pull itself apart under its own weight, revealing the separations between the pieces.

Once *Freedom* was disassembled and moved to the foundry, it was Reid who would supervise the careful casting of each piece into bronze, working most weeks without a break. From time to time, Walter and Franklin would climb into a carriage and ride together out to the foundry to check on *Freedom*'s progress and to watch Reid work. Bronze casting was, and is, a time-consuming process requiring a skilled and patient craftsman who was part metallurgist and part artist. Reid was all of the above—and Franklin and Walter agreed with Mills's assessment that Reid was "smart in mind, [and] a good workman in a foundry." Ironically, *Freedom*'s fate had been put in the highly skilled hands of the enslaved and oppressed.[34]

This issue of slavery, in fact, was very much on the American mind throughout most of 1860 as one of the defining issues in the race for the presidency. President James Buchanan—ineffective, indecisive, and exhausted—had vowed to serve only one term, and he was glad to be done with it; over the last four years, the country had become increasingly fractured, largely over the matter of extending slavery into new states and territories, and Southern states were turning up the volume on their calls for leaving the Union entirely.

Vying for the presidency in the 1860 election were two Democrats, one member of the upstart Constitutional Union party, and a former one-term Illinois Republican Congressman named Abraham Lincoln. On the issue of slavery—to many, the only issue that truly mattered—Lincoln, in the name of preserving the Union, had vowed to *contain* slavery, limiting it to only the states where it was currently practiced; he had not promised to *abolish* it. On the other hand, his closest rivals—former Democratic Vice President John Breckinridge and Senator Stephen Douglas—either openly supported slavery or embraced the concept of popular sovereignty.

On November 6—Election Day—Captain Franklin made his annual

report to the Congress, updating them on the building's progress over the last year. He acknowledged that work had proceeded slowly, pending funding from the Congress, but noted progress where he could: the foundations for several exterior arcades and porticos had been laid, work on most of the major stairways was underway, plastering was finished in all the committee rooms, and Rogers's bronze Columbus doors were nearly done. He also estimated that if money didn't run out, he felt certain the building could be completed by June 1863. While it would happen too late to get a mention in his end-of-the-year report, Franklin would also miss the guidance and experience of the versatile master carpenter Pringle Slight, who would die on November 27 at the age of seventy. The informal keeper of Bulfinch's copper dome had worked in the building for nearly half his life.

After making his report to Congress, Captain William B. Franklin—a lifelong Democrat but one who had grown disenchanted with the grift and corruption of the Buchanan administration—crossed party lines to cast his vote in the 1860 presidential election for Republican Abraham Lincoln.[35] So did enough other anti-secessionist Democrats—and Republicans and Constitutional Unionists—that Lincoln was elected the sixteenth president of the United States.

He had done so without carrying a single Southern state—and stunned Southerners responded by screaming even louder for secession. On December 20, following a brief state convention, South Carolina left the Union. That same day, on the grounds of the Capitol, one of the marble column shafts being shaped for placement on the building suddenly split. Walter was convinced it was an omen, writing that the column "went for *Secession*."[36]

Between the date of Lincoln's election and his inauguration on March 4, 1861, seven states seceded from the Union, including Jefferson Davis's home state of Mississippi. On January 21, 1861—a day he called "the saddest day of my life"[37]—Davis resigned from the Senate and went home. Two weeks later, he was elected president of the Confederacy. The man who had done so much to shape the Capitol building—to ensure it reflected the American character as well as the nation's potential for global prominence—now stood in direct defiance of the very government it represented.

Walter watched events unfold with dread and uncertainty. While he didn't consider himself pro-South, he wasn't necessarily a hardcore Union man either—and, in fact, based on newly uncovered records, Walter might have owned at least one enslaved worker who divided his time between working for Walter in D.C. and his family in Pennsylvania.[38] Slavery was still legal in Washington, D.C.—indeed, chained enslaved Africans were openly marched down Pennsylvania Avenue and South Capitol Street within plain sight of the Capitol—and Walter's own views on slavery seem to have been mostly ambivalent. As far as he was concerned, there was more than enough blame to go around for the current political divide. "I want to get away from this place," he wrote to a colleague. "I hate politicians of *every* stripe with a perfect hatred. . . . I very much fear that while we live in this country we are destined to live in the midst of its tumults and its broils wherever we may go."[39] For the moment, Walter would remain in Washington, but he was looking for any excuse to leave.

President Buchanan very nearly gave him one. Now in the final months of his presidency, Buchanan began a slow purge of secessionists in his cabinet, which included Walter's boss, Secretary of War John Floyd. Buchanan replaced him with his postmaster general, the pro-Union Republican Joseph Holt, who immediately appointed a trustworthy engineer to be the new head of the Capitol project—a Southern-born military man who had stayed loyal to the Union: Montgomery C. Meigs. The engineer practically wept tears of joy. "If God spared my life, I should place the Statue of American Freedom upon the Dome of the Capitol," he wrote.[40]

Meigs was back.

Walter, grumbling, went to pay his respects. Meigs "looked daggers at me," Walter reported, "and gave a grunt, gnashing his teeth."[41] Soon after, Meigs fired Walter, smugly notifying the architect that he had "the honor to inform you that your services are dispensed with." But Walter again reminded Meigs that he was a presidential appointee who couldn't be dismissed by a mere military captain. Walter would stay—and refuse to recognize Meigs's authority.[42] Their relationship was as toxic as ever.

On March 4, 1861, Abraham Lincoln was sworn in as president of the United States. The ceremony took place on the steps of the Capitol's central east portico, with the east lawn overflowing with spectators and fans who had come to see "the rail-splitter," as the press often called him, take the oath of office in person. As Lincoln was sworn in, the dome loomed overhead, barely complete beyond its first circular colonnade, with wooden derricks and struts still crawling its sides. It looked, noted Congressman Galusha Grow, "as if a cannon ball had cut it off."[43]

In his inaugural speech, Lincoln pled with both North and South to remember, "We are not enemies, but friends. We must not be enemies. Though passion may have strained, it must not break our bonds of affection." He urged all Americans to be guided "by the better angels of our nature." He could have been speaking directly to Meigs and Walter—for the two of them continued their squabbling even as Lincoln brought in the ambitious Senator Simon Cameron of Pennsylvania to serve as their new boss at the War Department.

That particular appointment was fine with Walter, who had urged his connections in Pennsylvania to buttonhole Cameron and let him know of his treatment at the hands of Meigs. The ploy seemed to have worked, as Cameron immediately clamped a ceasefire down on Meigs, prohibiting him from interfering with Walter in any way. Meigs, his feelings bruised and his ego stinging, responded with a lengthy letter in which he accused the new secretary of undermining his authority. Incredibly, Meigs failed to read the room and relied heavily on Jefferson Davis, now a pariah among Northerners, as his character reference. An annoyed Cameron brushed Meigs off without comment.

Despite Cameron's frustration with the engineer, President Lincoln appreciated Meigs's talents as an organizer and as a levelheaded military leader. On March 31, 1861—Easter Sunday—the engineer was called to the White House, where Lincoln tasked Meigs with helping to lead a secret mission to resupply federal troops in the Gulf of Mexico, eventually dispatching him on April 3. Nine days later, Confederate troops fired on Fort Sumter in South Carolina's Charleston Harbor. The nation was officially at war.

Lincoln quickly issued a call for seventy-five thousand soldiers to come to Washington, both to protect the capital city and to prepare to put down the rebellion, and he announced that troops would be permitted to camp in federal buildings—including the Capitol, where both the House and the Senate were presently adjourned. The first troops to arrive, a group of Pennsylvania volunteers, were put up in the Capitol's new House extension; several days later, nine hundred tired and dusty troops with the Sixth Regiment from Massachusetts arrived and were installed in the new Senate wing, where their commanding officer took over the Vice President's Room as his headquarters.

Next came the Eighth Massachusetts Regiment, who set up camp in the Rotunda, sleeping on the floor as moonlight, and sometimes spring rain, streamed in through the unfinished dome. As more and more troops filed in, they bivouacked anywhere in the building they could. "My office is at this moment while I write filled with soldiers," Walter wrote to his son. "The Capitol itself is turned into a barracks."[44]

Doorkeeper Isaac Bassett could barely watch as soldiers carelessly off-loaded their supplies in the Senate's pristine rooms and corridors. "It almost broke my heart to see the soldiers bring armfuls of bacon and hams and throw them down upon the floor of the Marble Room," he wrote. "Almost with tears in my eyes I begged them not to grease up the walls and the furniture."[45] Similarly, when soldiers in the Senate chambers began to use their bayonets to angrily hack at the desk that had belonged to Jefferson Davis, Bassett reminded them that the desk belonged *not* to the president of the Confederacy but to the government of the United States. "You were put here to protect, and not to destroy!" he shouted. "They stopped immediately and said I was right," Bassett wrote later.[46]

More troops continued to pour into the Capitol throughout the spring and summer, overworking the building's already limited water and sewer infrastructure. Congress, returning to session on July 4, cleared their chambers of soldiers but still had to step around discarded provisions and piles of trash. "There are 4,000 [troops] in the Capitol, with all their provisions, ammunition, and baggage, and the smell is awful," Walter wrote. "The building is like one grand water closet."[47] One police officer reported that there were cartloads of excrement piling up in the corners of nearly every room; elsewhere, men were plagued by lice and bedbugs. Gagging, Walter bolted from the building—and then left D.C. altogether.

Meigs completed his mission to the Gulf of Mexico on May 1, 1861—and on his arrival back in Washington on May 15, he immediately issued an order to stop all work underway at the Capitol. "The government has no money to spend except in self-defense," he declared.[48] That was disappointing news to the firm of Janes, Fowler & Kirtland Company, which still had stacked on the lawn in front of the Capitol 1.3 million pounds of iron plates, weighted down by barrels of sand and cement and ready for installation on the dome. The contractors feared that if they stopped their work and left the iron on the ground, it would be lost, damaged, or possibly taken by the government to be melted down for military use. And so even without pay, the firm decided to keep its workers on the job, hoisting up to the dome one plate of prefabricated iron after another, bolting the pieces in place, and hoping the government would reimburse them when it could. "[T]hey desired the honor and reputation of having their names associated with a work which, in design and execution, has no equal in the ornamental architecture of the world," Secretary of War Edwin Stanton explained later. Work might have stopped on the extensions, but progress on the dome would continue.

While the legend persists that it was President Lincoln who insisted that work at the Capitol continue throughout the war as a symbol of the grit and permanency of the Union, it was actually the commitment of the expert craftsmen at Janes, Fowler, & Kirtland Company, working without pay, who ensured that "the sound of the hammer" never stopped "during all of our civil troubles."[49] The firm would be fully reimbursed for their work by 1870.[50]

After his success in the Gulf of Mexico, Meigs moved quickly up the promotion ladder. He was appointed colonel of the 11th U.S. Infantry and then—thanks in no small part to President Lincoln, who continued to be impressed with the man's "qualities of masculine intellect, learning, and experience of the right sort"[51]—promoted to brigadier general and quartermaster general of the Army. It would be Meigs who—for the rest of the war and indeed for the next two decades—would ensure American troops remained effectively and efficiently fed, clothed, and armed. During the Civil War, Meigs would command Grant's base of supplies in several campaigns and would notably supervise the supplying of General William Tecumseh Sherman's army at Savannah. By some estimates, over the course of the war, Meigs would disburse more than $1.5 billion—all "accurately vouched and accounted for to the last cent," Speaker of the House James G. Blaine would later enthuse in admiration.[52]

In addition to his exemplary bookkeeping, Meigs was also a staunch Unionist—and it was Meigs who suggested that dead Union soldiers be interred in a cemetery on the property belonging to Confederate General Robert Lee on the Arlington side of the Potomac River, thus making the house and property forever uninhabitable by the Lees. "No man who ever took the oath to support the Constitution as an officer of our army or navy . . . should escape without loss of all his goods & civil rights & expatriation," Meigs wrote to his father. In January 1864, the federal government would seize Lee's property for use as a miliary cemetery; by May, the first Union soldiers would be laid to rest there.

In October 1864, Meigs's son, Lieutenant John Rodgers Meigs, would be killed while on a scouting mission for General Philip Sheridan in the Shenandoah Valley. Meigs would never forgive Lee, or the Confederates, for taking his son. "The rebels are all murderers of my son and the sons of hundreds of thousands," Meigs wrote in anguish.[53] He would bury his son in Arlington National Cemetery.

While cold weather usually meant the end of the building season, in the early winter of 1861, Janes's work crew was steadily continuing to raise the iron pieces onto the dome to complete its second story—a series of thirty-six arched windows encircling the level above the colonnade. At this height, workers carefully crawled along scaffolding mounted on both the inside and the outside of the dome as they bolted the ornate pieces together. One of these workers was Robert Slight, the forty-two-year-old son of the late carpenter Pringle Slight. In December, as Robert was working inside the dome, he slipped from the scaffolding and plummeted four stories to his death, his body landing heavily on the temporary wooden roof his own father had constructed over the opening of the Rotunda. While both Pringle and Robert Slight are buried at Congressional Cemetery on the far eastern end of Capitol Hill, a myth persists to this day that Robert's ghost lingers in the Rotunda.

And still the work continued, despite the bitter cold of early 1862. Snow and freezing rain drizzled into the open dome, running down the walls and puddling on the floor of the Rotunda. "Any gentleman who passes through the dome after a snow or rain storm, will see the injury that will be the result if the dome is left in its present unfinished condition," noted Congressman Robert McKnight of Pennsylvania.[54] Walter politely reminded impatient members that those currently working to finish the building—including Walter himself—were doing so without pay.

In January 1862, with Secretary of War Simon Cameron floundering amid charges of corruption and profiteering, President Lincoln officially brought in the no-nonsense Edwin Stanton as his new secretary of war, giving Meigs and Walter yet another new overseer at the War Department. At the same time, Benjamin B. French—who'd bounced from job to job after resigning as commissioner of public buildings under pressure from Franklin Pierce in 1855—was reinstated to the position by President Lincoln, returning one of Walter's allies to a position of prominence. With new personnel in two key places, Walter now made the rounds in Congress to push for moving oversight of the Capitol from the War Department over to *any* civilian agency. To members who might have been on the fence, the architect appealed to their patriotism, informing them that the decision to place the Capitol project under the War Department had been made by "that atrocious wretch Jeff Davis."[55] The point, he seemed to be saying, was that any *good* American would want the Capitol out from under the jurisdiction of the War Department.

Congress took up the debate in March, moving legislation that would reassign the Capitol to the Department of the Interior. Supporters argued that the War Department, which was conducting an actual war at the moment, had its hands full, as did Meigs, whose talents were put to better use moving military supplies across enemy territory than ordering building supplies for the Capitol. Predictably, supporters of Meigs took to the floor to disparage Walter and vice versa. Congressman

Charles R. Train, chairman of the House Committee on Public Buildings and Grounds, was particularly scathing of Meigs. "Everything is ready for the completion of the dome now, and I say that it ought to be completed," Train said, adding that he hoped the project would be finished under the supervision of Walter, "who has far more judgment and capacity than General Meigs, to complete the dome."[56]

The bill to transfer the Capitol to the Department of the Interior cleared the Congress in early April and was signed into law by President Lincoln on April 16, 1862. Shortly thereafter, Walter's new boss, Secretary of the Interior Caleb Smith, officially put Walter back in charge of the Capitol project. For Walter, it felt like vindication. "I feel very thankful for the providential turn our things have taken," he wrote to his wife.[57] This time, Meigs kept his mouth shut; he was far too busy helping coordinate the movement of supplies for more than a hundred thousand men making up the enormous but slow-moving Army of the Potomac.

On the same day Lincoln inked the legislation transferring the Capitol to the Department of the Interior, he also signed an act abolishing slavery in the District of Columbia. "I have ever desired to see the national capital freed from the institution [of slavery] in some satisfactory way," Lincoln wrote in his message to Congress.[58] With the stroke of a pen, more than three thousand enslaved persons were freed in the nation's capital eight months before the Emancipation Proclamation.

Among the three thousand freed was Philip Reid, who was casting the statue of *Freedom* at Clark Mills's foundry. On May 2, Walter traveled with Benjamin French, Secretary Smith, and Smith's wife out to Mills's foundry to inspect the nearly twenty-foot bronze statue Reid had finally finished casting in late April. Everyone was impressed. "Everything was done with propriety and dignity," wrote Walter—and Smith informed Reid that he wanted the statue brought to the Capitol's east garden so it could be admired by the public before it was placed on top of the completed dome. Reid would dutifully take the statue apart and have it shipped by cart back to the lawn of the Capitol for assembly and display before its installation atop the dome.[59]

Reid had begun casting *Statue of Freedom* in bronze out at Clark Mills's foundry as human chattel in 1860; fittingly, he would complete the job in April 1862 with his own freedom finally secured.[60]

Walter and Secretary of the Interior Caleb Smith got along well enough. As Walter gave the secretary a tour of the Capitol grounds, he was pleased to see that Smith seemed genuinely proud to have the building officially under the authority of his department. Smith also mostly left the architect alone, permitting Walter to appoint freely one of his chief assistants, thirty-nine-year-old Edward Clark, who had been with Walter for two decades, to replace Meigs as the building's new superintendent. Unlike Meigs—who had regarded himself as Walter's superior, even if he really wasn't—Clark understood that he was mostly on the job to carry out Walter's architectural plans and oversee the day-to-day management of the building's construction. It was almost with an audible sigh of relief, then, that Walter submitted to the Congress his reports detailing the work that remained to be done on the Capitol.

Apart from the dome, there were still columns that needed to be placed along the outer walls of the corridors connecting the old Capitol to the new additions, and stairs that needed to be completed on the east porticos of both new extensions. Walter also looked closely at how much had been spent on the dome before its construction had been stopped by Meigs in May 1861; he determined that there was likely enough unexpended funding to pay Janes, Fowler, & Kirtland Company to complete the dome after going without compensation for a year. At this time, too, Congress decided to start appropriations flowing into the building again, over objections from members who argued that Congress had better things to spend its money on while the nation was at war. But Vermont Senator Solomon Foot, chairman of the Senate Committee on Public Buildings and Grounds, insisted that "expediency requires that [construction of the Capitol] should be completed"[61] and argued convincingly that it was cheaper to continue construction on the building than to wait until after the war to repair all the damage currently being inflicted on the structure "in consequence of its present exposed condition."[62] But with skirmishes happening across the river, practically within sight of the Capitol, work was still going to proceed much more slowly than anyone liked, no matter how much funding was made available.

In late August 1862, a surprising and decisive Confederate victory at the Second Battle of Bull Run—the battlefield was only about thirty miles away from Capitol Hill—sent thousands of Union soldiers retreating back through the District, including more than eight thousand wounded. The Capitol, which had already been used as a barracks and a military headquarters, was now converted by the Union Army into a hospital. "The beds are now up in the rotunda, the old Hall of Rep's, and the passages—one thousand beds have been put up," Walter wrote. "It does not interfere with our work in the least, and I think the move is a good one."[63]

The building was also converted into a kitchen, as nearly twenty enormous brick ovens were built into the Capitol's basement for the purpose of providing federal troops camped in the city with a regular supply of bread and other rations. Stairways and hallways were lined with barrels of supplies, including pork, crackers, and flour; some stairways leading to the basement had been laid with planks, creating ramps so that full barrels of flour could be quickly rolled down the stairs to the basement ovens. More than sixteen thousand loaves were produced each day, filling the building with aromatic smoke that permeated committee rooms and meeting spaces before finally filtering out any open windows. Librarian of Congress John G. Stephenson fretted that the books in the Capitol library—*his* books, as far as he was concerned—would be permanently damaged. "I am pained to see a treasure instructed to my care—a treasure money cannot replace—receiving great damage from the smoke and soot that penetrates everywhere through that part of the Capitol which is under my charge," he wrote.[64]

Conditions inside the building continued to deteriorate; not only were there more than a thousand wounded in the building—many sleeping in the Rotunda, which was still open to the elements—but livestock now wandered the marble halls as well, rooting up the lawns or urinating on the Minton tiles Meigs had so proudly installed on the floors of the extensions. While Walter felt sorry for the wounded—"poor fellows, what they must suffer," he wrote—he thought the building had become "intolerable" and moved his Capitol office out to one of the shops on the lawn, away from the stench of defecation and the dying. He would eventually have a temporary wood-framed building constructed in the east garden for use by him and his staff, away from the suffering in the Rotunda.

With money flowing again, ironworkers from Janes, Fowler, & Kirtland Company had recently completed the second story of arched windows and were now bolting in place the white-painted iron pieces making up the final forty feet of the dome's curve sloping toward its top; one newspaper correspondent thought the scaffolding resembled "a huge skeleton skirt."[65] Progress on the rest of the building, however, had ground nearly to a halt by late fall, mostly because it was becoming impossible to get the marble needed to finish the columns on the exterior porticos. "The breaking out of the rebellion caused a total suspension of operations at the quarries," Walter reported to the Congress.[66] Both he and Public Buildings Commissioner Benjamin French wanted the building cleaned up and ready to receive the Congress when both bodies convened again in December. But the Capitol was a mess—and clearing out the Army was going to require someone with authority well above either Walter's or French's pay grade.

French finally appealed to just such a person, going directly to the president to ask for the removal of the military. Lincoln agreed; the smoky ovens were dismantled, and by late October 1862, the last of the wounded soldiers were transferred out of the Capitol and out of the city. It was finally quiet in the building again—but many of the rooms were almost hopelessly damaged, with marble mantels stolen and glass chandeliers shattered. French testily wrote to the Congress demanding funding to clean up the building and restore the "wreck of rooms" before the beginning of the next session of Congress.

Walter soon reported that workmen had scrubbed clean most of the exterior marble—including scouring away some of the scorching that still remained from the burning of the building in 1814—but he also noted that some of the stones had been defaced by "evil-disposed persons."[67] He was even angrier about the damage that had been done by the livestock roaming the compound, especially by the fat and bristly pigs that had scratched and rubbed themselves against the stacks of dome iron so forcefully that they had scoured off the white paint.

Walter and French would have the building cleaned up before Congress arrived, but the commissioner was out of patience. French politely but firmly informed the Congress that he sincerely hoped that in the future "the Capitol may hereafter be left to its legitimate uses and not defaced and disfigured by military occupation."[68]

With the dome still slowly going up, Walter was finally ready to talk with Brumidi about exactly what was needed for the *Apotheosis of Washington* painting at the top of the Rotunda. Writing to the artist in August, Walter explained that he needed a design for "a picture 65 feet in diameter, painted in fresco, on the concave canopy over the eye of the New Dome of the U.S. Capitol."[69] Viewed from the floor of the Rotunda a hundred eighty feet below, it would be the dramatic centerpiece of the Capitol building itself.

Walter was cleverly paying homage to William Thornton's 1793 original plan for the Capitol, which had called for visitors to peer down through a hole in the floor of the Rotunda at Washington's tomb. As Thornton had envisioned, Walter had indeed put Washington at the literal center of the Capitol building itself—but instead of visitors gazing down through an opening in the floor, Walter would have them looking up through an oculus in the ceiling, where they would see Washington benevolently regarding them from nearly the highest vantage point of the Capitol. A painting the size that Walter needed would take up about 4,664 square feet—and while Brumidi had painted some large surfaces in the past, he hadn't done anything *quite* that big yet. But Walter had confidence in the artist, giving him carte blanche on the design of the gigantic fresco based on little more than the title *The Apotheosis of Washington.*

In early September, Brumidi submitted to Walter his completed concept art for the painting, which featured two concentric circles of figures and scenes. Seated at the center of the inside circle was George Washington, decked out in military dress though still posed somewhat like Greenough's bathtub Washington, raising a sheathed sword with his left hand while his right hand beckoned the viewer. Flanking the first president on his left and right were the allegorical figures of Liberty and Victory—and without Jefferson Davis around to object, this depiction of Liberty would wear the liberty cap that Davis had found so offensive on Crawford's first sketches for his statue of *Freedom.* Extending beyond Liberty and Victory to finish up the interior circle were thirteen female figures, each with a star over her head, representing the original thirteen colonies. Two of them suspended a banner reading *"E Pluribus Unum"* directly over Washington.

Making up the larger outside circle, Brumidi had roughed out six scenes representing war, agriculture, manufacturing, commerce, marine—mostly depicting ways Americans had mastered the oceans—and the arts and sciences. It all looked good to Walter, who asked Brumidi to name his price for completing the work at full size. The artist, who needed the money, asked for $50,000—about $1.6 million today.

Walter assured the artist that he had certainly proven he was worth that kind of money, but he also told the painter that there was little chance of the Congress appropriating that much funding for decorating the Capitol—already a touchy topic—while it was also conducting a war. Brumidi patriotically agreed to reduce his fee to $40,000 instead—still a hefty $1.2 million in today's money—with nearly all of it going to Brumidi himself, though he would pay for supplies and any assistants out of his own pocket. After some discussion between Walter and John Usher, the genial Indiana attorney general who had just replaced Caleb Smith as secretary of the interior, Brumidi's fee was approved in January 1863, to be paid out in monthly installments of $2,000, equivalent to around $50,000 today. It was the nation's most expensive commission for public art up to that time and more money than Brumidi had ever seen in his life.[70] (Brumidi, always terrible with his finances and too generous with friends, would still run out of money within three years; he would also die broke in 1880.)

Walter had his carpenters prepare a full-sized model of the curved canopy for Brumidi to practice on and create the rough sketches—called "cartoons"—of his fresco at their actual finished sizes. There were multiple challenges for the artist; the figures, some of them as tall as fifteen feet, would be painted on a curved surface, requiring some distortion or foreshortening to make the figures appear legible when viewed from the floor of the Rotunda below. But Walter, who had designed the interior of the dome with a gallery in its upper region, *also* wanted the painting to be intelligible when viewed from that gallery, which was eighty-five feet closer to the curved surface of the ceiling. Brumidi thought he could do it and was anxious to get to work. But until the dome was completed—and until the gigantic canopy for him to paint on could be hung in the top of the exterior dome—there wasn't much for him to do apart from collect his handsome paychecks.

Nevertheless, Walter was optimistic about 1863; if things went as he hoped, he would have the dome completed just in time to have Crawford's *Statue of Freedom* mounted on top of the building for the Fourth of July—a symbolic deadline that Walter desperately wanted to hit. A completed dome would also mean he could put Brumidi to work painting *The Apotheosis of Washington* on the canopy in the top of the outer dome immediately.

Neither would happen. While the dome itself was very nearly finished, the tholus on which Crawford's statue was to stand was not. "Our 4th of July frolic is *no go*," Walter wrote sadly as the date approached.[71] And until the top of the dome was capped with an enclosed tholus to keep out the elements, there would be no hanging of the inner canopy on which Brumidi was to paint.

Still, while progress on the building had been slow, the work had, for the most part, never stopped. The craftsmen from Janes, Fowler, & Kirtland Company had kept the hammers clanging, and work had continued even as the building filled with smoke from military bread ovens, overflowed with wounded soldiers and excrement, and resounded with Congressional complaints about acoustics and art. Through it all, the Capitol had never stopped serving the people, the government, or the nation—a fact that had not gone unnoticed by President Lincoln. "If people see the Capitol going on," he remarked in 1863, "it is a sign we intend the Union shall go on."[72]

Walter was able to install in the building one major work of art that wasn't going in or on the dome: the gigantic bronze Columbus doors designed by Randolph Rogers, which had finally arrived at the Capitol nearly three years after being cast in Munich, Germany. Depicting the story of Christopher Columbus's life and voyages across eight panels, Rogers's doors were highly detailed and absolutely huge, with each one standing seventeen feet tall and weighing ten thousand pounds. The doors arrived in six pieces, and Walter had them assembled in the Rotunda before installing them in the doorway where the old House chamber connected to the new House extension. Walter thought the doors were beautiful—they were worth a trip to the Capitol in themselves, he informed his lawyer—and he told his wife that he was certain they would "attract more attention than any work of art ever seen in this country."[73]

Finally, in November 1863, Walter was satisfied that work on the dome had progressed enough that *Freedom* could at last be safely hoisted in pieces to the tholus at the top of the dome, where the 19.5-foot statue could be assembled one piece at a time as it was placed on its 18.5-foot cast-iron pedestal.

On November 24, 1863—a rainy Tuesday—Walter watched from the lawn of the Capitol as the first section of *Freedom* was raised three hundred feet off the ground by one of Meigs's remarkable and reliable cranes and carefully bolted in place atop the tholus, before bad weather prohibited any further work. On Wednesday the twenty-fifth, the second piece was installed in a steady rain, but with the weather getting increasingly colder and wetter, the third piece wouldn't make it to the top for another three days. After that, the fourth section was scheduled to go up on Monday, November 30, but it was so cold and windy that work crews finally gave up and headed inside. They had better luck the following day, and by the late afternoon of December 1, only the last four feet or so of the statue—*Freedom*'s head and shoulders—remained to be installed.

At precisely noon on Wednesday, December 2, 1863, the final piece of Thomas Crawford's *Statue of Freedom* was bolted into place by Charles F. Thomas, an experienced mechanical engineer unintimidated by heights. Thomas, a staunch Unionist, proudly placed a flag on top of the statue and stood stock-still to have his picture taken by a photographer at the intersection of First Street and New Jersey SE, nearly a mile away ("Mr. Thomas looks like a blackbird just lighted on Freedom's head," reported one journalist).[74]

Walter had wanted only a solemn ceremony to mark the occasion—with the nation at war, there would be no speeches or celebrating—but the event was still stirring enough in its understatement. The moment Thomas bolted *Freedom*'s head into place, there was a salute of thirty-five guns—one for each state; Walter had even included the states in rebellion in his head count. That salute was answered by the booming of guns from the twelve forts around the Federal city. Looking up at *Freedom*, more than three hundred feet from the ground, Walter thought she looked "placid and beautiful—and much better than I expected."[75]

He wasn't the only one who was moved. The American poet Walt Whitman, who was living in Washington at that time, had watched the dome slowly rising on Capitol Hill with awe. "I shall always identify Washington with that huge and delicate towering bulge of pure white, where it emerges calm and lofty from the hill, out of a dense mass of trees . . . ," wrote Whitman. "A vast eggshell, built of iron and glass, this dome—a beauteous bubble, caught and put in permanent form. I say a beauty and genuine success."[76]

Whitman also noted that *Freedom* faced east: with "her back to the city," the poet wrote—a positioning that still prompts questions from visitors. While a number of rumors and urban legends have persisted over the last century and a half—one said that Walter had mistakenly believed the city would eventually grow toward the east and thus had the statue aimed in that direction—the truth is much less entertaining: at the time *Freedom* was placed on top of the dome, the Capitol's main entrance was through the central east portico. Crawford's statue was simply facing the front side of the building.

Regardless, with *Freedom* firmly bolted in place atop the dome, the Capitol was, at last, finished.

Mostly.

After its completion in 1863, Thomas Walter remained unhappy with the proportions of the East Front—visible here tucked up under the base of the dome—worrying that the central east portico looked as if it were in danger of being crushed by the dome above it. To dispel the illusion, Walter suggested moving the East Front forward—a recommendation that would finally be realized nearly a century later.

CHAPTER 9

The Finest Building in the World

1863–1915

With *Statue of Freedom* firmly in place atop the Capitol dome, the Capitol building—to most, at least—looked finished. Thomas U. Walter knew better. As the architect walked around the building in January 1864, all he saw was what still needed work. The Senate extension was missing its porticos on the north and west sides, leaving the new Senate wing looking both unfinished and unbalanced, though at least its main east entrance, capped by Crawford's *Progress of Civilization* in its pediment, was finished. In far worse shape, the House extension had no exterior columns in place, and it lacked most of its exterior steps; members had to enter the House chamber by coming into the building through the main central doors at the Rotunda, then working their way south into their new wing. In his annual report to Congress, Walter explained that the absence of columns was due to delays in moving marble from the Lee quarry in Massachusetts. The Congress, while generally delighted with their new chambers, mostly now complained about the dust and debris and mud. They wanted the building completed and cleaned up. Now.

When the Congress convened again on December 7, 1863, Walter was hustling to put the finishing touches on the most obviously missing pieces of the building: enclosing the tholus at the top of the dome to prevent rain from pouring into the Rotunda, and setting in place the hundred Corinthian marble columns that marched along the exteriors of the House and Senate extensions. While Congressmen were still complaining about the ventilation system—temperature was no longer a point of contention, but some members thought the chamber stank—the main question in 1864, at least as it related to the Capitol, was what to do with the old House chamber.

Since the removal of the House to its new chamber in 1857, the old space had become mostly just a pass-through from the Rotunda to the new extension, a soaring, columned hall crammed with vendors, loiterers, lobbyists, and vagrants. Various proposals had been put forth at different times for its use, from giving it to the Library of Congress to enclosing it entirely and creating two floors of meeting and committee rooms. Benjamin French encouraged members to do something—anything—with the "magnificent room . . . now forlorn looking and dismantled."[1]

Eventually, the Congress settled on the idea of using the old chamber as an art gallery. While the lack of wall space in the room made it a difficult place to hang paintings—as had originally been suggested by Meigs's colleague Gouverneur Kemble—the room seemed better suited for statues; some recalled how magisterial the room had looked for the brief time when the heavy plaster model of *Freedom* had been on display only a few years earlier. On July 2, 1864, then, the Congress approved legislation proposed by Justin Morrill of Vermont to clean up and preserve the old House chamber, and it provided $15,000 to repurpose the space into a National Statuary Hall. As approved by the Congress, "each and all" states were invited to provide two statues made of either marble or bronze that celebrated citizens of their state who were "illustrious for their historic renown or for distinguished civic or military services."[2] The legislation also made clear the subject had to be dead.

The $15,000 appropriation was used mostly to pay for the removal of the chamber's old terraced wooden floor—which was "rotting and trembling under my tread," as Ohio Congressman Robert Schenck noted dramatically—and to install a new one made of marble. Congress put out the call for statues for the room later in 1864; the first to respond was Rhode Island, which in 1870 sent a statue of Revolutionary War hero Nathanael Greene beautifully carved by noted sculptor Henry Kirke Brown. Statues would come in slowly and regularly over the next sixty years; by 1933, the hall would be crammed with sixty-five statues displayed in rows three deep. At that point, the room looked like a cluttered attic full of bronze and marble figures—and apart from it being an eyesore, there was worry the floor would buckle under the slowly increasing weight.

In 1933, a concerned Congress authorized the display of the statues throughout the Capitol building, spreading them and their weight out beyond overloaded Statuary Hall. By 1971, all fifty states had sent at least one statue for display; it would take until 2005 for all states to be represented with the Congressionally sanctioned *two* statues—the last to arrive came from New Mexico, which sent a statue of Tewa spiritual leader Po'Pay. Today, statues can be seen in Statuary Hall as well as in various spots around the Capitol complex, including the Rotunda, the Hall of Columns, the Crypt, and the Capitol Visitor Center, completed in 2008. Since 2000, states have also been permitted to remove and replace their statues, with many swapping out figures of Confederates, enslavers, or segregationists. As of 2025, fourteen states have taken advantage of this option, using the opportunity to replace century-old statues with likenesses of more modern—and often less controversial—figures like Harry Truman, Gerald Ford, Johnny Cash, and Mary McLeod Bethune.

By late 1864, Thomas Walter was walking the corridors of the Capitol more deliberately, looking for unfinished business. Over the last twelve months, Captain Franklin and he had supervised the workers finishing up the exteriors, where solid brick walls were being faced with smooth white marble quarried in Massachusetts. Heavy marble Corinthian columns were being slowly raised into place around the sides of the extensions and their connecting corridors. And while there had been some initial scoffing at Walter's choice to design the extensions in the same neoclassical style that Thornton had used in 1790 because the look was considered dated and out of fashion by the 1860s, the building had a cohesive elegance that gave it an intentionally timeless architectural style. Working within the limitations of neoclassical design, both Walter and Meigs had sought to give the Capitol its own distinct character, ensuring that materials were of the highest quality, consistently colored—the slightest blemish on a column could cause it to be consigned to the junk pile—and well proportioned.

In fact, if Walter had any concern at all about the exterior of the building, it had to do with the proportions of the Capitol's east side. As he peered up at the building from the east plaza, tracing his eyes along the central portico and pediment, built in 1828, and then up onto the recently completed dome, Walter thought the marble portico looked particularly fragile in the shadow of the dome—as if it were in danger of being crushed by the nine million pounds of iron squatting on its shoulders. As a remedy, Walter recommended that the East Front of the central section be moved forward—extended "at least to the front line of the wings"—and he even drew up floor plans and provided a beautiful drawing of the Capitol completed in such a manner. Congress, however, was relieved to finally call the building finished; the only project they would approve at the moment had to do with moving the Library of Congress into some old committee rooms. Walter's proposal for the extended East Front was shelved, though his envisioned alteration would continue to be discussed for the next century.

Inside the building, in addition to the much-improved House and Senate chambers, there were more than a hundred new rooms spread over three floors in the finished extensions to use for committee meetings and offices. The rooms in the Senate wing were particularly striking, given all the work that had been done by Brumidi over the past decade. While the interference of the makeshift and xenophobic art commission established by the Congress in 1858 had often slowed down the funding that permitted Brumidi to work, many of the rooms and hallways were *mostly* complete. Among the still unfinished areas was the Senate Reception Room—the same room where Meigs had bid a teary farewell to his work crew in 1859—which had now been turned into the Senate post office, where each Senator had his own mailbox.

Similarly, one floor down, on the northern side of the extension, the committee room for the Senate Committee on Military Affairs and Militia was still incomplete. Brumidi had intended to decorate the space with scenes of the Revolutionary War, but he was only half finished at the moment, having completed one scene featuring the Battle of Lexington and another the death of General David Wooster, a largely forgotten Revolutionary hero whom Brumidi admired. Eventually, he would add images of the Boston Massacre and Washington's troops at Valley Forge. Brumidi's tableau of the Boston Massacre would include the first depiction of an African American anywhere in the Capitol when, at the center of his fresco, he painted the doomed Crispus Attucks about to be shot by British soldiers.

Most memorable, then as now, was a series of five connected corridors on the first floor of the Senate extension, referred to today as the "Brumidi Corridors" for the elaborate murals on the walls and ceilings painted or designed by the artist. Along with portraits of early revolutionaries like John Hancock and Robert Livingston, colorful, detailed scrollwork covers nearly every surface from floor to ceiling, with images of mice and birds among the ornately painted vines and vases. Along the ceiling, circular lunettes contain historical scenes like *Signing of the First Treaty of Peace with Great Britain*; most, however, wouldn't be completed until the late 1870s, and when Brumidi died in 1880, some spaces would still be empty, collateral damage in the continuing squabble between the art commission and the parsimonious Congress. Fortunately, this lack of funding left several empty lunettes in which later artists could paint images reflecting the ongoing story of the United States, including a flight of the Wright brothers, artist Allyn Cox's depiction of the 1969 Apollo moon landing, and Charles Schmidt's 1987 painting of the doomed crew of the space shuttle *Challenger.*

But now, in December 1864, after years of waiting, Brumidi would finally be put to work in the Rotunda—*way up* in the Rotunda—on what would be his grandest project of all, the gigantic fresco *The Apotheosis of Washington.* Walter had at last installed the enormous canopy in nearly the highest point of the dome, a hundred eighty feet from the floor, and mounted it firmly to the dome's interior ribs. To give Brumidi a workspace, he had placed a platform across the top of the oculus of the Rotunda's inner dome, then secured the platform against the same interior iron ribs holding up the canopy.

To reach it, Brumidi would ascend a staircase located between the interior and exterior domes, climbing about three hundred steps to the dome's interior gallery just above the oculus. From there, he'd access the platform covering the oculus, scaling the various struts that finally brought him close enough to the curved surface of the canopy to paint it. Much of the time, Brumidi, like Michelangelo adorning the ceiling of the Sistine Chapel, worked lying on his back. While the platform largely obscured the view of the Rotunda floor twelve stories down, clambering out onto it each day still required considerable nerve—as well as considerable faith in the engineers who had constructed it.

In early 1864, a change in military leadership by President Lincoln—who appointed the fearless Ulysses S. Grant as commander of all Union armies—led to several decisive Union victories that turned the tide in the Civil War. With the fall of Atlanta in July in particular—at the hands of the determined Union General William Tecumseh Sherman—the ability of the Confederacy to wage war was suddenly considerably diminished. By November 1864, with Northern optimism on the rise, Abraham Lincoln was reelected president in an electoral landslide.

On March 4, 1865, Lincoln took the oath of office on the east side of the Capitol, standing, as he had done in 1861, on a platform extending from the steps of the center section. The weather was overcast and slightly rainy as Lincoln, with a sheaf of papers in his hands, approached a small but ornate metal podium to read his prepared remarks. As he began speaking, the rain, as if on cue, suddenly ceased, and the newly completed white cast-iron dome of the Capitol building behind him seemed to glow in the sunshine. "He was just superstitious enough to consider it a happy omen," wrote reporter Noah Brooks.[3]

With an enthusiastic crowd of nearly forty thousand crammed onto the Capitol's east plaza, Lincoln delivered his second inaugural address—a short but conciliatory speech that awed the audience into such a "profound silence," as Brooks remembered, that Lincoln worried it had not gone over well. Quite the opposite was true. In his remarks, the president spoke of the costs of the war, of ending of the scourge of slavery, and of the importance of preserving the Union:

> With malice toward none, with charity for all, with firmness in the right as God gives us to see the right, let us strive on to finish the work we are in, to bind up the nation's wounds, to care for him who shall have borne the battle and for his widow and his orphan, to do all which may achieve and cherish a just and lasting peace among ourselves and with all nations.

A month later, on April 3, 1865, the news of the capture of the Confederate capital of Richmond reached Washington, D.C. Elated, the president ordered all public buildings to be illuminated in celebration.

Commissioner of Public Buildings Benjamin French—with a flair for the theatrical as well as an appreciation for the Capitol's location at the top of a hill overlooking the District—decided the Capitol needed something more dramatic than mere illumination. On an enormous banner more than a hundred feet long, French printed Psalm 118:23 ("This is the Lord's doing; it is marvelous in our eyes") in letters more than three feet high. He then had the banner stretched across the Capitol's entire western portico—the side facing the city—and lit it with gas spotlights. French noted proudly that it could be read from almost any point on Pennsylvania Avenue.

Less than two weeks later, Abraham Lincoln was shot in the head while attending a play at Ford's Theatre in Washington, D.C. He died on the morning of Saturday, April 15, 1865, in the back bedroom of a boardinghouse directly across the street from the theater. Benjamin French, distraught at hearing the news, closed and locked the Capitol.

Lincoln's casket was transported by an honor guard to the White House, where he lay in state in the East Room for three days, until Wednesday, April 19. At two o'clock that afternoon, the president's body was placed in a funeral carriage for a slow trip up Pennsylvania Avenue to the Capitol, accompanied by a solemn procession of more than thirty thousand soldiers, government leaders, and mourning citizens, led by the Twenty-second United States Colored Infantry. French had directed "clothing the Capitol in mourning,"[4] and as the procession made its way to Capitol Hill, they observed black bunting tied around every column on the exterior of the building. Under the dome, workmen had been instructed to cover all paintings and sculpture with black cloth; only a statue of George Washington was left deferentially uncovered, though a black sash had been carefully tied around him.

Inside the Rotunda, a large platform—called a catafalque—was waiting to receive the president's casket. Hastily designed by French's twenty-year-old son, Benjamin Jr., and assembled from pine boards hammered together by a team of carpenters led by French's assistant commissioner, Job W. Angus, the catafalque had been covered with a black cloth edged with silver fringe and silver stars. Now it was placed in the center of the Rotunda, where the president's casket was slowly lowered onto it to lie quite literally at the heart of the nation's government.

For two days, April 20 and April 21, more than forty thousand people filed through the Rotunda to pay their respects to the president, with many waiting in a line more than three miles long as they were soaked by steady spring rains.[5] "Thousands wended their way up the Capitol steps, into the grand rotunda, by the bier and coffin of the President, and then out at the eastern entrance," reported *The New York Times.* "The people clung to their friend with tenacity, and their silent homage was deep and tearful."[6]

Lincoln was not the first to lie in state in the Rotunda; Senator Henry Clay preceded the president in that distinction when he was mourned there on July 1, 1852, after dying of tuberculosis. But seeing Lincoln lying in state—the first president to do so and, indeed, the first American president to be assassinated—moved French profoundly. After the president's casket was removed and sent on its way to his hometown of Springfield, Illinois, French suggested to Meigs that the catafalque be preserved for posterity—and he knew exactly the right place for it. "It is my intention to have the mausoleum, intended for the remains of Washington, beneath the Crypt of the Capitol, thoroughly cleaned and properly fitted," French wrote Meigs on April 21, "and to place in it the *Catafalco* on which the body of our late beloved President lay in the rotunda, there to be preserved as a memento."[7]

As French suggested, the Lincoln catafalque was stored in the Crypt, where it would remain from 1865 until 2009, when it was moved to the Capitol Visitor Center. Since 1865, the Lincoln catafalque has been more than just a memento; it has been used every time an individual has lain in state in the Rotunda.[8] While the black fabric covering the catafalque has been replaced several times over the last century and a half—and the platform modified, as needed, to accommodate large or heavy coffins—the pine boards making up the basic structure are still the same ones that were nailed together by Job W. Angus and his carpenters in April 1865.

As of 2025, forty-seven figures[9] have lain in the Capitol[10]—but not all get to use the Lincoln catafalque. Generally, the catafalque is reserved for members of the Supreme Court and high-ranking military leaders and government officials—namely presidents, Senators, and Representatives. Private citizens placed in the Capitol—like Rosa Parks in 2005 or Billy Graham in 2018—are generally considered to lie in *honor* rather than in *state*, and they are not placed on the Lincoln catafalque.

Even as President Lincoln's body lay in state in the Rotunda in April 1865, anyone standing next to the catafalque who looked up into the top of the dome would have seen only the bottom of the wooden platform placed across the inner oculus, still supporting Brumidi as he lay on his back, painting more than a hundred eighty feet from the floor. The artist had worked steadily, and quickly, on the enormous fresco—and when Walter climbed the stairs to check on Brumidi in May, he found the painter was already finished with the center group of figures made up of Washington flanked by the figures of Liberty and Victory, encircled by the thirteen maidens representing the original colonies. Brumidi would finish the painting by November 1865, completing the enormous fresco in only eleven months.

Walter, meanwhile, was finding himself challenged on a new front. With the death of Lincoln, the presidency passed to his vice president, the irritable Andrew Johnson—and with a new administration came a new batch of cabinet secretaries. That included Johnson's pick for the Interior Department, James Harlan, a humorless Senator from Iowa who took it upon himself to purge his agency of employees he considered disloyal, ineffective, or insufficiently Christian. One of the first to go was clerk Walt Whitman, whose *Leaves of Grass* was considered by Harlan to be immoral. He next called Commissioner of Public Buildings Benjamin French on the carpet, asking for his honest assessment of the work going on in the Capitol compound. As part of his rambling reply, French suggested oversight of the Capitol be placed under his own office within the Interior Department—the office of the commissioner of public buildings—rather than as a direct report to the secretary.

To French's likely surprise, Harlan agreed to the reorganization—and on May 25, he transferred to French's office oversight not only of the Capitol, but of *all public works* in Washington, D.C. That was effectively it for Walter, who, with the stroke of Harlan's pen, found his authority and autonomy as Architect of the Capitol Extension essentially stripped away. Frustrated and hurt—Walter took the move as a vote of no confidence—the architect submitted his letter of resignation, offering to step down on June 1. Perhaps to his surprise, his offer was immediately accepted by Secretary Harlan. If Walter had been hoping Harlan was going to try to persuade him to stay, that clearly wasn't going to happen.

A little before noon on June 1, 1865, Thomas Ustick Walter climbed aboard a train leaving Washington, D.C., and bound for Philadelphia, where the architect would rejoin his family in their Germantown home by evening. The Capitol building that receded into the distance behind him was a very different building from the one he had encountered when hired by President Millard Fillmore as the building's fourth official Architect of the Capitol in 1851. His designs for the new House and Senate extensions, and their connecting corridors, had more than doubled the length of the original structure completed by Charles Bulfinch in 1829. He had given Congressmen and Senators larger, more comfortable, and more acoustically sound chambers, utilizing the era's most state-of-the-art technology. He had worked to modify and retrofit old spaces for new uses, such as constructing a redesigned Library of Congress with fireproof materials, converting the Senate's old chamber into a home for the Supreme Court, and transforming the old House chamber into a beautiful statuary hall.

More memorably, it had been Walter who had added what would become the building's most defining feature: its soaring iron dome, which he had sketched out as nearly an afterthought to replace Bulfinch's squatty and ill-proportioned copper dome. He had supervised its slow but regular construction under the watchful and sometimes skeptical eyes of four presidents, five secretaries of war, and multiple secretaries of the interior. He had scrambled for funding with distrustful legislators and committee chairmen, and clashed constantly with Meigs over design, decoration, materials, and credit. Ultimately, none of that would matter or even be remembered; practically overnight, Walter's dome gave the Capitol a memorable presence, provided the capital city with a defining and immediately recognizable silhouette, and endowed a nation recovering from a civil war with a new symbol of national pride.

In the final days leading up to his formal resignation, Walter had done his best to save face, tut-tutting to the secretary that all of his work was done anyway, so there was really no need for an Architect of the Capitol *at all.* Harlan filed that recommendation away without comment, likely to the relief of Walter's assistant Edward Clark, who Walter suspected was hoping to take his job.

As it turned out, he was right.

Just days after Walter's departure, French appointed his son Benjamin Jr. as the architect's replacement, only to be reminded by Interior Secretary Harlan that the position was still considered an executive appointment that could be filled only by President Johnson. In August, then, Edward Clark was named by the president as the newest Architect of the Capitol.

Clark's appointment to the position surprised no one. While the forty-three-year-old Clark wasn't necessarily ambitious, he had definitely put in time and effort to learn the basics of architecture from his uncle, an Army engineer, before serving as an apprentice in Walter's Philadelphia firm as a teenager. He had worked his way up through Walter's organization, in which he had lent a hand with the design and construction of Girard College. Then in 1851, he followed the architect to Washington, where he continued his service as one of Walter's primary assistants and most reliable draftsmen. He was polite and unassuming; with his bald head and dark eyebrows, he looked like a mild-mannered college instructor. Perhaps most important, he was considered a peacemaker and a great networker, and was liked by Republicans and Democrats. When Clark gave even the slightest indication that he was interested in the appointment following Walter's resignation, there was little to no opposition.

With most of the heavy lifting on the Capitol completed, Clark's immediate tasks at hand would involve finishing the detail work on the building: completing the porticos on the House and Senate wings, installing the new marble floor in Statuary Hall, and overseeing recently approved work to expand the Library of Congress. Over his long tenure as Architect of the Capitol, he would supervise the renovation and modernization of the building: replacing fireplaces with steam heat, and installing new gas and water lines as well as state-of-the-art technology like telephones, electric lights, and elevators.

He would also preside over the completion of *The Apotheosis of Washington*, which Brumidi started under Walter in December 1864 and put the final touches on under Clark in November 1865. Brumidi's speed was likely due partly to the fact that he had been left mostly on his own, with minimal interference or second opinions. The only real change the painter made to the fresco had come at the request of Meigs, who noticed that in the "Commerce" group—featuring Mercury handing a bag of money to a group of financiers—one of the heads visible in a crowd of figures looked exactly like his, a coy homage to Meigs by Brumidi. Perhaps concerned that his reputation might be tarnished by a depiction of him having money thrust in his face, Meigs asked Brumidi to remove his likeness from the group, and the artist complied, scraping the image of Meigs away and covering up the empty space with a patch of paint matching the color of the ceiling. Despite Brumidi's careful work, sharp eyes can still spot the cover-up on the ceiling.

Brumidi had also incorporated the image of a gray and bearded Thomas U. Walter into the fresco, with the architect standing in for Samuel F. B. Morse as one of the innovators clustered in the "Science" group—though if Walter noticed, he never mentioned it. Others have seen likenesses of Jefferson Davis and other Confederate leaders in the faces of the figures being trampled by Freedom in the "War" cluster, but if this was deliberate on Brumidi's part, he wasn't telling.

To illuminate the fresco, Walter had designed a lighting system of strategically placed mirrors to reflect sunshine streaming in through the dome's upper windows back up into the canopy to light it by day, while gas jet fixtures would illuminate the painting by night. Clark would finish installing the mirrors in January 1866, officially completing the dome. Shortly thereafter, the wooden platform across the oculus was carefully removed, revealing the painted ceiling to an impressed public. "Of all the fresco work ever yet done in America, this is the greatest," gushed one journalist, "and will be a most fitting covering piece to the finest building in the world."[11]

With the Capitol building close to complete, Clark, in his first report to Congress, now focused on the surrounding grounds, which were in need of more deliberate landscaping and better care. He suggested first that the boundaries of the Capitol grounds be extended several blocks to the north and south and that the sloping western lawn be extended the rest of the way down the hill to join up with the grassy Mall, presenting a uniform landscape from the Capitol building all the way down to the Washington Monument and the White House. It would take Congress several years to agree to even a modest extension of the grounds; some members considered enlarging the grounds to be a "luxury,"[12] while others—including James Harlan, who had returned to the Senate after his stint as secretary of the interior—were certain the Capitol wasn't long for Washington, D.C., anyway. Harlan was convinced the nation's capital would be relocated closer to the center of the nation as more and more states were added out west.

Maintenance continued to be an ongoing job, especially as the grounds around the building were still seen largely as a common area that was crisscrossed in several places by roads carrying carriages and foot traffic that trampled grass and left the grounds in general disarray. Clark tried to tidy things up by grading the roads and tearing down the remains of outbuildings and sheds that had been abandoned by work crews. But taking care of the property was becoming a big job, and when Benjamin French was removed as commissioner of public buildings in 1867, oversight of the Capitol was briefly transferred from his office to the chief engineer of the Army, who had larger work crews at his disposal to maintain the grounds.

Within a year, however, Congress moved oversight from the military—always a bone of contention—back to the civilian Clark, stripping away the title Architect of the Capitol Extension and officially designating him as simply Architect of the Capitol—the title that subsequent architects hold to this day. That new title meant Clark now had authority over everything from the interior and exterior of the physical building to the surrounding grounds and landscaping.

By 1872, Clark was finally making headway on the expansion of the Capitol grounds, thanks to the support of a key ally in the Senate, Justin Morrill, chair of the Senate Committee on Public Buildings and Grounds and the same member who had imagined creating Statuary

Hall from the old House chamber. Morrill introduced legislation extending the boundary of the Capitol grounds to B Street North and South—modern-day Constitution Avenue on the north and Independence Avenue on the south. The proposal involved condemning a saloon and several other unsightly private structures near the Capitol, giving the building room to breathe in both directions. The final bill, signed into law by President U. S. Grant in May, increased the size of the grounds surrounding the Capitol to 58.8 acres, its size today.

Morrill contacted an acquaintance of his in New York, the renowned and very famous landscape architect Fredrick Law Olmsted, who had designed New York City's Central Park and several other well-admired public spaces. "I hope you may feel sufficient interest in this rather national object not to have it botched,"[13] Morrill wrote to Olmsted, as he asked the architect if he would consider developing a preliminary design for the grounds of the Capitol. Morrill's appeal to Olmsted's patriotism worked; while Olmsted told Merrill he thought the current unplanned and unkempt nature of the Capitol grounds "manifests nothing so much as disunity," he liked the challenge that was being presented and saw it as a grand opportunity "to form and train the tastes of the nation."[14] He'd take the job. That was fine by Clark, who admitted he had no "practice or pretensions to skill as a landscape gardener"[15] and welcomed the opportunity to work with the nation's preeminent landscape architect.

At age fifty-one, Olmsted had already made his name and reputation designing outdoor spaces that drew the eye to the ground and then to the surrounding landscapes. This job, however, would be slightly different. "The ground is in design part of the Capitol," wrote Olmsted, "but in all respects subsidiary to the central structure."[16] For the grounds of the Capitol, then, the building itself was the showpiece; there would be no clusters of trees or obtrusive sculptures or anything else that would obscure or take the focus off it. Olmsted wanted the building visible and looking attractive no matter from where on the grounds it was viewed.

Olmsted asked Morrill for a payment of $1,500 for his design work—about $40,000 today—plus the costs of any travel from New York to Washington. His request was an absolute bargain that the Congress quickly approved. After some surveying and walking the grounds to look at trees—"the trees now growing about it were planted with no thought of the present building," he groused[17]—Olmsted handed in just a single-page drawing that would serve as the landscaping guide for the project for decades.

Leaning into his trademark curving paths and gently sloping terraces, Olmsted designed an approach to the Capitol's west side that aligned shaded walkways with the diagonal lines of Pennsylvania and Maryland Avenues so the walking paths began where the two roadways converged against the west lawn. Curving paths arced up the north and south sides of the building so visitors could stroll in the shade of carefully placed trees and bushes—but no showy flowering bushes that might draw the eye away from the building. On the expansive east side, Olmsted eliminated most of the access points that permitted carriages and visitors to cross the grounds haphazardly; instead, he funneled them up one main central north-south path extending from East Capitol Street. The look was informal yet highly organized. While he planned to incorporate hardscapes—fountains, lamps, and terraces—into his plan, everything would be placed deliberately to present the building in the best or most dramatic fashion, and designed in classical, Romanesque, and Oriental styles that would complement the neoclassical look of the Capitol rather than compete with it.

But Olmsted submitted more than just a plan for landscaping; as he had walked the grounds and viewed the Capitol from various angles, Olmsted thought the proportions of the building, especially with its new dome, made it appear as if the structure was perilously perched on the west side of Capitol Hill—"hanging upon the brow of a hill," he said[18]—and in danger of sliding down the slope. It was not a good look, in his opinion, for the centerpiece of American democracy. L'Enfant had once described Capitol Hill as a pedestal awaiting a monument—and so Olmsted proposed constructing a marble terrace surrounding the Capitol on its north, west, and south sides to literally serve as a kind of pedestal. "The building will appear as standing on a much firmer base and thus gain greatly in the supreme qualities of stability, endurance, and repose," he assured the Congress.[19]

Congress approved Olmsted's one-page plan in June 1874 and provided the landscape architect with an annual salary of $2,000—again, another good deal—along with a $200,000 appropriation that would be managed by the Architect of the Capitol. Clark, in fact, would begin to redefine the role of Architect of the Capitol with the landscaping project. He started to do less designing and more project management: overseeing Olmsted—at least on paper; dealing with the hiring of contractors; sorting through bids for materials; and basically taking on the role of an administrator.

Excavation and grading began almost immediately—nearly 300,000 cubic yards of material would eventually be removed—and new water, sewer, and gas lines would be installed while the ground was being reshaped. Olmsted would move some trees ("the more thrifty ones," he explained)[20] and order more than a thousand new ones for planting on the grounds over the next two decades; around forty of Olmsted's trees, in fact, remain standing on the Capitol lawn.

Olmsted's terrace, however, had gotten snarled in a debate about what to do with the rapidly expanding collection belonging to the Library of Congress. Ever since passage of the Copyright Act of 1870, which required that two copies of any item protected by law—not just books but also pamphlets, prints, maps, and sheet music—be deposited in the Library of Congress, the library had been inundated with materials and was outgrowing the allotted space in the Capitol at an alarming rate. While some members argued for an entirely new building to house the growing library, others pressed for extending the Capitol's western front farther out over the slope of Capitol Hill. Even Meigs weighed in on the matter, urging Congress *not* to extend the western front and expressing his support for Olmsted's terrace. But without resolution of the matter of whether the west side would be extended or the footprint in any other way altered, work on Olmsted's terrace would have to wait.

On the afternoon of May 19, 1876, as the Senate met in a closed session to consider articles of impeachment against William Belknap, President Grant's corrupt secretary of war, an explosion loudly rocked the chamber. Stunned Senators took a moment before peeking out the chamber doors and learning that a gas leak had ignited just downstairs in the hallway directly outside the Senate restaurant. As policemen cleared the halls and escorted rattled diners out, investigators traced the blast to a small, dark document room where a gas leak had detonated when John King, a Capitol Hill carpenter, struck a match to investigate the space. The explosion ripped doors from their hinges and threw King into a wall so violently that he left imprints of his head and hands in the plaster.[21] Senators went back to work, and no mention of the incident was made in the official record for the day.

The Senate adjourned at 4:50 p.m. King died in a Capitol Hill hospital an hour and ten minutes later. Two months later, the Congress would approve a private relief bill granting $3,000 to his widow and children.

Even as they debated what to do with the overflowing Library of Congress, members of Congress found the Capitol still had plenty of other quirks for them to complain about—starting with the enormous arched bronze Columbus doors, created by sculptor Randolph Rogers, that

Walter had installed in the south end of Statuary Hall at the entrance to the new House extension. The complaint wasn't with Rogers's work itself; if anything, it was *too* good. Every day, visitors would crowd around the doors, staring at Rogers's detailed work, tracing their fingers over the bronze—breaking pieces off in some cases—and creating in the hallway a bottleneck that annoyed Congressmen who had to push past on their way to the House chamber. Clark's solution was to remove the doors and put them where Walter had originally intended: at the front of the Capitol building. He placed them in the main entrance of the central east portico, where they would open directly into the Rotunda.

Sixty feet above the floor of the Rotunda, Clark had another issue to deal with: the empty eight-foot band encircling the Rotunda just below the thirty-six windows in the base of the dome. From his earliest drawings of the dome, Walter had intended for this space to contain decorative sculpture or a painting of some kind, but after Brumidi had become involved, Walter was going to, in a sense, get both of his preferences: namely, a two-dimensional frieze so skillfully painted by Brumidi that it would look as if the band were filled with three-dimensional figures in stone relief. The artist had prepared an initial sketch for the frieze in 1859, but delays and a near-perpetual lack of funding had postponed work for nearly two decades. Now, in 1877, Brumidi, at age seventy-two, had finally been authorized to begin working on the frieze.

As designed by Brumidi, the frieze would trace the history of the United States in sixteen panels, from the arrival of Columbus to the discovery of gold in California, with a focus on events from the Revolutionary War and exploration of the New World by Spanish colonizers. After scaling up his rough sketches of the first few panels and transferring them to the walls, Brumidi at last began painting in 1878.

The frieze was only fifty-eight feet from the floor of the Rotunda—significantly lower than the dizzying hundred eighty feet he'd braved to paint *The Apotheosis of Washington*, though still, said Brumidi, a "giddy height."[22] But the scaffolding on which he worked—two levels of narrow platforms clinging to the curved walls of the Rotunda with the help of struts and ropes—was perhaps more vertigo-inducing than the platform he'd worked from in the upper dome. Reaching it could be particularly perilous; one newspaper reporter watched in awe as Brumidi climbed the stairs to the upper gallery, then lowered himself over the railing nearly a hundred feet from the floor to make his way to a series of ladders he would use to climb the rest of the way down to his work scaffolding. There was little room for error. "If he should fall," wrote the reporter, "he would mash down yonder like a basket of eggs."[23]

In October 1879, Brumidi was painting while seated in a chair perched on the top platform of his scaffolding. As he leaned forward to touch up the wall, his chair suddenly slipped off the edge of the platform, pitching the artist forward and over the edge. Brumidi managed to save himself from mashing down yonder only by grabbing the rung of a ladder between the two platforms of his scaffolding. According to Brumidi's own understandably dramatic recounting of the accident, he dangled from the ladder for at least fifteen minutes until he was finally rescued by Capitol police officer Humphrey Lemon, who had been patrolling the dome and saw the artist tumble. But whether he dangled sixty feet in the air for five minutes or fifteen, Brumidi was understandably rattled, confessing to Clark that he'd had a "shock to the nerves."[24] He would shakily return to the scaffolding the following day to daub at the figure of William Penn presenting a treaty to the Lenape Indians, but Brumidi was never the same.

With his health deteriorating—he suffered from near-debilitating asthma and chronic diarrhea—the artist retired to work in his home studio at 921 G Street NW. "[I] have employed all the working days in drawing the cartoons for the frieze now in progress in the Rotunda of the Capitol," he told Clark.[25] With eight panels already completed, Brumidi hoped to spend the winter finishing detailed sketches of the remaining eight that another artist could transfer to the walls to complete the frieze. On February 18, 1880, he finished up a drawing of a scene depicting the Battle of Lexington. On the morning of February 19, Brumidi died at home, aged seventy-four. He had literally worked right to the very end.

To complete the remaining eight scenes Brumidi had sketched for the frieze, Clark brought in Filippo Costaggini, a classically trained Italian painter who had come highly recommended by Brumidi himself. While Costaggini could mimic Brumidi's style, his more detailed brand of painting didn't look as convincingly three-dimensional as Brumidi's. Costaggini began by painting the three Native Americans at the far right of the *William Penn and the Indians* panel, which Brumidi had been working on at the time of his accident. It's easy to spot where Brumidi stops and Costaggini begins.

Costaggini painted the next eight panels over nine years, completing Brumidi's vision for the frieze in 1889. However, Brumidi had made a major miscalculation, drawing his sketches under the incorrect assumption that the usable space in the fresco was nine feet high when it was actually only a little more than seven—and so, the downscaling of his sketches as they were transferred to the wall meant that the completed frieze was still thirty-one feet short of completely encircling the Rotunda. Costaggini pled with Congress to let him fill the space with panels of his own design—a request that was still unanswered when the painter died in 1904. The frieze would remain incomplete until 1953.

Despite the multiple hands on the frieze and the countless talented artists and sculptors whose art decorates the Capitol, it would be Brumidi whose work was, and is, forever associated with the Capitol. "He was the genius of the Capitol,"[26] declared *The Washington Post* in a front-page obituary in 1880. "The walls of the Capitol have been illuminated by his magic touch," enthused the *National Republican* in a similar page-one remembrance. "In every part of the building are traces of his presence."[27]

More than two hundred twenty years after his birth, Brumidi's work continues to amaze and inspire Capitol visitors, and his name is treated with no small amount of reverence by the Congress, especially in the

Senate, where his work still covers the walls of the Brumidi Corridors on the first floor of the Senate extension. Strolling the Brumidi Corridors today, visitors will also encounter a beautiful marble bust of the artist himself, commissioned by the Congress in 1967 from the noted sculptor Jimilu Mason. It presides nobly over the corridors that bear his name—the artist as art fittingly decorating his own hallways.

In 2008, the U.S. Congress and President George W. Bush approved Public Law 110-259, posthumously awarding the Congressional Gold Medal—the oldest and highest civilian award in the United States—to Constantino Brumidi. They noted in particular that his "life and work exemplify the lives of millions of immigrants who came to pursue the American dream."[28] Speaker of the House John Boehner was noticeably moved during the formal ceremony honoring the artist, and he more than once dabbed away tears. "The art here doesn't sit idly on display every day. It summons the building to life and replenishes the soul of the Congress," said Boehner. "This of course is the legacy of Brumidi, who filled his work with such color and attention to detail and tradition that it is unavoidable and too captivating to be ignored."[29]

By 1880, much of the landscaping work on the Capitol grounds was complete. Over the previous six years, Olmsted had installed more than seventy-eight hundred trees and plants, hundreds of which had been stolen by trespassers or eaten and trampled by the cattle that still invaded the grounds from time to time even as low stone walls surrounding the campus were being installed. On the west side, the shaded pathways extending from Pennsylvania and Maryland Avenues were underway.

Olmsted had also added some other features to the grounds, including a small hexagonal structure that he called the "Summer-house," which was artfully constructed from red brick and enclosed a cool man-made grotto just off the northwest corner of the Senate extension. "There has been much complaint from the want of a resting place for those who walk from the bottom of the hill to the [Capitol] building," Olmsted wrote in a report to the Congress in 1880. "To meet this want, a structure is now being erected, designed to combine both drinking fountain and a secluded and cool retreat."[30] While the Summerhouse is a sleeper favorite of many visitors to the Capitol grounds today, at the time, some Congressmen weren't sure what to make of it. "I heard it was built for a monkey-house," hooted Senator James Beck of Kentucky. "I do not know what it is."[31] Others complained that Olmsted had overstepped his authority, as he had designed and built the structure without ever alerting the Congress or seeking its approval. Congressmen made it clear to Olmsted that there would be no more architectural ad-libbing. The architect quietly canceled plans for a similar structure on the House side.

The only part of the landscaping project that remained unfinished—in fact, it hadn't been started at all—was the western terrace, because the Congress still hadn't made up its mind what to do with the Library of Congress. Some progress *had* been made; Librarian of Congress Ainsworth Spofford had at last convinced legislators the library's collection was growing so quickly that a new building was needed to shelve and store all of it—a suggestion that President Rutherford B. Hayes also echoed in his first message to Congress.[32]

With momentum growing in favor of a new library building, Senator Morrill slid funding into an appropriations bill permitting construction of one corner of the terrace, gambling that once work on the terrace had started, Congress would be obligated to complete it. While recognizing the fait accompli of Morrill's maneuver, Congress simply demanded Olmsted provide them with a detailed work plan, which the architect did. As described by Olmsted, the new terrace would have two grand staircases, allowing access to the foot of Capitol Hill from the West Front, and—the icing on the cake for some legislators—would house seventy-four storage rooms and ten new committee meeting rooms. That was enough to get Congress enthusiastically on board.

Morrill's strategy also empowered Spofford to redouble his efforts to persuade Congress to move the library out of the Capitol; he eventually badgered legislators into making a much-needed formal decision. In 1886, Congress authorized construction of a new building for the Library of Congress on First Street directly east of the Capitol, and provided a hefty $585,000 to acquire the site and another $500,000 to begin construction. The new library—built in a heavily ornamented style reflecting the architecture of the Italian Renaissance and now called Beaux Arts—would open in 1897 to great acclaim. In the minds of some visitors, it would give the Capitol a run for the title of most beautiful building in Washington, D.C.

Olmsted didn't seem intimidated or even all that impressed with the ornate library building slowly going up across the street. Instead, he concentrated on completing the terrace and doing for the Capitol compound what he had done for New York with his design for Central Park: he would make it a vibrant, walkable, and must-see destination and a defining feature of the growing city's distinct personality.

In addition to the terrace and its much-desired office and storage space, Olmsted had also taken on the regular complaint from legislators about the air quality in their respective chambers. Olmsted agreed the air in the chambers could be stuffy or unpleasant, even going so far as to declare the air in the House as a "poisonous miasma."[33] While Clark worked inside the building to renovate the House extension, creating a spacious lobby just behind the House chamber and entirely rebuilding the House floor, Olmsted worked outside, installing ventilated towers and ductwork on the south lawn of the Capitol to funnel fresh air into the inner chamber—a novel idea that the Senate soon embraced as well, asking Olmsted for a similar setup on the north side.

By the mid-1880s, things were far enough along on the construction of the terrace that Olmsted tried to step down from his post overseeing its construction. Clark, knowing it was better to have the savvy landscaper close at hand, insisted on keeping Olmsted on as a consultant, essentially putting him back in charge of the project for the next five years. Olmsted immediately had a crisis of sorts on his hands, as Congress decided it wanted the committee rooms being built under the new terrace to have windows looking west out over the Mall—"out toward the west where all the winds blow, where the air is pure and sweet and clear," Senator Eugene Hale of Maine cooed dramatically.

Olmsted blanched at the very idea, arguing that windows anywhere in the terrace platform would look like "the opening of holes in a dam" and make the Capitol appear "less secure in its foundations."[34] It was an argument Olmsted would lose; today, the Capitol's western terrace still has six tall, arched windows flanking a central arched entry. Perhaps to Olmsted's disappointment, the building does not appear any less secure in its foundations.

"The Capitol grounds, which formerly were homely and formal in appearance, have been transformed into a beautiful park," enthused Washington's *Critic and Record*, "and are now most exquisitely beautiful."[35] Most seemed to agree; Olmsted's design and careful eye for detail, from the ornate gas lamps that could be lit with the touch of a button to the sloping paths lined with trees that seemed to frame any view of the building, had transformed the grounds from monotonous to majestic. He had also blended the Capitol grounds nearly seamlessly into the Mall—which was still mostly just a series of parks and pathways to the west. In this way, he presented a unified vista from Capitol Hill toward the Washington Monument, which had finally opened to the public in 1888.

Recently, too, the Potomac River had been dredged by the Army Corps of Engineers to make the river more easily navigable, and the removed sediment was used to extend the Mall farther to the west and south. In doing so, engineers created a scenic overlook at the western end of the Mall where the Lincoln Memorial would be constructed beginning in 1914; to the south was the newly formed Tidal Basin, over which the Jefferson Memorial would preside starting in 1943. Anchoring the Mall then, as now, was the Capitol, perched securely atop Olmsted's new terrace. Nearly three decades after a civil war, Olmsted's message was clear: the Capitol, and the republic, weren't going *anywhere.*

As Olmsted's carefully selected flora took hold in its carefully planned settings, it required regular attention from Capitol groundskeepers to ensure trees, lawns, bushes, and other plants remained neatly trimmed and pruned. In no time at all, Olmsted's trees were flourishing—so much so that some parts of the grounds were so darkly shaded that Clark recommended a regular night patrol to keep evening visitors safe.

There were some, however, who thought the extra security might be put to better use inside the building.

In December 1887, William Preston Taulbee, a thirty-six-year-old Kentucky minister and Congressman, was taking a political beating at the hands of his home state's newspapers, based on the reporting of *Louisville Times* journalist Charles E. Kincaid, who had caught Taulbee in "a most compromising position" with a young woman in the U.S. Patent Office.[36] The affair cost Taulbee his marriage and so damaged what had been a rising political reputation that he opted not to run for reelection in 1888 and became a lobbyist instead. While he was modestly successful at his new job, Taulbee was never going to forgive Kincaid for ruining him.

Taulbee was a big man, standing a robust six foot two, while Kincaid—described by even the most sympathetic of newspapers as "small and frail"[37]—was barely over five feet tall. For two years, the two men publicly traded highly personal insults that nearly always turned into physical assaults, with the diminutive Kincaid receiving the worst of it, whether he was getting shoved into railings or having his nose pulled by the larger man. While Kincaid usually did his best to avoid Taulbee, the two of them eventually crossed paths in the Capitol at noon on Friday, February 28, 1890, just outside the entrance to the House chamber. Predictably, Taulbee began taunting Kincaid, growing angrier and more animated as he loomed over the smaller man. Even as House doorkeeper Samuel Donaldson tried to keep the peace and pulled the two men apart, Taulbee seized Kincaid by the collar and threw him against the wall. A rattled Kincaid slowly hauled himself to his feet, then went home for his pistol.

Around 1:40 p.m., Taulbee and Donaldson emerged from the House chamber and headed down the gallery stairs for the House dining room, taking one arm of the Y-shaped staircase that led from the second floor to the first. As Taulbee passed the landing and began descending the single marble stairway near the restaurant, Kincaid, now gripping a revolver in his pocket, quietly approached his nemesis on the stairs. When he was just behind Taulbee, Kincaid called his name; when the big man turned around to look, Kincaid fired a single shot directly into his face. Taulbee staggered away with his face in his hands, spattering blood on the marble steps. Kincaid, unmoved, calmly turned himself over to the Capitol policeman who had rushed to the stairs at the sound of the gunshot.[38]

Incredibly, Taulbee would survive for another eleven days, eventually succumbing to his wound on March 11. Nearly everyone agreed it was a well-deserved comeuppance. "Taulbee played the coward's part attacking a man who was physically his inferior and Kincaid was compelled to defend himself as best he could," went one typical editorial. "It may teach other burly ruffians a lesson."[39] A jury agreed and acquitted Kincaid, determining he had acted in self-defense. Meanwhile, the marble steps where Taulbee was shot are still visibly stained with a dark spatter that may or may not be from Taulbee's blood and that, some say, defies even the harshest scrubbing.

Monday, September 18, 1893, was a holiday in Washington, D.C., set aside on the city's calendar to celebrate the hundredth anniversary of the laying of the cornerstone of the U.S. Capitol building. Even the weather was obliging, with clear and sunny skies—"a more perfect day could not be desired," declared Washington's *Evening Star.*[40] At one p.m., every bell in the city rang out. With his cabinet and members of the Supreme Court just behind him, President Grover Cleveland—now in his second, nonconsecutive term—climbed into a carriage at the front of a steady procession up Pennsylvania Avenue toward the Capitol. It was the very same route taken by George Washington a century earlier, though the dirt road hacked into the countryside of 1793 was now a major thoroughfare paved with asphalt. More than 150,000 spectators lined Pennsylvania Avenue, cheering wildly as the president passed by.

American flags with forty-four stars hung from the upper-story windows of buildings along the parade route, while others were draped in red, white, and blue bunting. Programs had been printed so onlookers could keep track of all the military units and civic organizations marching by and read the names of every committee member who had planned events for the day. It truly seemed as if the entire city had turned out for the occasion, either to participate in the parade or to watch it.

At two p.m., Cleveland arrived at the East Front of the Capitol building, where a crowd of more than a hundred thousand packed the plaza, sitting on Olmsted's carefully designed lawns or clambering for any spot on the building they could find. Spectators crammed themselves into every last inch of the stairways and porticos, some watched from the large windows at the base of the dome, and others—in a move that would send modern-day Secret Service agents scrambling—climbed daringly out onto the roof overlooking the plaza and the president below.[41]

Cleveland, framed against the columns and portico of the East Front, stood before the crowd with his hat in his hand to deliver brief remarks.

Rising to the occasion, the president hailed the Capitol as "a magnificent structure" with a noble pedigree, "designed and planned by great and good men as a place where the principles of a free representative government should be developed in patriotic legislation for the benefit of the people." More important, he stressed, it had been built, like the government itself, on the foundational principles of decency, honesty, and selflessness:

> If representatives who here assemble to make laws for their fellow-countrymen forget the duty of broad and disinterested patriotism and legislate in prejudice and passion or in behalf of sectional and selfish interests, the time when the corner stone of our Capitol was laid and the circumstances surrounding it will not be worth commemorating.[42]

Afterward, Architect of the Capitol Edward Clark mounted a plaque commemorating the laying of the first cornerstone in 1793, putting it in the south face of the southeast corner of the Old Senate wing. As noted earlier, he most likely installed it in the wrong place.

November 6, 1898, was cold and rainy—typical late-fall weather in Washington, D.C. Neither the House nor the Senate was in session—it was a Sunday—so it was quiet in the building as Lieutenant Robert Akers, a Capitol policeman, settled into a chair in his office just west of the Senate chambers. At 5:22 p.m., Akers heard a thunderous explosion that shook the building so violently, it knocked him from his chair. Akers sounded the alarm immediately, though help was already on the way, as the enormous bang had been heard for blocks. He then ran for the Supreme Court chamber, where he was certain the blast had come from. As he entered the corridor outside the courtroom, he found the way clogged with debris and a choking dark smoke.

"EXPLOSION AT CAPITOL," screamed an all-caps headline in a special evening edition of *The Washington Post* published less than four hours later. "SUPREME COURT CHAMBER IN RUINS."[43] For a moment, there were suspicions that the explosion had been the result of a bomb, an act of retribution against U.S. involvement in Cuba during the ongoing Spanish-American War. Further investigation, however, revealed the cause as a leaking gas line in the cellar just below the Supreme Court that had been accidentally ignited by a lamp—shades of the gas leak that had killed carpenter John King twenty-two years earlier. The blast heaved up portions of the floor in the courtroom and the Small Senate Rotunda, blew out windows and doors throughout the old north wing, and slightly damaged some of Latrobe's colorful tobacco capitals. The resulting fire took several hours to put out and burned much of the law library. It was an "irreparable loss," wrote *The Washington Post*. "Flames and destruction know no sentiment."[44]

During the cleanup, more than twenty tons of damaged brick, mortar, and plaster were removed from the building. As work crews repaired the floors in the courtroom and in the Small Senate Rotunda, some of the original stone laid by Latrobe was replaced with concrete—a change in building materials that has empowered one of the more enduring urban legends involving the Capitol building. While the wet concrete was still drying in the floor of the Small Senate Rotunda, a cat sprinted through the space, leaving several small paw prints that are still clearly visible near the base of one of Latrobe's columns. Local folklorists say the prints belonged to a supernatural demon cat first reported in the early 1890s by a terrified night watchman who claimed the cat grew to a monstrous size as it stalked him. "A truly horrific apparition," journalist René Bache wrote in 1898, even as he noted that some of the Capitol's scariest ghost stories were spread by Capitol employees "discharged finally for drunkenness."[45] Visitors still scan the floor in the Small Senate Rotunda, excitedly looking for the cat's prints.

In the days and weeks following the explosion and fire, Congress was anxious enough to ask for an assessment of the condition of the materials in the rest of the old section of the building, with an eye toward fireproofing. Of particular concern was the roof, which was still constructed mostly out of wood and which firefighters had scrambled to protect as the blaze in the Supreme Court chambers swirled up toward the ceiling. It was determined that a new, fireproof roof was indeed in order—and while the building was being so carefully evaluated, Congress also asked that the Architect of the Capitol figure out what to do with the space that had been vacated by the Library of Congress a year earlier.

At this point, however, the architect overseeing the assorted Capitol projects wasn't going to be Edward Clark. Now seventy-six years old, Clark was in bad health and had for several years handed most of his duties over to thirty-three-year-old Elliott Woods, who had served as his chief clerk and right-hand man since 1885. Woods's role as de facto Architect of the Capitol was no secret—"[Woods] is practically in charge of the building, as Architect Clark is not in good health," noted *The Washington Post*—but there were many in the architecture community who were watching Woods warily for one simple reason: Woods wasn't a trained architect. In fact, he had only a high school education. But he had proven himself to be a highly competent and organized administrator, and for now, that was enough.

While Clark continued to maintain the title of Architect of the Capitol, then, it would be Woods who would do the actual work over the next few years, overseeing the fireproofing of the Capitol roof and the reconfiguring of the space in the west side of the center section formerly occupied by the Library of Congress. By early 1901, the wooden roofs and low domes over the old north and south wings had been removed and rebuilt with fireproof materials, mostly steel and copper. Removing the roof of the old House wing also presented Woods with an opportunity to make some improvements to Statuary Hall, where the old wooden ceiling, which had been painted to look as if it were decorated with indented coffers, could finally be replaced with an ornate ceiling with *real* coffers. Removing the smooth wooden ceiling was certain to change the famously unusual acoustics in the chamber, but Woods promised that "the echoes have been saved to a great extent."[46] Thanks to Woods, visitors to Statuary Hall who stand in just the right spot can still experience the odd acoustics that bounce a whisper across the chamber with absolute clarity.

In his renovation of the old Library of Congress, Woods stunned the Congress with his efficiency, completing the job in only six months, during which he converted the formerly cavernous west center section into three floors of meeting spaces, offices, and storage rooms for use by both the House and the Senate. Meanwhile, the cast-iron library that Thomas Walter had been so proud of was unceremoniously disassembled and sold for scrap at a profit.

Woods also began responding to other complaints and requests from the Congress, returning to what seemed to be the never-ending matter of the airflow in the House chamber; even Olmsted's ventilation towers had failed to appease perpetually unhappy House members. Once again, the entire floor of the chamber was removed so work crews could install air grills at each member's desk—and while the room was being torn apart, Woods took the opportunity to incorporate other upgrades like call buttons to signal for assistance from House pages. The chamber was also repainted, getting rid of Brumidi's showy colors and painted decorations, which had annoyed members for decades.

In January 1902, Edward Clark died at home in Washington, D.C., at age seventy-nine, marking the end of a thirty-six-year tenure as Architect of the Capitol—he's still the longest-serving architect in the position's history. The efficient and well-liked Elliott Woods had been serving as acting architect for at least four years, and most assumed his permanent elevation to the post was both imminent and well deserved. Pushback came immediately, however, from members of the American Institute of Architects—most notably from its secretary, Glenn Brown, an accomplished architect who had recently published the first volume of what would be his two-part magnum opus, *History of the United States Capitol*. The forty-seven-year-old Brown, offended at the very idea that such a position would go to a nonarchitect, appealed directly to President Theodore Roosevelt, recently ascended to the office following the assassination of William McKinley, to appoint an actual architect, and enthusiastically recommended himself as the best man for the job.

At the same time, supporters of Woods whirled into action, stuffing Roosevelt's White House mailbox with countless letters of support for the de facto Architect of the Capitol. Among Woods's staunchest supporters was the powerful Republican Congressman Joseph Cannon, who had been in the House almost nonstop since the Grant administration, was serving as the chairman of the powerful appropriations committee, and would later be elected Speaker of the House. While Roosevelt and he were both Republicans, there was no love lost between them—the two repeatedly clashed over issues like the environment and government regulation—and Cannon would derisively refer to the president as "that fellow at the other end of the Avenue."[47] Still, Cannon's endorsement was certain to carry significant weight with the president and nearly anyone else.

Cannon didn't necessarily know all that much about Woods, but he did know that he didn't like Glenn Brown and the American Institute of Architects presuming they had any say whatsoever over who the next Architect of the Capitol should be; in Cannon's opinion, that decision was solely up to the Congress. Cannon went to the White House for a conversation with Roosevelt, who agreed to formally appoint Woods to the post on the condition that—in a sop to the professional architects—his title be changed from "Architect" to "Superintendent." Otherwise, the position belonged to Woods and would remain parked under the jurisdiction of the secretary of the interior, as it had been since the 1862 rebuke of Meigs. That was all fine by Woods; Brown, meanwhile, would disparage Woods for the rest of his career, chalking up Woods's promotion solely to the inexperience and naivete of Teddy Roosevelt, who he thought was clearly in over his head.

Elliott Woods was a man of many talents and many interests. A lack of formal training never diminished his enthusiasm for architecture any more than it did his interest and excitement in countless other pastimes, from chemistry to music. When he wasn't in his office in the Capitol, Woods could be found in his private laboratory at Delaware and C Street NE, conducting science experiments or playing the violin. For relaxation, he wrote operas and played in a kazoo band. He was outgoing and modest, and when it came to his professional duties, he seemed to be perpetually in motion, whether he was overseeing the regular painting of the dome every four years (it took thirty-five men two months and forty-two hundred gallons of paint), ordering signs reading "Pull the Chain" to be installed over the toilets, or hiring dogs and ferrets to hunt down rats in the Capitol's cellars and dark hallways. He truly was, as many called him, "the busiest man in Washington."[48]

Woods would preside over a number of false starts regarding the extension of the Capitol's East Front—an item that had been on Thomas Walter's wish list for the building since the 1860s. In March 1901, Congress even provided funding for Woods to prepare plans for renovating the center section of the Capitol, which would involve not only pushing the East Front forward but also refacing the West Front in marble as part of a grand new western entrance to the building. The self-aware Woods, fully understanding he was a better administrator than architect, hired as consultants the noted New York–based architects John Carrère and Thomas Hastings, who had gained national attention for their 1897 design for the main branch of the New York Public Library. While Carrère and Hastings developed the detailed plans for the renovation and the new western entrance, Woods concentrated intently on the one piece of the project he had assigned himself: a set of enormous bronze doors he envisioned being installed in the new West Front entrance.

For his doors, Woods collaborated with Louis Amateis, chairman of the fine arts department at Columbian University—now George Washington University—to design a set of doors depicting key scenes, and key players, involved in the story of America's contributions to the arts and sciences, law, engineering, agriculture, and other subject areas. Amateis's ambitious and extremely detailed drawings were eventually scaled up and created in three dimensions, then cast in bronze in 1910. By that time, however, Congress had decided against the new western entrance, giving Woods two enormous bronze doors, thirteen feet tall, with nowhere to go. The elaborately carved doors would go on display at the Corcoran Gallery of Art in Washington, D.C., from 1910 to 1914, and then at the Smithsonian for several decades before finally being moved back into the Capitol, where they are now mounted against a flat wall—there's no hallway or chamber behind them—near the Memorial Door entrance in the House wing adjacent to the Rotunda. Given their highly detailed carved panels, Capitol visitors can't resist stopping to stare at what are now called the Amateis Doors—nor can they keep their hands off them, with the oil from generations of probing fingers polishing a number of features to a high shine, including the bare butt of a young boy depicted in the bottom right of the Fine Arts panel.[49]

Ultimately, the Congress approved only one improvement recommended by Carrère and Hastings in their proposed design. They signed off on the sculpture to be used in the pediment of the east entrance of the House extension, which had stood empty since its completion in the 1850s. In 1908, Woods hired for the task the American sculptor Paul Wayland Bartlett, who had worked on a similar pediment for the New York Stock Exchange. With the enthusiastic approval of the Congress, Bartlett began work on a piece called *The Apotheosis of Democracy*, featuring at the center of the triangular pediment a personification of Peace with her right arm outstretched to protect the figure of Genius. On either side of her are depictions of the two primary sources of America's wealth; to her left are representatives of industry—a printer, an ironworker, foundry workers, a textile worker, and a young boy catching a fish—and on her right are figures depicting agriculture, including a reaper, a farmer with a bull, and a woman and her children harvesting a field. After some delay—it took Bartlett longer to finish the work than he had anticipated—the completed pediment was finally unveiled on August 2, 1916.

Despite the lack of progress on the center section, the Woods era would be one of efficient restoration and renovation—and beyond the building itself, Woods would oversee the construction of two important Capitol-adjacent structures during his tenure. Much of the new work would be driven by the results of the 1900 census, which called for even *more* Congressional representation to meet the needs of the nation's rapidly growing population, which had more than doubled from just over thirty-one million in 1860 to seventy-six million in 1900. That expansion in the citizenry had upped the number of Representatives from 148 in 1860 to 386 in 1900, while the addition of twelve new states in that same period had bumped the number of Senators up from sixty-six to ninety.

The increasing ranks of legislators meant that committee rooms in the Capitol were getting cramped, and amenities like restaurants and barbershops were often full beyond their original capacity. While Congressmen and Senators continued to work at their desks in the House and Senate chambers—just as their predecessors had since the 1790s—increased responsibilities for members meant a growing need for staff, clerks, and aides. Latrobe, Bulfinch, Walter, Clark, and even Olmsted had worked to carve out as much space as they could for private offices for members, but they had managed to make room for only about fifty on the House side—not even close to meeting their needs. And even with their smaller numbers, things weren't much better on the Senate side. Clearly, dedicated office space for legislators and their staffs was going to be needed.

In the early 1890s, the Senate, anticipating the problem, had purchased the Maltby Building, a somewhat rickety U-shaped apartment building at the corner of New Jersey Avenue NW and B Street, and converted it for their use, eventually creating enough rooms to provide a personal office for every Senator as well as additional committee meeting spaces. That had abated the issue somewhat on the Senate side of Capitol Hill, so Woods, once again consulting with Carrère and Hastings, focused on providing a brand-new freestanding office building for anxious Congressmen. At this point, the Senate decided it wanted a new building, too, especially as the Maltby Building was found to be sinking rapidly on one side and was determined to be a firetrap. Carrère and Hastings obligingly designed a matching building for the Senate on the north side of Capitol Hill. The Maltby Building would eventually be torn down; close to its site today is the Taft Memorial and Carillion, honoring Senator Robert A. Taft and located just west of the current trio of Senate office buildings.

With the detailed work being carried out by Carrère and Hastings under Woods's supervision, construction on both the House and Senate office buildings proceeded quickly, with the new House building opening on December 12, 1908, and the Senate building opening only four months later, on March 5, 1909. For the first time ever, every House member would have an office. The offices for members weren't much—each House office was only about fifteen feet by twenty feet, with slightly more space given to Senate offices—but they were private and equipped with the latest state-of-the-art technologies: telephones, individual lavatories, hot and cold running water, steam heat, and forced-air ventilation. Committee rooms were set up like executive boardrooms—usually just a tasteful meeting table surrounded by leather chairs, with witnesses expected to pull up a seat to squeeze in alongside members to address the committee.

From the start, members on both sides of the Hill had insisted on an underground tunnel connecting their new office buildings with the Capitol—and Woods delivered, creating not just an underground walkway but an underground subway system of sorts. As originally envisioned, each building was to be connected to the Capitol by a real subway with a dedicated track. However, with costs escalating and members concerned about public criticism of an underground train as an unnecessary luxury, Woods arranged instead for members to be whisked from one building to the other on lemon yellow battery-powered vehicles built by the Studebaker Company in their South Bend, Indiana, factory; they could carry eight people and reach speeds of up to twelve miles per hour. Senators, in particular, were fond of the yellow electric cars, naming the vehicles Peg and Tommy.

Within a few years, members would finally have a real subway system, when Woods had the yellow cars replaced with an electric monorail system made up of a single car suspended from an overhead electrical rail. While the monorail was slower—it went only eight miles an hour—it moved eighteen people at a time, making it more efficient than the yellow cars. Here, too, Senators couldn't resist naming their monorail, christening it the Toonerville Trolley as a nod to the train in cartoonist Fontaine Fox's immensely popular comic strip, *Toonerville Folks.*

Still, there would always be complaints that members of Congress spent too much time, attention, and taxpayer money on providing themselves with luxurious spaces—complaints that continue to echo down the decades anytime Congress seeks to improve its own facilities. But Woods was a good manager. The buildings were brought in on time and under budget; by some estimates, Woods saved the federal government more than $100,000 through his care and diligence. It was enough for Congress to grant Woods a healthy bonus of $15,000—a little more than half a million dollars in today's money.

Woods's new House and Senate office buildings would begin to get crowded almost immediately. Following the census of 1910, the size of the House of Representatives swelled to 433 members; by 1920, its ranks would increase to 435 members, where they remain frozen more than a century later, thanks to the Reapportionment Act of 1929—and despite the fact that the population of the United States has more than tripled since that time.[50] In the Senate, the addition of Oklahoma in 1907 had nudged their numbers up to ninety-two; the admission of New Mexico and Arizona to the Union would push that number up to ninety-six by early 1912.

A slight rethinking of the space in the Senate office building could have made room for new Senators, but accommodating the swollen House required a serious reconfiguration of its still pristine office building. New Representatives and their staffs would be shoehorned into the building by cutting ceiling beams out of the attic, then raising the roof just high enough to create forty-eight new but cramped offices. The House chamber, as well, was almost too packed to function. Woods addressed this challenge by removing all individual desks and replacing them with fanned-out rows of fixed, conjoined upholstered seats—without desks—creating more room, and more aisle space, for members. This solution defines the layout of the House floor to this day.

The growth of the population of the United States—and the Congress—was a sign of the growing influence of the nation itself, as the country began to make its way confidently into the twentieth century, striding onto the global stage as an economic and political force to be reckoned with. Personal animosities would certainly continue to play out under the dome, but as the United States began to involve itself in international affairs, it was inevitable that unrest in the Capitol would become more political than personal.

The first act of genuine terrorism in the Capitol featured one of its strangest characters, the sad and haunted Erich Muenter, a forty-four-year-old former Harvard professor and a hardcore German nationalist. Muenter was plagued by mental illness and had already killed once; in 1906, he had poisoned his pregnant wife with arsenic, then spent the better part of the next decade evading police by bouncing around the country in and out of various teaching jobs while changing his name several times.

In 1914, while pursuing a Ph.D. at Cornell under the name of Frank Holt, Muenter became involved with the German espionage organization Abteilung III b. His views toward the United States and its engagement in the war against Germany—which, in 1914, mostly consisted of sending arms to Great Britain and France to fight the Germans—subsequently hardened, then radicalized him. Declaring himself "an old-fashioned American with a conscience,"[51] Muenter planned to make a political statement by bombing the Congress, destroying munitions bound for the war in Europe, and killing the American financiers who funded such efforts.

On the afternoon of Friday, July 2, 1915, Muenter quietly entered the Capitol and headed for the Senate chamber, where he intended to plant three sticks of dynamite connected to a timer. He found the chamber doors locked; had he bothered to check the Senate's schedule, Muenter would have realized the Senate had been out of session since March and wasn't due to reconvene until winter. Undeterred, Muenter instead planted his time bomb under the telephone switchboard in the Senate Reception Room, which was also vacant in anticipation of the July 4 holiday weekend; then he set the timer on his package for midnight. After wandering around the Capitol grounds for a while, he eventually headed for nearby Union Station to catch a late train to New York City.

At 11:23 p.m., Muenter's bomb exploded spectacularly, though harmlessly, inside the Senate Reception Room. In a letter he'd mailed to the press, Muenter said he hoped the explosion would "make enough noise to be heard above the voices that clamor for war. This explosion is an exclamation point in my appeal for peace." Capitol police officer Frank Jones, on patrol in the building, definitely heard the noise—"It sounded like several cannon[s] going off," he said later[52]—and ran to find the opulently decorated reception room in ruins, with broken mirrors, shattered windows, and splintered wood littering the floor. Overhead, cracked chandeliers still swayed in the smoke and swirling dust; Brumidi's fresco had been scorched and, in some places, blasted off the ceiling.

Muenter might have heard the explosion as he boarded his train at Union Station for New York City,[53] but he was on a different mission now. After arriving in New York, he planted a small bomb on the ship S.S. *Minnehaha*, bound for Liverpool with a hull full of American munitions. Then, in the early-morning hours of July 3, Muenter armed himself with a pair of revolvers, took a cab out to Long Island, and politely knocked on the door of forty-six-year-old financier J. Pierpont Morgan Jr., son of the esteemed and similarly named millionaire and philanthropist who had passed away only two years earlier. Muenter blamed the younger Morgan for bankrolling Germany's enemies—an accusation that was mostly true—and was determined to make the financier pay for it.

Morgan's door was answered by Henry C. Physick, the inscrutable family butler. Muenter presented himself to Physick as an associate of the millionaire and demanded to see Morgan. When he was refused entry by the skeptical butler, Muenter forced his way past Physick and into the house. As he brandished both revolvers, Muenter raced through the gigantic mansion searching for Morgan, eventually finding him on a second-floor landing. The millionaire lunged at the gunman, and the two scuffled violently, throwing punches as they rolled around on the floor of the landing. Muenter managed to fire two shots, hitting the financier in the thigh and groin, but the much stronger and larger Morgan eventually got the better of the professor, pinning him down while Physick pummeled Muenter into unconsciousness with a large piece of coal.

It took police several days to realize that the Capitol bombing and the attempt on Morgan's life were related; Muenter had signed his letter of confession to the newspapers as "R. Pearce" while he had identified himself to Physick as "Thomas C. Lester." Fortunately, it took only a few days—as well as some careful handwriting analysis—before police were able to determine that Muenter, Pearce, and Lester were all the same person.

Newspapers of the era were certain that the bomb at the Capitol had to be part of a political statement. It was not unreasonable to think so; less than three months earlier, a German U-boat had torpedoed the British ocean liner R.M.S. *Lusitania,* killing nearly twelve hundred people, including 128 Americans. "Some persons in the crowd which had gathered around the Capitol were inclined to believe that the bomb had been placed by some war fanatic as an act of resentment against the United States government," wrote the New York *Sun.* "It was recalled that just such an incident as this had been feared and guarded against in Washington since the early days after the outbreak of the European war."[54]

Muenter died in police custody on July 6 after diving head-first from the cross-bars of his jail cell onto the concrete floor; witnesses reported that he hit the pavement so hard that it sounded like a gunshot. The day after Muenter's death, the bomb he had planted aboard the S.S. *Minnehaha* exploded while the ship was at sea, starting a small fire but otherwise causing no injuries and barely harming the ship. By then, Muenter and his cause had sparked a growing "anti-Hun" movement. In fact, Muenter's bomb in the Senate Reception Room had the effect of nudging the United States toward engagement in the European war with Germany—exactly the opposite of Muenter's intent.

Two years later, on April 2, 1917, President Woodrow Wilson appeared before a joint session of Congress to make the case for entering the war in Europe by declaring war against Germany. "The world must be made safe for democracy," Wilson thundered. "Its peace must be planted upon the tested foundations of political liberty." Two days later, the U.S. Senate voted to declare war on Germany by a vote of eighty-two to six.

One of the six opposing the declaration was Robert La Follette, the progressive-minded Senator from Wisconsin. The war would be paid for not by the industries who stood to profit the most from it, he argued, but rather by the taxpayers who could afford it the least. He would similarly vote against President Wilson's Espionage Act—which prohibited any criticism of the government—calling it nothing short of an erosion of First Amendment rights. "The right to control their own Government according to constitutional forms is not one of the rights that the citizens of this country are called upon to surrender in time of war," La Follette said later. "In this government, the people are the rulers in war no less than in peace."

La Follette's dissent was regarded by many at the time as treason—he was spit on and hanged in effigy, and some argued that he should have been executed by a firing squad—though time would be kinder to his reputation. If opponents wanted to accuse him of treason, then "Fighting Bob" La Follette had a ready response. "Collective homicide can not establish human rights," he said. "For our country to enter the European war would be treason to humanity."

For his daring, forthright, and consistent advocacy for progressive causes, human rights, and freedom of speech, La Follette—who died in 1925—was honored by his home state of Wisconsin in 1929 as the subject of one of its two statues in the U.S. Capitol's National Statuary Hall Collection. In 1957, La Follette was selected by a Senate Special Committee—chaired by a young Senator from Massachusetts named John F. Kennedy—as one of the five most outstanding Senators in the history of the United States Senate. Kennedy cited La Follette's commitment to "social and economic reforms which ultimately proved essential to American progress in the 20th century." La Follette was honored—along with Senators Clay, Webster, Calhoun, and Robert Taft—by having his portrait hung permanently on the walls of the room chosen by the U.S. Senate to house its Hall of Fame. "[His portrait] bears witness to the proceedings of this body," proclaimed Wisconsin Senator Russ Feingold in 2007, "and perhaps challenges his successors here to continue fighting for the social and government reforms he championed."[55]

La Follette's portrait hangs just off the floor of the Senate, in the Senate Reception Room—the very same room where Muenter's bomb exploded in 1915.

After decades of often acrimonious debate, the restoration of the Capitol's decaying West Front was finally completed in 1987 under the oversight of architect George M. White, who ensured that Frederick Olmsted's grand terraces remained intact. White also pushed to move presidential inaugurations from the East Front to this side of the Capitol, permitting larger crowds to witness the peaceful transfer of executive power starting with the inauguration of Ronald Reagan in 1981.

CHAPTER 10

A Masterpiece

1917–1998

On the morning of Monday, April 2, 1917—hours before President Woodrow Wilson was scheduled to address a joint session of Congress to seek a declaration of war against Germany—more than fifteen hundred protestors, most of them pacifists, occupied the central east portico and steps of the Capitol. Men and women alike, many dressed solemnly in black and wearing sashes reading "We Want Peace," spread themselves out across the steps, blocking access to the bronze doors that led into the Rotunda.

Capitol police moved in quickly to disperse the crowd, carefully corralling them onto the Capitol's east plaza, where police mounted on horseback kept a watchful eye on the protestors. One young protestor was shaken nearly to tears—"They have discriminated against us," she told *The Washington Times*—but Senator Atlee Pomerene of Ohio was unmoved. "You're the best ally the Germans have got!" he screamed at the protestors.[1]

Many of the protestors, part of a group organized by the Emergency Peace Federation, planned to meet with their Congressmen and Senators, including thirty-six-year-old Massachusettsian Alexander Bannwart, a Swiss-born businessman, part-time minor-league baseball manager, and—until recently—an admirer of Woodrow Wilson. While police broke up the protestors, Bannwart was already inside the building, tracking down one of his Senators, the long-serving conservative

Henry Cabot Lodge, who had recently announced his intention to support Wilson and vote for war.

Bannwart caught up with the sixty-six-year-old Lodge just outside a committee room, where the two of them got into an increasingly heated discussion. As their voices rose, Bannwart called Cabot a "damned coward" for his pro-war stance; Lodge shouted, "You are a damned liar!" and launched himself at the larger and much younger man, pummeling him in the face. Several members of Lodge's staff and a number of policemen jumped into the fray as well and, as one reporter diplomatically put it, "severely handled" Bannwart for nearly five minutes. Bannwart was eventually dragged away, bleeding from his face and head, and taken to a police station, where he was charged with assault. Lodge—the aggressor but sounding like the aggrieved—loudly stated that he would not press charges.[2]

Newspapers at the time, perhaps delighting in the irony that a pacifist demonstration had ended in violence, falsely reported that Bannwart had thrown the first punch—a narrative Lodge was more than happy to perpetuate, and one that so frustrated Bannwart that he eventually sued Lodge for defamation. Before the matter could be settled in court, Lodge, through his private secretary, admitted that Bannwart's recounting of events—in which Lodge had hit him first—"is now in accordance with actual facts."[3]

Even today, the fistfight remains the only time a sitting United States Senator has openly assaulted a constituent in the Capitol.

Responding to Woodrow Wilson's plea, Congress gave its consent to go to war against Germany, ending years of American neutrality and helping not only to turn the tide of the war in Europe, but also to churn the American economy to life. Architect of the Capitol Elliott Woods kept the lights on through it all, bathing the dome of the Capitol with floodlights from sundown to midnight every night during the course of the war, a literal beacon of freedom and optimism on the shores of the Potomac.

And for those who wondered how the Capitol could afford all those lights, Woods had in 1910 overseen the construction of a Capitol power plant, just south of the Capitol building, a few blocks down the hill near New Jersey Avenue SE and E Street SE. The plant had been authorized by Congress in 1904 specifically to generate steam and electricity for the Capitol and its surrounding buildings—which, by the time the structure was completed in 1910, included the House and Senate office buildings and the Library of Congress.

Woods prided himself on building a state-of-the-art facility, and the plant would be regularly expanded and improved over the next hundred years to keep pace with new technology, going from electric to steam to coal to natural gas. By 1951, it would stop generating power altogether, transferring the Capitol and its buildings over to PEPCO, the local power company, though it would continue to provide the steam and cold water needed to heat and cool the Capitol compound—a responsibility it still fulfills.

While Woods's power plant was a half mile from the Capitol building, the architect, always a fan of repurposing useful materials, had brought a bit of the old Capitol compound to this new, if slightly removed, Capitol facility. In 1908, as Woods was designing the plant, Congress had approved a resolution to rid itself at last of one of its old eyesores: Horatio Greenough's twelve-ton, toga-clad marble statue of George Washington, which had been baking on the east lawn since its banishment from the Rotunda in 1843. Left behind on the east lawn was only its enormous granite pedestal, inscribed with the words "First in War, First in Peace, First in the Hearts of His Countrymen." Woods would take Washington's abandoned granite pedestal and use it as the cornerstone of the new Capitol power plant when construction started in 1909; the engraved words "First in Peace" are visible on it on the building's ground level.

For most of his term, Woods had concentrated mainly on building

Capitol-adjacent structures, overseeing construction of the House and Senate office buildings and the new power plant. Now, however, as the war in Europe wound down and came to an official end by November 1919, Woods turned his eye toward the Capitol itself, and he began to consider extending the structure's east central front. It was a project that had been proposed by Walter, endorsed by Clark, and promoted by Woods since his days as Clark's right-hand man. A war-weary Congress, however, was in no mood to pursue such an ambitious undertaking; Woods's fingerprints in the Capitol would end up mainly on improved heating, circulation, and lighting. For most members of Congress, that was enough.

As he approached twenty years on the job, Woods remained well-liked by members and had even earned the grudging respect of the American Institute of Architects, which bestowed on the self-taught Woods honorary membership in its ranks in 1921. That same year, former Speaker Joseph Cannon, with whom Woods had always had a good working relationship, moved to change Woods's title from "Superintendent of the Capitol" back to "Architect." "He is the best architect that I ever met," Cannon said affectionately of Woods on the floor of the House. "He is not a very old man, but as he is getting along in years, he would like to be called 'architect.'"[4]

Woods would enjoy the title of Architect of the Capitol for only two more years. In May 1923, he died of a heart attack while vacationing in Spring Lake, New Jersey. He was fifty-nine years old.

Once again, the search for the next Architect of the Capitol would extend no further than the prior architect's right hand. This time, the position was occupied by forty-nine-year-old David Lynn, a civil engineer who had worked in Woods's office for more than two decades. Like Woods before him, Lynn wasn't a trained architect, but he had come up through the ranks, doing nearly every job, from watchman to cleaning crew, and he was regarded as the heir apparent to the position. But given Lynn's lack of an architectural degree, Glenn Brown of the American Institute of Architects once again rose in protest. He was told in no uncertain terms by the Congress to butt out.

What Lynn might have lacked in professional training, he more than made up for with pedigree and enthusiasm. Lynn came from one of Maryland's old established families and carried himself like old money—tall, handsome, and well-spoken. In his more than twenty years in Washington, he had made plenty of friends on both sides of the political aisle, and he was well-liked by his colleagues in the Office of the Architect of the Capitol. Lynn also genuinely appreciated the distinguished history of the office and the responsibilities that had come with the job since the time of George Washington. To most members of Congress, he was a shoo-in for the job, and President Calvin Coolidge—also a fan—moved to officially appoint Lynn to the position in August 1923.

To perhaps no one's surprise, one of the first issues Congress raised with Lynn had to do with the air quality in the chambers—this time, it was Senators who were complaining that the air in their chambers was stale and toxic. Senator Royal Copeland of New York, a practicing physician, noted that twenty-two incumbent Senators had died between 1916 and 1924, an alarming statistic he blamed, without any actual proof, on the air quality in the Senate chamber. Unlike with prior complaints about the circulation, when the Congress had generally been content to let engineers fiddle with new fans or tear up the floors to install new ductwork, this time the Senate was determined to have its entire wing reconfigured. Senators requested that Lynn figure out how to incorporate the exterior wall on the north side of the wing—the one with all the windows in it—as part of the Senate chamber. That modification would let in natural light and, more important, give them the ability to open the windows to allow in outside air.

Doing so, however, would involve tearing out three of the Senate's most beautiful rooms just north of the chamber: the President's Room, the Marble Room, and the Vice President's Room. But members remained determined, and therefore Lynn engaged Carrère and Hastings, the architects who had designed the first House and Senate office buildings, to determine the best way to lay out the new chamber. Over the course of a year, Carrère and Hastings carefully mapped out their vision, designing a beautiful space lit by the northern windows and giving the chamber a striking though more casual look that some thought made it resemble a train station. And then, just as quickly as the proposed new space had gained momentum and supporters, it was suddenly abandoned, thanks to a relatively new invention: air-conditioning.

The House of Representatives had actually embraced the new technology first, contracting with the Carrier Engineering Corporation—whose founder, Willis Carrier, had invented modern air-conditioning in 1902—to bring what the company promoted as "manufactured weather" to the Capitol. Cool air started blowing in the House in late 1928, followed by the Senate by the summer of 1929; even better, along with the cool air came controlled humidity, which would take the edge off the hot, sticky summers that traditionally had members abandoning the District until early fall. The reactions of some members were akin to those of nervous cavemen skeptically eyeing fire; Lynn had to circulate to concerned Congressmen a memo assuring them that moving from the humid outside air into the Capitol's cooler, drier air would not be fatal to their health.

The chamber's "manufactured weather" convinced the Senate that it no longer needed to reconfigure its chamber to incorporate the north windows, so it abandoned the Carrère and Hastings floor plans and thus spared the three elegant, marbled suites at the rear from the sledgehammer. Air-conditioning would also fundamentally change the way the House and Senate did business, making it possible to stay in session well into the summer. "Summer work," one reporter noted, "is no longer the broiling death-dealing business for elder Congressmen that it used to be."[5] With members more than satisfied by their new controlled climate, the rest of the Capitol as well as the House and Senate office buildings would be air-conditioned by 1935.

At the same time Lynn was working to keep the Congress happy, he was also taking marching orders from William Howard Taft, former president of the United States and now chief justice of the Supreme Court. Taft wanted a new home for the nation's highest court, which had been sharing space with the legislative branch since 1793. Originally housed in the bottom floor of the Capitol—in a space now serving as a judicial library and all-purpose storage room—the Supreme Court had been working out of the Old Senate Chamber since 1860, when that body had left its old space and headed into the new, more modern extension. While the court had picked up some rooms and offices for justices and clerks in the center-west section formerly occupied by the Library of Congress, most justices still worked out of their homes. Taft thought this was all beneath the dignity of the nation's highest court. His justices, he argued, deserved a dedicated building of their own.

And so a commission was put together to study the issue and recommend potential new sites for the court, while the distinguished architect Cass Gilbert was assigned the task of designing the court's new home. The commission eventually settled on a location directly across from the Capitol on First Street: a large plot of land that Gilbert didn't like very much, as one side of it was cut on a diagonal by Maryland Avenue. But Gilbert, tasked by Taft with imagining "a building of dignity and importance suitable for its use as the permanent home of the Supreme Court,"[6] dutifully went to work anyway, eventually drawing a modest structure in neoclassical style that could fit onto the awkwardly shaped parcel of land within the shadow of the Capitol. Gilbert's dignified court building would be nowhere near as flashy as the Library of Congress—sitting directly across East Capitol Street and decked out in festive Beaux Arts style—but it was perfectly suitable for the highest court in the land.

In the summer of 1930, the hatchet-shaped property on First Street was cleared, which required razing several creaky apartment buildings as well as one older structure of some historical importance: the Old Brick Capitol, which had recently been converted into row houses. Its demise did not go unacknowledged nor unopposed; the National Women's Party, which had used the building for its headquarters in the early 1920s, tried its best to save it, but was unsuccessful. Accepting the inevitable, supporters celebrated the edifice with a farewell luncheon in May 1930, shortly before it was torn down in June.[7] "Finis for the Old Brick Capitol," wrote the Washington *Sunday Star* respectfully.[8] To stand on the site of the Old Brick Capitol today, simply head for the Supreme Court building.

Work on the court's new home proceeded quickly; its cornerstone would be laid in 1932, and the Supreme Court would sit for the first time in its own dedicated structure on October 7, 1935. Unfortunately, neither architect Cass Gilbert nor Chief Justice William Howard Taft would be there to see it. Gilbert had died of a heart attack while visiting family in England in 1934 at age seventy-four; Taft, already in declining health and with a weak heart, died at home in Washington, D.C., in March 1930 at age seventy-two. On March 11, 1930, Taft would lie in state in the Rotunda of the U.S. Capitol; later that day, he would be the first president of the United States to be buried in Arlington National Cemetery.

Even as the national economy soured into the Great Depression in the late 1920s and on into the 1930s, spiking unemployment to nearly 25 percent, work of some kind would always seem to be underway at the Capitol complex. Indeed, federal contracts and projects would keep workers in the region actively employed; it was one of the few places in the United States where work was relatively steady. One of the major projects in the complex, in addition to the work underway on the Supreme Court, was the construction of another House office building just west of the first one. Lynn, like Clark before him, relied on the expertise of consulting architectural firms for the design and planning of the building. Many in Congress thought the first House office building was too opulent—not a good look for "the people's body," especially during the Depression—and asked for something more restrained and less showy.

Congress would eventually settle on designs submitted by a local firm known as the Allied Architects of Washington that provided a concept in the popular neoclassical revival style, which was similar in look and feel to Cass Gilbert's conservative design for the Supreme Court. The building would be under construction by June 1932 and completed at a staggeringly fast clip, with the Congress occupying the building less than a year later, in April 1933. Under David Lynn's careful supervision, the building came in more than a million dollars under budget—and yet there were still some members of Congress who found the cheaper and less lavish building a bit too much. "I won't like it when some unemployed constituent finds me here," one Congressman confessed to the *Washington Herald*. "There'll be remarks and criticism of the expense." (Reporters at the *Herald* were inclined to be forgiving, even as they reminded Congress to be "just as considerate" when it came to providing funding to the District's public schools.)[9]

A similar kind of economic anxiety, in fact, would prompt a life-threatening outburst in the House chamber in the winter of 1932. On the cold and snowy afternoon of Tuesday, December 13, as House members defeated a motion to impeach President Herbert Hoover, twenty-five-year-old Marlin Kemmerer, dressed impeccably in a suit and bow tie, took a seat in the front row of the House visitor gallery. In his pocket was a ten-page speech—a manifesto of sorts—and a loaded .38-caliber pistol. "I got to thinking about the operation of the government and decided to make the speech," Kemmerer said later. "I thought the most effective way to get recognition was to bring the gun."

Days earlier, before leaving his hometown of Allentown, Pennsylvania, Kemmerer, a clerk at the local Sears department store, had posted for his supervisor a note explaining his upcoming absence from work: "Will be back as soon as I can attend to business for the relief of the unemployed and the depression in general," he wrote. Now, looking down on the House floor from the crowded gallery, Kemmerer slowly stood up, slung one leg over the gallery railing, and waved his pistol at the Congress seated below. "I want 20 minutes to address the House!" he shouted.

Members scrambled for cover or sprinted for the doors. "The chamber was in wild confusion," reported the *Evening Star.* "Members of the House forgot the vote they were engaged in and most of their dignity."[10] As the Speaker of the House pounded the gavel and shouted lamely for order, members continued to dive for cover. "I demand the floor!" Kemmerer shouted again.

Amid the chaos, two members remained calm: Representative Edith Rogers of Massachusetts, who had counseled shell-shocked veterans of World War I at Walter Reed Hospital and recognized the symptoms of mental illness, and Minnesota Congressman Melvin Maas, a World War I veteran still serving in the Marine Corps Reserve. Rogers and Maas coolly crossed the House floor and stood directly below Kemmerer.

"You won't do anything," Rogers told Kemmerer quietly as the young man continued waving his gun.

"All right, son," Maas said. "I'll give you twenty minutes. But we have rules here. You can't speak with a gun. Come on, give me the gun."

Kemmerer, an expert marksman, pointed the pistol directly at Rogers, then at Maas—neither of whom even flinched. Then he dropped the gun, still cocked and loaded, about fifteen feet down into Maas's open hands. Before Kemmerer could deliver a word of his speech—which began with "Okay America! For the next 20 minutes you will listen to a speech which has the interest of the American people. The first man that tries to stop me will die. Is that understood?"—he was grabbed from behind by Representative Fiorello La Guardia of New York, who had run from the floor to the gallery and now seized Kemmerer with the help of an off-duty police officer. "I am for *all* the people!" Kemmerer screamed as he was dragged away by Capitol police.

In Kemmerer's rented room a few blocks away, police found two sticks of dynamite that Kemmerer said he'd planned to use but feared would kill bystanders. "I expected to get arrested," he calmly told police later. "I was not personally mistreated by the Congress, but Congress has mistreated the whole country." The clearly mentally ill Kemmerer, in fact, would earn the sympathies of the House of Representatives, which would lobby for his release from prison after serving only a year. Kemmerer would recover, marry, have a large family, and pass away peacefully in Philadelphia in the year 2000, aged ninety-three.

Edith Rogers would go on to become one of the longest-serving women in the U.S. Congress, holding her seat for thirty-five years through eighteen consecutive terms before her death in 1960. Her record would stand until 2012, when it was surpassed by Maryland Senator Barbara Mikulski. During World War II, Rogers would author legislation creating the Women's Army Auxiliary Corps, which permitted women to serve their country in a noncombat capacity; after the war, she promoted the physical and mental health needs of veterans returning home. So effective was the Republican Rogers in steering a veterans' unemployment compensation bill through the Congress that Democratic President Franklin Roosevelt invited her to the White House ceremony when he signed the bill into law—and handed her his pen immediately after affixing his signature.

As for Melvin Maas, he would serve with distinction in the South Pacific during World War II while still a sitting Congressman, then go on to work for the Sperry Corporation in New York City. Eventually blinded by injuries sustained during World War II, he would serve as the chairman of President Eisenhower's Committee on Employment of the

Physically Handicapped, becoming a strong advocate for the mentally ill. At his death in 1964 at the age sixty-five, nearly every obituary would mention the incident with Kemmerer. For his entire life, Maas had been called a hero for his actions that afternoon, even receiving a silver medal from the Carnegie Hero Fund for his valor. But Maas would almost always dismiss any such applause, confessing he'd been scared to death. "I wasn't a hero," he said. "That pistol looked like a 105 howitzer to me. When I heard afterwards that the fellow was a pistol instructor and expert shot, I almost fainted."[11]

The structural engineer had bad news for Architect of the Capitol David Lynn. In 1938, the roofs of the House and the Senate chambers had been thoroughly examined—and both were found to be "entirely obsolete." The iron beams that Montgomery Meigs had so confidently installed in the 1850s were now "greatly overstressed" and needed to be entirely replaced.[12] In 1940, Congress appropriated the funding needed to build new roofs of concrete and steel—two construction materials that were in increasingly short supply as the United States began ramping up for involvement in another war in Europe. But with the roofs in both the House and the Senate failing, Lynn, in the name of safety, constructed steel frames to support the sagging ceilings over each chamber, bracing their weight on columns mounted on the visitor galleries. It made each chamber resemble a warehouse. Some Senators complained that it looked like they were working out of a barn, but at least members wouldn't have to worry about the ceilings crashing down on their heads while they waited for work on the new roof to begin.

The world war—and then postwar priorities—would delay work on the new ceilings until 1949, at which point each chamber would be given a total overhaul, with Lynn insisting on not just new ceilings but completely renovating and redesigning the interiors. For two years, the

Senate returned to its old chambers, while the House worked out of the enormous meeting room for the Ways and Means Committee in the newest House office building. Work crews tore into the spaces in the extensions that had been so carefully designed and constructed by Thomas Walter and Montgomery Meigs nearly a century earlier. In 1951, the legislators returned to their respective chambers to find them sleeker, modernized, and—in the opinions of some—distinctly lacking in character.

Gone were the ornate ceilings with skylights that illuminated the spaces dramatically but unreliably; they had been replaced with flat ceilings—finally cleaning up the acoustics in each chamber—and recessed electric lights that lit the spaces brightly and evenly. Out, too, were Walter's interior designs and Meigs's color schemes of the 1850s, which had been deemed too Victorian; they had been traded for mostly straight lines and neutral colors. "There seemed to be no point in preserving the existing character of the architecture of the two chambers of the period of 1860," one Congressional commission noted. "Therefore, it was agreed to return to the architectures of the Early Republic."[13]

Whether the new style truly reflected the neoclassical look of the Capitol's earliest era was debatable—one modern historian thought it was architecturally messy, derisively referring to the chamber design as "pastiches of vaguely classical designs, pursued without conviction or vigor"[14]—but nearly all admitted the look was cleaner, lighter, and more modern. The walls of the Senate were now covered with simple red and tan panels, separated by marble pilasters; in the House, light-colored paneling, also separated with marble pilasters, had been replaced with darker, richer tones. At the front of the Senate chamber, the vice president's podium was now made of black marble rather than wood. In the House, the Speaker's rostrum was backed with Ionic columns of black marble topped with white marble capitals from Alabama. Over the doors of House chamber were new marble relief portraits of historical figures considered to be great lawmakers, from Moses to Edward I to Thomas Jefferson.

David Lynn proudly celebrated the chambers for their "quiet, simple beauty and dignity." Local newspapers, however, seemed split. While Washington's *Evening Star* thought the Senate in particular was "brilliantly decorated,"[15] the *Daily News* snickered that both chambers resembled nothing so much as "a couple of Hollywood boudoirs."[16]

Lynn would find the critics much kinder to another project undertaken on his watch, the completion of Brumidi's *Frieze of American History*, which, circling the high inner wall of the Rotunda, had been left unfinished in 1889. The last section completed by Filippo Costaggini, following Brumidi's designs, depicted the discovery of gold in California, but to its right were still thirty-one feet of blank wall. "This vacant space with all its bleak bareness confronted the millions of people who visited the Capitol for the 65 years from 1888 [*sic*] to 1953," groaned Congressman Thomas Jenkins of Ohio.[17] Congress had been trying to fill the space since 1939, regularly introducing legislation authorizing completion of the frieze; Jenkins finally steered the bill to passage in August 1950.

Selected for the job of filling the gap was fifty-four-year-old artist Allyn Cox, a talented New York muralist who had studied at the American Academy in Rome. Over the course of thirty months, Cox cleaned the original frieze, then completed three new panels that carefully mimicked the artistic style of Brumidi and Costaggini, ensuring a unified look. As specified by the Congress, Cox added panels depicting the Civil War, the Spanish-American War, and the birth of flight at Kitty Hawk—the first depiction of twentieth-century technology in Walter's neoclassical dome. In Cox's panel, the *Wright Flyer* seems to soar into the air just behind Brumidi's first panel, literally bringing the frieze back full circle to reconnect with itself.

The completed and cleaned frieze would be dedicated on May 11, 1954, in a celebration in the Rotunda attended by President Dwight D.

Eisenhower. In his remarks for the occasion, Eisenhower noted the diversity of races and cultures represented in the frieze. "We find here represented the great fusion of foreign bloods that brought about this Nation that became America," said the president. "These are representative of the bloodstreams that, joining here in this great country of promise and opportunity, have produced the great Nation that is symbolized here in this Rotunda."

Eisenhower closed by reminding the audience that the Capitol was more than just a place; it was the very embodiment of the nation itself. "Here, indeed, is not only a spot that reminds us of America, of her past, and her achievements," said Eisenhower, "but it is one that in a very real sense *is* America."[18]

Among the important but eye-glazing details of the Twentieth Amendment to the United States Constitution—the amendment that sets the start date of a president's term at January 20—is language similarly starting each session of Congress on January 3. Following the ratification of the Twentieth Amendment in 1933, Congress approved legislation further providing that each session of Congress should last from January 3 until July 31. That rarely happened, however; with the growing needs of a post–World War II nation, Congress usually found itself staying in session well into late summer, often into autumn, and sometimes working Saturdays and Sunday as it attempted to end the session in something close to a timely manner. That likely made members especially thankful that they were working in a building with a central air-conditioning system—a luxury most Americans of the time still did *not* have.[19]

It wasn't unusual, then, for the Senate to be in session on July 12, 1947, a moderately warm Saturday, with temperatures rising into the middle eighties. Shortly after eleven a.m., Senator John Bricker of Ohio—who had been the 1944 vice presidential candidate on the ticket with Republican Thomas Dewey—left his suite in the Senate office building and headed for the building's underground subway. He was about fifteen feet from the waiting subway car when a calm and bespectacled constituent—and former Capitol police officer—named William Kaiser drew a .22-caliber pistol, fired directly at Bricker . . . and missed.

Bricker, stunned but unhurt, leapt onto the subway, ducked under a seat, and screamed for the driver to pull away as quickly as possible. (Newspapers of the era delighted in reporting that Bricker had allegedly yelled, "Let's get the hell out of here!") The train could move at a top speed of only about eight miles an hour, but it was fast enough; as the train chugged away, Kaiser fired another shot, missing again. Bricker, winded but none the worse for wear, jumped off the train when it arrived at the Capitol and calmly went to the floor to vote on a tax bill.

Kaiser was taken into custody without a fight, looking so cool and collected as he was booked and photographed by police that newspapers dubbed him "the Grinning Gunman." Capitol police had seen Kaiser in the building earlier that morning acting "most queerly." Under questioning, Kaiser revealed that he had an ax to grind with Bricker; in 1934, while serving as the attorney general of Ohio, Bricker had liquidated a building and loan association, bankrupting its investors, including Kaiser; and Kaiser had spent the next thirteen years angry with Bricker for "stealing" from him. Kaiser later told police that he had fired at Bricker simply to "to refresh his memory."[20] As it turned out, Kaiser likely hadn't fired any shots at Bricker at all, only blanks. While indicted for the shooting, Kaiser would be determined to be insane and sent to St. Elizabeths psychiatric hospital in south Washington, D.C., where he would die less than a year later of heart disease.

His assault on Bricker had come fifteen years after Marlin Kemmerer had brandished a weapon in the House gallery—and yet Capitol police still saw no reason to improve security in the Capitol compound. "I don't see why this incident should require more police protections," said the Senate sergeant at arms, blaming the thin police force on the need to "stretch it over the Capitol and Senate and House Office Buildings as well as the grounds"[21]—a problem that wasn't going to go away.

A different kind of interloper would arrive in the halls of Congress in 1947: television, which allowed the previously inscrutable proceedings of Congressional committees to be seen by the public at large—and the public at large couldn't get enough, with an estimated thirty million viewers watching the live proceedings of the Special Committee on Organized Crime in Interstate Commerce in 1951.[22] Live broadcasts of Congressional hearings would shape American politics, and the American character, in the mid-twentieth century, whether the people were rooting for Senator Estes Kefauver as he interrogated nervous mob bosses in 1951 or cheering as the Communist-chasing Senator Joseph McCarthy finally got his comeuppance in a dressing-down by Army attorney Joseph Welch in 1954. Still, committee hearings were one thing; the floor was quite another—and Congress would keep the new technology off the floor of each chamber for another twenty-five years, finally permitting their daily floor proceedings to be televised live starting in 1979.

And so there were no cameras trained on the House gallery in 1954 to broadcast yet another brazen act of political violence. It would be left instead to newspapers to report the story, most under inch-tall headlines screaming variations of FIVE CONGRESSMEN SHOT.

On Monday, March 1, Speaker Joe Martin of Massachusetts was at the Speaker's dais in the House, presiding over an afternoon floor debate on immigration, when four well-dressed individuals—three men, one woman—sat down in the southwest corner of the House gallery. When the four had entered the gallery, there were no metal detectors to pass through and no real screening process to ensure the safety of members or the public. Instead, the doorkeeper on duty simply asked the woman—a striking thirty-four-year-old named Lolita Lebrón—if she had a camera in her purse, reminding her of House rules prohibiting photography. Assuring the doorkeeper she did not, Lebrón and her colleagues were admitted into the gallery to find seats. Lebrón had told the doorkeeper the truth; there was no camera inside her purse. Instead, there was a loaded semiautomatic pistol. Her colleagues were also armed with concealed guns.

Lebrón and her three coconspirators—Rafael Cancel Miranda, Andrés Figueroa Cordero, and Irvin Flores Rodríguez—were all Puerto Rican nationalists, part of an active and radical movement devoted to the cause of Puerto Rico's independence. Following the annexation of Puerto Rico by the United States at the end of the Spanish-American War in 1898, the relationship between the two had been complicated and, at times, fractious. On the island itself, Puerto Ricans had divided into roughly two factions: one that leaned toward U.S. statehood and another that vowed to fight for independence—sometimes by any means necessary.

In November 1950, two Puerto Rican nationalists had sought to draw international attention to the Puerto Rican independence movement by assassinating President Harry Truman—a thwarted attempt that left one policeman and one nationalist dead, though Truman was untouched. But the attempt had gotten Truman's attention, and in 1952, he supported permitting Puerto Ricans to vote on a new constitution—though independence itself was not on the ballot. That omission remained a bone of contention for Puerto Rican nationalists, who continued to revolt—and now, two years later, Lebrón intended to make another similarly dramatic statement, hoping to draw attention to the "imperial rule" of the island by the United States.

Her three coconspirators and she sat in the House gallery for some time as debate continued on a bill regarding the status of Mexican agricultural workers. Then, at two thirty p.m., the four quietly said the Lord's Prayer and stood up in unison. Lebrón shouted, "*Viva Puerto Rico libre!*"—"Long live free Puerto Rico!"—and unfurled a Puerto Rican flag, draping it sloppily over the gallery railing. Then the shooting began, with the four nationalists firing more than thirty rounds into the House chamber below. Wooden chairs splintered under the spray of bullets. Majority Leader Charles Halleck dove under a desk as several bullets riddled the table where he'd just been working.

"It was bedlam on the floor," recalled Mike Michaelson, a reporter seated in the House press gallery. "There was debris. . . . Everybody was screaming and yelling and ducking."[23] Most shots were fired by Cancel Miranda; one gunman's pistol jammed, while Lebrón fired her shots into the ceiling. "I didn't come to kill anyone," she said later. "I came to die for Puerto Rico."[24] It was all over in a matter of minutes, as bystanders, police, House staff, and even Congressman James Van Zandt of Pennsylvania tackled the shooters. As one gunman sprinted out of the gallery, he was intercepted by a policeman who, according to one eyewitness, "just hauled off and slugged him good and flattened him."[25]

The House floor remained in a state of pandemonium as members scrambled for help. Five Congressmen had been shot—two Republicans and three Democrats—with the most critically wounded being thirty-five-year-old Republican Alvin Bentley of Michigan, who had taken a bullet in the chest. While Representative Walter Judd of Minnesota, a physician, attended to the wounded, House pages—mostly young men in their late teens and early twenties—moved quickly to load Bentley onto a stretcher and haul him out of the chamber. As the group of pages carried Bentley down the rain-slicked steps of the east House portico toward a waiting ambulance, a United Press photographer began taking pictures, sending page Bill Emerson into a fury. "No photographs!" Emerson screamed, jabbing a finger in the direction of the photojournalist. The next day, front pages everywhere carried the image of Bentley being borne on the shoulders of several pages—only his feet are visible on the stretcher—as Emerson, his mouth wide open, angrily points and shouts at reporters.

All wounded members would recover, though it was touch-and-go for Bentley, who was initially given "a little better than a 50-50 chance."[26] His revival likely spared the conspirators a death sentence, especially as neither Lebrón nor any of her coconspirators showed any remorse for their actions. In federal court, all four were quickly found guilty of assault with intent to kill, with additional convictions for seditious conspiracy. The three men were sentenced to seventy-five years in prison, while Lebrón was given fifty years; her sentence was slightly mitigated because she had fired her pistol into the ceiling rather than at members. Defiant to the end, none would apply for parole. In 1977, a terminally ill Cordero would be granted clemency and released from prison; two years later, citing "humane considerations," President Jimmy Carter commuted the sentences of the remaining three conspirators. "I freed them because I thought 25 years was enough," Carter said.[27]

Decades later, Joe Bartlett, who'd been one of the House reading clerks in the chamber at the time of the shooting, was still outraged that anyone would violate the House chamber with such an act of violence. "Most common was the emotion of anger," he recalled. "How dare they do this?" In the days following the shooting, there was some serious consideration given to the idea of enclosing the gallery behind bulletproof glass. But "that was overruled," said Michaelson. "They said, 'No, this is the People's House, and it's got to be opened up. We can't do that.'"[28] Instead, Congress began professionalizing the Capitol police force, starting with abolishing the patronage system and providing a more structured training program[29]—a long process that would eventually shape the modern United States Capitol Police.

Today, reminders of the 1954 shooting can still be found in the House chamber. The drawer in the desk used by the Republican leadership is still scarred by a bullet hole. And inside each cloakroom hangs the United Press photo of Alvin Bentley being carried down the Capitol steps by House pages, the admonishing scream of Bill Emerson forever frozen in time.

In September 1954, in one of his final acts as Architect of the Capitol, David Lynn would oversee the repair of the holes left in the House ceiling where Lolita Lebrón had fired her pistol overhead. Eight days later, Lynn quietly retired at age eighty, after serving as Architect of the Capitol for thirty-one years. While he had asked his colleagues to let him retire without a fuss, they couldn't resist swinging by his home in northwest D.C. to drop off farewell gifts, presenting him with an FM radio and a large television set.

At practically the very moment Lynn was walking out the door, Speaker of the House Joe Martin fired off a letter to President Eisenhower with his pick for the new Architect of the Capitol, a former one-term Republican member of Congress from Delaware named John George Stewart. Like Lynn and Woods before him, Stewart wasn't an architect. But unlike Lynn and Woods, Stewart hadn't come up through the ranks of the Office of the Architect of the Capitol; his practical experience was limited mostly to civil engineering at the Department of Justice. And as a former elected official, Stewart was more politician than architect, a distinction that would come to define his often rocky tenure overseeing the Capitol complex. His nomination was enthusiastically supported by key Republicans, and his appointment was approved so quickly that the always watchful American Institute of Architects didn't even have time to object to his lack of experience.

Taking his new office on October 1, 1954, Stewart would hit the ground running and oversee the construction of a second Senate office building, a project that had been formally approved in 1949 but delayed by the Korean War. Ironically, the rapidly expanding needs of the Senate were the result of new reforms intended to make the Congress more effective and more efficient. Following a reorganization of the Congress in 1946, the number of standing committees in the House had been reduced from forty-eight to nineteen, while the number in the

Senate had gone from thirty-three to fifteen. However, reducing the total number of committees had led to an increase in oversight responsibilities, which meant a need for larger staffs and more clerks. The new office building, then, would provide significantly more room for committees and committee staff.

Lynn had already done most of the work for Stewart, having selected a site for the new Senate office building directly east of the first one and purchasing and condemning properties in an area known locally as "Slum's Row." He had also hired the New York architectural firm of Eggers & Higgins to design the building in their trademark blend of contemporary and classical styles. Members wanted their new space to complement the first Senate office building without embracing its showiness; there would be no soaring rotundas or staid marble columns in committee rooms. Like their House counterparts, Senators didn't want constituents walking into a workspace that was *too* extravagant.

To reflect the increasing role of committees, the previous "boardroom" layout of their hearing rooms—in which members sat facing one another around a large table—was abandoned in favor of placing a rostrum at the head of the room, with members, grouped by political party, seated on either side of the chairman and facing the witnesses and the audience. To connect the new building to the Capitol, the existing underground subway was renovated and expanded. Work on the new 750,000-square-foot building would proceed at a steady pace and without controversy, with Senators ready to move in by October 1958.

That same year, Stewart would finally get his hands on the Capitol itself—and for perhaps the first time, an architect wouldn't be working to address complaints about air quality in the chambers. Instead, Steward would preside over the last major modification of the Capitol building, an extension of the central East Front—an alteration to the Capitol's footprint that had been proposed and actively lobbied for by Thomas U. Walter nearly a century earlier.

Walter's concerns about the East Front had always been mostly aesthetic; he thought the central portico looked too fragile to support the weight of the enormous dome that practically squatted down right on top of its triangular pediment. Clark, during his long tenure, regularly mentioned the proposed extension in his reports to Congress and went beyond aesthetics to push for the purely practical, usually framing the extended front as a means for picking up the extra space that his Congressional supervisors seemed always to be demanding. But there was concern, too, that the original Virginia sandstone that had been installed in the East Front by Bulfinch in the 1820s was beginning to crumble and would need to be replaced with a more durable material, preferably marble.

As early as 1904, while designing the first House and Senate office buildings, the architecture firm of Carrère and Hastings had been tasked with coming up with some options for extending the East Front. Among their proposals was a plan to push the East Front forward by a little more than thirty feet and to add a new facade that maintained the general look of the original front. While House Speaker Joseph Cannon had come close to getting the extension authorized at that time, the project had been shelved for the next five decades.

It would take a new and resolute Speaker of the House to take it off the shelf again. Sam Rayburn, a long-serving Democrat from Texas, had led the House Democrats since 1940 and been Speaker twice already when the election of 1954 put Democrats once again back in control of the House. Rayburn's House colleagues elected him to serve as their Speaker when the new Congress convened in 1955; now that he was back in the Speaker's chair, Rayburn was determined to get the extension of the East Front done—and done quickly. Rayburn saw it as a logical solution for meeting the growing space and office needs of the Congress—but he also agreed with Walter's assessment that the building would just plain *look* better with the East Front pushed forward.

Rayburn, with Stewart as his enthusiastic agent and right hand, intended to stick mostly to the plan submitted by Carrère and Hastings, which involved pushing the center East Front forward 32.5 feet. But rather than removing or refacing the worn sandstone walls, which had been installed by Bulfinch nearly a hundred thirty years before, Stewart proposed simply attaching the extended front directly to the face of the old one. That would leave Bulfinch's original exterior sandstone walls intact to serve as interior walls for the new extension. And there would be no need to design a new East Front; the face of the extension would be an exact replica of the current structure—what Rayburn called "archaeological reproduction"—with every detail faithfully replicated in sturdy marble instead of fragile sandstone, all the way down to Luigi Persico's *Genius of America* pediment, which John Quincy Adams had personally designed generations ago.

The Speaker wanted quick action, not debate, so he made sure to stack a commission overseeing the new construction with Congressional allies—and with Stewart. While Rayburn was not inclined to take complaints from naysayers too seriously, opponents were just as determined not to be ignored. The Capitol had been altered countless times in the past, but until now, no one had ever objected to modifying the building by waving the banner of historic significance—a war cry that might have saved the Old Brick Capitol from its demolition in 1930. By 1958, however, things had changed; defenders of Bulfinch's original East Front loudly reminded Rayburn that the steps of the East Front—the actual steps and not some marble reproduction as Rayburn and Stewart were proposing—had been the site of every presidential inauguration since 1829. Abraham Lincoln had stood on those steps as he called for "malice toward none." Andrew Jackson had thwarted an assassination attempt in the sandstone portico and not in a marble copy 32.5 feet to the east of it. They weren't concerned that the dome hung over the east portico; they objected to history being replaced with a marble duplicate. One member of the Committee to Preserve the National Capitol complained that "the proponents of this controversial plan care nothing at all for the most important symbol of our national heritage."[30]

Stewart, however, thought that argument was nonsense. "The Capitol is not a museum," he sniffed. "It is the live seat of a great government."[31] Rayburn was equally unsentimental, arguing that the Capitol should grow and evolve with the nation. The Speaker was going to move forward with the extension, opposition be damned, though to try to sweeten the deal, he added some much-needed improvements to the funding list, including repairs to the dome and better lighting. They would never be enough to appease opponents, but Rayburn, a nimble legislative tactician, moved his bills for the extension through the Congress with little opposition.[32] *The New York Times* made it clear that it considered replacing the eastern front to be a "deliberate desecration" of the building and branded Rayburn and Stewart "architectural vandals."[33]

Both Rayburn and Stewart would run into similarly loud grumbling when it came to another of Rayburn's pet projects of the era, a third House office building. Following a feasibility study in 1955, Rayburn annoyed his colleagues by inserting language in an appropriations bill permitting such sums "as may be necessary" to be spent on the building, essentially giving the project managers—in this case, Rayburn and Stewart—a bottomless pit of money with which to work. As envisioned by Rayburn; designed by the Philadelphia architectural firm of Harbeson, Hough, Livingston, & Larson; and overseen by Stewart, the new building would be constructed with state-of-the-art amenities and conveniences, making it immediately popular with members. It would also be gigantic, with an underground garage for sixteen hundred cars, room for 169 member offices, hearing rooms and staff offices for twenty-five committees and subcommittees, men's and women's gymnasiums, a swimming pool, press and television facilities, maintenance shops, and—always in demand—plenty of storage.

The building would be plagued by delays, finally opening a decade later in February 1965. At its opening, it was so closely associated with the Speaker that it was already being called the Rayburn House Office Building—the name it still bears today. Critics thought it was the ugliest building in the city. Senator Stephen Young of Ohio derided it as "the most stupendous architectural monstrosity of our times," while Illinois Senator Paul Douglas called it an "architectural abomination."[34] While a suspicious comptroller later audited Stewart's books—which were spotlessly clean—and discovered that Rayburn hadn't exploited the such-sums clause, the building was generally regarded as Rayburn's folly, a memorial to one man's power. Rayburn dismissed such criticism; his job, as he saw it, was to take care of his colleagues and their staffs and, by extension, the Congress. Today, members of Congress still vie for space in the building.

Before any construction on the Capitol's extended East Front could begin, the old East Front had to be dismantled, leaving behind the sandstone front wall but removing everything else. The twenty-four sandstone Corinthian columns on the portico, each of which had taken months for Bulfinch's craftsmen and work crews to move and cut and polish and install, were removed by Stewart's crew in a matter of days, to be replaced by much sturdier marble copies. (Today, twenty-two of the original sandstone columns stand in dignified display at the U.S. National Arboretum in northeast Washington, where they overlook a reflecting pool.) Artisans set up a shed on the east grounds to begin repairing the ornate sandstone cornices and sculpture—all of which, including Persico's *Genius of America* figures, were badly corroded by weather—and re-creating them in marble. Not everything was saved and reproduced, however. As already mentioned, the problematic sculptures *Discovery of America* and *Rescue*—with their offensive depictions of Natives—were removed for good, thanks largely to the efforts of Leta

Myers Smart, a member of the Omaha Tribe of Nebraska who for years had barraged lawmakers with letters making the case that the statues were "a great source of humiliation to every Indian who has set foot in Washington."[35]

On July 4, 1959, President Eisenhower was on hand to lay the eastern extension's cornerstone, a gigantic piece of red granite quarried in Marble Falls, Texas, and inscribed "A.D. 1959." The ceremony was all business—there were no parades—and Eisenhower, who had flown in from Camp David just for the celebration, quickly and solemnly spread cement on the stone with the same trowel used by George Washington and Millard Fillmore for similar ceremonies. "By this symbolic gesture . . . we rededicate ourselves to the principle of representative government," Eisenhower promised the crowd. "We reaffirm our devotion to the values upon which this republic rests."[36]

With work officially underway on the extended front, the long-overdue restoration of the Capitol dome, now just several years shy of its hundredth birthday, could also finally begin. Scaffolding crawled along the outside of the dome for much of 1959 and 1960 as workers stripped the old white paint off the dome's iron pieces with pneumatic hammers, then further sandblasted each down to its base. In this unprotected condition, bare iron can rust within five hours, so every piece was immediately treated with a red-tinted rust inhibitor, giving the dome a red hue for several months as repairs and restoration continued. The dome would be returned to pristine, gleaming white by spring 1960.

At the same time, the first marble column shafts were being installed on the newly extended center east portico, with modern gas-powered cranes easily moving each eighteen-ton column into place. The columns of the new colonnade were installed in less than four weeks; the same task had taken Bulfinch and his crew more than two years to complete. While pushing the eastern face out only a little more than thirty feet might seem like an insignificant nudge forward, doing so dramatically changed the feel of the center section. The old front had been tightly pressed up against the base of the dome so it looked like a belt buckle straining against a protruding gut. The new extended front suddenly gave the dome room to breathe on its east side, as if the belt had been loosened. In addition, the front of the center section was now nearly even with those of the House and Senate wings on its flanks, making the entire building appear more balanced.

The exterior of the extension would be completed in time for the swearing in of President John F. Kennedy, who stood on the marble steps of the new extension in the shadow of the newly cleaned and restored Capitol dome on a frigid January 20, 1961, to deliver one of the great inaugural addresses of all time. As he urged American citizens to "ask not what your country can do for you—ask what you can do for your country," it was clear that history was already being made on the steps.

The interior of the extension would take slightly longer to complete, formally opening in early 1962. Rayburn, however, would never get to enjoy the space he had worked so hard to see to completion. He succumbed to pancreatic cancer in November 1961 at the age of seventy-nine.

Already referred to in deferential tones as "Sam Rayburn's East Front," the extension would contain large new offices for the Speaker, of course, as well as for the vice president, both housed behind five tall windows looking out onto the Capitol's east lawn. There was also space for the House Appropriations Committee as well as the Joint Atomic Energy Committee, which occupied most of the fourth floor of the extension. More than ninety rooms had been added to the Capitol, some of which would remain unmarked and designated as hideaways—small, private offices in the Capitol allocated to members by seniority. Most impressive, perhaps, in the north portion of the extension was a gleaming new Senate Reception Room—a gigantic formal space with wood paneling, parquetry flooring, and crystal chandeliers; it was matched on the south end of the extension with a similar space for the House.[37]

The expansive and elegant Senate Reception Room was a particularly welcome addition, as the Senate had grown accustomed to hosting high-ranking officials in either the small reception room just off the Senate floor—the same one rocked by Erich Muenter's bomb in 1915—or the cramped Old Senate Chamber, which was often hastily decorated to suit each occasion. Senator John Stennis of Mississippi, in fact, had been particularly upset with the use of the old chamber as an entertainment space; the inaugural lunch for President Kennedy had recently been held in the space, complete with chefs and servers working from the vice president's rostrum—a use of the old chamber that Stennis considered undignified. He wasn't the only one; as another member privately put it, "We've given so many parties there, and switched furniture around so much, it's beginning to look like a barroom."[38]

Stennis was determined to restore the Old Senate Chamber to the condition it had been in when the Senate abandoned it for its new chamber in 1859. "It seems to me that we should make full restoration," Stennis told his colleagues in a 1960 floor speech, "and that this is a small cost indeed for preservation and restoration of a national shrine in which all Americans take pride."[39] At the same time, he also wanted to bring the Old Supreme Court Chamber back to its prior glory; the space, used as a library when the court had left to take over the Old Senate Chamber in 1859, had since been converted into several run-of-the-mill offices, with a drop ceiling installed to hide the unique vaulted, arched ceiling that Benjamin Latrobe had been so pleased with. The current state of both chambers, said Stennis, reflected a "degradation of our American culture."[40]

Stennis was persistent—and eventually persuasive. In 1962, Senate Democratic Leader Mike Mansfield vowed to "kick out the cocktail parties,"[41] but it would take nearly a decade for all members to get there—some still thought the space was perfectly serviceable for receptions. Eventually, Lady Bird Johnson—who as First Lady made a mission of beautifying spaces in the nation's capital—made a phone call to the chairman of the House Appropriations Committee to voice her support for allowing renovation of the historic rooms to move forward.

Restoration of the Old Supreme Court would be completed by May 1975. The courtroom was restored to look almost exactly as it had when the court had sat in session in the late 1850s; public records, period art, and old guidebooks had been referenced to help re-create the look and decor of that era. (One careful observer noticed that a painting of Chief Justice John Marshall showed a small bit of the carpet in the chamber, which allowed curators to ensure the rug in the room was restored to the correct color.) The only liberties taken with the room's decor were the new busts of the first four chief justices carefully installed on brackets throughout the chamber.

A little more than a year later, on June 16, 1976, the Senate convened in its similarly restored old chamber to celebrate the opening of the newly renovated space. "History makers served in this room," Vice President Nelson Rockefeller reminded his colleagues as they walked the terraced floor with rows of desks arranged as they had been in Daniel Webster's time.[42] Faithful reproductions of furniture of the era had been crafted and installed using old prints and guidebooks for reference. The portrait of George Washington by Rembrandt Peale, which the Senate had purchased in 1832 and removed in 1859, was hung at the center of the room on the wall just above the vice president's elegantly draped rostrum—returning it to the place of prominence it had occupied during the Senate's golden age.

The space was christened with a formal dedication to "those American statesmen who again and again have emerged amidst the storms of their times to hold together and to weld a Nation worthy of the highest aspirations of its people and of the world." As Mike Mansfield reminded his colleagues, the institution was bigger than any one of them or the chamber itself. "The Senate's responsibilities go on," said Mansfield, "even though the faces and, yes, even the rooms in which they gather fade into history."[43]

★★★

Just as he had recommended extending the East Front of the Capitol to better balance the scale of the portico with the dome, Thomas U. Walter had also recommended a similar extension of the West Front—as had Clark in his ongoing efforts to make space anywhere he could for the Congress, its committees, and its staff. In 1963, just months after completion of the eastern extension, Congress appropriated funding for Stewart to study the West Front, both to assess its condition and to come up with several options for its possible expansion.

Surprising no one, the sandstone walls of the West Front, like those of the East Front, were found to be in the same weather-worn condition, contributing to some slight sagging in the entablature above the central colonnade, which prompted some worry that the entire west side of the building was in danger of collapsing. While assuring the doomsayers that this outcome was unlikely, Stewart nevertheless installed wooden braces on the Capitol's western face to prop up the drooping entablature.

Stewart proposed some additions to the West Front that went far beyond the committee and office spaces envisioned by Walter and Clark, suggesting pushing the front out more than eighty feet to make room for a number of restaurants and other facilities. That was unacceptable to Senator Stephen Young of Ohio, who accused Stewart of trying to "make the Capitol into a king-sized Howard Johnson's."[44] More problematic, every plan for the extended West Front involved ripping out some or all of Olmsted's carefully designed terraces—a recommendation that alarmed preservationists.

Bolstering preservationists even further, in 1960, the Capitol had been declared a National Historic Landmark by the National Park Service. While such a designation didn't necessarily restrict the Congress's ability to alter the building, it did send a message that this was no ordinary structure; it was an *icon*. Any changes to the building, therefore, were going to demand careful thought and deliberation—and would be watched closely by the public. The Senate at least seemed to get it, shooting down their House counterparts' recommendations to expand the West Front and voting instead to simply renovate and restore the crumbling sandstone walls.

As the matter was still being discussed, Stewart died of cancer on May 24, 1970, at age seventy-nine. His nearly sixteen-year tenure as Architect of the Capitol had been productive: he had overseen the extension of the East Front, the restoration and preservation of the dome, and the construction of two office buildings. But his loyalty—some would say fealty—to Speaker Rayburn was cause for resentment among some members, who accused him of simply rubber-stamping anything Rayburn wanted. Stewart had always responded to such criticism by stating he was simply doing his job. "As an agent of the Congress, I stand ready to carry out, to the best of my ability, any duties which the Congress may see fit to place upon me at any time," he said proudly.[45]

Nevertheless, there were still some who pushed for reforming the process through which the Architect of the Capitol was recruited and appointed, making the position more professional and less political. Even President Nixon seemed to agree when he assigned levelheaded advisor Daniel Patrick Moynihan the task of searching for a replacement for Stewart—preferably someone who was an actual architect. Moynihan shrewdly co-opted the American Institute of Architects for assistance, and the organization was quick to recommend its own vice president, fifty-year-old George M. White, for the job.

Finally, the institute had one of its own in the nation's most prominent public architectural job—and White would prove to be an excellent choice for the gig. The easygoing White was not only an architect, but also a lawyer and electrical engineer, with an M.B.A. from Harvard. Fond of colorful bow ties, he looked more professorial than political—and, indeed, White would strive to keep his office free from political influence, preferring instead to celebrate the Capitol's history as part of his optimism for the future. "We want to preserve our past so we can tell where we came from," he said later, "so that maybe will put us in the direction of where we want to go."[46]

But being apolitical didn't mean he was going to shy away from giving members his frank opinion—and shortly after taking office on January 27, 1971, White fearlessly leapt into the fray over the West Front, pushing back against any option that would tear into Olmsted's terraces and coming down in favor of only a minor renovation. The increasingly acrimonious debate over restoration versus revision would even spill over into the pages of the nation's largest newspapers, with editors at *The Washington Post* applauding the Senate for continuing to torpedo House efforts to extend the West Front. Even *The New York Times* jumped into the debate, demanding that Congress "stop all the foolishness, once and for all, about extending the West Front."[47]

While White had come to the conversation late, he had surprisingly strong feelings about the Capitol's west side. He found it majestic, because it housed one of the best views in all of Washington, D.C., as it looked straight down the Mall toward the Washington Monument and the Lincoln Memorial. White, in fact, would recommend that presidential inaugurations be moved from the east side to the west, not only for the spectacular view but because there was more space for spectators to witness the swearing in. President-elect Ronald Reagan seemed to agree, and at his inauguration on January 20, 1981, Reagan, as the first president to be sworn in on the West Front, acknowledged the history that was being made. "This is the first time in our history that this ceremony has been held . . . on this West Front of the Capitol Building," he said. "Standing here, one faces a magnificent vista opening up on this city's special beauty and history."[48] White nodded in satisfaction.

The debate over whether to restore or renovate the West Front would continue to rage for more than a decade until April 27, 1983, when the Capitol itself seemed to have decided to force the issue. Around nine o'clock that evening, an enormous chunk of sandstone, about ninety square feet, broke away from the Capitol's west face and tumbled loudly into a courtyard below. Twelve weeks later, Reagan signed into law legislation approved by the Congress providing $49 million for restoration—not renovation—of the West Front.

With funding secured, refurbishment proceeded smoothly. Scaffolding was constructed along the sandstone walls, and work crews used it to carefully remove layers of white paint that had been applied to the building over the last hundred sixty years. The sandstone blocks installed by Bulfinch in the 1820s were shored up with cement grout or strengthened by the insertion of stainless steel rods. Stones that were deemed too damaged to reuse—about 40 percent of the original sandstone—were replaced with Indiana limestone. Olmsted's open courtyards, tucked away just behind the terraces, were enclosed under glass roofs, carving out new indoor spaces in the lowest levels of the Capitol while still leaving the terraces intact. Under White's supervision, the restoration was completed in November 1987. The job was also brought in under budget.

White had been on the job for only a little more than thirty days when a Capitol operator received an ominous phone call around one a.m. on March 1, 1971. "Evacuate the building immediately," a man's voice warned her, then informed the stunned operator that a bomb had been planted in the Capitol building. "This is the real thing. This is in retaliation for the Laos decision," the man said, referencing U.S. support for the invasion of Laos by the South Vietnamese. "The bomb will go off in thirty minutes," he warned. The line went dead.

At 1:32 a.m., a time bomb made of fifteen pounds of dynamite exploded in a small restroom in a northwest corner of the ground floor of the old Senate wing. No one was hurt—no surprise, given the early hour and that police, given the heads-up, had evacuated the building—and the Old Senate Chamber, still undergoing restoration, was thankfully undamaged. Still, the explosion had blown out four windows in the Capitol's West Front—glass was found more than forty feet away from the building—and the swinging doors of the nearby Capitol barbershop had been blasted off their hinges. Oddly, amid the scattered debris and damaged walls, every mirror in the barbershop was unbroken.

White sprinted to the Capitol to assess the damage—he was particularly worried that the blast might have cracked the outer walls of the West Front—but he reported with relief to Democratic Leader Mike Mansfield that he had found "no damage to the structural integrity of the building." But the explosion had left a mess—broken stained glass windows, damaged lights, cracked walls—that White estimated would cost more than $300,000 to clean up and repair. Mansfield would consider himself, and the building, lucky. "There have been threats, as many as five a week, over a period of months," he said later.

In a five-page letter sent to the Associated Press, the radical, militant organization the Weather Underground claimed credit for the bombing, boasting that it had attacked "the very seat of U.S. white arrogance." By bombing the Capitol, they said, they hoped to "freak out the warmongers." But mostly, the response was relief and some defiance, with President Nixon vowing that bomb threats would not "close these great public buildings to the people." Coincidentally, the bombing occurred seventeen years to the day after Lolita Lebrón and her three co-conspirators had opened fire in the House gallery. Unlike that day in 1954, however, no arrests would be made—in fact, members of the Weather Underground were notoriously good at *not* getting caught. As Architect of the Capitol David Lynn had done before him, White would oversee the cleanup, checking on work crews as they patched broken window frames, replaced split doorjambs, and carted away wheelbarrow after wheelbarrow of broken stone and plaster.

At the same time, White was supervising two more projects: one in the Capitol building and the other just across Constitution Avenue to the north. There, work had begun on a third Senate office building to give breathing room to the staff of nearly three thousand presently stuffed into the other two office buildings. Initially, Congress had intended simply to add space to the second office building but had quickly realized, after seeing Senators rent out office space in nearby hotels and town houses, that a new building was clearly needed.

And so Congress authorized construction of another Senate office building, sending White to interview several architectural firms for the design. White came back with a contractor with a distinguished pedigree, the San Francisco firm of John Carl Warnecke & Associates, which had designed the John F. Kennedy Eternal Flame grave site at Arlington National Cemetery. Warnecke, who brought a modern sensibility to his buildings, designed a nine-story structure—with three more stories underground—of more than one million square feet; he provided Senators with large open-floor suites with modular walls and doors that members could snap into place however they liked to give their office floor plan almost any configuration. On the exterior, the building was all straight lines and stacked rectangles. It looked like a marble radiator.

It was the most practical and energy efficient of all the Congressional office buildings, though, to many, the least charismatic. "It's just a sump to hold the overflow caused by Congress's relentless expansion," *The New York Times* complained as Senators began to occupy the building in 1982. "A building whose banality is exceeded only by its expense," sighed a disappointed Senator Daniel Patrick Moynihan.[49] The usual crush of Senators jockeying for offices in the new space didn't happen as expected; senior Senators, entitled by their rank to have first choice of offices in the new building, simply refused to move in, allowing junior members to occupy some of the newest and largest offices on the Hill. But White was proud of the building's design and defended its sterile facade as a deliberate effort not to outshine the Capitol building across the street.[50]

Having a third office building created a new and unexpected problem for Senators. For years, constituents could send mail to their elected officials by addressing their letters to their member at either the "Old Senate Office Building" or the "New Senate Office Building." (Harry Truman, while serving as a Senator in an era when there was only *one* Senate office building, took great delight in informing his constituents that all they had to do was address their letters to "Harry Truman, SOB, Washington.") With the completion of a third building, however, something was needed to differentiate the three.

The old and new Senate office buildings, then, would be named after two recently deceased Senate leaders, Richard Russell and Everett Dirksen, respectively, while the newest building would be designated at the time of its groundbreaking for the much-admired and terminally ill Senator Philip Hart of Michigan, who would die of cancer before the building was completed. On the House side, the matter was formally settled in 1962, when the three House office buildings were dedicated to former Speakers. The oldest was named for Joseph Cannon of Illinois, the second for Nicholas Longworth of Ohio, and the newest and largest—fittingly—for the larger-than-life Sam Rayburn, who had overseen its construction.

The other active project under White's jurisdiction was underway on the first floor of the House extension in a series of three long corridors that interconnected to form a capital "I." It was here that the artist Allyn Cox—who had completed Brumidi's *Frieze of American History* twenty years earlier—was at work painting the halls in an ornate style to complement the Brumidi Corridors on the opposite side of the building. Cox had started work on the east side of the extension in the north-south hallway—a hallway running parallel to the magisterial Hall of Columns at the center of the wing. He was painting what would come to be known as the Hall of Capitols; in it, Cox depicted sixteen different sites that had served as the home of Congress, starting with the old Stadt Huys in Albany, where colonial representatives had met in 1754, and running at intervals down the length of the hallway to end with the Capitol as it had appeared in 1867 with the completion of Walter's dome.

Up in the hallway's barrel ceiling, Cox was also working on scenes depicting key historic events from the Capitol's first seven decades, from Washington choosing the site for the building to wounded Union soldiers recovering in the Rotunda, on through to the 1866 passage of the Civil Rights Bill. And in the vaults of the ceiling, Cox painted portraits of key contributors to the Capitol's design and function, including Pierre L'Enfant, Frederick Olmsted, and the nine men who had served as Architect of the Capitol since 1793—including White himself, who was depicted in a blue suit and red bow tie and with a wry smile on his face.

A fast worker, Cox would finish the Hall of Capitols in less than two years, and he would dab at the remaining two corridors at intervals for nearly a decade, painting sixteen murals in the wing's central east-west corridor, which bisected the Hall of Columns. This central corridor would come to be called the Great Experiment Hall for its depiction of three centuries of key legislative and executive accomplishments that had contributed to the American experiment, starting with Pilgrim leader William Brewster signing the 1620 Mayflower Compact and running through suffragist Anna Howard Shaw leading a march for women's suffrage in New York in 1917.

Like Brumidi before him, Cox would die before he could complete his work; after his death from a stroke in 1982 at age eighty-six, artists from EverGreene Painting Studios—a firm that then, as now, specialized in the restoration and preservation of historic art and architecture—would finish the work in the wing's western north-south corridor using Cox's designs. Finally completed in 1994, the Westward Expansion Corridor includes maps and other scenes of exploration that opened up the nation, including Lewis and Clark surveying a Native village on the Missouri River and the completion of the transcontinental railroad in Utah in 1869.

On Cox's passing in 1982, the *Los Angeles Times* mourned the loss of "a latter-day Michaelangelo,"[51] while Speaker of the House Tip O'Neill, in reverent tones, called Cox "a great artist."[52] Brumidi might be the

Capitol's best-known and most respected painter, but Cox deserves his accolades, too; while his figures and faces aren't always of the same quality as Brumidi's—they're slightly more cartoony, as if drawn for *The New Yorker*—Cox remains a superb storyteller, conveying emotion, movement, and drama in his single panels. Senate Majority Leader Howard Baker rightly called Cox's work "splendid" and deserving of "a special place in the art history of the world."[53]

It all seemed eerily familiar: at 10:48 p.m. on the evening of Monday, November 7, 1983, a phone call came through to the Capitol switchboard. "Listen carefully, I'm only going to tell you one time," a man's voice told the Capitol operator. "There is a bomb in the Capitol building. It will go off in five minutes. Evacuate the building."[54]

Ten minutes later, a bomb ripped through the corridor just outside the Senate chamber's south entrance. The force of the explosion tore the mahogany doors leading to the offices of Minority Leader Robert C. Byrd off their hinges and blasted a hole in the wall of the Senate Republican cloakroom, leaving a fifteen-foot crater behind it. The explosion was loud enough to be heard outside the building—one bystander said he thought there had been a sonic boom—and as police ran to investigate the sound, they found the hallways outside the Senate chamber filled with dark smoke and smoldering debris.

Fortunately, the Senate wing was empty—though according to its own schedule, it shouldn't have been. The Senate had taken up a military appropriations bill at nine that morning and expected to vote on amendments late into the evening; members had worked so quickly, however, that they had completed their business earlier than expected and adjourned at 7:02 p.m. "It was indeed fortunate that the Senate was not in session last night," Majority Leader Howard Baker noted the next morning. "Had we been in session at 11 o'clock, undoubtedly there would have been grave injury and perhaps loss of life."[55] After adjourning, some members had attended an event in the new reception room, just across the hall from where the bomb had been planted. But that gathering, too, had wrapped earlier than expected, sending members and guests home well before the eleven p.m. explosion.[56]

As he had done in 1971, White went immediately to the Capitol to assess the damage. While the blast had shattered chandeliers and furniture and damaged several paintings—including a portrait of Daniel Webster that was irreparably shredded[57]—the building had once again held; White reported that there was no structural damage, though repairs and cleaning would likely run to nearly a million dollars. And while reporters who rushed to the scene had initially reported that the stately Ohio Clock had been destroyed by the blast, they had gotten it wrong; it was only the glass of its case that had cracked. When the smoke cleared, the 166-year-old clock was still ticking.[58]

The next day, the local National Public Radio station received a message from an organization calling itself the Armed Resistance Unit. "Tonight we bombed the U.S. Capitol," the message said. The bombers made clear that it had not been their intent to kill anyone, hence their warning to evacuate; they had directed their attack toward the Capitol building as one of the U.S. government's "institutions of imperialist rule" and in protest of American involvement in Grenada, Lebanon, and Central America.[59]

In truth, the attack had been planned and executed not by the Armed Resistance Unit—that was a red herring to throw off police and the FBI—but by a radical far-left domestic terrorist group called the May 19th Communist Organization, which took its name from the birthdays of Malcolm X and Ho Chi Minh. The group was small and made up mostly of women who were experienced bomb makers as well as masters of disguise and subterfuge. In fact, it would take the FBI almost five years to make an arrest, finally indicting seven May 19th members for the Capitol bombing in May 1988. At that point, nearly all were already serving time for other crimes, including the 1981 armed robbery of a Brink's armored truck. In a March 1990 deal with prosecutors for their roles in the 1983 bombing of the Capitol, forty-five-year-old Laura Whitehorn was sentenced to twenty years in prison, while forty-three-year-old Linda Sue Evans was sent away for forty.

On August 6, 1999, Whitehorn was released on parole after serving a little more than fourteen years of her sentence. Evans, meanwhile, had her sentence commuted by President Bill Clinton on January 20, 2001, one of several controversial pardons and commutations issued on his last day in office. In a *New York Times* op-ed, Clinton defended his decision, saying individuals like Evans "seemed to me deserving of executive clemency. Overwhelmingly, the pardons went to people who had been convicted and served their time."[60] Members of the Senate Judiciary Committee were unconvinced, pondering, in the words of Republican chairman Orrin Hatch, "some serious questions as to whether some of them [the pardons] were appropriate."[61]

The May 19th organization's bombing would also mark the beginning of a new era of increasingly rigid security measures in and around the Capitol. In the months following the 1971 bombing, Capitol visitors were finally required to pass through metal detectors before entering the House and Senate galleries, but not the building itself. Now Congress would tighten security even further, installing metal detectors at all public entrances to the Capitol and restricting access to much of the building's interior. The hallways around the Senate and House chambers, once open to tourists and lobbyists, were closed to the public. Staff and other officials would be permitted in these areas only by displaying identification at all times.

But the Congress remained as conflicted as ever over its decision to limit any access to the Capitol. "I think a free society such as ours owes a degree of access of the public to the public buildings," said House Majority Leader Jim Wright. "This is not our building. It's the building of the people of the United States." Senate Sergeant at Arms Larry Smith was more realistic than idealistic. "God forbid anyone should lose their life visiting the Capitol," Smith said. "[But] it is impossible to make any building entirely secure unless you close it down."[62]

It was a question the Congress would continue to struggle with for the next three decades.

On September 18, 1993, the U.S. Capitol turned two hundred years old. To commemorate its bicentennial, a symbolic cornerstone was dedicated in a ceremony at the West Front, with Masons from all fifty states reenacting the ritualistic laying of the cornerstone two centuries earlier. Architect George White was there wearing a Masonic apron and watching in a steady rain as Senator Strom Thurmond of South Carolina, using George Washington's trowel, spread concrete on the cornerstone. There were no parades or big speeches; White had saved those for a different bicentennial celebration, focusing on *Statue of Freedom*, which he was having restored.

Two years earlier, the architect had asked conservationists to examine Thomas Crawford's *Statue of Freedom*, which had stood atop the dome exposed to the elements since 1863. To no one's surprise, the statue was corroding, its pedestal rusting. Between the five pieces of the statue, the joints—which had been so cleverly revealed by the enslaved Philip Reid a hundred thirty years before—had been clumsily caulked and recaulked over the years, leaving dark lines that were visible from the ground. In short, she was a mess. So on May 9, 1993, White climbed to the top of the dome to personally help loosen her from her perch before a jet-powered Skycrane helicopter lifted her from the tholus and carefully set her down on the Capitol's east lawn.

For five months, tourists could watch as workers repaired more than seven hundred holes in the 19.5-foot bronze statue. She was blasted clean with high-pressure water hoses and then finally restored to a dark bronze-green color. On the morning of October 23, a bright orange heavy-lift helicopter returned to the lawn, prepared to move the statue back to its perch—and this time, there was plenty of pomp and circumstance, with cannon fire and remarks from notable VIPs like President Bill Clinton and Vice President Al Gore.

Among the speeches given that day, the most poignant came from Poet Laureate Rita Dove, who read aloud the poem "Lady Freedom Among Us," which she had written for the occasion. "Don't think you can ever forget her," Dove read, her voice soaring, ". . . for she is one of the many / and she is each of us." At that, *Freedom* was slowly lifted from the plaza and gently returned to the top of the dome, 287 feet above the ground. Steelworkers at the top carefully moved the statue into place, then turned and bowed to the thousands of cheering spectators in the plaza below.

Having successfully guided the building through its bicentennial era, Architect of the Capitol George White retired on November 21, 1995. His tenure had spanned the terms of six presidents, from Nixon to Clinton, and—apart from his cleaning up after two explosions—had been marked mostly by relative calm and a lack of controversy, which was much appreciated by members of Congress after the politically tinged tenure of George Stewart. "Our finest architect since William Thornton," Daniel Patrick Moynihan said of White as the architect retired to his home in Bethesda.[63]

White was the last Architect of the Capitol to be selected solely by a president. In 1990, Congress approved new rules to define the appointment process for the Architect of the Capitol as well as the position's length of term, which until 1990 had always been open-ended. Under the 1990 rules, each Architect of the Capitol would be appointed for a fixed ten-year term by the president, with the advice and consent of a bicameral, bipartisan Congressional advisory commission. White's only advice to the Congress on finding an Architect of the Capitol was to "[choose] someone who is beyond reproach in connection with moral standards. There is [*sic*] hundreds of millions of dollars passed through the Office of the Architect and it needs to be known that he is untouchable, or she."[64]

The revised appointment process worked mostly fine for the next three decades, though there would often be long gaps between appointments. White's successor, Alan Hantman, would begin his ten-year term in January 1997, over a year after White's retirement. And at the conclusion of Hantman's term in February 2007, the position would be filled by Stephen T. Ayers on an interim basis until his formal appointment to the post in May 2010, more than three years later.

Things changed, however, with the early retirement of Ayers and the confirmation of J. Brett Blanton, appointed by President Donald Trump on December 9, 2019. Barely three years into Blanton's term, the Office of the Inspector General reported a long list of Blanton's ethics abuses, such as theft, waste, fraud, and, in the days leading up to the November 2020 election, his wife giving unauthorized personal tours to fringe groups that created "the appearance of impropriety and using a public position for private gain, which is a violation of [the Office of the Architect of the Capitol] policy."[65] Blanton denied the allegations, but with calls for his resignation coming from both sides of the Hill and both sides of the political aisle, the architect was doomed; he was terminated in February 2023 by President Joe Biden, who selected Chere Rexroat, an accomplished engineer, as interim Architect of the Capitol, the first woman to serve in the role, though she was never formally appointed to the position.

In 2023, Congress again revised its own rules, clarifying the proper methods of hiring *and* firing the architect and devising a system that removed the president of the United States entirely from the appointment process. Under the new rules, the architect is appointed to a ten-year term by a bipartisan, bicameral Congressional commission and may, at the discretion of that commission, be reappointed for an additional term. Similarly, the architect can also be removed at any time by a majority vote of the commission members.[66]

The first architect appointed by the new Congressional commission, Thomas E. Austin, began his term as the thirteenth Architect of the Capitol in June 2024. A former director of engineering at Arlington National Cemetery, Austin seems to have a healthy respect for the unique aspects of his job—"It's definitely a working piece of historic architecture," he said of the Capitol[67]—as well as an appreciation for the building's ability to inspire and awe. "It is hard to overstate the impact of seeing the Dome of the Capitol with the *Statue of Freedom* at the top," said Austin. "Every morning when I come in, I am in awe of the building and what it represents. Inside the Capitol, I am truly amazed by the artwork throughout the building—everything from the tiles on the floor to the paintings on the walls and the state statues along the corridors.

"The whole Capitol," said the architect, "is a masterpiece."[68]

CHAPTER 11

Irresponsibility and Madmen

1998–Present

Like George White before him, whose first month on the job sent him sprinting to the Capitol to check on damage from a bomb planted by the Weather Underground in 1971, Architect of the Capitol Alan Hantman would have to deal with violence in the building—which included the murder of two Capitol policemen—in the early years of his term.

On Friday, July 24, 1998, forty-one-year-old Russell Eugene Weston approached one of the Capitol's lesser used public entrances tucked away on the ground floor of the East Front just south of the majestic main center steps. Weston had driven to Washington, D.C., from his father's home in Illinois, bringing little with him except the .38-caliber pistol he had stolen from his father's bedside table. Weston had a history of paranoid schizophrenia—he had been placed on a watch list for writing threatening letters to President Clinton—and now, as he walked toward the Capitol's ground-floor entrance, Weston was convinced that once he was inside, he would find somewhere in the building an iron safe containing a time machine he could use to travel back to the past and expose the president as a clone.

As Weston entered the building, he passed through and set off the metal detector just inside the door. That alarm caught the attention of a police officer stationed near the entrance, fifty-eight-year-old Jacob "JJ" Chestnut, an eighteen-year veteran of the Capitol Police as well as a former Air Force policeman who had served two tours of duty in Vietnam.

Chestnut, who was giving directions to a group of tourists, turned toward the metal detector; as he did so, Weston shot him in the back of the head at close range. Another officer at the door, Douglas McMillan, quickly returned fire but missed; Weston fired back, wounding McMillan and a tourist. "The sound was like firecrackers, *bang bang bang*," one House committee staffer reported later.[1] Amid the screams, Weston pushed open a door to his left marked "Do Not Enter" and began to move down the long corridor in the private suite belonging to the House Republican Whip Tom DeLay of Texas.

Weston hadn't made it very far when he was met by John Gibson, a forty-two-year-old plainclothes Capitol Police detective assigned to protect DeLay. Hearing the shots, Gibson had ordered staff to take cover before moving down the narrow corridor toward the sound. Weston spotted Gibson immediately and fired at the detective several times, staggering Gibson backward with a fatal shot to the chest. Heroically, Gibson still managed to fire four shots at Weston, who fell to the ground with wounds in the stomach and both legs. Mortally wounded, Gibson collapsed behind a desk as Capitol Police swarmed the suite and subdued and arrested Weston.

Weston would be determined incompetent to stand trial and, as of 2026, remains in a mental institution. Chestnut and Gibson were laid in honor together in the Rotunda on July 28, 1998, making Chestnut the first African American to lie in honor in the Capitol.[2] In a solemn thirty-minute ceremony, some of the most powerful men and women in the nation gathered to pay tribute to the two slain police officers who had given their lives protecting the building at the heart of the American democracy. "It is fitting that we gather here to honor these two American heroes," said President Clinton, "in this Capitol they gave their lives to defend."[3]

It was becoming clear to the Congress, however, that the bravery of police officers—along with metal detectors, color-coded ID cards, and limited entry points—wasn't going to be enough to guarantee the safety of members and visitors to the Capitol. Something had to be done to limit, or better control, access to the Capitol building. But members faced the same dilemma as always: how can you keep the People's House both *open* and *secure*?

Congress did have a plan—or at least the start of one. In 1991, it had authorized funding for the planning and design of a visitor center: a place where the millions of visitors to the Capitol each year could learn more about the building, its architecture, its history, and the role of the Congress—but also a place to control the flow of traffic into the building. The center would be located entirely underground, buried beneath the lawn on the east side of the Capitol and accessed by a sloping walkway that would take visiors through an open glass pavilion sunk fifty feet below the surface, keeping the views of the Capitol—as Frederick Olmsted had intended—as uncluttered as possible. Once inside, visitors would be funneled into the Capitol through a secured passageway and entrance. The Capitol, then, would remain very much a public building, but instead of having visitors enter the structure through any of several exterior entrances, the new center would ensure they all came in through *one* secure entrance underground. In 1995, a report had even been issued on the design—one of the last overseen by George White before his retirement—but the estimated price tag of $70 million to $100 million had spooked members into shelving the report indefinitely.

The recent killing of two Capitol policemen, however, persuaded even the most fiscally conservative members to reconsider things—and in October 1998, Congress formally authorized construction of the Capitol Visitor Center, working off the specifications and recommendations of their own 1995 report. In 2000, there was a groundbreaking; preconstruction activities were to begin in the fall of 2001, with the center planned for completion by late 2005.

Then, on September 11, 2001, al-Qaeda terrorists hijacked American Airlines Flight 77 and deliberately crashed it into the Pentagon at 9:37 a.m.; twenty-six minutes later, at 10:03 a.m., the similarly hijacked

United Airlines Flight 93 was heroically brought down by a passenger revolt, plunging it into a field near Shanksville, Pennsylvania, instead of into its likely intended target: the U.S. Capitol.

At 10:15 a.m., with smoke from the Pentagon blackening the skies just southwest of the Capitol, Capitol Police ordered members of Congress and their staffs to evacuate all buildings in the Capitol compound—not just the Capitol but all Congressional office buildings, the Library of Congress, and the Supreme Court. The Senate, which suspended its business at the moment of the evacuation order, returned to session in the early hours of September 12 to defiantly conduct the people's business. In the weeks and months after the attacks, Washington, D.C., resembled a war zone, with military vehicles at street intersections, soldiers from the D.C. Army National Guard mobilized around the city, and access to all federal buildings tightly controlled, sometimes by a show of force.

Through it all, Congressional leaders insisted the Capitol would remain open even as they demanded greater security measures for the just underway visitor center. Estimated costs climbed from $265 million to $621 million. But despite some occasional complaints about the rising costs—"a monument to government inefficiency, ineptitude and excessiveness," sniffed Georgia Congressman Jack Kingston[4]—support remained solid and work continued without interruption under the oversight of Architect of the Capitol Alan Hantman until 2007, then under the direction of his replacement, Stephen Ayers. The center would open to the public on December 2, 2008—a date that deliberately reflected the official completion of the Capitol back on December 2, 1863, when *Freedom* was finally secured atop the dome. Thomas U. Walter would have approved.

The visitor center was constructed as an official extension of the Capitol and is considered just as much a part of the Capitol building as its dome or the House and Senate chambers. As such, the materials used for its construction and design match those of the Capitol, from Pennsylvania sandstone to Virginia granite and Tennessee marble. It also conforms to Olmsted's landscaping designs, as it is tucked between the swooping curves of pathways laid out by the landscape architect in the 1870s. And at nearly 580,000 square feet, it's the largest project undertaken in the Capitol's history, with a footprint nearly as large as that of the Capitol building itself.

The centerpiece of the Capitol Visitor Center is Emancipation Hall, named to formally honor—at last—the contributions of the enslaved laborers who helped build the Capitol. Prominently on display is a Slave Labor Commemorative Marker, a single block of Aquia Creek sandstone originally laid as part of the Capitol's East Front in 1826 and still scuffed with visible chisel marks left by the hands that did its quarrying and shaping. It is "a fitting and lasting tribute to these men, black men, slaves," said Congressman John Lewis, "in a permanent place here in the United State Capitol."[5] Dotted around the space are overflow statues from the National Statuary Hall Collection, usually the newest additions submitted to the collection by the states. And at the center of the hall is the full-sized plaster model of *Statue of Freedom* executed by sculptor Thomas Crawford in his Rome studio in the 1850s—a tacit reminder of the contributions of the enslaved Philip Reid, who helped to elevate *Freedom* to her appropriate perch at the top of the people's shrine to democracy.

"We trust that this whole building will stand throughout the ages," Speaker Sam Rayburn said of the Capitol at the laying of the cornerstone for the East Front extension in 1959. "And it will unless irresponsibility and madmen determine to destroy everything. We express the hope here today that this will never happen."[6]

On January 6, 2021, it happened.

By the time of the 2020 election, President Donald Trump had browbeaten and blustered his way through a tumultuous four-year presidency marked by chaos and discontent. Citizens enraged by the killing of young Black men had taken to the streets to protest outside the White House in the name of social justice—and Trump had had them tear-gassed. More than 200,000 Americans had died of COVID-19 during his presidency;[7] Trump, meanwhile, had continued to assert that the virus "affects virtually nobody."[8]

And Trump—as unwilling to accept the truth as Andrew Jackson had been following his election loss in 1824—didn't want to hear about it when he lost the election of 2020 to former Vice President Joe Biden. Winning, and the adulation that he thought winners deserved, always mattered most to Trump. And if he didn't win . . . well, that was because someone else had clearly cheated. As the host of the popular reality shows *The Apprentice* and *The Celebrity Apprentice* from 2004 to 2015, Trump never won an Emmy Award—a loss he attributed to the awards being rigged against him; he had thus regularly taken to social media to accuse the Emmys of being "dishonest" and a "con game."[9] To Trump, losing was for chumps—and now that he had lost the 2020 election and the presidency, he was going to do whatever it took—tell whatever lie he needed to tell—to get it back.

On the afternoon of Wednesday, January 6, 2021, Congress was scheduled to meet in a joint session in the House chamber to certify the results of the 2020 election—an election Trump had lost to Biden in the Electoral College 306 to 232 and in the popular vote 51 percent to 47 percent. But at a noon rally convened by him within sight of the Capitol, he urged a crowd of thousands of cheering supporters to "Stop the Steal," alleging that the election had been stolen from him due to voter fraud in several pivotal states. None of that was true, but it didn't matter—the outgoing president's supporters were worked up into a lather.

And now Trump was encouraging Republicans in Congress to overturn the results of the election, even pressuring his own vice president, former Indiana Governor Mike Pence, not to certify the results. That unprecedented move would have tossed the election back to the states; Trump felt certain he could overturn his losses in swing states like

Georgia. He'd already been caught on tape trying to convince Georgia's secretary of state to "find 11,780 votes" to overturn the state's election results and add its coveted sixteen electoral votes to his tally.

Fifteen minutes into his remarks on January 6, he urged the growing crowd of supporters to move on the Capitol. "I know that everyone here will soon be marching over to the Capitol building to make your voice peacefully and patriotically heard," he told them, and prodded them to "give our Republicans the kind of pride and boldness that they need."[10]

Just after one p.m., as Congress began the process of certifying the election, Trump shouted for his supporters to "fight like hell! And if you don't fight like hell, you're not going to have a country anymore. So, let's walk down Pennsylvania Avenue!"[11] As his supporters surged toward the Capitol, Trump returned to the White House to keep an eye on the action on television. The mob grew louder as it moved to the Capitol's West Front. Some in the throng brandished makeshift weapons; others carried plastic zip ties, intending to use them to handcuff members of Congress—especially House Speaker Nancy Pelosi.[12] On the west lawn, someone constructed a makeshift gallows—and shouts of "Hang Mike Pence!" began, suggesting the fate of the vice president if he certified the election for anyone other than Trump.

With the crowd—peppered with members of far-right extremist groups like the Proud Boys and the Oath Keepers—getting louder and more agitated, one Capitol police officer nervously radioed for backup. "They're throwing metal poles at us," he said, and then, his voice rising, added, "Multiple law-enforcement injuries." At one fifteen, another officer radioed that the mob was "now effectively a riot."

As rioters moved up the Capitol's west lawn, Senate Majority Leader Mitch McConnell, a Republican from Kentucky, took to the Senate floor to warn that overturning Biden's election—which he acknowledged had been legitimate—would "damage our republic forever. . . . If this election were overturned by mere allegations from the losing side," he said, "our democracy would enter a death spiral." Shortly thereafter, rioters reached the Capitol's West Front, where they scaled its walls and pounded on doors as they pushed back Capitol police. The scaffolding and stages constructed by the Architect of the Capitol's office for Biden's scheduled swearing in on January 20 were angrily torn down and destroyed.

At two fifteen, the mob finally forced its way into the building through broken windows and kicked-in doors on the Capitol's West Front. Capitol police were battered backward; one officer was crushed in the doorway. At that moment, the Secret Service swooped in to remove Vice President Pence from the Senate floor and rushed him off to a safe location. Senators could hear the crowd in the building and they began running for the exits. "This is what you've gotten, guys!" Senator Mitt Romney shouted at his colleagues who had argued in favor of overturning the election. In the House chamber, Nancy Pelosi was hustled away by police.

It was chaos inside the Capitol as rioters began scrambling through the building. Capitol Police officer Eugene Goodman, trying to buy time for Senators to finish evacuating the chamber, confronted the converging crowd and tricked rioters into following him away from the entrance to the Senate. Within moments of Goodman's ploy, rioters would enter the now abandoned chamber, poring through papers and speeches Senators had left behind on podiums, looking for . . . Well, no one was quite sure—just "something we can use against these scumbags," one rioter growled as he rifled through a member's prepared remarks. In the Speaker's Lobby, another group attempted to force open a set of locked doors to gain access to the floor of the House, where many members were still hunkered down. As the glass in the doors was broken in, a thirty-five-year-old Air Force veteran named Ashli Babbitt began to crawl through the opening and was shot dead by Capitol police.

Trump, now watching the riot from the White House dining room, refused to call off the mob of his supporters. Instead, he took to social media to complain, "Mike Pence didn't have the courage to do what should have been done"—red meat for the crowd in the Capitol scrolling through Trump's social media feed for direction and motivation.

Rioters stormed inside the Capitol for nearly three hours, some taking selfies on their phones while others continued to ransack Capitol offices. One man was photographed gleefully strolling through the Rotunda with Speaker Pelosi's stolen podium, another with his feet up on Pelosi's office desk. The so-called QAnon Shaman—a right-wing conspiracy theorist in a horned helmet and a face smeared with red, white, and blue paint—was seen bellowing in the gallery of the Senate chamber and later from the vice president's chair.

On the second floor, a Delaware drywall mechanic named Kevin Seefried was photographed strolling with a Confederate flag dangling from a flagpole slung over his shoulder—the first time in the Capitol's history the building had ever been breached by anyone carrying the official colors of the Confederacy. On the wall behind Seefried was a portrait of Senator Charles Sumner, who in 1856 had taken the beating of his life for standing against everything the Confederate flag represented. "I saw the Confederate flag there," New Jersey Senator Cory Booker, one of the chamber's few Black members, said later. "What will we do? How will we confront this shame?"

Finally, at 4:17 p.m., Trump called off his supporters via a video statement posted on his social media account. "It was a landslide election and everyone knows it," he glowered, telling yet another lie about the election. "But you have to go home now."

It would take several more hours before the building and the grounds were cleared. As members returned to the Capitol around eight p.m., they stepped carefully around shattered furniture and broken glass and tried to avoid skidding on floors that had been slickened by residue from fire extinguishers. In Statuary Hall—the old House chamber—some marble statues had been smeared with blood or paint. In other places, floors were streaked with muddy footprints. Trump flags still leaned against walls; in one corridor, a handmade banner reading

"TREASON!" had been abandoned.[13] Members pushed aside discarded water bottles and other trash as they returned to their seats in the House chamber.

At 3:42 a.m. on the morning of Thursday, January 7, Vice President Mike Pence officially affirmed the election of Joe Biden as the forty-sixth president of the United States.

But the damage was done. "We can now add January 6, 2021, to that very short list of dates in American history that will live forever in infamy," New York Senator Chuck Schumer said solemnly. More than a hundred seventy police officers had been injured in the riot;[14] five would die in the days and weeks after, including four who took their own lives. It would cost more than $3 million to clean up the mess and repair the damage to the Capitol.

And once again, the Congress had to do some self-reflection on its own security systems and protocols and to ponder how it had been caught so flat-footed. Over the next few years, the Capitol Police would see its budget steadily increase as it began to transition from a regular police force to what it called a "protective force" built on intelligence gathering and threat assessment. "We were not sharing intel the way we should have," said Police Chief Tom Manger. "We were not operationalizing it. All of those things are being done now."[15]

The FBI estimated that more than two thousand individuals had participated in the storming of the Capitol on January 6; by a year later, 1,583 people had been arrested, with 1,270 convicted.[16] Trump, however, would continue to falsely assert that the rioters were merely tourists—or, if you weren't buying that, that the violence had been committed by paid actors or left-wing organizations disguised in the familiar red MAGA hats of Trump supporters. "They were patriots as far as I was concerned," Trump said of the rioters. "I talk about them a lot. They were treated very unfairly."[17]

Talk like that was too much for President Joe Biden to stomach. As far as he was concerned, January 6 had been "a day we nearly lost America—lost it all," he said. "And what's Trump done? He's called these insurrectionists 'patriots,' and he promised to pardon them if he returns to office."[18]

On January 20, 2025, Donald Trump returned to office. As promised, on his very first day as president, Trump issued full commutations and pardons to all January 6 rioters, including those convicted of violent offenses.

The events of January 6 were not the first time violence rocked the U.S. Capitol—nor, as we have seen, even the first time Americans inflicted violence against their fellow Americans within its walls. As both the symbol and the epicenter of the American experiment, the Capitol houses not just the government but the American psyche. Since 1790, when it was still just a scribbled word on a map of the new Federal district, the Capitol—even the very idea of it—has always been a reflection of the American character, including its mood and mindset. A disturbance in the American collective consciousness—be it political crisis or cultural chaos—seems to inevitably ricochet through the halls of the Capitol.

It has always been this way. Like with the United States itself, both the design and the construction of the Capitol have often been messy, disorganized, and, at times, largely improvised. The Capitol's very location was a matter of political expediency. Several times, its very look was defined by a wonderful, almost charming faith in the American people: contests in which any American could submit a design showed a genuine trust in the American people to determine their own identity by creating their own American iconography.

The building's growing footprint and profile mirrored the growing size, and growing needs, of the United States as the country expanded westward, adding new states and new citizens from nearly every background, culture, and nationality. Some improvements—such as the types of materials used, from marble to Minton tiles—were carefully deliberated; others—like an architect hanging a drawing of a dome no one had asked for in his office . . . and suddenly having everyone ask for it—were happy accidents. The American experiment, too, is both methodical and spontaneous.

And like the nation the Capitol embodies, it is an imperfect structure. Our monument to the ideals of American democracy was built, in part, by enslaved workers, who had neither liberty nor equality. And it was built of imperfect materials—foundations that crumbled and had to be repoured; wooden struts and beams that rotted, sagged, or caught fire; and sandstone that needed constant replacement over two centuries. While the Capitol has since been strengthened and shored up—with marble walls and terraces and iron struts—it still requires continual maintenance, care, and upkeep. So, too, does the American experiment.

The Capitol is a place where some of the nation's finest moments have been realized—where Americans have been at their best—from Samuel F. B. Morse, in a nondescript committee room, changing the speed at which information traveled, to John F. Kennedy, from the Capitol's grand east steps, appealing to a new generation of Americans to answer the call to service. It is also a place where Americans have brutalized one another in the name of ego or self-righteousness, leaving Senator Charles Sumner bloodied and beaten on the floor of the U.S. Senate and Capitol Police officers pummeled and pepper-sprayed inside the Rotunda.

In its nearly two and a half centuries, it has been burned down, torn down, bombed, and rocked by explosions. Its halls have echoed with gunfire and been blackened by gas fires. And each time, the building has been reimagined, rebuilt, and reconstructed to be stronger and better than before.

And through it all, *Freedom* stands atop the Capitol dome, still facing east and still gazing hopefully toward the rising sun of every new morning.

Acknowledgments

While writers often like to say that writing is the loneliest of professions—it's just you and the blank page, day after day, especially on those days when you're stuck—we're mostly just being dramatic. Because as anyone who does this knows, once you get beyond putting your own butt in the chair and your name at the top of the page, a book doesn't happen without the support, patience, understanding, hard work, and enthusiasm of countless others.

I began this project in the wake of the events of January 6; as a former Congressional staffer who worked in the Capitol compound for nearly a decade, that day hit me like a punch in the gut. This project was my way of responding and coping, of giving something back to the building that was such an important part of my first years as an actual adult. And writing it, I remembered again how much I loved that building and the people I worked with in it all those years ago.

And so, I want to thank them first: that special group of friends and colleagues I lived and labored with during those years in Washington, D.C., who made working in that building—and in those buildings around it—a joy and a privilege: Rod and Kimberly Barnes-O'Connor, Kerry Bertram, Allegra Carpenter, my late mentor Kay Davies, Leah DiMarco, Chris Gallegos, Ginny and Paul Gilman, Marco Gonzales, Stan and Stephanie Harris, Kathy Kersting, Mike and Cassie Knapp, Lisa Meyer-Hagen, Loren Monroe, Keith Nelson, Mike and Marron

Nelson, Gail and Dave Noren, Mark and Aggie Saltman, Mike Westphal and Gary (miss you, man!) and Anne-Kathryn Ziehe. I know there are plenty of you I'm forgetting, but it's late as I write this. Know that I loved every moment of our working together. This book is for all of you.

Naturally, once I was ready to take on this iconic subject, I looked for guidance and wisdom from my fantastic agent, Jonathan Lyons, who's been at my side, and had my back, for more than twenty years. It's also been a privilege to work again with John Parsley, one of the best editors to ever do it, and who always takes the time to chitchat on the phone with me, even when I know he's super busy, because that's the kind of human being he is. I've also had the good fortune of taking on this project with Jill Schwartzman, an incredible editor I've wanted to work with for years; the stars finally aligned for this one, and I couldn't be happier. Assistant editor Charlotte Peters kept me on track and on task and never flinched when I e-mailed her *just one last time, I promise.* Thanks to all of you, and to the rest of the crack team at Dutton who always do their best to support their writers. I also want to send a huge thanks to copyeditor Frank Walgren, who saved me from myself more than once. Any other mistakes you might spot are all mine.

I'm also so appreciative of the support and enthusiasm I received regularly from my colleagues and work family at the University of New Mexico: Terry Babbitt, Cinnamon Blair, Steve Carr, Ben Cloutier, Mitch Garrity, Faith Gresham, Madison Hernandez, Bridgette Noonen, Ethan Rule, and President Garnett Stokes. Thanks for putting up with me.

Finally, I couldn't have made it through my five years with this project without the support and inspiration I regularly received from the folks I'm fortunate enough to call friends and colleagues. Apart from those who've been mentioned already, my thanks to Michael Burgan, Melissa Harman, Heath Lee, James McGrath Morris, Scott Phillips, and especially my writing wingman Simon Read, whom I can always count on to send me photos of one amazing martini after another.

I'm particularly grateful, too, for the love and support of those I'm even luckier to have as family and loved ones. My warmest thanks to Chuck and Kelly Evans, Jennifer German, Barb Jones, and Kris Villaca, all of whom always made a point of checking in on me and kindly asking, "How are things going?" I especially want to thank Colleen Herst for her constant love and care and heroic patience—I hope you know that this book couldn't have happened without you. My dad, Larry Jones, and stepfather, Wayne Miller, both passed away while I was writing this, and I think each of them would've really liked this one—know you're both loved and missed. My mom, Elaine Miller, along with my brother, Cris, and his family, also remain my most steadfast fans. Finally, my daughter, Madi, and her husband, Chris, make me feel supported and loved even as they continue to make me really, really proud of them. Thank you all for going on this journey with me; I love and adore all of you.

Brian Jay Jones
Albuquerque, New Mexico, December 2025

Notes

Chapter 1

1. Pierre L'Enfant to George Washington, September 11, 1789, quoted in William C. Allen, *History of the United States Capitol* (Washington, D.C.: U.S. Government Printing Office, 2001), 8, https://babel.hathitrust.org/cgi/pt?id=umn.31951d02020559a&seq=7.

2. George Washington to David Stuart, November 20, 1791, Founders Online, National Archives, https://founders.archives.gov/documents/Washington/05-09-02-0118.

3. See "XIII. The Proclamation by the President, 30 March 1791," Founders Online, National Archives, https://founders.archives.gov/documents/Jefferson/01-19-02-0001-0015.

4. Or, as it was called then, the Eastern Branch.

5. Pierre Charles L'Enfant to Thomas Jefferson, 11 March 1791, Founders Online, National Archives, https://founders.archives.gov/documents/Jefferson/01-20-02-0001-0004.

6. Who was Jenkins? Historians, and D.C. locals, have been speculating for nearly two centuries. One story posits that there was a local farmer named Thomas Jenkins who had once grazed his cattle on the site—unlikely, given the heavily wooded nature of the area. Recently, some careful detective work by members of the Capitol Hill Historical Society found that Jenkins owned fifty-four acres of property about a mile east of the Capitol, and they thought it likely that L'Enfant might have simply applied the name to the entire area. See John Michael Vlach, "The Mysterious Mr. Jenkins of Jenkins Hill," *The Capitol Dome*, 2004, https://web.archive.org/web/20081023082234/http://uschscapitolhistory.uschs.org/articles/uschs_dome-02.htm.

7. Unclear, though historian Bob Arnebeck is doing his best to dig into it. See "Carroll of Duddington vs. Jenkins of the Hill," Washington Examined, December 31, 2018, https://dcswamp.blogspot.com/2018/12/carroll-of-duddington-vs-jenkins-of-hill.html.

8. This is often misquoted as "a pedestal waiting for a monument." Pierre-Charles L'Enfant to George Washington, 22 June 1791, Founders Online, National Archives, https://founders.archives.gov/documents/Washington/05-08-02-0199. See also Ron Chernow, *Washington: A Life* (New York: The Penguin Press, 2010), 662.

9. In fact, he misspelled it nearly every time as "presidial palace."

10. Pierre Charles L'Enfant, Library of Congress, U.S. Geological Survey, and U.S. National Geographic Society, "Plan of the city intended for the permanent seat of the government of the United States: projected agreeable to the direction of the President of the United States, in pursuance of an act of Congress, passed on the sixteenth day of July, MDCCXC, 'establishing the permanent seat on the bank of the Potowmac'" (Washington, D.C.: Library of Congress, 1991), map, https://www.loc.gov/item/97683585/.

11. XII. Thomas Jefferson to Pierre Charles L'Enfant, 10 April 1791, Founders

Online, National Archives, https://founders.archives.gov/documents/Jefferson/01-20-02-0001-0015.

12. Chernow, *Washington*, 630.

13. Chernow, *Washington*, 630.

14. John Adams, Diary, September 23, 1789, Massachusetts Historical Society, Adams Family Papers, https://www.masshist.org/digitaladams/archive/doc?id=D46.

15. Chernow, *Washington*, 630.

16. See "Thomas Jefferson's Explanations of the Three Volumes Bound in Marbled Paper (the So-called 'Anas'), 4 February 1818," Founders Online, National Archives, https://founders.archives.gov/documents/Jefferson/03-12-02-0343-0002.

17. "Thomas Jefferson's Explanations."

18. William Maclay, *Journal of William Maclay, United States Senator from Pennsylvania, 1789–1791*, ed. Edgar S. Maclay (New York: D. Appleton and Company, 1890), 305, https://catalog.hathitrust.org/Record/001142328.

19. *Journal of William Maclay*, 328.

20. Well, sort of. The text of the legislation only got as specific as "on the river Potomac, at some place between the mouths of the Eastern Branch and Connogochegue." See "An Act for establishing the temporary and permanent seat of the Government of the United States," *Record of the First Congress*, Sess. II, 1790, Ch. 28, 130, https://tile.loc.gov/storage-services/service/ll/llsl//llsl-c1/llsl-c1.pdf#page=249.

21. James Monroe to Thomas Jefferson, 26 July 1790, Founders Online, National Archives, https://founders.archives.gov/documents/Jefferson/01-17-02-0051.

22. Bob Arnebeck, *Through a Fiery Trial: Building Washington 1790–1800* (Lanham, MD: Madison Books, 1991), 50.

23. Arnebeck, *Through a Fiery Trial*, 46.

24. Commissioners to George Washington, October 21, 1791. See Glenn Brown, *History of the United States Capitol* (New York: Da Capo Press, 1970), 4.

25. See Arnebeck, *Through a Fiery Trial*, 74.

26. Arnebeck, *Through a Fiery Trial*, 78. Emphasis in original.

27. Chernow, *Washington*, 664. Emphasis in original.

28. Arnebeck, *Through a Fiery Trial*, 80.

29. Chernow, *Washington*, 664.

30. Kimberly Prothro Williams, "Capitol Hill Historic District" (Washington, D.C.: Capitol Hill Restoration Society, 2003), https://dcpreservation.org/wp-content/uploads/2023/01/Capitol_Hill_Brochure_0.pdf.

31. Thomas Jefferson to Pierre L'Enfant, February 22, 1792, quoted in Saul K. Padover, ed., *Thomas Jefferson and the National Capital* (Washington, D.C.: U.S. Government Printing Office, 1946), 93.

32. Padover, *Jefferson and the National Capital*, 98.

33. See Arnebeck, *Through a Fiery Trial*, 98.

34. Thomas Jefferson to the Commissioners, March 6, 1792. See Glenn Brown, *History of the United States Capitol*, 5.

35. Arnebeck, *Through a Fiery Trial*, 105.

36. See "Enclosure II: An Advertisement for the Capitol, 6 March 1792," Founders Online, National Archives, https://founders.archives.gov/documents/Jefferson/01-23-02-0188. Jefferson's original handwritten version of the ad can be seen on the Library of Congress website at www.loc.gov/exhibits/jefferson/images/vc103a.jpg.

37. "XII. Jefferson to L'Enfant."

38. Chernow, *Washington*, 665.

39. Thirty-six entries submitted by thirteen different men have been found so far.

40. All conversions of historical financial figures to modern equivalents were done using the online tool "How Much Is That Worth?" at https://www.measuringworth.com.

41. Allen, *History of the United States Capitol*, 17.

42. Arnebeck, *Through a Fiery Trial*, 101.

43. Arnebeck, *Through a Fiery Trial*, 127.

44. "Thirtysomething," because Hallet's precise birth date is uncertain, listed in most places as "c. 1760."

45. Glenn Brown, *History of the United States Capitol*, 6.

46. See Gordon S. Brown, *Incidental Architect* (Columbus: Ohio University Press, 2009).

47. Ihna Thayer Frary, *They Built the Capitol* (Richmond, VA: Garrett and Massie, 1940), 33.

48. Glenn Brown, *History of the United States Capitol*, 19.

49. Glenn Brown, *History of the United States Capitol*, 19.

50. Arnebeck, *Through a Fiery Trial*, 133.

51. Allen, *History of the United States Capitol*, 22.

52. Frary, *They Built the Capitol*, 35.

53. George Washington to Thomas Jefferson, June 30, 1793, quoted in Allen, *History of the United States Capitol*, 23.

54. "The President to the Commissioners," July 25, 1793, *Documentary History of the Construction and Development of the United States Capitol Building and Grounds* (Washington, D.C.: Government Printing Office, 1904), 28.

55. Donald Carlson, U.S. Capitol Historical Society Board of Trustees Chair, remarks, U.S. Capitol Cornerstone 225th Anniversary, September 18, 2019. See https://www.c-span.org/video/?451601-1/us-capitol-cornerstone-225th-anniversary.

56. Daniel Webster, "An Address Delivered at the Laying of the Corner Stone of the Addition to the Capitol of the United States," July 4, 1851, quoted in Glenn Brown, *History of the United States Capitol*, xvii.

57. See "The First Cornerstone," Architect of the Capitol, https://www.aoc.gov/explore-capitol-campus/buildings-grounds/capitol-building/first-cornerstone.

58. According to Masonic tradition, corn symbolizes nourishment and wine represents refreshment while oil is an emblem of joy, peace, love, and happiness. For further reference, see U.S. Capitol Cornerstone 225th Anniversary.

59. "The First Cornerstone."

60. Lawrence Knutson, "OK, Where Did It Go? Search Is On for the Capitol Cornerstone," *The Daily Tribune* (Grand Rapids, MI), June 8, 1993, 4A.

61. Thornton's report to the U.S. Congress, January 1, 1805, quoted in Glenn Brown, *History of the United States Capitol*, 35.

62. Glenn Brown, *History of the United States Capitol*, 17.

63. Frary, *They Built the Capitol*, 46.

64. Frary, *They Built the Capitol*, 36.

65. Allen, *History of the United States Capitol*, 29.

66. Tobias Lear to George Washington, September 5, 1794, cited in Gordon Brown, *Incidental Architect*, 10.

67. William Thornton to John Coakely Lettsom, January 8, 1795, cited in Gordon Brown, *Incidental Architect*, 11.

Chapter 2

1. Allen, *History of the United States Capitol*, 14.

2. William C. Allen, "History of Slave Laborers in the Construction of the United States Capitol," Office of the Architect of the Capitol, Washington, D.C., 2005, 7, https://emancipation.dc.gov/sites/default/files/dc/sites/emancipation/publication/attachments/History_of_Slave_Laborers_in_the_Construction_of_the_US_Capitol.pdf.

3. Lee H. Nelson, *White House Stone Carving: Builders and Restorers* (Washington, D.C.: U.S. Department of the Interior, 1992), 6.

4. Arnebeck, *Through a Fiery Trial*, 348.

5. Arnebeck, *Through a Fiery Trial*, 233.

6. Lina Mann, "The Complexities of Slavery in the Nation's Capital," White House Historical Association, https://www.whitehousehistory.org/the-complexities-of-slavery-in-the-nations-capital.

7. See Allen, "History of Slave Laborers," 8. Similar records were not kept after 1801.

8. Henry Hope Reed, *The United States Capitol: Its Architecture and Decorations* (New York: W. W. Norton & Company, 2005), 7.

9. Allen, "History of Slave Laborers," 10.

10. See John Kelly, "A New Book Tells the Remarkable Story of a Former Enslaved Person—and Much More," *The Washington Post*, August 11, 2021, https://www.washingtonpost.com/local/george-pointer-dc-history/2021/08/11/1f632f54-fac6-11eb-943a-c5cf30d50e6a_story.html. Also, "Captain George Pointer," National Park Service, https://www.nps.gov/grfa/learn/historyculture/captain-george-pointer.htm.

11. Allen, *History of the United States Capitol*, 30.

12. Allen, *History of the United States Capitol*, 32.

13. Glenn Brown, *History of the United States Capitol*, 21.

14. Allen, *History of the United States Capitol*, 33.

15. George Washington to the Commissioners of the Federal District, January 29, 1797. See *Documentary History*, 77.

16. Frary, *They Built the Capitol*, 48.

17. Allen, *History of the United States Capitol*, 38.

18. Allen, *History of the United States Capitol*, 40.

19. Frary, *They Built the Capitol*, 7.

20. Mary V. Thompson, "Death Defied," George Washington's Mount Vernon, https://www.mountvernon.org/george-washington/death/death-defied-dr-thorntons-radical-idea-of-bringing-george-washington-back-to-life/.

21. David Ramsay, *The Life of George Washington* (Baltimore: Cushing and Jewett, 1825), 233.

22. "The Resolution to Bury President George Washington at the U.S. Capitol," United States House of Representatives History, Art & Archives, https://history.house.gov/Historical-Highlights/1700s/The-resolution-to-bury-President-George-Washington-at-the-U-S—Capitol/.

23. Frary, *They Built the Capitol*, 57.

24. Gordon Brown, *Incidental Architect*, 27.

25. Frary, *They Built the Capitol*, 57.

26. "November 22, 1800: Fourth Annual Message," University of Virginia, Miller

Center, Presidential Speeches: John Adams Presidency, https://millercenter.org/the-presidency/presidential-speeches/november-22-1800-fourth-annual-message.

27. Quoted in Don Kennon, "March 4, 1801: The First Inauguration at the Capitol in Washington, D.C.," U.S. Capitol Historical Society, January 11, 2013, https://uschs.wordpress.com/2013/01/11/march-4-1801-the-first-inauguration-at-the-capitol-in-washington-d-c/.

28. Gaillard Hunt, ed., *The First Forty Years of Washington Society, Portrayed by the Family Letters of Mrs. Samuel Harrison Smith (Margaret Bayard) from the Collection of Her Grandson, J. Henley Smith* (New York: Charles Scribner's Sons, 1906), 25.

29. This shared power structure is still in place today and still causing D.C. residents considerable heartburn.

30. Lovering and Dyer signed a contract for $4,789 on June 20, 1801. The building was occupied by the Congress on December 1, 1801, which means that the project was completed in less than six months. See Matt Guilfoyle, "Constructing the Capitol: The Oven," June 18, 2013, Architect of the Capitol, https://www.aoc.gov/explore-capitol-campus/blog/constructing-capitol-oven.

31. Guilfoyle, "Constructing the Capitol."

32. George C. Hazelton Jr., *The National Capitol: Its Architecture, Art and History* (New York: J. F. Taylor & Company, 1897), 145.

33. Talbot Hamlin, *Benjamin Henry Latrobe* (New York: Oxford University Press, 1955), 230.

34. B. H. Latrobe, "A Private Letter to Individual Members of Congress on the Subject of the Public Buildings of the United States, November 28, 1806," quoted in Glenn Brown, *History of the United States Capitol*, 34.

35. Gordon Brown, *Incidental Architect*, 36.

36. Hamlin, *Benjamin Henry Latrobe,* 265.

37. Hamlin, *Benjamn Henry Latrobe*, 263.

38. It was common enough by 1800 that a notice in the *National Intelligencer and Washington Advertiser* dated December 12, 1800, casually mentioned a house for rent on "New Jersey Avenue of Capitol Hill."

39. Lawrence Knutson, "Democracy's Stage Hits 200," *The Post-Star* (Glens Falls, NY), September 12, 1993, A5.

40. Allen, *History of the United States Capitol*, 33.

41. Glenn Brown, *History of the United States Capitol*, 47.

42. See Allen, *History of the United States Capitol*, 66.

43. See Richard Chenoweth, "The Very First Miss Liberty: Latrobe, Franzoni, and the First Statue of Liberty, 1807–1814," *The Capitol Dome*, Summer 2016, 2–15.

44. Philip Mazzei to Thomas Jefferson, 12 September 1805, Founders Online, National Archives, https://founders.archives.gov/documents/Jefferson/99-01-02-2373.

45. Hamlin, *Benjamin Henry Latrobe,* 268.

46. John H. B. Latrobe, "The Capitol at Washington at the Beginning of the Present Century," in *An Address by John H. B. Latrobe Before the American Institute of Architects* (Baltimore: William K. Boyle, 1881).

47. Chenoweth, "First Miss Liberty," 11.

48. Chenoweth "First Miss Liberty," 12.

49. Hamlin, *Benjamin Henry Latrobe,* 274.

50. Hamlin, *Benjamin Henry Latrobe,* 271.

51. Thomas Jefferson to Benjamin Latrobe, October 10, 1809, quoted in Richard Chenoweth, "The Most Beautiful Room in the World? Latrobe, Jefferson, and the First Capitol," *Le Libellio* 7, no. 3 (2011): 39–48.

52. Hazelton, *The National Capitol*, 28.

53. Chenoweth, "First Miss Liberty." 13.

54. See Allen, *History of the United States Capitol*, 71.

55. Hamlin, *Benjamin Henry Latrobe*, 289.

56. See Allen, *History of the United States Capitol*, 74.

57. Thomas Jefferson to Benjamin Latrobe, April 25, 1808. See *Documentary History*, 145.

58. Hazelton, *The National Capitol*, 31.

59. Benjamin Latrobe to Thomas Jefferson, August 28, 1809, quoted in "Corncob or Cornstalk Columns and Capitols," Architect of the Capitol, https://www.aoc.gov/explore-capitol-campus/art/corncob-or-cornstalk-columns-and-capitals.

60. See Hamlin, *Benjamin Henry Latrobe*, 283–86. Also, Allen, *History of the United States Capitol*, 94–95.

61. Gordon Brown, *Incidental Architect*, 37.

62. Glenn Brown, *History of the United States Capitol*, 42.

63. See Allen, *History of the United States Capitol*, 82–84; Hamlin, *Benjamin Henry Latrobe*, 277–78.

64. Quoted in Hamlin, *Benjamin Henry Latrobe*, 278.

65. Jim Abrams, "Haunted House on the Hill," CBS News, October 31, 2003, https://www.cbsnews.com/news/haunted-house-on-the-hill/.

66. "Report of the Committee on the President's Message communicating a report of the Surveyor of the Public Buildings, accompanying a bill making further appropriations for completing the Capitol and for other purposes, communicated to the House January 11, 1810." See *Documentary History*, 160. Emphasis in original.

67. Thomas Jefferson to B. H. Latrobe, July 12, 1812, quoted in Hamlin, *Benjamin Henry Latrobe*, 291–92.

68. Hamlin, *Benjamin Henry Latrobe*, 292.

69. B. H. Latrobe to Robert Fulton, March 12, 1813, quoted in Allen, *History of the United States Capitol*, 94.

70. "June 1, 1812: Special Message to Congress on the Foreign Policy Crisis—War Message," University of Virginia, Miller Center, Presidential Speeches: James Madison Presidency, https://millercenter.org/the-presidency/presidential-speeches/june-1-1812-special-message-congress-foreign-policy-crisis-war.

71. John C. Calhoun, "Relations with Great Britain," *Annals of Congress*, House of Representatives, 12th Congress, 1st Session, June 1812, 1545–46.

72. Allen, *History of the United States Capitol*, 108.

Chapter 3

1. Secretary of War John Armstrong to the D.C. Militia's commander, Major General John Peter Van Ness, quoted in "Prelude," The White House Historical Association, https://www.whitehousehistory.org/prelude.

2. Major General John Peter Van Ness, quoted in "Prelude."

3. Anthony S. Pitch, *The Burning of Washington* (Annapolis, MD: Naval Institute Press, 1998), 19.

4. Pitch, *Burning of Washington*, 97.

5. Pitch, *Burning of Washington*, 104.

6. Hazelton, *The National Capitol*, 35.

7. Pitch, *Burning of Washington*, 104.

8. Glenn Brown, *History of the United States Capitol*, 39.

9. Pitch, *Burning of Washington*, 106.

10. Daniel Sheldon Jr. to Dr. Daniel Sheldon, August 26, 1814. See Pitch, *Burning of Washington*, 126.

11. David Winchester to James Winchester, August 25, 1814. See Pitch, *Burning of Washington*, 126.

12. Thomas Jefferson to Marquis de Lafayette, Monticello, February 14, 1815, quoted in Hazelton, *The National Capitol*, 37.

13. John R. Elting, *Amateurs to Arms! A Military History of the War of 1812* (New York: Da Capo Press, 1995), 220.

14. Francis F. Beirne, *The War of 1812* (New York: E. P. Dutton & Co., Inc., 1949), https://penelope.uchicago.edu/Thayer/E/Gazetteer/Places/America/United_States/_Topics/history/_Texts/BEI1812/22*.html.

15. James Madison to Congress, September 20, 1814. See *Documentary History*, 172.

16. "Senate proceedings of February 3, 1815." See *Documentary History*, 178.

17. "Special message of President James Madison, September 17, 1814." See *Documentary History*, 172.

18. See Hazelton, *The National Capitol*, 38.

19. Hazelton, *The National Capitol*, 38.

20. Hazelton, *The National Capitol*, 39.

21. "Senate proceedings of February 3, 1815." See *Documentary History*, 178.

22. "Report from the Superintendent of the Public Buildings, October 29, 1914." See *Documentary History*, 174.

23. Hazelton, *The National Capitol*, 39.

24. B. H. Latrobe to Nathanial Ingraham, September 9, 1813. See Paul Kreingold, *Potomac Marble: History of the Search for the Ideal Stone* (Charleston, SC: History Press, 2023), 25.

25. B. H. Latrobe to _____, September 24, 1814. See Hamlin, *Benjamin Henry Latrobe*, 433.

26. Allen, *History of the United States Capitol*, 93.

27. For Mary's account, see Hamlin, *Benjamin Henry Latrobe*, 435–36.

28. Allen, *History of the United States Capitol*, 102.

29. B. H. Latrobe to Thomas Jefferson, July 12, 1815, quoted in Glenn Brown, *History of the United States Capitol*, 48.

30. Allen, *History of the United States Capitol*, 108.

31. Allen, *History of the United States Capitol*, 103. Emphasis in original.

32. Allen, *History of the United States Capitol*, 104.

33. Gordon Brown, *Incidental Architect*, 37.

34. Kreingold, *Potomac Marble*, 44.

35. Hazelton, *The National Capitol*, 39.

36. Thomas Jefferson to Samuel H. Smith, 21 September 1814, Founders Online, National Archives, https://founders.archives.gov/documents/Jefferson/03-07-02-0484-0003.

37. Jefferson to Smith.

38. Jefferson to Smith.

39. William Johnston, *History of the Library of Congress, Volume I (1800–1804)* (Washington, D.C.: Government Printing Office, 1904), 86.

40. Editors of *American Register*, circa July 1817, quoted in Johnston, *History of the Library of Congress*, 90.

41. Jefferson to Smith.
42. Kreingold, *Potomac Marble*, 44.
43. Kreingold, *Potomac Marble*, 162.
44. Hazelton, *The National Capitol*, 41.
45. Kreingold, *Potomac Marble*, 72.
46. Kreingold, *Potomac Marble*, 45.
47. Samuel Lane, "Report to Committee on the Expenditures of the Public Buildings, January 24, 1818." See Kreingold, *Potomac Marble*, 46–47.
48. Allen, *History of the United States Capitol*, 112.
49. Hamlin, *Benjamin Henry Latrobe*, 442.
50. Allen, *History of the United States Capitol*, 112–13.
51. There's actually another figure of Justice without a blindfold on one of the friezes sculpted by Adolph Weinman on the west wall of the Supreme Court chamber. See "Figures of *Justice* Information Sheet," Office of the Curator, Supreme Court of the United States, May 22, 2003, https://www.supremecourt.gov/about/figuresofjustice.pdf.
52. B. H. Latrobe to Samuel Lane, May 30, 1816. See Hamlin, *Benjamin Henry Latrobe*, 445.
53. B. H. Latrobe to Isaac Hazlehurst, July 27, 1816. See Hamlin, *Benjamin Henry Latrobe*, 446.
54. "8th Inaugural Ceremonies," Joint Congressional Committee on Inaugural Ceremonies, https://www.inaugural.senate.gov/8th-inaugural-ceremonies/. See also the *National Intelligencer*, March 8, 1817, which reported on the squabble with great interest.
55. Hamlin, *Benjamin Henry Latrobe*, 447.
56. James Monroe to George Bomford and Joseph Swift, March 17, 1817. See *Documentary History*, 220–21.
57. Samuel Lane to the Congress, January 24, 1818. See *Documentary History*, 204–5.
58. James Monroe to Samuel Lane, April 4, 1815. See *Documentary History*, 198.
59. Kreingold, *Potomac Marble*, 177.
60. B. H. Latrobe to Thomas Jefferson, July 24, 1817. See Kreingold, *Potomac Marble*, 51.
61. Samuel Lane to the U.S. Congress, December 20, 1819. See *Documentary History*, 220.
62. Allen, *History of the United States Capitol*, 116.
63. Allen, *History of the United States Capitol*, 117.
64. Allen, *History of the United States Capitol*, 118.
65. The "miniature" was twenty inches by thirty inches and presently hangs in the Yale University Art Gallery in New Haven, Connecticut.
66. Hazelton, *The National Capitol*, 105.
67. That's about $740,000 today.
68. Hazelton, *The National Capitol*, 105.
69. B. H. Latrobe to John Trumbull, January 22, 1817. See Allen, *History of the United States Capitol*, 135.
70. Kreingold, *Potomac Marble*, 164.
71. B. H. Latrobe to John Trumbull, October 10, 1817. See Charles E. Fairman, *Art and Artists of the Capitol of the United States of America* (Washington, D.C.: U.S. Government Printing Office, 1927), 37.

72. Hamlin, *Benjamin Henry Latrobe,* 451.
73. James Monroe, Annual Message to Congress, 1817, quoted in Hazelton, *The National Capitol,* 40.
74. Latrobe to Trumbull, October 10, 1817. See Fairman, *Art and Artists of the* Capitol, 37.
75. Frary, *They Built the Capitol,* 101.
76. William Lee to Charles Bulfinch, September 14, 1817. See Hamlin, *Benjamin Henry Latrobe,* 452.
77. B. H. Latrobe to Thomas Jefferson, November 20, 1817. See Kreingold, *Potomac Marble,* 189.
78. As reported by B. H. Latrobe to Robert Goodloe Harper, November 24, 1817. See Allen, *History of the United States Capitol,* 123.
79. Account of the Lane-Latrobe meeting as described by Latrobe's wife. See Hamlin, *Benjamin Henry Latrobe,* 477.
80. B. H. Latrobe to James Monroe, November 20, 1817. See Hamlin, *Benjamin Henry Latrobe,* 478.
81. Frary, *They Built the Capitol,* 102.
82. B. H. Latrobe to James Monroe, December 18, 1817. See Hamlin, *Benjamin Henry Latrobe,* 478.
83. Frary, *They Built the Capitol,*141.

Chapter 4

1. Hamlin, *Benjamin Henry Latrobe,* 451.
2. Hamlin, *Benjamin Henry Latrobe,* 452.
3. Allen, *History of the United States Capitol,* 125.
4. Frary, *They Built the Capitol,* 141.
5. Charles Bulfinch to John Quincy Adams, January 25, 1823, Ellen Susan Bulfinch, *The Life and Letters of Charles Bulfinch, Architect, with Other Family Papers* (Boston: Houghton, Mifflin and Company, 1896), 245.
6. That's about $68,000 today.
7. Frary, *They Built the Capitol,*139.
8. Gordon Brown, *Incidental Architect,* 100.
9. Gordon Brown, *Incidental Architect,* 97.
10. Charles Bulfinch to Hannah Bulfinch, February 7, 1817. See *Life and Letters of Charles Bulfinch,* 196.
11. Charles Bulfinch to Hannah Bulfinch, February 7, 1817. See *Life and Letters of Charles Bulfinch,* 196.
12. Frary, *They Built the Capitol,* 141.
13. Allen, *History of the United States Capitol,* 128.
14. Frary, *They Built the Capitol,* 143.
15. Hazelton, *The National Capitol,* 45.
16. Hazelton, *The National Capitol,* 45.
17. Allen, *History of the United States Capitol,* 129.
18. Charles Bulfinch, Report to Congress, November 1818, quoted in Hazelton, *The National Capitol,* 46.
19. Allen, *History of the United States Capitol,* 143.
20. *Life and Letters of Charles Bulfinch,* 299.
21. James Monroe, "Third Annual Message," December 7, 1819, The American

Presidency Project, https://www.presidency.ucsb.edu/documents/third-annual-message-1.

22. Gordon Brown, *Incidental Architect*, 111.

23. John Trumbull to Charles Bulfinch, January 28, 1818, quoted in Hazelton, *The National Capitol*, 47–48.

24. Hazelton, *The National Capitol*, 48.

25. John Trumbull to Charles Bulfinch, July 25, 1818, quoted in Allen, *History of the United States Capitol*, 137.

26. *National Intelligencer*, August 27, 1818.

27. Charles Bulfinch to Thomas Bulfinch[?], c. 1843. See *Life and Letters of Charles Bulfinch*, 299.

28. Hazelton, *The National Capitol*, 50.

29. Charles Bulfinch to Joseph Elgar, December 9, 1822. See *Documentary History*, 251.

30. *Documentary History*, 251.

31. *Life and Letters of Charles Bulfinch*, 299. Emphasis in original.

32. See S. D. Wyeth, *Rotunda and Dome of the U.S. Capitol* (Washington, D.C.: Gibson Brothers, 1869), 199.

33. *Documentary History*, 251.

34. Joseph Elgar to Charles Bulfinch, September 30, 1822. See *Life and Letters of Charles Bulfinch*, 245.

35. *Documentary History*, 245–46.

36. See Allen, *History of the United States Capitol*, 147.

37. "The New Library Room at the Capitol," *Daily National Intelligencer and Washington Express*, January 1, 1825, 3.

38. George Blagden to Joseph Elgar, April 21, 1824. See Allen, *History of the United States Capitol*, 150.

39. "Report of the Committee on the Public Buildings, in relation to the operations on said buildings during the last year, and to their present state, February 13, 1824." See *Documentary History*, 258.

40. Editor of the *New-York Statesman*, "Public Buildings at Washington," *The Pittsfield* (MA) *Sun*, June 3, 1824, 1.

41. Commissioner Elgar to John Quincy Adams, May 6, 1825. See Egon Verheyen, "'Unenlightened by a Single Ray from Antiquity': John Quincy Adams and the Design of the Pediment for the United States Capitol," *International Journal for the Classical Tradition* 3, no. 2 (1996): 223.

42. Charles Bulfinch to Thomas Bulfinch, June 22, 1825. See *Life and Letters of Charles Bulfinch*, 249.

43. Verheyen, "'Unenlightened,'" 223.

44. *Life and Letters of Charles Bulfinch*, 249.

45. Verheyen, "'Unenlightened,'" 226.

46. *Life and Letters of Charles Bulfinch*, 249.

47. *Life and Letters of Charles Bulfinch*, 249.

48. The decaying figures were removed in 1958 when the Capitol's East Front was extended, and plaster models were made from the original sandstone. The current sculpture on the Capitol is a reproduction carved from Georgia marble.

49. An early Capitol guidebook explained: "However Hope may flatter, America will regard only that prosperity which is founded on public right and the preservation of the Constitution." Not even close.

50. *Life and Letters of Charles Bulfinch*, 249.

51. Hannah Bulfinch to her sons, December 25, 1825. See *Life and Letters of Charles Bulfinch*, 250.

52. Hannah Bulfinch to Stephen Greenleaf Bulfinch, December 16, 1827. See *Life and Letters of Charles Bulfinch*, 259.

53. Joseph Elgar to the president, December 7, 1826. See *Documentary History*, 279.

54. Cost of the 1828 version of the Capitol provided by the Office of the Architect of the Capitol. See "How Much Did It Cost to Build the Capitol?," Architect of the Capitol, https://www.aoc.gov/explore-capitol-campus/capitol-hill-facts/how-much-did-it-cost-build-capitol.

55. The scenes depicted are *Conflict of Daniel Boone and the Indians* by Enrico Causici; *The Landing of the Pilgrims* by Causici; *The Preservation of Captain Smith by Pocahontas* by Antonio Capellano; and *William Penn's Treaty with the Indians* by Nicholas Gevelot.

56. Hazelton, *The National Capitol*, 125.

57. Hazelton, *The National Capitol*, 125.

58. In 2020, Congress, in a funding bill for the Office of the Architect of the Capitol (AOC), reported that "there are depictions of Native Americans throughout the Capitol that do not portray Native Americans as equals or Indian nations as independent sovereigns" and urged the AOC to reconsider how its tour guides interpret the art for visitors.

59. Hazelton, *The National Capitol*, 109.

60. "Estimate for Work on the Capitol of the United States for 1828, House Document 180, February 1, 1828." See *Documentary History*, 296.

61. Allen, *History of the United States Capitol*, 164.

62. Frary, *They Built the Capitol*,153.

63. Charles Bulfinch to Stephen Greenleaf Bulfinch, June 3, 1830. See *Life and Letters of Charles Bulfinch*, 260.

Chapter 5

1. Adams had merely replied to a question from a White House guest who had spotted Jarvis's wife at the gathering and asked in a stage whisper, "Who is that lady?" Adams responded, loudly enough to be heard, "That is the wife of one Russell Jarvis . . . a man who, if he had any idea of propriety in the conduct of a gentleman, ought not to show his face in this house." See Samuel Flagg Bemis, "The Scuffle in the Rotunda: A Footnote to the Presidency of John Quincy Adams and to the History of Dueling," *Proceedings of the Massachusetts Historical Society* 71 (1953): 159.

2. Account taken from Bemis, "The Scuffle," 156–66.

3. Bemis, "The Scuffle," 156–66.

4. "Mission & History," United States Capitol Police, https://www.uscp.gov/the-department/our-history.

5. Jon Meacham, *American Lion* (New York: Random House, 2008), 59.

6. Meacham, *American Lion*, 57.

7. See John Horace Pratt, "Authentic Account of All the Proceedings on the Fourth of July, 1815, with Regards to Laying the Corner Stone of the Washington Monument Now Erecting in the City of Baltimore," self-published pamphlet (Baltimore, 1815), 5.

8. House proceedings of February 16, 1832. See *Documentary History*, 317.

9. Wyeth, *Rotunda and Dome*, 200.

10. Wyeth, *Rotunda and Dome*, 202.

11. Hazelton, *The National Capitol*, 75.

12. Hazelton, *The National Capitol*, 74.

13. Allen, *History of the United States Capitol*, 174.

14. Ronald G. Shafer, "The First Statue Removed from the Capitol: George Washington in a Toga," *The Washington Post*, January 22, 2023, https://www.washingtonpost.com/history/2023/01/22/george-washington-statue-toga-capitol/.

15. Hazelton, *The National Capitol*, 77.

16. *Life and Letters of Charles Bulfinch*, 293.

17. See, for example, Edward Everett, "Greenough's Statue of Washington," *The Charleston* (SC) *Daily Courier*, December 10, 1841, 2.

18. Ralph Waldo Emerson to Margaret Fuller, January 1843. See *The Letters of Ralph Waldo Emerson*, Volume III, ed. Ralph L. Rusk (New York: Columbia University Press, 1939), 122, https://archive.org/stream/in.ernet.dli.2015.184813/2015.184813.The-Letters-Of-Ralph-Wald-Emersonsix-Vol3_djvu.txt.

19. Hazelton, *The National Capitol*, 77.

20. Vivien Green Fryd, "Two Sculptures for the Capitol: Horatio Greenough's 'Rescue' and Luigi Persico's 'Discovery of America,'" *The American Art Journal* 19, no. 2 (1987): 25.

21. See *New-York Evening Post*, February 2, 1835, 2.

22. Lawrence's birth date is uncertain. He is believed to have been born in 1800 or 1801.

23. Thomas Hart Benton, *Thirty Years' View or, A History of the Working of the American Government for Thirty Years, from 1820 to 1850*, Volume I (New York: D. Appleton and Company, 1854), 521.

24. Well, probably. There is some disagreement on whether Crockett was one of the two men who wrestled Lawrence down.

25. Edwin A. Miles, "Andrew Jackson and Senator George Poindexter," *The Journal of Southern History* 24, no. 1 (1958): 62.

26. Meacham, *American Lion*, 300.

27. Hezekiah Niles, "Assault on the President," *Niles' Weekly Register*, February 7, 1835, 391.

28. See Charles Dickens, *American Notes for General Circulation and Pictures from Italy* (London: Chapman and Hall, 1880), 297–312.

29. Alexis de Tocqueville, *Democracy in America*, Volume II, chapter XII, https://www.gutenberg.org/files/816/816-h/816-h.htm#link2HCH0012.

30. Tocqueville, *Democracy in America*, Volume II, chapter XXI, https://www.gutenberg.org/files/816/816-h/816-h.htm#link2HCH0012.

31. Daniel Webster, however, was rumored to have had, on the Capitol's third floor directly above the Senate chambers, a small room that served mostly as his private wine cellar and saloon.

32. See Dickens, *American Notes*, 297–312.

33. Joanne B. Freeman, *The Field of Blood: Violence in Congress and the Road to Civil War* (New York: Picador, 2018), 43.

34. *Journal of the House of Representatives of the United States*, September 9, 1841, 488.

35. Hazelton, *The National Capitol*, 52.

36. Dickens, *American Notes*, 297–312.

37. Joseph Stromberg, "How Samuel Morse Got His Big Idea," *Smithsonian Magazine*, January 6, 2012, https://www.smithsonianmag.com/smithsonian-institution/how-samuel-morse-got-his-big-idea-16403094/.

38. Tom Standage, *The Victorian Internet: The Remarkable Story of the Telegraph and the Nineteenth Century's On-Line Pioneers* (New York: Walker and Company, 1998), 49.

39. Traditionally, it has been reported that the message was sent from the Old Supreme Court Chamber in the Capitol, but the U.S. Senate historian believes it is more likely that Morse was given one of the smaller rooms directly across from the chamber, where he could have puttered without interfering with the business of the court. See Senate Historical Office, "Senate Stories: 'What Hath God Wrought': Morse's Telegraph in the Capitol," May 7, 2024, https://www.senate.gov/artandhistory/senate-stories/morses-telegraph-in-the-capitol.htm.

40. Today, the Mount Clare station is part of the B&O Railroad Museum in Baltimore.

41. "The Electro Magnetic Telegraph," attributed to *Baltimore Patriot & Commercial Gazette*, May 25, 1844. Reprinted in the *Martinsburg* (WV) *Gazette*, May 30, 1844, 2.

42. "The Magnetic Telegraph," *Baltimore Sun*, May 31, 1844.

43. "'What Hath God Wrought.'"

44. "Solar Gas Lights on Capitol Hill," *Daily National Intelligencer and Washington Express*, January 15, 1847, 1.

45. John Fairfield to Anna Paine Fairfield, Washington, D.C., December 4, 1847. See Arthur G. Staples, ed., *The Letters of John Fairfield* (Lewiston, ME: Lewiston Journal Company, 1922), 445.

46. Martha M. Hamilton, "Created by Congress, Company Brought D.C. Out of the Dark," *The Washington Post*, January 23, 1989, https://www.washingtonpost.com/archive/business/1989/01/23/created-by-congress-company-brought-dc-out-of-the-dark/61defd3a-8c9a-4710-a61e-fb1633aa2cbb/.

47. Staples, *Letters of John Fairfield*, 445.

48. "The Capitol Illuminated," *Washington Union*, November 19, 1847, 2.

49. "Items," *New York Daily Herald*, June 23, 1848, 4.

50. Gilbert King, "The Day Henry Clay Refused to Compromise," *Smithsonian Magazine*, December 6, 2012, https://www.smithsonianmag.com/history/the-day-henry-clay-refused-to-compromise-153589853/.

Chapter 6

1. Committee on Public Buildings report, May 28, 1850. *Documentary History*, 430.

2. House proceedings of July 22, 1850: *Congressional Globe* 31–1, 1425. See *Documentary History*, 438.

3. Robert Mills, "Report on the Extension of the Capitol of the United States," May 1, 1850. See *Documentary History*, 435.

4. Senate proceedings of September 23, 1850: *Congressional Globe* 31–1, 1944. See *Documentary History*, 443.

5. House proceedings of July 22, 1850: *Congressional Globe*, 31–1, 1425. See *Documentary History*, 439.

6. "An Act making Appropriations for the Civil and Diplomatic Expenses of the Government for the Year ending the thirtieth of June, eighteen hundred and fifty-one, and for other Purposes, approved Sept. 30, 1850." See *Documentary History*, 445.

7. Glenn Brown, *History of the United States Capitol*, 116.

8. See the notice in *The Daily Republic*, October 9, 1850, 4.

9. Allen, *History of the United States Capitol*, 192.

10. Allen, *History of the United States Capitol*, 193

11. Reed, *The United States Capitol,* 14.

12. Thomas U. Walter, Report to the Secretary of the Interior, December 28, 1851. See *Documentary History*, 465.

13. "The National Anniversary," *Weekly National Intelligencer,* July 12, 1851, 1.

14. *Mr. Webster's Address at the Laying of the Corner Stone of the Addition to the Capitol, July 4, 1851* (Washington, D.C.: Gideon and Co., 1851), 28.

15. *Mr. Webster's Address*, 13.

16. Architect's Office to the president of the United States, September 13, 1851. See *Documentary History*, 451.

17. House proceedings of March 12, 1852: *Congressional Globe*, 32–1, 730. See *Documentary History*, 469.

18. Allen, *History of the United States Capitol*, 203.

19. House proceedings of March 12, 1852: *Congressional Globe,* 32–1, 730. See *Documentary History*, 470.

20. House proceedings of March 12, 1852, *Documentary History*, 471–72.

21. Senate Rep. Com. No. 163. 32nd Congress, 1st Session. In the Senate of the United States, April 2, 1852. See *Documentary History*, 507–8.

22. Extension of the Capitol, Senate proceedings of March 24, 1852. See *Documentary History*, 509.

23. See "Fire in the Capitol—Library of Congress Burnt," *The Washington Union*, December 25, 1851, 3.

24. John Y. Cole, *America's Greatest Library: An Illustrated History of the Library of Congress* (Washington, D.C.: The Library of Congress, in association with D. Giles, Limited, London, 2017), 28.

25. "Fire in the Capitol," 3.

26. "John Silva Meehan (1790–1863)," Library of Congress, https://www.loc.gov/item/n86070561/john-silva-meehan-1790-1863/.

27. Cole, *America's Greatest Library*, 17.

28. "Our Washington Correspondence," *The Raleigh* (SC) *Register*, September 21, 1853, 3.

29. "The Congressional Library," *New Orleans Crescent*, September 9, 1853, 2.

30. "The Congressional Library," 2.

31. Senate proceedings of February 15, 1853: *Congressional Globe* 32–2, 625. See *Documentary History*, 570.

32. William C. Allen, *The United States Capitol: A Brief Architectural History* (Washington, D.C.: U.S. Government Printing Office, 1990), 37.

33. House proceedings of March 12, 1832, *Documentary History*, 472.

34. Allen, *History of the United States Capitol*, 213.

35. Peter A. Wallner, *Franklin Pierce: Martyr for the Union* (Concord, NH: Plaidswede, 2009), 210–13.

36. Allen, *History of the United States Capitol*, 216.

37. John M. Bryan, *Robert Mills: America's First Architect* (New York: Princeton Architectural Press, 2001), 314.

38. Thomas U. Walter to Amanda Walter, May 22, 1858. See Allen, *History of the United States Capitol*, 282.

39. Michele Cohen, "New Perspective, New Discoveries: A Close-up Look at Crawford's *Progress of Civilization*," Architect of the Capitol, September 28, 2016, https://www.aoc.gov/explore-capitol-campus/blog/new-perspective-new-discoveries-close-look-crawfords-progress.

40. Architect of the Capitol staff, "The Liberty Cap: Symbol of American Freedom," Architect of the Capitol, July 26, 2024, https://www.aoc.gov/explore-capitol-campus/blog/liberty-cap-symbol-american-freedom.

41. "Crawford and His Last Work," *The Crayon*, March 14, 1855, 167–68.

42. November 29, 1853, journal entry in Montgomery C. Meigs, *Capitol Builder: The Shorthand Journals of Montgomery C. Meigs, 1853–1859, 1861. A Project to Commemorate the United States Bicentennial, 1800–2000*, ed. Wendy Wolff (Washington, D.C.: U.S. Government Printing Office, 2001), 52.

43. "Crawford and His Last Work," 167–68.

44. November 30, 1853, entry in Meigs, *Journals*, 25.

45. Allen, *History of the United States Capitol*, 219.

46. House proceedings of June 14, 1854: *Congressional Globe* 33–1, 1393–1402. See *Documentary History*, 615.

47. Senate proceedings of February 20, 1854: *Congressional Globe* 33–1, 448. See *Documentary History*, 609.

48. Senate proceedings of January 24, 1854: *Congressional Globe* 33–1, 383. See *Documentary History*, 603.

49. Reed, *The United States Capitol*, 22.

50. Reed, *The United States Capitol*, 22.

51. November 4, 1854, entry in Meigs, *Journals*, 140–41.

52. November 4, 1854, entry in Meigs, *Journals*, 140–41.

53. October 13, 1854, entry in Meigs, *Journals*, 129.

54. May 31, 1954, entry in Meigs, *Journals*, 75.

Chapter 7

1. Allen, *History of the United States Capitol*, 226.

2. Reed, *The United States Capitol*, 15.

3. House proceedings of February 22, 1855. See *Documentary History*, 991.

4. June 8, 1854, entry in Meigs, *Journals*, 76–77.

5. *Documentary History*, 609.

6. Allen, *History of the United States Capitol*, 225.

7. December 11, 1854, entry in Meigs, *Journals*, 164.

8. December 11, 1854, entry in Meigs, *Journals*, 164.

9. Allen, *History of the United States Capitol*, 226.

10. December 21, 1854, entry in Meigs, *Journals*, 173.

11. December 24, 1854, entry in Meigs, *Journals*, 176.

12. December 26, 1854, entry in Meigs, *Journals*, 176.

13. December 28, 1854, entry in Meigs, *Journals*, 181.

14. December 29, 1854, entry in Meigs, *Journals*, 183.

15. House proceedings of February 20, 1855: *Congressional Globe* 33–2. See *Documentary History*, 620.

16. Allen, *History of the United States Capitol*, 230.

17. *Documentary History*, 991.

18. *Documentary History*, 991.

19. Annual report of Jefferson Davis, December 3, 1855. See *Documentary History*, 997.

20. Robert O'Harrow Jr., "Montgomery Meigs's Vital Influence on the

Civil War—and Washington," *The Washington Post,* July 1, 2011, https://www.washingtonpost.com/lifestyle/magazine/montgomery-meigss-vital-influence-on-the-civil-war—and-washington/2011/06/10/AGTLu3tH_story.html.

21. Allen, *History of the United States Capitol,* 223.

22. *Documentary History,* 992.

23. "About the Senate Chamber: Historical Overview," United States Senate, https://www.senate.gov/about/historic-buildings-spaces/chamber/overview.htm#:~:text=In%201861%20Hale%20urged%20creation,the%20Chamber%2C%20continued%20for%20decades.

24. Thomas U. Walter to Jefferson Davis, March 17, 1856. See *Documentary History,* 1000. Emphasis in original.

25. Annual report of M. C. Meigs to the Congress, November 16, 1855. See *Documentary History,* 994.

26. M. C. Meigs to Jefferson Davis, March 5, 1856. See *Documentary History,* 999.

27. M. C. Meigs to Jefferson Davis, March 8, 1856. See *Documentary History,* 1002.

28. See "Capitol Dome," Architect of the Capitol, https://www.aoc.gov/explore-capitol-campus/buildings-grounds/capitol-building/capitol-dome.

29. M. C. Meigs to L. D. Campbell, March 5, 1856. See *Documentary History,* 999.

30. December 29, 1854, entry in Meigs, *Journals,* 183.

31. August 28, 1854, entry in Meigs, *Journals,* 106.

32. Reed, *The United States Capitol,* 23.

33. December 28, 1854, entry in Meigs, *Journals,* 180.

34. December 28, 1854, entry in Meigs, *Journals,* 180.

35. Barbara Wolanin, *Constantino Brumidi: Artist of the Capitol* (Washington, D.C.: Government Printing Office, 1998), 9.

36. December 28, 1854, entry in Meigs, *Journals,* 180.

37. Wolanin, *Constantino Brumidi,* 21.

38. See the July 12, 1854, entry in Meigs, *Journals,* 86.

39. There is some disagreement over who was the main force behind the selection of the Minton tile, with the Office of the Architect of the Capitol promoting Walter and historians like Allen strongly making the case for Meigs.

40. Wolanin, *Constantino Brumidi,* 3.

41. Wolanin, *Constantino Brumidi,* 9.

42. Wolanin, *Constantino Brumidi,* 9.

43. Wolanin, *Constantino Brumidi,* 45.

44. Allen, *History of the United States Capitol,* 252.

45. "Statue of Freedom," Architect of the Capitol, https://www.aoc.gov/explore-capitol-campus/art/statue-freedom.

46. *Documentary History,* 997–98.

47. Allen, *History of the United States Capitol,* 255.

48. Edward Ball, May 26, 1856, *Documentary History,* 639.

49. *Documentary History,* 992.

50. Joanne B. Freeman, *The Field of Blood: Violence in Congress and the Road to Civil War* (New York: Picador, 2018), 167.

51. Freeman, *The Field of Blood,* 167.

52. Freeman, *The Field of Blood,* 216.

53. Charles Sumner, *The Crime Against Kansas. The Apologies for the Crime. The True Remedy. Speech of Hon. Charles Sumner, in the Senate of the United States, 19th and 20th May, 1856* (Cleveland: John P. Jewett & Company, 1856), 9.

54. Sumner, *The Crime Against Kansas.*

55. Eric H. Walther, *The Shattering of the Union: America in the 1850s* (Lanham, MD: SR Books, 2004), 97.

56. Freeman, *The Field of Blood*, 219.

57. There is some confusion over whether there were several ladies present or just one and whether they were in the chamber or in the lobby. Some versions of the confrontation also have Brooks waiting for the lady (or ladies) to clear out before assaulting Sumner. I have relied on the eyewitness testimony of Senate clerk Colonel Joseph H. Nicholson, who told a Senate select committee that Brooks had almost immediately proceeded up the aisle after asking if a young woman could be cleared away. See U.S. Senate Committee Report, 34th Congress, 1st Session, Rep. Com. No. 191, May 28, 1856, https://www.senate.gov/artandhistory/history/common/image/SumnerInvestigation1856.htm.

58. Freeman, *The Field of Blood*, 220; Hazelton, *The National Capitol*, 153.

59. Walther, *The Shattering of the Union*, 99.

60. Accounts of the caning are taken from Williamjames Hull Hoffer, *The Caning of Charles Sumner: Honor, Idealism, and the Origins of the Civil War* (Baltimore: Johns Hopkins University Press, 2010), as well as from Walther, Freeman, and Nicholson's 1856 testimony. Again, details vary from account to account—did Brooks enter the lobby first or proceed directly into the chamber?—so I have tried to settle on the points that are generally agreed upon.

61. Asher C. Hinds, *Hinds' Precedents of the House of Representatives of the United States: Including References to Provisions of the Constitution, the Laws, and Decisions of the United States Senate*, Volume 2 (Washington, D.C.: U.S. Government Printing Office, 1907), 1094.

62. Freeman, *The Field of Blood*, 222. Emphasis in original.

63. Freeman, *The Field of Blood*, 223. Emphasis in original.

64. William Cullen Bryant, "The Outrage on Mr. Sumner," reprinted in *New-York Tribune*, May 24, 1856, 7.

65. Freeman, *The Field of Blood*, 223.

Chapter 8

1. See, for example, "Speech of Hon. Edward Ball, of Ohio, on the profligate and wasteful expenditures upon the public buildings," delivered in the House of Representatives, May 26, 1856, https://search.law.villanova.edu/Record/174554?testvufw=1.

2. "From the annual report of Capt. M. C. Meigs, in charge of construction of the New Dome, Nov. 30, 1857." See *Documentary History*, 1010.

3. Allen, *History of the United States Capitol*, 272.

4. December 20, 1857, entry in Meigs, *Journals*, 560.

5. December 26, 1857, entry in Meigs, *Journals*, 568.

6. January 21, 1858, entry in Meigs, *Journals*, 583.

7. "A Night Scene in the House of Representatives," *The Republican* (Holmes County, OH), February 11, 1858, 2.

8. "A Night Scene," 2.

9. Accounts of the fight taken from Grow's recollection: Jeff Nilsson, "Beatings, Brawls, and Lawmaking: Mayhem in Congress," *Saturday Evening Post*, December 4, 2010, https://www.saturdayeveningpost.com/2010/12/beatings-brawls-lawmaking-mayhem-congress/; and "Fight in the House of Representatives," *Alexandria Gazette*, February 8, 1858, 2.

10. Noah Brooks, *Mr. Lincoln's Washington* (South Brunswick, NJ: T. Yoseloff, 1967), 112.

11. While some newspapers of the era recorded Grow as referring to Keitt as a "nigger-driver," Grow, recalling the incident years later, insisted he had used the term "negro-driver." See "Fight in the House of Representatives."

12. As a young man, Elihu B. Washburne opted to change the spelling of his last name to "Washburne," believing it aligned more closely with the traditional English spelling.

13. Allen, *History of the United States Capitol*, 279.

14. Allen, *History of the United States Capitol*, 281.

15. Thomas Walter to Rev. Israel D. Ring, April 19, 1858, quoted in Allen, *History of the United States Capitol*, 278.

16. January 3, 1859, entry in Meigs, *Journals*, 691.

17. January 4, 1859, entry in Meigs, *Journals,* 692.

18. Senate Historical Office, "United States Senate Chamber, 1859–2009," Secretary of the Senate. S. Pub. 110–21, 2009, 6.

19. Hazelton, *The National Capitol*, 178.

20. Busts of twenty of the first twenty-one vice presidents are in the Senate chamber; the bust of the eighteenth vice president, Henry Wilson, who served under Ulysses S. Grant, is in the U.S. Capitol in the Vice President's Room—the same room where he died in 1875.

21. The desk is usually called "the Wilson desk," though it was never actually associated with Henry Wilson (and, in fact, it was purchased for the room by Vice President Hobart). As president, Richard Nixon asked that the desk be moved to the Oval Office, perhaps thinking it had belonged to Woodrow Wilson. This was the desk that was wired for recording at the press of a button. In 1977, the desk was returned to the Vice President's Room in the Capitol.

22. "The President's Room," U.S. Senate Commission on Art by the Office of the Senate Curator, https://www.senate.gov/artandhistory/art/resources/pdf/President_s_Room.pdf.

23. January 4, 1859, entry in Meigs, *Journals,* 692.

24. Allen, *History of the United States Capitol*, 286.

25. Thomas Walter to Amanda G. Walter, January 4, 1859. See Allen, *History of the United States Capitol*, 286.

26. January 6, 1859, entry in Meigs, *Journals,* 694.

27. Allen, *History of the United States Capitol*, 293.

28. October 28, 1859, entry in Meigs, *Journals,* 749

29. November 2, 1859, entry in Meigs, *Journals*, 753.

30. Thomas Walter to John Rice, November 3, 1859, quoted in Allen, *History of the United States Capitol,* 298.

31. Allen, *History of the United States Capitol*, 301.

32. Thomas Walter to Janes, Fowler, & Kirtland Company, March 23, 1860, quoted in Allen, *History of the Capitol,* 302. Emphasis in original.

33. Architect of the Capitol staff, "Philip Reid and the Statue of Freedom," Architect of the Capitol, https://www.aoc.gov/explore-capitol-campus/art/statue-freedom/philip-reid.

34. Information on Philip Reid comes from the following sources: Architect of the Capitol staff, "Philip Reid," and Senate Historical Office, "Senate Stories—in Form and Spirit: Creating the Statue of Freedom," United States Senate, December 11,

2023, https://www.senate.gov/artandhistory/senate-stories/in-form-and-spirit-creating-the-statue-of-freedom.htm.

35. See Allen, *History of the United States Capitol*, 308.

36. Thomas Walter to John Rice, December 24, 1860. See Allen, *History of the Capitol*, 309. Emphasis in original.

37. William J. Cooper Jr., *Jefferson Davis, American* (New York: Knopf, 2000), 3.

38. See the comments of Bruce Laverty, curator of architecture at the Athenaeum, regarding Thomas Walter, in Lauren Drapala, "A Building Is Never Completely Lost," Hidden City: Exploring Philadelphia's Urban Landscape, September 29, 2011, https://hiddencityphila.org/2011/09/into-the-archives-part-ii/.

39. Thomas Walter to George Anderson, February 4, 1861, quoted in Allen, *History of the United States Capitol*, 310.

40. Allen, *History of the United States Capitol*, 310.

41. Thomas Walter to Charles Fowler, March 1, 1861, quoted in Allen, *History of the United States Capitol*, 310.

42. Allen, *History of the United States Capitol*, 310–11.

43. Galusha Grow, House proceedings of June 15, 1860. See *Documentary History*, 769.

44. Thomas Walter to Robert Walter, April 19, 1861, quoted in Allen, *History of the United States Capitol*, 313.

45. Senate Historical Office, *The Senate's Civil War* (Washington, D.C.: United States Senate, 2011), 13, https://www.senate.gov/artandhistory/history/resources/pdf/SenatesCivilWar.pdf.

46. Senate Historical Office, *The Senate's Civil War*, 9.

47. Senate Historical Office, *The Senate's Civil War*, 13.

48. "Constructing a National Symbol," United States Senate, https://www.senate.gov/about/historic-buildings-spaces/capitol/dome-national-symbol.htm.

49. "Constructing a National Symbol."

50. Ellen Terrell, "The Capitol Dome: Janes, Fowler & Kirtland Co.," Library of Congress Blogs, May 30, 2015, https://blogs.loc.gov/inside_adams/2015/05/the-capitol-dome-janes-fowler-kirtland-co/.

51. Abraham Lincoln to General Winfield Scott, June 5, 1861. See Robert O'Harrow Jr., *The Quartermaster: Montgomery C. Meigs, Lincoln's General, Master Builder of the Union Army* (New York: Simon & Schuster, 2016), 115–16.

52. See "14th Quartermaster General: Brigadier General Montgomery C. Meigs, Quartermaster General, May 1861–February 1882," U.S. Army Quartermaster Corps, https://quartermaster.army.mil/bios/previous-qm-generals/quartermaster_general_bio-meigs.html.

53. Robert M. Poole, "How Arlington National Cemetery Came to Be," *Smithsonian Magazine*, November 2009, https://www.smithsonianmag.com/history/how-arlington-national-cemetery-came-to-be-145147007/.

54. "The Capitol Extension," House proceedings of April 14, 1862: *Congressional Globe*, 37–2, 1658. See *Documentary History*, 806.

55. Allen, *History of the United States Capitol*, 317.

56. *Documentary History*, 807.

57. Allen, *History of the United States Capitol*, 319.

58. Abraham Lincoln, "Message to Congress on Signing an Act Abolishing Slavery in Washington, D.C," April 16, 1862, The American Presidency Project, https://www.presidency.ucsb.edu/node/201897.

59. The total cost of *Freedom*, exclusive of installation, was $23,796.82—nearly $700,000 today.

60. Later in 1862, he would marry; three years later, he would have his own business working as an in-demand plasterer in Washington, where he was "highly esteemed," wrote author S. D. Wyeth, "by all who know him." See S. D. Wyeth, *The Federal City; or, Ins and Abouts of Washington* (Washington, D.C.: Gibson Brothers, 1868), 195.

61. "Constructing a National Symbol."

62. Senate proceedings of March 5, 1862, *Documentary History*, 791.

63. Senate Historical Office, *The Senate's Civil War*, 14.

64. Senate Historical Office, *The Senate's Civil War*, 15.

65. "From Washington: The Dome of the Capitol—Crawford's Goddess of Liberty—The Old Capitol—A Sketch of the New Edifice—Interesting Details," *Wisconsin State Journal*, December 11, 1863, 2.

66. Thomas Walter to Congress, November 1, 1862, *Documentary History*, 815.

67. *Documentary History*, 816.

68. Matt Guilfoyle, "Path to Capitol During the Civil War," Architect of the Capitol, August 28, 2012, https://www.aoc.gov/explore-capitol-campus/blog/path-capitol-during-civil-war.

69. Wolanin, *Constantino Brumidi*, 125.

70. "Artist Constantino Brumidi's 'Study for the Apotheosis of Washington in the Rotunda of the United States Capitol Building,'" Smithsonian American Art Museum and Its Renwick Gallery, https://americanart.si.edu/videos/artist-constantino-brumidis-study-apotheosis-washington-rotunda-united-states-capitol.

71. Allen, *History of the United States Capitol*, 323. Emphasis in original.

72. Lincoln's remarks were reported by John Eaton, chaplain of the 27th Ohio, in his memoir, *Grant, Lincoln, and the Freedmen: Reminiscences of the Civil War with Special Reference to the Work for the Contrabands and Freedmen of the Mississippi Valley* (New York: Longmans, Green, and Co., 1907), 89.

73. Thomas Walter to Amanda Walter, August 29, 1863, quoted in Allen, *History of the United States Capitol*, 325.

74. "The Capitol Dome: Interesting Account of Its Construction and Surmounting," *The Savannah Morning News*, September 24, 1893, 15. In this newspaper article, in which the eighty-year-old Thomas recounts the events of thirty years earlier, he refers to himself as "Superintendent of the Construction of the New Dome." Fortunately for Thomas, neither Walter nor Meigs was around to take issue with this title.

75. Allen, *History of the United States Capitol*, 327.

76. Walt Whitman, The Walt Whitman Archive, https://whitmanarchive.org/item/per.00198.

Chapter 9

1. Annual report of B. B. French, Commissioner of Public Buildings, October 13, 1863. See *Documentary History*, 356.

2. See Section 1814 of the United States Revised Statutes, https://www.law.cornell.edu/uscode/text/2/2131#:~:text=And%20the%20President%20is%20authorized,for%20the%20purpose%20herein%20indicate.

3. Erin Allen, "Here Comes the Sun: Seeing Omens in the Weather at Abraham Lincoln's Second Inauguration," March 4, 2015, Library of Congress Blogs, https://blogs.loc.gov/loc/2015/03/here-comes-the-sun-seeing-omens-in-the-weather-at-abraham-lincolns-second-inauguration/.

4. Curator Division, "The Lincoln Catafalque in the U.S. Capitol," Architect of the Capitol, April 15, 2015, https://www.aoc.gov/explore-capitol-campus/blog/lincoln-catafalque-us-capitol.

5. See Senate Historical Office, *The Senate's Civil War*, 25.

6. Franklin Bradley, "Profile in History: Job W. Angus," Architect of the Capitol, June 28, 2018, https://www.aoc.gov/explore-capitol-campus/blog/profile-history-job-w-angus.

7. Curator Division, "Lincoln Catafalque."

8. Well, not *every* time, but there's a technicality. When the Unknowns of World War II and the Korean War lay in state, an additional catafalque was built, with corners of each coffin resting on the Lincoln catafalque.

9. I'm using "figures" instead of "individuals," as there have been several times that the remains of multiple Unknown Soldiers have been placed to lie in state.

10. While most individuals have lain in state or in honor in the Rotunda since 2019, three individuals—Representative Elijah Cummings, Associate Supreme Court Justice Ruth Bader Ginsburg, and Representative Donald Young—have lain in state in National Statuary Hall.

11. "From Washington," *The Leavenworth* (KS) *Times*, January 4, 1866, 1.

12. Allen, *History of the United States Capitol*, 342.

13. Allen, *History of the United States Capitol*, 345.

14. Justin Martin, *Genius of Place: The Life of Frederick Law Olmsted* (Boston: Da Capo Press, 2011), 320.

15. Allen, *History of the United States Capitol*, 345.

16. Olmsted report to Congress, submitted by Edward Clark in his annual report, June 30, 1882. See *Documentary History*, 1191.

17. Allen, *History of the United States Capitol*, 346.

18. Allen, *History of the United States Capitol*, 356.

19. Martin, *Genius of Place*, 321.

20. National Association for Olmsted Parks, "Frederick Law Olmsted on the Landscape Design for the Capitol Grounds, 1874," 2009, https://olmsted.org/wp-content/uploads/2023/06/Reprints_Spring_2009_Vol_11_No_1.pdf.

21. See "Fatal Accident. Terrible Explosion of Gas at the Capitol—One Man Killed and Another Badly Burned," *Washington Chronicle*, May 20, 1876, 5.

22. Jane Armstrong Hudiburg, "'From the Giddy Height Above': Investigating Constantino Brumidi's Final Days in the Capitol Rotunda," *The Capitol Dome*, 2014, 30.

23. See Hudiburg, "'From the Giddy Height Above,'" 28–35, and Jane Armstrong Hudiburg, "The Artist of the Capitol: Constantino Brumidi's Near-Death Experience," United States Capitol Historical Society, https://capitolhistory.org/USCHS-Capitol-Stories-files/USCHS-Capitol-Stories-Constantino-Brumidi.pdf.

24. Hudiburg, "'From the Giddy Height Above,'" 28–35, and Hudiburg, "The Artist of the Capitol."

25. Hudiburg, "'From the Giddy Height Above,'" 34.

26. "Death of a Great Artist," *The Washington Post*, February 20, 1880, 1.

27. "Constantino Brumidi: Death of the Distinguished Artist in This City Yesterday," *National Republican*, February 20, 1880, 1.

28. Public Law 110-259 (122 Stat. 2430), approved July 1, 2008, https://www.congress.gov/110/statute/STATUTE-122/STATUTE-122-Pg2430.pdf.

29. Ian Duncan, "A High Honor for Capitol Artist," *Los Angeles Times*, July 12, 2012, AA2.

30. Franklin Bradley, "Olmsted's Never-Built Retreat," Architect of the Capitol, September 21, 2021, https://www.aoc.gov/explore-capitol-campus/blog/olmsteds-never-built-retreat-south-summerhouse.

31. Senate proceedings of August 1, 1882. See *Documentary History*, 1214.

32. "December 3, 1877: First Annual Message," University of Virginia, Miller Center, Presidential Speeches: Rutherford B. Hayes Presidency, https://millercenter.org/the-presidency/presidential-speeches/december-3-1877-first-annual-message.

33. Letter from Mr. Fred. Law Olmstead [*sic*], Landscape Architect of the Capitol grounds, to Hon. E. H. Rollins, Chairman of the Committee on Public Buildings and Grounds, January 11, 1882. See *Documentary History*, 1182.

34. Frederick Olmsted to Hon. William B. Allison, Chairman of Committee of Appropriations, U.S. Senate, July 15, 1886. See *Documentary History*, 1240.

35. "The Visitor's Guide," *The Critic and Record*, May 3, 1890, 3.

36. W. P. Walton, untitled article, *Semi-Weekly Interior Journal* (Stanford, KY), December 13, 1887, 2. One version of the story—from Taulbee's brother—says the disagreement stemmed from Taulbee's refusal to endorse Kincaid for a political post.

37. "The Kincaid-Taulbee Affair," *The Kentucky Advocate*, March 7, 1890, 7.

38. See "The Shooting of Congressman William Taulbee on the Steps of the U.S. Capitol," United States House of Representatives History, Art & Archives, February 28, 1890, https://history.house.gov/Historical-Highlights/1851-1900/The-death-of-Congressman-William-Taulbee-on-the-steps-of-the-U-S—Capitol/. See also Peter Overby, "A Historic Killing in the Capitol Building," NPR, February 19, 2007, https://www.npr.org/2007/02/19/7447550/a-historic-killing-in-the-capitol-building.

39. "The Public," *The Clinton* (IL) *Public*, March 7, 1890, 2.

40. "A Century: The Capitol's Celebration Today," *Evening Star*, September 18, 1893, 1.

41. See, among others, Duncan S. Walker, ed., *Celebration of the One Hundredth Anniversary of the Laying of the Corner Stone of the Capitol of the United States* (Washington, D.C.: U.S. Government Printing Office, 1896). Also see newspaper accounts of the day, such as "A Century: The Capitol's Celebration Today," *Evening Star*, September 18, 1893.

42. Walker, *Celebration of the One Hundredth Anniversary*, 47.

43. "EXPLOSION AT CAPITOL," *The Washington Post*, November 6, 1898, 1.

44. "EXPLOSION AT CAPITOL," 1.

45. René Bache, "Ghosts of the Capitol," *Boston Evening Transcript*, October 1, 1898, 28.

46. Annual Report of the Superintendent of the United States Capitol Building and Grounds, 1902, 7, https://babel.hathitrust.org/cgi/pt?id=nyp.33433124361225&seq=7.

47. Booth Mooney, *Mr. Speaker: Four Men Who Shaped the United States House of Representatives* (Chicago: Follett Publishing Company, 1964), 97.

48. Allen, *History of the United States Capitol*, 387.

49. In 2013, the doors were finally professionally cleaned and conserved with a protective wax coating applied to protect them from the oils from probing and rubbing hands.

50. The 1910 census put the U.S. total population at 92,228,496. By 2020, the population was officially at 331,449,281.

51. "Letter Sent to the Post Justifies Capitol Bomb; Gives Name 'R. Pierce,'" *The Washington Post*, July 4, 1915, 2.

52. Daniel E. Russell, "The Day Morgan Was Shot," Glen Cove Heritage, http://www.glencoveheritage.com/legacy_site/morganshooting.pdf.

53. Accounts vary on whether Muenter actually witnessed the explosion from Union Station.

54. "Bomb Exploded in U.S. Capitol Wrecks a Reception Room; . . . Explosion Attracts Big Crowd to the Scene," *The Sun*, July 3, 1915, 1.

55. Russ Feingold, "Honoring Robert M. La Follette," *Congressional Record*, July 24, 2007, 15415–16, https://www.govinfo.gov/content/pkg/CREC-2007-07-24/pdf/CREC-2007-07-24-pt1-PgS9835-2.pdf.

Chapter 10

1. "Police Drive Pacifists Off Capitol Steps," *The Washington Times*, April 2, 1917, 1.

2. Charles S. Groves, "Senator Lodge Right There with the Punch; Returns Blow of Boston Pacifist Who Hit Him in the Face," *The Boston Globe*, April 2, 1917, 1.

3. Massachusetts Historical Society, "President of the Massachusetts Historical Society in a Fistfight: War Declared," April 2017, https://www.masshist.org/object-of-the-month/2017-april. See also "Lodge and Pacifist 'Kiss and Make Up,'" *The Washington Times*, April 15, 1919, 6.

4. *Congressional Record*, January 13, 1921, 1485.

5. Senate Historical Office, "Senate Stories: Cooling Off the Senate," United States Senate, August 2, 2021, https://www.senate.gov/artandhistory/senate-stories/cooling-off-the-senate.htm#9.

6. "Building History," Supreme Court of the United States, https://www.supremecourt.gov/about/buildinghistory.aspx.

7. While many sources list the demolition date for the Old Brick Capitol as 1929, D.C. newspapers of the era make it clear the building was still standing as late as May 1930. See Philip Plyler, "Finis for the Old Brick Capitol," *The Sunday Star Magazine*, May 25, 1930, 1; "Historical Pageant Given, to Be Repeated; Tuesday Selected for Program by Persons Who Would Preserve Old Capitol," Washington *Sunday Star*, May 25, 1930, 1.

8. Plyler, "Finis for the Old Brick Capitol."

9. Edward T. Folliard, "Lawmakers Who Gave Themselves New Annex, Skimp on Schools," *The Washington Herald*, April 24, 1933, 2.

10. "Check on Visitors to House Urged," *Evening Star*, December 14, 1932, 3.

11. Quotes and story details from this section taken from "A Gunman in the House Gallery, 1932," United States House of Representatives History, Art & Archives, December 13, 1932, https://history.house.gov/HistoricalHighlight/Detail/35649; "Check on Visitors," 3; Jack El-Hai, "A Disarming Congressman," "Impulse," December 2006, https://www.carnegiehero.org/wp-content/uploads/2020/08/issue8.pdf; Dustin Waters, "The Depression-Era Gunman Who Tried to Hold the House of Representatives Hostage: 'I Demand the Right to the Floor for 20 Minutes,'" *The Washington Post*, January 19, 2020, https://www.washingtonpost.com/history/2020/01/19/gunman-congress-marlin-kemmerer/.

12. Allen, *History of the United States Capitol*, 411.

13. "Report of the Commission of Fine Arts, 1944–1948," 21, https://babel.hathitrust.org/cgi/pt?id=mdp.39015068260358&seq=1.

14. Allen, *History of the United States Capitol*, 414.

15. Robert K. Walsh, "Tradition Vies with Splendor as New Congress Opens," *Evening Star*, January 4, 1951, 1.

16. Andrew Tully, "Boudoirs or Not, Our 5 Million Capitol Chambers Are Completed," *The Washington Daily News*, January 2, 1951, 21.

17. "Introductory Address by Hon. Thomas A. Jenkins," *Congressional Record*, May 11, 1954, 6370.

18. Dwight D. Eisenhower, "Remarks at the Capitol at the Dedication of the Rotunda Frieze," May 11, 1954, The American Presidency Project, https://www.presidency.ucsb.edu/documents/remarks-the-capitol-the-dedication-the-rotunda-frieze. Emphasis added.

19. While the Capitol had been operating with a central air-conditioning system since 1935, most American businesses and homes of the era weren't yet constructed with such a system—and while smaller window units had been available since 1932, only forty-three thousand had been sold by 1947. See "History of Air Conditioning," U.S. Department of Energy, July 20, 2015, https://www.energy.gov/articles/history-air-conditioning.

20. Quotes and account taken from various news sources of the era, including "Crank Fires Two Wild Shots at Sen. Bricker," *Times-Herald* (Washington, D.C.), July 13, 1947, 4, and "Bricker Escapes Subway Shots; Ex-Guard Held as Assailant," *Evening Star*, July 13, 1947, 1.

21. "Bricker Escapes Subway Shots."

22. "Special Committee on Organized Crime in Interstate Commerce," United States Senate, https://www.senate.gov/about/powers-procedures/investigations/kefauver.htm.

23. "Whereas: Stories from the People's House: 'Firecrackers' in the House Chamber," United States House of Representatives History, Art & Archives, February 26, 2014, https://history.house.gov/Blog/Detail/15032401528.

24. Warren Bratter, "*Lolita Lebrón: Ejemplo de Varón*," Hofstra, September 29, 2020, https://sites.hofstra.edu/un-poco-de-todo/2020/09/29/lolita-lebron-ejemplo-de-varon/.

25. "Bill Goodwin: Recollections of the 1954 Shooting in the House Chamber: Part One," United States House of Representatives History, Art & Archives, November 2, 2009, https://history.house.gov/Oral-History/Events/1954-Shooting/.

26. Donn Munson, "Devoted Friends, Kin Keep Hopeful Vigil at Hospital for Rep. Bentley," *Times-Herald* (Washington, D.C.), March 3, 1954, 6.

27. Frederic J. Frommer, "Puerto Rican Nationalists Attacked the Capitol. Jimmy Carter Freed Them," *The Washington Post*, January 5, 2025, https://www.washingtonpost.com/history/2025/01/05/jimmy-carter-puerto-rico-capitol-attack/.

28. "'Firecrackers' in the House Chamber."

29. Robert K. Walsh, "'Capitol Hill Precinct' to Increase Police Guard Under Study," *Evening Star*, March 3, 1954, 1.

30. "Face-Changing Nearer for Capitol's East Front," *The New York Times*, January 30, 1958, https://www.nytimes.com/1958/01/30/archives/facechanging-nearer-for-capitols-east-front.html.

31. "Art: Defeat on the East Front," *Time*, March 3, 1958, https://time.com/archive/6828897/art-defeat-on-the-east-front/.

32. See "Fight on Alteration of Capitol Lost," in *CQ Almanac 1958* (Washington, D.C.: Congressional Quarterly, 1959).

33. "Capitol Folly," *The New York Times*, February 16, 1958, https://www.nytimes.com/1958/02/16/archives/capitol-folly.html.

34. Associated Press, "J. George Stewart Dies; Stormy Capitol Architect," *Bridgeport* (CT) *Post*, May 25, 1970, 8.

35. C. Joseph Genetin-Pilawa, "A Curious Removal: Leta Myers Smart, *The Rescue*, and *The Discovery of America*," *The Capitol Dome*, 2015, https://capitolhistory.org/wp-content/uploads/2012/07/USCHS-Capitol-Dome-2015-Spring-1-24.pdf.

36. "Eisenhower Text," *The Boston Globe*, July 5, 1959, 39.

37. The new Senate Reception Room, commonly referred to as the Mansfield Room, is S-207. The House Reception Room, named for Rayburn, is H-207.

38. Isabelle Shelton, "Capitol Footnotes: East Front or Texas Front?," *Evening Star*, September 10, 1961, 86.

39. Senator John Stennis, "Use of the Old Supreme Court Chamber," *Congressional Record*, May 10, 1960, 9824.

40. Stennis, "Use of the Old Supreme Court Chamber," 9824.

41. "Senate's Old Chamber to Become a New Shrine," *The Washington Post*, April 1, 1962.

42. See *Congressional Record*, June 16, 1976, 18534–36.

43. *Congressional Record*, June 16, 1976, 18534–36.

44. "J. George Stewart Dies," 8.

45. "Capitol Architect Stewart Dies," *The Morning News* (Wilmington, Delaware), May 25, 1970, 1.

46. Matt Schudel, "George White, Influential and Long-Serving Architect of the Capitol, Dies at 90," *The Washington Post*, June 23, 2011, https://www.washingtonpost.com/local/obituaries/george-white-influential-and-long-serving-architect-of-the-capitol-dies-at-90/2011/06/23/AGGvvHiH_story.html.

47. "A Capitol Crime," *The New York Times*, July 4, 1977, https://www.nytimes.com/1977/07/04/archives/a-capitol-crime.html.

48. Ronald Reagan, "Inaugural Address 1981," Ronald Reagan Presidential Library & Museum, https://www.reaganlibrary.gov/archives/speech/inaugural-address-1981.

49. "Hart Building Opens Under Protest," United States Senate, November 22, 1982, https://www.senate.gov/about/historic-buildings-spaces/office-buildings/hart-building-opens.htm.

50. Bruce Weber, "George M. White, Architect of Capitol, Dies at 90," *The New York Times*, June 23, 2011, https://www.nytimes.com/2011/06/23/us/23white.html.

51. "Noted U.S. Capitol Muralist Dead at 86," *Los Angeles Times*, September 29. 1982.

52. William P. Coughlin, "Allyn Cox, 86; Worked on US Capitol Murals," *The Boston Globe*, September 29, 1982, 30.

53. Coughlin, "Allyn Cox."

54. William Rosenau, *Tonight We Bombed the U.S. Capitol: The Explosive Story of M19, America's First Female Terrorist Group* (New York: Atria, 2019), 183.

55. "Terrorist Bomb Explosion Rocks Capitol," in *CQ Almanac 1983* (Washington, D.C.: Congressional Quarterly, 1984), 592–94.

56. See Robert Pear, "Bomb Explodes in Senate's Wing of Capitol; No Injuries

Reported," *The New York Times*, November 8, 1983, https://www.nytimes.com/1983/11/08/us/bomb-explodes-in-senate-s-wing-of-capitol-no-injuries-reported.html.

57. While the missing shreds would be found and painstakingly restored, the painting would never be the same.

58. "Old Clock in Senate Is Alive and Ticking," *The New York Times*, November 30, 1983, https://www.nytimes.com/1983/11/30/us/old-clock-in-senate-is-alive-and-ticking.html.

59. Rosenau, *Tonight We Bombed the U.S. Capitol*, 184.

60. William Jefferson Clinton, "My Reasons for the Pardons," *The New York Times*, February 18, 2001, https://www.nytimes.com/2001/02/18/opinion/my-reasons-for-the-pardons.html.

61. U.S. Congress, Senate, Committee on the Judiciary, *President Clinton's Eleventh-Hour Pardons*, 107th Congress, 1st Session, S. Hrg. 107–194, https://www.govinfo.gov/content/pkg/CHRG-107shrg76344/pdf/CHRG-107shrg76344.pdf.

62. "Terrorist Bomb Explosion Rocks Capitol," 592–94.

63. Schudel, "George White."

64. Ron Sarasin, "Interview with George M. White," U.S. Capitol Historical Society, September 8, 2008, https://capitolhistory.org/wp-content/uploads/2017/03/USCHS-Oral-History-Architect-Capitol-George-White.pdf.

65. Architect of the Capitol, Office of the Inspector General, "J. Brett Blanton, Architect of the Capitol, Abused His Authority, Misused Government Property and Wasted Taxpayer Money, Among Other Substantiated Violations" (Investigation 2021-0011-INVI-P), September 2023, https://en.wikisource.org/wiki/J._Brett_Blanton,_Architect_of_the_Capitol,_Abused_His_Authority,_Misused_Government_Property_and_Wasted_Taxpayer_Money,_Among_Other_Substantiated_Violations.

66. See "Architect of the Capitol Appointment Procedure: Evolution and Recent Changes" (CRS Report R41074), Congressional Research Service, July 17, 2024, https://www.congress.gov/crs_external_products/R/PDF/R41074/R41074.14.pdf.

67. "The Capitol Building Looks Like It Always Has but It Has a New Architect," *Federal Drive with Tom Temin*, Federal News Network, April 28, 2025, https://federalnewsnetwork.com/facilities-construction/2025/04/the-capitol-building-looks-like-it-always-has-but-it-has-a-new-architect/.

68. Architect of the Capitol staff, "Meet the Architect: Q&A with Thomas E. Austin," Architect of the Capitol, September 30, 2024, https://www.aoc.gov/explore-capitol-campus/blog/meet-13th-architect-thomas-e-austin.

Chapter 11

1. Connie Cass, "Tourists Caught in Scene of Panic," *The Kansas City Star*, July 25, 1998, A1.

2. Since then, Rosa Parks, Elijah Cummings, and John Lewis have all lain in honor or in state.

3. William J. Clinton, "Remarks at the Congressional Tribute Honoring Officer Jacob J. Chestnut and Detective John M. Gibson," July 28, 1998, The American Presidency Project, https://www.presidency.ucsb.edu/documents/remarks-the-congressional-tribute-honoring-officer-jacob-j-chestnut-and-detective-john-m.

4. Ashley Halsey III, "6 Years Later, Capitol Visitor Center Puts Out Long-

Awaited Welcome Mat," *The Washington Post*, December 1, 2008, https://www.washingtonpost.com/archive/national/2008/12/01/6-years-later-capitol-visitor-center-puts-out-longawaited-welcome-mat/4e9e4ddb-aa55-428b-adf1-a0aec6028e37/.

5. John Lewis, "Recognition for Slave Laborers Who Worked on Construction of United States Capitol," *Congressional Record*, September 12, 2000, https://www.congress.gov/congressional-record/volume-146/issue-106/house-section/article/H7444-3?s=1&r=7425.

6. Associated Press, "Must Battle Despotism, He Reminds; Speaks at Rites for Capitol Cornerstone," *St. Louis Globe–Democrat*, July 5, 1959, 1.

7. Bill Chappell, "'Enormous and Tragic': U.S. Has Lost More Than 200,000 People to COVID-19," NPR, September 22, 2020, https://www.npr.org/sections/coronavirus-live-updates/2020/09/22/911934489/enormous-and-tragic-u-s-has-lost-more-than-200-000-people-to-covid-19.

8. Caitlin O'Kane, "Trump Said Coronavirus 'Affects Virtually Nobody,' as U.S. Surpasses 200,000 Deaths," CBS News, September 22, 2020, https://www.cbsnews.com/news/covid-it-affects-virutally-nobody-trump-coronavirus-rally/.

9. Liam Stack, "Trump and the 'Rigged' Emmy Awards: A History of Snubs," *The New York Times*, October 20, 2016, https://www.nytimes.com/2016/10/21/us/politics/trump-apprentice-emmy.html.

10. Laurie Kellman and Zeke Miller, "Trump, Pelosi Trade Insults as Their Feud Heats Up," Associated Press, May 23, 2019, https://apnews.com/article/ce08485cee37470db8983b8bd06c40a0.

11. Brian Naylor, "Read Trump's Jan. 6 Speech, a Key Part of Impeachment Trial," NPR, February 10, 2021, https://www.npr.org/2021/02/10/966396848/read-trumps-jan-6-speech-a-key-part-of-impeachment-trial.

12. Kellman and Miller, "Trump, Pelosi Trade Insults."

13. See *Washington Post* staff, "Cleaning Up the Damage and Destruction at the U.S. Capitol," *The Washington Post*, January 8, 2021, https://www.washingtonpost.com/graphics/photography/2021/01/07/photos-aftermath-capitol-riot/.

14. This number includes both Capitol police and Metropolitan police. See U.S. General Accountability Office, Report to Congressional Requesters, "Capitol Attack: Federal Agencies Identified Some Threats, but Did Not Fully Process and Share Information Prior to January 6, 2021" (GAO-23-106625), February 2023, https://www.gao.gov/assets/gao-23-106625.pdf.

15. Joe Davidson, "Capitol 'Absolutely' Is Safer Now Than on Jan. 6, Police Chief Says," *The Washington Post*, January 19, 2024, https://www.washingtonpost.com/politics/2024/01/19/capitol-police-chief-safety-improvements-jan6/.

16. Roger Parloff, "The High-Water Mark of the Jan. 6 Prosecutions," Lawfare, January 6, 2025, https://www.lawfaremedia.org/article/the-high-water-mark-of-the-jan.-6-prosecutions.

17. Erica L. Green. "Trump Administration Considers Money for Pardoned Jan. 6 Rioters," *The New York Times*, March 26, 2025, https://www.nytimes.com/2025/03/26/us/politics/trumo-jan6-rioters-compensation.html.

18. Colleen Long and Zeke Miller, "Biden Warns Against Trump Reelection After Jan. 6 Capitol Riot, a Day 'We Nearly Lost America,'" Associated Press, January 5, 2024, https://apnews.com/article/jan-6-biden-capitol-riot-trump-b3706850266109be341a2cce783931e6.

Illustration Credits

Chapter 1

Courtesy of the Library of Congress, Geography and Map Division. L'Enfant, Pierre Charles. *Plan of the city intended for the permanent seat of the government of the United States: projected agreeable to the direction of the President of the United States, in pursuance of an act of Congress, passed on the sixteenth day of July, MDCCXC, "establishing the permanent seat on the bank of the Potowmac."* Washington, D.C., 1991. Map. https://www.loc.gov/item/97683585/.

Chapter 2

Courtesy of the Library of Congress, Prints and Photographs Division. Thornton, William, architect. *U.S. Capitol, Washington, D.C. East elevation, low dome.* Washington, D.C., between 1793 and 1800. Photograph. https://www.loc.gov/item/92519533/.

Chapter 3

Courtesy of the Library of Congress, Prints and Photographs Division. Munger, George, artist. *U.S. Capitol after burning by the British.* Washington D.C., 1814. Photograph. https://www.loc.gov/item/2004662324/.

Chapter 4

Courtesy of the Library of Congress, Prints and Photographs Division. Bulfinch, Charles, artist. *Capitol, east front / from a sketch by Charles Bullfinch* [*sic*]. Washington, D.C., 1904. Photograph. https://www.loc.gov/item/2014649264/.

Chapter 5

Courtesy of the Library of Congress, Prints and Photographs Division. Plumbe, John (likely). *United States Capitol, Washington, D.C., east front elevation.* Washington, D.C., ca. 1846. Daguerreotype. https://www.loc.gov/item/2004664419/.

Chapter 6

Courtesy of the Library of Congress, Prints and Photographs Division. Walter, Thomas Ustick, architect. Wood, John, photographer. *Original design, adopted by the President A.D. 1851.* Washington, D.C., 1851. Photograph. https://www.loc.gov/item/2009631409/.

Chapter 7

Courtesy of the Library of Congress, Prints and Photographs Division. Schoenborn, August G., architect. Walter, Thomas Ustick, architect. *U.S. Capitol. Washington, D.C. Perspective projection.* Washington, D.C., between 1850 and 1860. Photograph. https://www.loc.gov/item/2025163248/.

Chapter 8

Courtesy of the Library of Congress, Prints and Photographs Division. Wood, John, photographer. *Inauguration of Mr. Lincoln.* Washington, D.C., 1861. Photograph. https://www.loc.gov/item/96511712/.

Chapter 9

Courtesy of the Library of Congress, Prints and Photographs Division. *The Capitol, East Front from the Northeast Corner.* Washington, D.C. [between 1860 and 1930]. Photograph. https://www.loc.gov/item/2017647069/.

Chapter 10

Courtesy of the Library of Congress, Prints and Photographs Division. Highsmith, Carol M., photographer. *Dome, U.S. Capitol, Washington, D.C.* Washington, D.C., between 1980 and 2006. Photograph. https://www.loc.gov/item/2011633827.

Chapter 11

Courtesy of the Library of Congress, Prints and Photographs Division. Horydczak, Theodor, photographer. *U.S. Capitol exteriors. Dome of U.S. Capitol through trees at night.* Washington, D.C., ca. 1920–ca. 1950. Photograph. https://www.loc.gov/item/2019681978/.

Index

Note: Italicized page numbers indicate material in photographs or illustrations.

About the Author

Brian Jay Jones is the critically acclaimed bestselling biographer of some of the world's most iconic creative geniuses. Born in the Midwest and raised in the Southwest, Brian has a degree in English from the University of New Mexico. He spent more than two decades as a public policy analyst and speechwriter for thought leaders and elected officials at all levels of government, including nearly ten years in the U.S. Senate. He presently lives in New Mexico.